The Complete Pug Handbook

LINDA WHITWAM

ISBN-13: 978-1500439194

Acknowledgements

My sincere thanks to all the Pug organisations, breeders, owners and canine experts who have generously contributed their time, expertise and, between them, centuries of experience with the breed. Without them The Complete Pug Handbook. would not have been possible. Special thanks to: The Pug Dog Welfare and Rescue Association, The Pug Dog Club of America, Robert and Holly Hitchcock, Donna Shank, Brenda Schuettenberg, Roberta Kelley-Martin, Saran Evans, Carly Firth, Erin Ford, Catherine Jones-Kyle, Deborah Beecham, Deborah Hayman, Holly Attwood, Laura Libner, Linda Guy, Linda Wright, Melanie Clark, Tony Glover, Sandra Mayoh, Sue Wragg, J. Candy Schlieper, Jo Cousins, Amber Lea Morgan and Dr Sara Skiwski of The Western Dragon. Kennels of contributor breeders are listed at the back of the book.

Copyright

Table of Contents

1. Get to Know the Pug

To anyone who is not familiar with Pugs, they may seem like strange little animals with flat faces, barrel bodies and short legs. Yet they are one of the most popular breeds and, as anyone who has owned a Pug will tell you, they are simply unlike any other dog. Indeed, a recognised hazard is that if you're not careful, you get so attached to these affectionate little critters that you end up with 'a pile of Pugs.' So what's so special about them?

The breed is quite unique - not only in terms of appearance, but also in personality. If it is possible for a dog to have a sense of humour, then the Pug has it in spades. And the Pug excels at what he has been bred for, and that is to be a companion to humans.

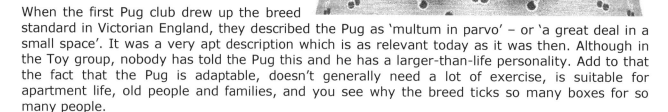

Extremely affectionate, the Pug is happiest when with his owners. If you haven't decided on a name for yours yet, 'Shadow' could be a good choice, as they often follow you everywhere - even to the bathroom. The Pug's other great love is food, and it's a constant challenge to maintain that sturdy body at a healthy weight.

When the first Pug club drew up the breed standard in Victorian England, they described the Pug as 'multum in parvo' – or 'a great deal in a small space'. It was a very apt description which is as relevant today as it was then. Although in the Toy group, nobody has told the Pug this and he has a larger-than-life personality. Add to that the fact that the Pug is adaptable, doesn't generally need a lot of exercise, is suitable for apartment life, old people and families, and you see why the breed ticks so many boxes for so many people.

The big doe eyes, flat, wrinkly face and an expression that says he's seen it all before prove an irresistible combination for many dog lovers. And if you're out and about with your Pug, you may well find that he's a people magnet. The Pug is a companion dog without equal. He loves to be with his people and he'll keep you amused with his antics and sense of fun. If you are out at work all day, don't get a Pug; go for a breed which is less dependent on humans for happiness.

This is a breed with a mind of its own, sometimes unpredictable in that you can't guess what he might do next – but it will probably make you smile. Underneath all of that is a huge heart from a companion who is loving and only too eager to please you.

But be warned that the Pug is not a lapdog who will obediently hang on to your every word and unquestioningly follow commands. No, the Pug has a mind of his own, so you must be prepared to be patient when housebreaking and teaching basic commands.

Pugs also have a reputation for being very good with children.

Typical Traits

Your Pug's character will depend largely on two things. The first is his temperament, which he inherits - and presumably one of the reasons why you have chosen a Pug. The American Kennel Club describes the Pug as "even-tempered, charming, alert, mischievous and loving."

However, what many new owners do not realise is that, as well as being born with those wrinkles, big eyes and other trademark physical features, your dog also inherits his temperament from his parents and ancestors. Good breeders select their breeding stock based not only on appearance, but also on what sort of disposition he or she has. And that's another reason to take your time to find a good, responsible breeder. The breed standard states: "This is an even-tempered breed, exhibiting stability, playfulness, great charm, dignity, and an outgoing, loving disposition."

The second factor is environment – or how you rear and treat your dog. In other words, it's a combination of **Nature and Nurture**. The first few months in a dog's life are so important. Once he has left the litter, he takes his lead from you as he learns to react to the world around him. One essential aspect of nurture is socialisation. Even though Pugs generally start out affectionate and even-tempered, it is essential to spend time introducing yours to other dogs and humans, as well as noises and traffic, from an early age. A dog comfortable in his surroundings without fear or anxieties is less likely to display unwanted behaviour such as biting, growling or switching off.

Through your guidance and good socialisation your Pug learns whom he can trust, whether to be afraid - which in turn may cause an aggressive or fearful reaction in him - how much he can get away with, and so on. He also learns not to be selfish and to share you, as well as his food and toys, with others.

To say all dogs of the same breed are alike would be akin to saying that all Americans are optimistic and friendly and all Brits are polite and reserved. It is, of course, a huge generalisation. There are grumpy, unfriendly Americans or rude in-your-face Brits. However, it is also true to say that being friendly and optimistic are general American traits, as is being polite in Britain. It's the same with the Pug. Each individual dog has his or her unique character, but there are certain traits which are common within the breed. So here are some typical Pug traits:

- ❖ They are very loving, eager to please and want to be with their owners. They are also tactile and like to lick and be close

- ❖ They do not like being left alone for hours on end. They may suffer from separation anxiety if left for long periods

- ❖ They make wonderful companions, provided you can give them the attention they need and teach them some ground rules

- ❖ They are even tempered and adaptable to your lifestyle. Raised properly they are very affectionate without being needy

- ❖ They are **extremely** greedy and prone to putting on weight

- ❖ They can demand your attention. If not properly socialised they can become jealous of you showing

affection to others and may aggressively guard food and toys

❖ They have a sense of fun and clownish personality. They may do funny, illogical things. Some Pugs love to have a mad few minutes and dash around, grabbing things in their mouths, play bowing or chasing

❖ Energy levels vary greatly from one dog to another. Although they are regarded as having fairly low exercise requirements, all Pugs need some daily exercise, preferably out of the garden or yard

❖ Generally blacks have higher energy levels - and are often more mischievous - than fawns

❖ **ALL Pug puppies are lively.** Some will settle down, others may have high energy levels all of their lives. If a Pug is energetic it is usually in short bursts, as the breed is not known for its stamina

❖ Young Pugs, like all puppies, like to chew, especially when young or bored

❖ They are predominantly indoor dogs, which makes them suitable for apartment life

❖ They need stimulation to stop them getting bored; they love playing games. They can also be persistent (wilful, even) if they set their mind to something

❖ This is not the easiest bred to housebreak or obedience train. It takes a lot of repetition for them to easily obey commands – and they hate doing anything in the rain - although they are eager to please their owners and highly motivated by food

❖ They are known for being good with babies and children – but, like any dog, they should be supervised with young children, who should learn not to be rough. The Pug, despite its robust appearance, has small, delicate limbs and protruding eyes which can be easily injured

❖ They can be quite sensitive emotionally, picking up on the mood in the household, and do not respond well to shouting or violence

❖ Pugs do not bark a lot, although many of them are quite noisy. They snuffle, snort, snore - and make a range of strange noises, especially when demanding attention, or expressing their displeasure at something. This can sometimes sound like screaming

❖ They don't make good guard dogs as they will greet strangers like old friends, although some make better watch dogs and will bark if somebody comes to the door

❖ They are not generally one-man dogs, being friendly with everybody. They have big hearts and will respond to anyone who shows them kindness – or food

❖ They overheat easily and need air conditioning in hot climates

❖ They are often good with other dogs and cats, especially if introduced at an early age. Sometimes a male will not get on well with another male Pug in the house, and a female might not get on with another female Pug – but again this depends on the temperament of the dogs

❖ Some can be possessive – you don't own them, they own you!

❖ They have short easy-to-groom coats - although **they shed short hairs all year round**

- ❖ Many suffer from breathing, spine or eye problems, allergies and/or skin problems

- ❖ They require regular personal care, e.g. eye, wrinkle and tail cleaning

- ❖ Most Pugs can't swim, so be very careful near water -or buy a canine lifejacket if you visit water regularly

- ❖ The Pug can be expensive when it comes to vets' bills. Don't get one unless you can afford annual pet insurance right from the beginning

- ❖ They can have a high tolerance to pain, so you need to keep an eye on your Pug for any signs of ill health or discomfort

If we haven't managed to put you off, then read on and learn more about this unique breed and how to fulfil your part of the bargain by taking good care of these entertaining, loving little dogs.

Is a Pug the Right Dog for Me?

Many owners forge a bond so deep with their Pug that they wouldn't consider any other breed. But taking on any dog is a big commitment. Before you take the plunge, make sure the Pug is the right breed for you. After all, with any luck they will be your trusty companion for the next decade or more. Answering the following questions will help you to make up your mind:

1. Are you looking for a dog to take on long walks every day or to go jogging with?

2. Do you want to spend a lot of time outdoors with your dog?

3. Do you want a dog you can take to agility classes and competitions?

4. Do you want to spend many hours playing with your dog?

5. Are you looking for a guard dog?

6. Do you want to breed from your dog?

7. Do you live in an extremely hot or cold climate?

8. Are you out at work all day?

9. Do you have a swimming pool or live by water?

10. Are you very house-proud or easily embarrassed?

11. Are you a first-time dog owner?

12. Do you want a breed that is easy to train and housebreak?

If the answer is YES to any of these questions, then the Pug may not be the breed for you – and here's why:

1. Although energy levels vary greatly from one Pug to another - and blacks often have higher energy levels than fawns - the breed is generally regarded as having low to medium energy levels. Pugs are not known for their stamina and are usually content with short walks. They overheat easily and the shape of their heads and bodies do not naturally lend them to jogging, swimming or other strenuous activity. If you enjoy walking or the Great Outdoors and want your Pug to be part of this, choose a puppy from a more athletic bloodline and gradually build up the amount of daily exercise.

2. The Pug is a canine which spends most of its time indoors, and is suitable for apartment life as long as there is regular access to the outdoors. Although they are playful and may run around very energetically when young, most Pugs soon run out of steam. There are other breeds more suited to regular strenuous outdoor activity.

3. Occasionally Pugs do compete in activity classes, but they are not known for it. They lack stamina due to their physical make up and can be a bit stubborn to train. You may have a dog which loves to jump through hoops – if that's the case, great. But if your Pug doesn't want to do it, you'll have a difficult task to persuade him otherwise. Be aware that some Pugs are deceptively agile, so your garden fence may need to be as high as four or five feet!

4. Many Pugs are playful, some breeders say that the Pug is a perpetual child; he never grows up. He may love playing with you and his toys, but it will be in short bursts of high energy activity and he soon tires.

5. Some Pugs may bark when somebody comes to the door, but they generally want to be friends with everyone and would be quite happy to watch a burglar walk off with your prize possessions, rather than try to deter them – especially if food is on offer

6. Breeding Pugs is a difficult and complex – not to mention expensive – business and it is a practice best left to the experts. If you are interested in breeding Pugs at some future stage, see **Chapter 13. The Birds and the Bees.**

7. People living in extreme climates can own Pugs, but it requires more effort on their part to ensure that the dog does not become overheated, a condition which the breed is prone to. In hot weather they should be in an air conditioned room. Neither can they tolerate extremely cold conditions.

8. Above all, the Pug is a companion dog; they were originally bred specifically for this purpose. One left alone will be unhappy at the separation. If you are out at work all day, consider delaying getting a dog until you have more time.

9. Due to their conformation (body shape) and respiratory system, most Pugs cannot swim, although they often don't realise that. If you have a pool or live by water, it should be fenced off for the safety of the dog. Some owners buy lifejackets for their dogs.

10. The vast majority of Pugs - God bless 'em - pass wind, make odd noises and snore! They can also be messy eaters and drinkers, leaving trails across the floor, and they often shed hair all year round. Some are difficult to housetrain. If you are extremely house-proud, prim and proper, a less gassy canine with elegant table manners would be a better choice.

11. Like all brachycephalic (flat-faced) breeds, the Pug has special needs. Some have health issues as well as intolerance to temperature fluctuations and excessive exercise, as well as a high pain threshold which can mask underlying problems. Others may need a specialised diet and extra personal care to keep them healthy. If you are a first-time or inexperienced dog owner, make sure you get plenty of advice from your breeder, go on the online Pug forums and read books to learn more about the breed.

12. Pugs can have a stubborn streak and while some owners find them perfectly easy to housetrain, others find it can take a long time. Some of this will depend of the bloodline, but more often it depends on how much time you are prepared to put in at the beginning. Vigilance and consistency are the keys. All Pugs generally hate going outside in the rain to do their business; creating a sheltered area outdoors is ideal. Similarly with obedience training, patience and repetition are needed - along with lots of treats. Try carrot or apple to keep the weight in check.

On the other hand, if you answer YES to the next set of questions, then the Pug could be just the dog for you.

1. Are you looking for a companion dog?

2. Do you want a dog that is suitable with children or old people?

3. Have you got the finances to cover medical problems which may well run into thousands of dollars – or pounds? (Not all conditions may be covered by insurance).

4. Are you prepared to put in the time to train your dog – even if he is a bit stubborn?

5. Are you prepared to clean your dog's eyes, ears and skin folds regularly – i.e. more than once a week?

6. Does everyone in your house like Pugs?

7. Are you around a lot of the time?

The Pug's stand-out feature – apart from his unique looks - is his deeply affectionate companionship. As long as you are around and he is not left alone for long periods, he will enjoy nothing more than snuggling up and snoring away happily.

The breed is suitable for the elderly, as most Pugs are happy with relatively little exercise, although it all depends what they have got used to as a puppy. A dog accustomed to two daily walks will come to expect them, whereas another which has only lived in the house and yard or had 15 minutes a day in the park since puppyhood will probably be equally as content.

Pugs are known for being good with children. They will become playmates for them. Although care should be taken with small puppies, which can easily get injured, and time with small children and any dog should always be supervised.

The breed can suffer from a range of inherited illnesses, some of which are due to the trademark flat faces and protruding eyes. Responsible breeders are making great strides in improving the health of the breed, but you would be a rare owner indeed if you did not need to visit the vet several times during your dog's life - and that's in addition to annual injections and check-up.

Monthly health insurance for a Pug may cost in the region of £25 to £30 in the UK, or up to $45 in the US. We highly recommend insuring your healthy Pug as soon as he or she arrives home and before any health problems develop, as most insurers will refuse to cover pre-existing conditions, so start with a clean bill of health and everything should be covered. Over their lifetimes, many Pugs will rack up thousands of pounds' or dollars' worth of insurance payments and veterinary bills in terms of health checks, vaccinations, preventative care and extra medical attention.

Training a Pug requires a lot of patience - if you expect yours to immediately jump to your every command, you're in for a disappointment. According to canine psychologist Dr Stanley Coren, Pugs require 40 to 80 repetitions before they understand a new command. Pugs ARE intelligent, but they may prefer to consider the command - and then ruminate on it a little longer - before deciding whether or not to respond. Patience is the key if your little treasure is proving to be a tad strong-willed.

Before getting a Pug or any other breed of dog, it's important that all family members want this new addition to the household. There are far too many dogs who become surplus to requirements and end up in rescue shelters or looking for a new home through no fault of their own.

The lifespan of the Pug varies, depending on the bloodline - ask your breeder how long her Pugs generally live. The Kennel Club (UK) gives a very generally verdict of "over 10 years," while others say 10 to 15 years. With lots of TLC from their owners, some Pugs have been known to live until their late teens.

What The Breeders Say

You bring your new Pug home and you have so many questions. You can ring the breeder for advice, but don't want to be bothering her every five minutes. So imagine how wonderful it would be if you had a couple of dozen expert Pug breeders on hand to give you advice along the way. Well you have, right here!

Experienced breeders, most from around the UK and USA, have helped to produce The Complete Pug Handbook. Between them they have hundreds of years' experience of breeding and living with Pugs, and they have generously given their time to answer questions and give advice to help new owners take good care of their Pugs. Here's some of them talking about the typical Pug temperament and best things about the breed.

Deborah Beecham, of Fizzlewick Pugs, South Wales, UK, has been involved with the breed since 2001 and said: "The typical Pug has a lively, happy disposition; they are incredibly nosey little creatures, which is apt to get them into mischief if left unchecked. They are very loyal and love people, they like nothing better than to be centre of attention, and they make good watchdogs as nothing much gets past them, but are not prone to bark excessively for no good reason. They have a deep, throaty unmistakable little bark which is not shrill, high pitched or annoying like many Toy breeds. They are very good with children and like to be everyone's pal and nothing pleases them more than to be around their family; they hate being left alone and will not thrive if left without company."

Saran Evans, Sephina Pugs, Carmarthenshire, UK: "They have boundless enthusiasm, they are little clowns that thrive on making you laugh. They crave human companionship and the closer to you they can get, the better. This includes joining you in the bathroom and attempting to join you in the bath! They are happy dogs, always so upbeat and enthusiastic, they never fail to lift your spirits."

Carly Firth, Mumandau Pugs, Greater Manchester, UK: "For me the best and most appealing thing about Pugs is quite obviously the look of the breed. Their face and expression makes them unique, and their shape, right down to those double curled tails. They may be small and compact, but they certainly don't feel like they are. I can confidently say once you've had a Pug 'you've been Pugged!' and you'll never want to go without. They are addictive little characters.

"However, a Pug can be quite demanding of your companionship and attention at times. They can be playful, intelligent and have moments of even being a little on the wilful side, due to those underlying sensitivities. They are fabulous around children. And I would also say they are a good breed to start with if you have never had a dog before.

"From personal experience, I have found the bitches to be more dominant, and dogs to be more of a sensitive nature. My bitch is quite content to go off on her own and keep herself entertained with toys and bones, my dog will show interest with these, but generally only if it involves human interaction. However this could also be linked with their bloodlines. In addition to this, I also think socialisation is an important factor. If done in the right socialisation window, with the appropriate

opportunities, then later on in their life Pugs really can be confident little things.

"Interestingly I have also found when Pugs are an only dog, they are very manageable, and can also be little slobs even. Yet when they are in a pack of at least three dogs, they can be wild little things expressing lots of natural instinctive traits."

Breeders Robert and Holly Hitchcock, of Bobitch Pugs, Derbyshire, UK, sums the breed up as: "Happy, lively, mischievous, loving and loyal. The most unique thing about them is their look and the fact that they are a big dog in a small package, adaptable to most lifestyles." Pictured is their splendid Decaylite King Louie at Bobitch JW ShCM.

Deborah Beecham Fizzlewick Pugs South Wales, UK, said: "The most appealing thing about Pugs…hmm…where to start!? They make excellent companions, they are almost human in some ways, they are clever, funny, loyal and just so happy to do 'whatever' as long as they have your company. I think the Pug dog motto "Multum in Parvo" (meaning much in little) sums them up perfectly."

Holly Attwood, Taftazini, Sheffield, UK: "They are fun loving with a lively disposition. Pugs are full of character, highly intelligent, and cheeky with a touch of naughtiness, and they make you laugh every day. They are also even-tempered, friendly with dogs and people; a true companion. The most unique things about them are their quirky traits, like 'the pug run,' their tenacity and their love of life! They are always happy but have a mind of their own."

Melanie Clark, Pugginpugs, Lincolnshire, UK: "The Pug as a breed has the most adorable character which is full of mischief. It is not long before they melt your heart with their big doughy eyes and wrinkled faces - the face of innocence... or are they? I would say although they can be stubborn at times, they're a fun loving breed eager to please their humans."

Linda Guy, Londonderry Pugs, Northern Ireland: "They are stubborn, loving, friendly, courageous, playful, and lazy at times. Sometimes they go 'supersonic' and take mad fits of running around the house at full pelt. Their beautiful eyes are the window into their souls. They can tell you how they are feeling and you feel like they understand you when they look into your eyes. They love physical affection and really bond with you. They are brave and funny dogs." Pictured is Linda's Roxie sporting her new fur coat.

Sandra Mayoh, Drumlinfold Pugs, North Yorkshire, UK: "Pugs are outgoing, happy-go-lucky, comical and they love all people and other animals. What makes them unique and special are their cute faces, their ability to make you laugh and their devotion to the family."

Sue Wragg, of Glammarags Pugs, Cheshire, UK: "They are happy, confident, loving and amusing. Pugs make you smile every day with their comical behaviour and appealing expressions."

Deborah Hayman, of Fawnydawn Pugs, Malta, added: "Regarding temperament, the typical Pug should be of good nature, calm and relaxed. Throughout the years I found out that female puppies are more hyper than the males, but eventually they will settle down with maturity. Pugs are great family dogs, I have had two babies since I started with Pugs and they have always been great."

Here's what some US breeders have to say on the breed, starting with Donna Shank and Brenda Schuettenberg of RoKuCiera Pugs, California, who have been breeding Pugs since 1962: "When you think about describing the Pug temperament, think about a three-year-old child in a dog suit! There is laughter, tears, games of tag and temper tantrums when over-tired. They are the most loving companions.

"They are the smallest Mastiff-like breed and they don't think that they are little, this can be dangerous for them sometimes if their owner is not careful. Pugs act like a large working dog that doesn't take up so much of the couch or bed when you share that space with them. Most normal

Pugs love children and make great playmates that are more than willing to get into any adventure the child can think up - the Pug will help them think up even more variations."

J. Candy Schlieper, of CandyLand Pugs, Ohio, has been breeding Pugs for more than 30 years. She said: "They are funny, very loving, compassionate, sweet and very devoted to their owners. They make wonderful companions and do well with kids, people and all breeds of dogs. They are a wonderful breed - there's no other like them - and you just can't live without them."

Roberta Kelley-Martin, of HRH Pugs, California, has been involved with purebred dogs for more than 30 years and has bred Pugs since 2003. She said: They are easy going, loving, playful, loving, stubborn, loving, comical, loving, entertaining, loving, loyal, and fun loving! They need to be in your lap, and are little dogs with a big attitude. Pugs are (or should be) very confident dogs that handle a multitude of situations well. They easily adapt to new people, new animals, and changes in their lives. (At least mine do.) They are best summed up as: 'Unconditional love and devotion'."

Catherine Jones-Kyle, Dixie Darlings, Tennessee, said: "Pugs are loyal to a fault, they are loving and a constant companion all through the house. They should be relaxed and easy going. They are fun and have a wicked sense of humour, being intelligent but stubborn. They may know what they are supposed to do, but if they don't feel like doing it, they'll find a reason not to - like opting to chew on a bone they 'lost' ages ago and just found.

"Pugs love to be loved, spoiled and are attention hogs. They are patient, allowing even toddlers to do what they want with them without complaint. Everything about them is unique and special: they are great with children, they do well in small spaces like apartments, but love a big yard to run in - even if it only a few steps. The have a way of looking at you; you can have an entire conversation with them just by watching their eyes."

Erin Ford, of Fur-N-Feathers, Florida: "Pugs are very gentle, attentive and love to be centre of attention, As puppies Pugs are very hyper and social, they love to spend lots of time outside, As they get older they enjoy spending time with their family cuddling on the couch, They are harder than most breeds to potty train and have a very strong will and are stubborn at times, They don't listen very well unless trained.

"What appealed to me was their little eyes and nose, they have the sweetest little face and look up with such admiration and complete love. What makes them unique is how they can light up the darkest of lives with just their personality, which is so big for such a small dog, and they demand to be loved."

Laura Libner, of Loralar Pugs, Michigan, added: "The typical Pug temperament is impish and very personable. What makes them special is their love of life - being silly, fun loving, easy going and trustworthy companions."

Linda and Kim Wright, of Wright's Pugs, Michigan have the last word: "Pugs are funny, lovable, busy, lively cuddle bugs. They love to be on your lap and are jealous if anyone else is getting attention. We call them the clowns of the dog world. They don't know they are a little dog, they are larger than life and have a wonderful temperament.

"Three words to sum them up? An absolute delight."

The Pug is a very loving and rewarding companion, but it is also a breed whose happiness relies on a committed owner. Are you ready for the challenge? Read on to find out.

2. History of the Pug

Chinese Whispers

The exact history of the Pug has been lost in the mists of time. There is some recent evidence that, although the Pug may have originated in China, its current genetic make-up owes more to European breeds of dogs than Chinese ones.

According to most historians and the London Zoological Society, the Pug's origins lie in China and it is one of the oldest dog breeds in the world. Ancient Chinese documents state that short-nosed dogs with a description similar to that of the Pug existed there around 700-400BC.

From these earliest times the Pug's sole function was to live in luxury as a companion dog. They were bred and owned by emperors, and there was an ancient Chinese law stating that only the Emperor was allowed to own a Pug. Other people could only own one if it was a gift from the Emperor himself; illegal ownership was punishable by death.

Pugs had their own living quarters and servants within the Royal Palace and were held in the highest regard. Emperor Ling (168-190 AD) was so taken with these little dogs that that he gave them ranks. Males were given the rank of Kai-Fu, or viceroy, ruling in the name of the king or queen. Females were given the same rank as the wives of high officials. Soldiers guarded the dogs, who were fed only the best meat and rice – Puggy heaven!

During the Yuan Dynasty (1271-1368) it was customary to parade all the Emperor's animals in front of his guests. Immediately after the lions, the "golden-coated nimble dogs" were presented.

Many historians believe the modern breed originated from the Lo-Chiang-Sze dog, later shortened to Lo-Sze. Others believe its ancestor was a little short-haired dog with a flat nose and a tail curled on its back called the Ha-Pa, or Happa. Dogs similar to Pugs were popular in the Imperial court during the Song Dynasty, 960-1279. (Pictured is Emperor Taizong of Song).

In his 1921 book "Dogs of China and Japan in Nature and Art" 1921, V.W.F. Collier devotes a whole chapter to 'The Chinese Pug', in which he refers to the Pug as the Lo-Sze. He writes: "One of the most important characteristics of the Chinese Lo-sze dog, in addition to universal shortness of coat, is elasticity of skin existing in a far greater degree than with the 'Pekingese.'

"The point most sought after by Chinese breeders was the 'Prince' mark, formed by three wrinkles on the forehead with a vertical bar in imitation of the Chinese character for Prince (today called the thumbprint). This same character is distinguished by the Chinese in the stripes on the forehead of the tiger, which, in consequence, is the object of superstitious veneration among the ignorant. The button, or white blaze, on the forehead was also encouraged in the Lo-sze dog, but was not of the same importance as the wrinkles.

"Other points — such as compactness of body, flatness of face, squareness of jaw and soundness of bone — are similar to those of Pekingese, except as regards the ears, which were small and likened to a dried half apricot, set with the outer face on the side of the head and pointing slightly backwards. "The 'Chiao-tzu,' or horn-ear, is also admissible. The legs are but slightly bent at the elbow. The tail is docked by the Chinese, with a view to symmetrical form. The curly tail, however, is known to have existed ('sze kuo chu-erh'), and the double curl was also known.

LO-SZE DOG. "SHEN CHEN-LIN. CAREFUL DRAWING"

"The most admired and rarest of the breed was the 'loong chua lo-sze' (dragon-claw pug), which was short-coated except for the ears, the toes, behind the legs, and the chrysanthemum flower tail, all of which were very well feathered. This appears to have been a distinct race which became extinct about fifty years ago.
"The pug-dog occurred in any colour, and was bred as small as possible."

The breed spread to Tibet, where they were kept by monks in monasteries, then to Japan and centuries later to Europe. It is generally agreed that modern Pugs are descended from dogs imported to Europe in the 16th or early 17th centuries, initially smuggled out of China by sailors of the Dutch East India Company. The sailors took the little dogs home, where they soon became popular as companions for the upper classes and nobility. They were known as Mops or Mopshond in Dutch and Mopshund in Germany (literally 'roly poly dog!')

During The Eighty Years' War against Philip II of Spain, the life of William the Silent, Prince of Orange (1533-1584), pictured, was saved by his Pug, Pompey. While the prince slept one night at Hermigny, France, assassins crept toward his tent. Pompey heard them and began barking and scratching to warn his master, finally jumping on the prince's face to alert him to the impending danger.

Sir Roger Williams' 1618 book *"Actions in the Low Countries"* describes the attack: "The Prince of Orange (...) being retired into the camp. Julian Romero, with earnest persuasions, procured license of the Duke D'Alva to hazard a camisado, or night attack, upon the Prince. At midnight Julian sallied out of the trenches with a thousand armed men, mostly pikes, who forced all the guards that they found in their way into the place of arms before the Prince's tent, and killed two of his secretaries.

"The Prince himself escaped very narrowly, for I have often heard him say that he thought but for a dog he should have been taken or slain. The attack was made with such resolution, that the guards took no alarm until their fellows were running to the place of arms, with their enemies at their heels, when this dog, hearing a great noise, fell to scratching and crying, and awakened him before any of his men; and though the Prince slept armed, with a lacquey always holding one of his horses ready bridled and saddled, yet, at the going out of his tent, with much ado he recovered his horse before the enemy arrived.

"Nevertheless, one of his equerries was slain taking horse presently after him, as were divers of his servants. The Prince, to show his gratitude, until his dying day kept one of that dog's race, and so did many of his friends and followers. These animals were not remarkable for their beauty, being little white dogs, with crooked noses, called Camuses." (The French word camus meant 'a person with a short, flat nose.')

This incident would permanently link the Pug with the Dutch House of Orange and cause the breed to travel to England from Holland with another Prince of Orange, William III, over a century later.

William and his cousin and wife Mary (pictured), were both Protestants. They became joint sovereigns of the Kingdoms of England, Scotland and Ireland in 1689, an event which came to be known as 'The Glorious Revolution' after they succeeded the Catholic James II (Mary's father and William's uncle). It is said that William's Pugs attended his coronation ceremony wearing orange ribbons.

These first dogs were often referred to as 'Dutch Pugs' or 'Dutch Mastiffs.' Although the term 'mastiff' technically refers only to the English Mastiff breed, the word 'mastiff' or 'molosser' was and still is used to describe certain types of dog which share a common ancestor. Molossers are solidly built, large dog breeds, typically with heavy bones, pendant ears, a relatively short and well-muscled neck and a short muzzle. Larger molossers today include all the Mastiffs, including Dogue de Bordeaux (French Mastiff), Great Dane (German Mastiff), Cane Corso (Italian Mastiff) and Tosa Inu (Japanese Mastiff). The Pug, Bulldog, French Bulldog and Boston Terrier are regarded as the small molossers or mastiffs.

The Order of the Pugs

Pugs eventually became popular in other European countries. They were painted by famous European artists and in Italy they rode on the front of private carriages dressed in jackets and pantaloons which matched those of the coachman. Some time around 1736, the Pug became the symbol of a strange group known as the Mops Orden, or Order of the Pug, believed to have started in Bavaria, Germany. This was a secret society, a fraternal group for Roman Catholics who had been forbidden to join the Freemasons by Pope Clement XII.

The constitution of the Order of the Pug allowed women to become members as long as they were Catholic. The Grand Master was a man, but each lodge required two Lodge Masters or 'Big Pugs,' a man and a woman who shared the governing role. Members called themselves Pugs (or Mops, the German word for Pug), and members of the Order carried a silver Pug medallion.

Novices were initiated in a bizarre ceremony at which they wore a dog collar and had to scratch at the door to get in. The novices were then blindfolded and led nine times around a carpet decorated with symbols while the Pugs of the Order barked loudly and shouted: "Memento mori" - Remember you shall die! – to test the steadiness of the newcomers. During the initiation, novices also had to kiss a porcelain Pug's backside under its tail (see picture) as an expression of total devotion. It is thought that this ritual may have been a deliberate parody of the mysterious Freemason rituals, which the Mops were excluded from.

Around 1740, German sculptor Johann Joachim Kaendler, master model maker at the famous Meissen porcelain factory in Germany, was commissioned to create a group of porcelain Pug dogs which were used in the rituals of the Order of the Mops. It is thought the secret society chose the Pug as their emblem as a symbol of loyalty, trustworthiness and steadiness. However, the breed also came to represent a subversive element.

Pugs had been brought to England by the Protestant King William III who replaced the Catholic king, who was banished to France. The English Parliament were unsure of this new Dutch king following the so-called 'Glorious Revolution' and created a new type of constitutional monarchy in which they very carefully watched over the king and his actions. Intellectuals from other European countries began to admire this new style of government and free thinking, and owning a Pug was a subtle way of showing solidarity with England's revolution without getting locked in the stocks or hurled into a dungeon.

There are other interesting 18th century stories involving Pugs. One of them relates to Josephine de Beauharnais, wife of Napoleon Bonaparte. Before her marriage to Napoleon, Josephine was married to Alexandre de Beauharnais. He was guillotined during the Reign of Terror and Josephine was imprisoned in Carmes Prison until five days after Alexandre's execution. At that time she had a Pug named Fortune who was her only permitted visitor at Carmes. Josephine used the little dog to carry secret messages to her two children, Eugene and Hortense.

When she married Napoleon in 1796, he supposedly refused to let the Pug come on to their bed on their wedding night. The Pug then reportedly bit Napoleon in the leg and Josephine announced that if the dog could not stay in the bed, then neither would she. From then on Napoleon shared his bed with a Pug as well as Josephine (except when she had a headache!)

Pugs in Art

During the 18th century Pugs were very fashionable, particularly among the higher echelons of society, and famous painters wasted no time in committing the breed to canvas. One of the earliest European paintings of a Pug was by French artist Nicolas de Largillière, entitled Louis XIV and His Heirs (right), painted between 1710 and 1714, now in the Wallace Collection, London. The black Pug is just visible at the lower right of the painting, the dog at the front is a Papillon.

In France at that time Pugs were known as Carlins after Carlo "Carlin" Bertinazzi, an Italian actor famous for playing the role of Harlequin, or buffoon, in the French theatre. The Harlequin wore a black mask during the performance and the Pug's black mask was a characteristic of the breed at this time.

Spanish romantic painter Francisco Goya (1746-1828) had a penchant for Pugs. His 1786 oil on canvas 'The Marquesa de Pontejos' features the wasp–waisted figure of María Ana de Pontejos y Sandoval, Marquesa de Pontejos, in shepherdess style, complete with her faithful fawn Pug, suitably bedecked in a fancy bow with three bells at the front (next page, left).

Centrepiece of Flemish artist Louis-Michel van Loo's striking 1759 portrait of Russian aristocrat Catherina Golitsyna (centre) is the Pug. The princess's clothes and pearls signified luxury and good taste – even the Pug has pearls on his collar. In his critique of the painting, Stephen Pain says: "Since the time of Peter the Great, pugs in Russia had been a favoured symbol of aristocrats, like the toy breeds of today, and in their proximity to the ladies one could read sometimes an erotic undertone – the hair and nape was an erogenous zone in the eighteenth century, hence those curly locks that fall from her hair."

English painter William Hogarth was the devoted owner of a series of Pugs and a great fan of the breed. He used to take his pet Pug along with him whenever he painted the high society ladies and gentlemen of the day – and many of his Pugs made it into the final painting. His 1745 self-portrait (above, right), now in London's Tate Gallery, includes his beloved Pug, Trump.

Hogarth's love of Pugs has recently surprised art experts. In 1757 he painted his final self-portrait, entitled 'Hogarth Painting the Comic Muse' which shows the artist at his easel on which is an unfinished sketch of the Muse of Comedy. When curators at London's National Portrait Gallery X-rayed the painting for a new catalogue, they got quite a surprise. Hidden underneath the oil paint was another painting, no longer visible, of the artist painting a nude woman and in one corner was none other than a cheeky Pug leaping over a pile of canvasses and peeing on them!

When English artist George Reynolds' 1766 painted George Selwyn with his pug, Raton in 1766, he deliberately aligned the heads of man and animal so they were both staring directly at the artist. It was said to provide a "witty counterpoint between Selwyn's languid expression and Raton's alertness to the artist's or the viewer's presence."

The paintings of Pugs below are all from the 1700s and early 1800s. All of them show how much the Pug has changed physically over time – similar to what has happened to the English Bulldog. Historically, the Pug was a far more athletic dog with longer legs, a lighter body and longer muzzle. Two of the artworks show Pugs which have been subjected to the cruel practice of ear cropping, explained later. Gainsborough's painting of a Pug, far left, fetched almost £1 million (around $1.5 million) at auction in 2009.

Pictured is a pair of Pugs from the acclaimed Meissen porcelain factory. Today a valuable collection of the original Meissen Pugs and human figurines with their Pug dogs, all mementoes of the Order of the Mops, can be found at the headquarters of the Freemasons in Great Queen Street, between Holborn and Covent Garden in London.

The Pug has also appeared in literature, Lady Bertram had a pet Pug in Jane Austen's novel Mansfield Park, published in 1814.

Ear Cropping and Names

In *"A History And Description Of The Modern Dogs Of Great Britain And Ireland. (Non-Sporting Division)"* 1894, Rawdon Briggs Lee writes of the rise in popularity of the breed in England: "The pug has never been claimed in this country as a native breed, but was supposed to have been a native of Holland, and even to this day is sometimes called the Dutch pug. As it happens, at present more of them are with us now than is the case in any other country on the Continent, although the pug has a wide range, extending pretty much from the east to the west of Europe.

"In France and Italy it is a favourite with the ladies, and at one period of its existence, but for a short time only, it was known in the former country as the Carlin, owing to its black mask or muzzle, a name given it in honour of a popular harlequin named Carlin. This, of course, was but a passing fancy, and prior to Carlin's popularity they had been known as doguins or roquets, but afterwards they obtained the commoner, if less euphonious, name of pugs."

A certain Mrs Piozzi confirmed the popularity of Pugs in Italy, as she wrote in her journal of 1789: "The little Pug dog or Dutch mastiff has quitted London for Padua, I perceive. Every carriage I meet here has a Pug in it." There is also evidence that Pugs were popular in Russia and that some British strains may also have come from Russia.

Rawdon Briggs Lee went on to describe a cruel historical practice which may explain how the Pug got its name: "Unfortunately, prior to the introduction of dog shows (1859), cruel custom had insisted that the pug dog looked most lovely when robbed of its ears. They were not merely cut off and artistically trimmed, as is the common practice with the bull terrier and one or two other varieties at the present time, the pug's ears were shorn off, and rounded close to the head; so close, indeed, in some instances as to give the impression, which was curiously believed to be correct, that they had been torn out by the roots.

"The vagaries of fashion are certainly most difficult to comprehend, and why a delicate lady's pet dog should have been tortured in this way there is not the slightest reason to show. Fighting dogs had their ears cut off to prevent their offering a hold for the teeth of an opponent; ears of terriers had been cut to produce a smarter and brighter appearance, and perhaps the tail had been docked in the first instance under the vulgar superstition that the "distemper worm "was thereby destroyed!

"A pug with the ears shorn off was rendered hideous, though may be its profile thus looked more like the shadow of a clenched fist than it would with the ears on; the pug no doubt obtaining its name from the Latin word pugnus, a fist."

Writing in 1903 in *"British Dogs, Their Points, Selection, And Show Preparation"* W. D. Drury puts forward another explanation for the name: "Although the word pug originally meant an imp, or little demon, the name is not applied to the dog in a sinister sense, but with a kindly feeling, as we playfully call a spirited child a little imp."

His explanation is based on the theory that the word 'pug' was a corruption of Puck, a mischievous nature sprite in Celtic folklore. There are other theories as to how the breed got its name.

The word 'pug' was commonly in the second half of the sixteenth century as a term of endearment and the word may have been transferred to the cute little dogs. In England, the dog breed wasn't known as a Pug until the mid-1700s, and even then it was referred to as the' pug dog'. M. Bailey's Dictionary of 1731 stated: "Pug, a nickname for a Monkey or Dog." The word 'pug' may have been given to the breed because the face somewhat resembled that of a marmoset monkey, also called a pug, which was a popular pet of the day.

However the name came about, today we can't imagine the Pug being called anything else. It's short and sweet, just like the breed itself!

Two Types of Pugs

During the 19th century, two types of Pugs developed: the Willoughby and the Morrison strains had been developed, and were rivals for many years.

The Morrison line developed from a pure Dutch Pug. It is said that this strain descended from Pugs of Queen Charlotte and George III, who obtained their original stock from the continent. From this line Charles Morrison, a tavern owner from Walham Green, developed the Morrison Pug. The Morrison Pugs had cobby bodies, rich apricot-fawn coats and heads with a trademark black mask. Morrison's two famous Pugs, Punch and Tetty were the foundation stock for many of today's modern Pugs.

In an attempt to improve the breed, Lord Willougby d'Eresby (or his wife Lady Willoughby, according to some accounts) went to St. Petersburg and contacted a, a lady tightrope walker known as the female Blondin, who sold him two Russian Pugs. (Others claim he obtained a pug from Vienna that belonged to a Hungarian countess.) Mops, one of the dogs purchased from the tightrope walker was bred to Nell, a fawn bitch from Holland, that had a shorter face, more wrinkles and a heavier jowl.

It was thought Nell's attributes were just what was needed to improve the line, and the crossing of the two dogs produced a line of Pugs noted for their smutty, cold-stone fawn colour with entire, or nearly entire, black heads. The Willoughby Pugs were sometimes called pepper and salt because of their smutty coats. They had wide saddle marks or traces and were leggier, slimmer and 'small in the eye.' These characteristics can still appear in litters today, indicating that the Willoughby influence is still around.

According to reports at the time, few fanciers considered the Willoughby-type Pugs an asset to the breed. There were, however, those who boasted about them and Victorian judges were also instrumental in promoting the line.

After much selective breeding, the Morrison and Willoughby lines were crossed and re-crossed, and the bloodlines fused into one, but breeders today can still recognise the individual characteristics of the two types of Pugs.

Another important development came about in 1860. Two Pugs were stolen from the palace of the Emperor of China during the siege of Peking, and soldiers or members of the embassy are thought to have brought them back to England. In any case, a Mrs St. John received these pure Chinese Pugs as a gift. Laura Mayhew, a distinguished breeder and a friend of Mrs St. John, was thrilled about the arrival of these Pugs from China, and had them brought to her home in Twickenham. The two Pugs, Lamb and Moss, looked like twins - clear apricot fawn, no white and beautiful heads. It is said: "They were lovely dogs, although they needed a bit more leg and shorter backs."

CLICK

This fresh Oriental blood interbred into the Willoughby and Morrison lines made their strains stronger. Lamb and Moss produced a son, Click, (pictured, right) and Mrs Mayhew became his owner. Click bred with many bitches to produce top-quality Pugs, especially valuable females. Click's lines were the thought to be the finest of the 19th century. In fact, in both England and America the majority of modern Pug dogs trace back to Click.

Victorian Times

Queen Victoria, who ruled from 1837 to 1901, was a great dog lover. Her Pugs, many of which she bred herself, included Olga, Pedro, Minka, Fatima and Venus. The Queen favoured fawns. She passed her love of the breed on to many other members of the Royal family, including grandson King George V and his son, King Edward VIII, who became the Duke of Windsor after his abdication. Her influence contributed to the outlawing of the cruel habit of cropping Pugs' ears, although this did not happen until 1895.

Queen Victoria's passion for dogs in general helped to establish the world's first Kennel Club in London on April 4th 1873. The original 13 gentlemen members wanted to have a consistent set of rules for governing the popular new activities of dog showing and field trials.

The Victorians' love of both dogs and hobbies meant that dog showing and activities became very popular extremely quickly. The first conformation Dog Show in the world was held in the Town Hall, Newcastle-on-Tyne, in 1859 and the next 14 years saw explosive growth in this new and fashionable hobby.

Although a class was reserved for Pugs at the 1860 show, none were entered. The Pug's appearance probably changed after around 1860 when a new wave of the breed was imported directly from China. These dogs had shorter legs and a flatter nose. This smaller, less athletic and non-functional breed fell out of favour with the public for a while. Although later in the 19th century, British aristocrat

Lady Brassey is credited with making black Pugs fashionable for a while after she brought some back from China in 1886.

In the 19th century, opinions were divided about the breed. In his 1894 *"A History And Description Of The Modern Dogs Of Great Britain And Ireland. (Non-Sporting Division),"* Rawdon Briggs Lee wrote a full description of the Pug and its merits: "As a companion in the house, and for an occasional run into the country, no dog is better fitted than the pug. He is cleanly in his habits, has a pretty, soft coat, and nice skin; no foul smell hangs about him, and he is gentleness itself. He shows no ill-temper or moppishness, and the objectionable lolling out of the tongue and unpleasant snorting, which at one time were so common in this variety, is quickly disappearing. "Of several pugs that I have owned or known, not more than one of them was addicted to either of these unpleasant habits.

"All were lively and tractable, and if not actually as intelligent as a highly-trained poodle, one pug I knew was quite accomplished in many little tricks he used to perform. No doubt had a professional trainer taken this little dog in hand it would have been able to earn more than its own living on the stage. Again, a pug can remain sweet and healthy on less open-air exercise than any other dog, and two of them will play about the dining room or nursery and amuse themselves as much as two terriers would by a scamper in the green fields.

"The pug is not a hunting dog, except so far as tracking the footsteps of his fair mistress is concerned, but he has been known to take to the unladylike occupation of killing rats, which he has done as well as a terrier. Still, it is no part of the duties of a lady's lap-dog to soil his pretty mouth by contact with the most obnoxious of creatures, because we all know that perhaps the next minute he may be fondled and caressed by his owner.

"Although I have said a pug dog can do with comparatively little out-door exercise, still, he is better for as much as he can be given, for no dog has a greater tendency to put on fat, and reach a state of obesity, than the one of which I write. Whoever saw a pug dog thin and gaunt, with its ribs and backbone almost sticking through the skin? He always looks smooth, contented, and comfortable, eats well, and he should have as little meat and fat-producing food as possible. Some writers have given him the reputation of stupidity, but I do not believe him deserving of such an epithet. In the house and out of doors he is as sensible as any other dog, follows well in a crowd when properly trained, and is no more liable to lose himself than an ordinary terrier.

"For a long time there was a fallacy abroad that the sex of the pug could be determined by the carriage and curl of the tail, the dog having his over on the right side and the bitch on the left. As a matter of fact, I have repeatedly observed dogs with the curl to the left, and bitches with theirs to the right. Sundry peculiarities in the pug are that it is essential for the toe nails to be black (this is often overlooked by the judges), and that they should have a black mole or spot on each cheek. Of course, all dogs have the latter, but in the pug it is much more clearly defined than is the case in other varieties. The dark trace along the back is another peculiarity, as is, of course, the quaintly-curled tail."

He added: "The quaint-looking, courtly little dogs were quite the rage for a time, but I fancy that for one reason or another they did not make a great deal of headway in Britain, possibly because in-breeding had made them delicate. However, every now and then some fresh blood was introduced from both France and Italy, as well as from Holland, and so the breed was continued, although it did not become particularly common."

W D Drury disagreed with this affectionate portrait of the Pug, writing in *"British Dogs, Their Points, Selection, And Show Preparation"* in 1903: "The popularity of the Pug seems to have been at neap tide at the beginning of last century, if we may judge from the following remarks of a cynical writer of that period: 'Perhaps in the whole catalogue of the canine species there is not one of less utility, or possessing less the power of attraction, than the Pug dog; applicable to no sport, appropriated to no useful purpose, susceptible of no predominant passion, and in no way remarkable for any extra eminence, he is continued from era to era for what alone he might have been originally intended - the patient follower of a ruminating philosopher, or the adulating and consolatory companion of an old maid'."

"With these views and sentiments Pug-lovers, whether "ruminating philosophers," maids, or matrons, are not likely to be in sympathy. One would suppose the writer to have been a cantankerous old bachelor, caring for nothing but his pipe, his Pointer, and his gun."

In the American *"Book Of Dogs - An Intimate Study Of Mankind's Best Friend"* published by the National Geographic Society (US) in 1919, authors Ernest Harold Baynes and Louis Agassiz Fuertes stated: "The pug was once a great favorite with those who like pet dogs, but he has long since been supplanted by other and more attractive breeds. Almost obsolete in America, at least, the pug is now most often encountered in his china image, which still graces the mantel in many a mid-Victorian home.

"Mastiff colors characterize this curly tailed stocky, stiff-legged little dog, "apricot fawn" with black face and ears being the invariable rule, except for the all-black variety, which was never popular here. On fawn dogs, a black "trace" down the back is very greatly prized. The face is very short and cobby, the chest wide, neck short and loose of skin, and the legs straight and well boned, but not too heavy. The eyes are set wide apart and quite low. They are rather full and prominent. The ears are small, thin, and soft, and the coat is short, fine, and hard. They are clean, companionable dogs, with a tendency to get fat, blind, and asthmatic as they get old."

According to 'Every Woman's Encyclopaedia', written 1910-1912: "Time was when the pug reigned supreme in Mayfair. Now, however, his place has been usurped by other breeds; but still the pug has many adherents, and at no time have his interests been more jealously guarded. Has he not clubs to see to his representation and secure the awarding to him of "specials" at our great shows. As a pet, the pug has many merits, not the least of which are the facts that his coat and breath are free from any sort of unpleasant odour, his size is suitable for the average house or flat, and his short coat does not require the grooming and attention of the Pekinese and other long-haired toys now in vogue."

The next two paragraphs ring as true today as they did over 100 years ago: "The popular idea of the pug seems, unhappily, to be that of an obese, panting, and more or less snappy little beast. Any truth that may lurk in this fallacy only proves that the pug, like the rest of us, has 'the defects of his qualities.' Treated on rational principles, he is a merry, cheery creature, full of affection, and an alert house-dog.

"True, he has a tendency towards embonpoint (plumpness) beyond most small dogs, but careful dieting and sufficient exercise will keep him in good trim. Like many short-nosed dogs, he has a habit of snorting and snuffling if he contracts a cold. It is necessary, therefore, to see that he is protected from draughts, and at the same time to keep him as hardy and fit as possible."

Pictured above is Miss L Burnett's Champion Master Jasper, which 'Every Woman's Encyclopaedia' describes as "an excellent example of correct expression."

"And, in conclusion, let those breeds whose doggish day seems over remember that Fashion's wheel, like that of Fortune, is ever rolling, and the day will surely return when the Toys that were the joy of the Early Victorian lady will supplant some of their foreign rivals, and we shall see the Italian greyhound, the pug, and the Maltese again lords of the boudoirs and, doubtless, occupants of the best seats in the aeroplanes of Park Lane."

Incidentally, the lady authors had some advice for new Pug owners, most of which is still relevant over a century later: "It is advisable to buy pugs as young as possible, and then only from someone in whom you can place complete confidence - a well-known breeder, if you can, rather than an unknown dog-dealer. Do not be above asking the vendor or the doggy friend of experience how to feed the youngster. See that the instructions you receive are as carefully carried out as would be those of your medical man.

"If possible, feed and exercise and train your dog yourself. Groom him daily, and be as firm as kind -if not more so. The result will be a dog of which you need not be ashamed, affectionate and intelligent, good-looking, and reasonably hardy, and it will be your own fault if he resembles the disgusting, unhappy obesity of popular fiction and caricature."

At the turn of the 20th century, leading dog expert W. D. Drury, known as 'Stonehenge,' gave the breed this ringing endorsement in *British Dogs, Their Points, Selection, And Show Preparation*: "The pug, when made a companion of, shows a high intelligence; as house dogs they are ever on the alert, and promptly give notice of a stranger's approach, and from their extremely active, I may say merry, habits, they are most interesting pets, and well repay by their gratitude any affection and kindness bestowed on them. One quality they possess above most breeds, which is a strong recommendation of them as lap dogs, and that is their cleanliness and freedom from any offensive smell of breath or skin."

Wide Variations

In his 1897 British Dogs book, book Hugh Dalziel complains about the wide variation of Pugs being shown at the end of the 19th century: "I have attended many of our shows in various parts of the country, but have failed to discover the type of dog required, there being such a discrepancy in the decisions at shows. One judge seems to favour one dog and another judge prefers another, and in many instances, I will not say all, they seem to ignore altogether the points as laid down by the authors before named." (Pictured is the original Pug Breeder's Challenge Cup)

PUG BREEDER'S CHALLENGE CUP.

"At one show you will see a big dog, with a turned-up tail, not the 'curl,' win; at another, one with a long muzzle and leggy, or a black face and the coat all 'smutty,' instead of a distinct trace. Now, I think, and have no doubt most of the fancy will bear me out, that what I may term the modern pug should, in the first place, be 'small' - being a toy, the smaller the better. I adopt myself the standard weight of 12lb, and if a little less all the better; but I contend if they are much over that it is a fault, and should be looked upon as such."

He goes on to give some statistics for the top dogs of the day: Miss Alicia A. L. Jaquet's Tum-Tum: Age, 2 years 4 months; weight, 19lb; height at shoulder, 13in; length from nose to set on of tail, 22in; length of tail, 6½in; girth of chest, 20in; girth of loin, 17¾in; girth of head, 14½in; girth of arm 1in. above elbow, 5¾in; girth of leg 1in below elbow, 5in; length of head from occiput to tip of nose,

5in; girth of muzzle midway between eyes and tip of nose, 7 ½in; from corner of eye to tip of nose, 1in.; between eyes, 1¾in; depth of chap, 1¾in; colour and markings, stone fawn, black points.

Mr T. Morris's Punch: Weight, 17½lb; height at shoulder, 12in; chest to stern, 16in; length of leg, 6½in; girth of chest, 19½in; muzzle, ⅞in; girth of muzzle, 7in.

Mr S. B. Witchell's Young Friday: Weight, 14¾lb; length of leg, 6in; height at shoulder, 12in; length from chest to stern, 12½in; girth of chest, 20in; ditto of loins, 16in; around skull, 14½in; length of nose, 1⅛in; around snout, 8in; width between ears, 4½in.

Mr E. Weekly-Vic: Age, 3 years 11 months; weight, 20 pounds; height at shoulder, 12 inches; length from nose to set on tail, 21 inches; length of tail, 8 inches; girth of chest, 22 inches; girth of loin, 16 3/4 inches; girth of head, 12 3/4 inches; girth of arm I inch above elbow, 5 inches; girth of leg I inch below elbow, 4 inches; length of head from occiput to tip of nose, 5 inches; girth of muzzle midway between eyes and tip of nose, 6 inches; colour and markings, apricot fawn.

These measurements illustrate not only the wide variations in the Pug at that time, but also how much the conformation of the breed changed over the next century. All of the dogs had narrower legs than those of today, their weight varied tremendously and some had much longer bodies than today's Pug.

The Black Pug

The history of the black Pug is outlined by Rawdon Briggs Lee *in "A History And Description Of The Modern Dogs Of Great Britain And Ireland. (Non-Sporting Division)"* 1894 and, just as with the fawn Pug, there is a lack of clarity as to its origins: "Here is a new variety, which has certainly appeared and obtained identity as such within the past two or three years, although we must go back a little further for the time when a few specimens were occasionally exhibited in our show rings; these being the property of the late Lady Brassey, and they were first shown at Maidstone in 1886.

"Perhaps to form a direct contrast to these early specimens, some kind of an attempt had been made to produce white pugs; but herein success was not achieved, the nearest approach thereto being one that a couple of years ago was shown in New York, and another sent to the Birmingham show in 1892, by Miss Dalziel, of Woking, but neither was of that snowy whiteness which one would require, and both I should take to be more "sports" than anything else. Still I do not see any reason why white pugs could not be produced by judicious crossing with the palest fawn specimens, with a slight dash of white bulldog or bull terrier to assist matters. However, this is digression.

"It seems strange that with such a modern variety of dog there should be serious doubts about its origin, and there are certainly differences of opinion on the matter. On one side it is stated to have come from the North of China, and that Lady Brassey brought a specimen therefrom when she was touring round the world in her yacht, the "Sunbeam." Again it is said the breed first sprang up accidentally, it being a "sport" produced in the north of London by one of the working fanciers in that locality, who had a particularly dark-coloured strain of the ordinary pug.

"Mrs W. H. B. Warner, of Northallerton, at the close of 1893, showed a little black dog which she had brought from Japan, where it was said to be of a rare and choice breed. This is nothing else than a long-coated pug- i.e., pug in character and shape, but with a jacket such as is seen on a Pomeranian. But there is no reason to doubt that in the East there are as many varieties of the dog as we have here. However, it is only in place that this latest of importations should be mentioned here. In, however, suggesting that our black pugs may have come from some such dog as this, it must not be forgotten that they have very short and thin jackets, the antipodes of this little fellow of Mrs Warner's.

"Personally, I believe there may be truth in both statements, that a black pug was accidentally produced, and at the same time a specimen or two had been brought from the East. Although Lady Brassey makes no allusion to a black pug in her published journals of the voyage of the "Sunbeam," still I know as a fact that two or three similar dogs were on her yacht, but whether they were then called black pugs is another question. More likely they were known as Chinese pugs.

"A writer in a recent number of Black and White says: 'It is rather unfortunate that the late Lady Brassey should have allowed the origin of the new pug to remain a mystery, but there seems little doubt that it hailed from China, as in a weekly contemporary, only the other day, I saw a copy of an advertisement which had been appearing in the North China Daily News:

> "LOST, NEAR THE HONG KONG AND SYEZCHEN ROADS, LAST EVENING, A SMALL PEKING PUG, BLACK BODY AND HEAD, WHITE PAWS. ANYONE FINDING SAME WILL BE REWARDED ON BRINGING

"The white paws were evidently uncommon, and were the lost dog's distinguishing marks. I have also learned that a lady in the West End bought a black pug bitch from a sailor on one of the cargo ships just in the docks from China. Another lady at Willesden also bought one in the same way. This one was, however, unfortunately burnt in a fire, and before the purchaser had bred from her; but it is an undoubted fact that these pugs came off a Chinese vessel just arrived in port, and were sold to them as Chinese pugs. One lady describes hers as ' very short in face, good curl tail, and a beautiful jet black' - a perfect pug in points. Again, I have heard of a 'Chinese pug' being bought at Portsmouth from a ship calling there.

1870

"It is, therefore, not improbable that Lady Brassey's black pugs Jack Spratt and Mahdi were brought home from China by Lady Brassey, and were of the breed mentioned in that stray advertisement for a lost pet, viz. a 'Peking ' pug".

"That the variety is, at any rate, now quite a distinct one I do not doubt at all, for the following reasons. Mrs Fifield, of Eastleigh, Southampton, who has some excellent specimens, which originally came from the Brassey strain, says that when blacks are mated together they breed true to type and colour, although in almost every litter a perfectly-marked grey specimen appears, but Mrs Fifield never bred a black one from grey parents. Most of the blacks have, however, a little patch of white on the chest or toes, but others are perfectly black.

"Miss 'Mortivals' (Miss M. D. Robinson), Takeley, Essex, writes in a similar strain, and as these two ladies have had a greater experience of black pugs than any one else, their opinions must be highly valued. Indeed, they, with Mr Alfred Bond, of Gravesend, appear to be the only persons who have given much attention to the variety, and to them all credit is due for the improvement brought about in the appearance of the animal since it first came upon the scene.

"The black pug is now a more cobbily and thickly-made dog than was the case three or four years ago; he is lower on the legs, and his head, face, and skull are more characteristic of our own pug dog, and he is likely in the future to breed quite as true to type as any other of our modern varieties; thus in due course he will popularise himself.

"Although it was not until 1886 that black pugs first appeared at our shows, long before this time Lady Brassey had them at Normanhurst. A pair was given to a lady in Liverpool. Lord Londonderry was likewise presented with a specimen, and later I hear that Her Majesty the Queen took one, amongst her other canine companions, to Balmoral, on the usual royal visit to the Highlands. The royal pug, which bore the name of "Brassey" in honour of its donor, died at Windsor in 1891, and, so far as I can learn, not one of these four animals left any progeny behind."

"After Lady Brassey's tragical death in the Southern seas in 1887, several of her black pugs were purchased by Mr A. Bond, already alluded to. One of these dogs was Jack Spratt, who is said to be pretty well the progenitor of the present strains, though of course other blood was introduced. Mr Bond had the misfortune to lose Jack Spratt in 1888, both he and Bessie Spratt falling victims to that scourge of the pet dog, inflammation of the lungs.

"Fortunately, ere this occurred, Mr Bond had been successful in rearing Lino, from Jack and Bessie Spratt, a handsome black dog, which he subsequently sold to Mrs Fifield, of Southampton, and which has since sired the notable Doatie Darling and Black Gem, two of the best blacks we have had. What had become of Nap. II. - Lady Brassey's especial favourite - and his sister Black Bess, no one could find out, until the Crystal Palace Committee, in their show for 1891, provided two classes for black pugs. Then for the first time Normanhurst Nap, who had become the property of Miss Mortivals, met his brother, the Gravesend Lino, who beat the old favourite. Singularly, the first prize went to quite an outsider, believed to have come from the East End of London, as breeder and pedigree were stated unknown and the type had nothing of the Jack Spratt about it.

"This dog, Nigger, now better known as Surprise, attracted, however, the attention of the judge, and its black coat, tightly curled tail, coupled with a smart carriage, quite overbalanced his somewhat long, terrier-like face, and placed him first in the open class for dogs, in which there were twelve entries. The other dogs shown, the true lineal descendants of Jack Spratt were so shy as to render themselves ridiculously unassertive, their tails dangling under their bodies, so they were quite out of the running. Nap II, however, was consoled by winning the first stud medal ever given to a black pug, he being awarded one of the two bronze medals offered by the Crystal Palace for stud pugs. (pictured is Champion Impi).

"These two well-filled classes of odd-looking, but remarkably handsome, jet black pugs created considerable attention, and since that time classes have been provided for them at our leading exhibitions. Such is all that is known as to the history of the black pug.

"Mrs Fifield and Miss Mortivals both accord the black pugs excellent characters. They say they are hardier than the fawn, especially when past puppyhood, and even when young they are not much trouble to rear. Oily food suits them best, and Miss Mortivals gives hers linseed once a week, it improving their coats and making them appear smarter and cleanlier than they would without it.

"Mrs Fifield writes that 'the black pugs differ materially from the fawns; firstly they are not so susceptible to cold. The prettiest sight I remember was seeing the delight of an exquisite litter of black puppies in their first snowstorm; they simply revelled in it. They are much more tenacious in affection, for, while the fawns freely make friends, no enticements will induce the blacks to leave their owners, and, although very timid, they are wonderfully intelligent and easily learn tricks. "They are cleanly in their habits, but, whilst the fawns are proverbially greedy, the blacks are extremely dainty feeders. A combination of such excellent traits makes them the most perfect companions ladies can possibly wish for'.

"I think I have produced sufficient evidence to satisfy carpers that no wrong has been done in introducing in this volume the Black Pug as a distinct variety. The evidence of those who keep him proves this, not only because the blacks are, even in disposition, unlike the fawns, but because the former breed equally true to type as the latter.

"So far as the points and description are concerned, excepting in colour the two should be alike, but whether by introducing the "fawn" strain one or two of the distinguishing traits in the blacks may be ultimately lost is a question upon which there may be two opinions. The blacker the black pug is the better; he should be free from white, and any brown or bronze tinge is a very severe handicap when being judged in the ring."

Pugs in America

The first Pugs arrived in America shortly after the Civil War (1861-5). The breed grew rapidly in popularity due to its unique appearance and the American Kennel Club was quick to recognise the breed in 1885. Initially the Pug's popularity grew in leaps and bounds, with fierce competition among new Pug breeders. The American Pug fanciers imported prizewinning dogs from England to form the mainstay of today's bloodlines.

In England at the time there were actually two breed standards, one compiled by the Pug Dog Club and the other by leading dog expert and author W.D. Drury, known as Stonehenge. This in turn led to a range of very different looking dogs winning prizes in America initially, which was naturally not without controversy, until the Americans drew up their own breed standard, which varied slightly from the English version - as, indeed, it does today.

The Celebrated Stud Pug Dog

Champion Kash,

The Sire of many Winners.

Stud Fee, $20.00.

Puppies for Sale from Celebrated Prize Winning Stock. Price, $15 00 to $50.00.

A. E. PITTS,

Indianola Kennels,

COLUMBUS, OHIO.

The Show Ring

A leading figure in the breeding of Pugs in the US was Dr Cryer, who published a book called Prize Pugs in 1891 which claimed that up to that time half of all winning Pugs in America at that time had Click's blood in them. His home bred dogs Max and Bessie came from imported dog Dolly, whose father was the Click dog Toby. Other famous imports, all English champions, included Master Tragedy, Othello, Little Banjo, Lord Clover and Effie, who went on to win three championships at New York, but unfortunately was a non-breeder.

One of the most famous of them all was Bradford Ruby, an

imported silver fawn male with English Champion parents, owned by Walter D. Peck of City View Kennels, New Haven, Connecticut. He is listed as having been shown a total of 46 times with great consistency, being placed second and sometimes third in his first 30 or so shows in England. But his fortunes really took off when he reached the North American show scene and went on to win championships in New York, Toronto, Philadelphia, Newark, New Haven and Hartford.

Pictured right are Mrs Foster's Diamond and Bradford Ruby. The champion dogs of this time had slimmer bodies and longer legs than today's Pug.

Another early Pug was known as Joe, but whose proper name was Zulu II, the change of name being the result of an error on the part of the young man sent over from England in charge of owner Miss Lee's dogs. The real Joe was sold as Zulu II before the dogs went to Pittsburgh Show and Zulu II was shown as Joe and came second.

In 1879 there were 24 Pugs exhibited at New York and Philadelphia Kennel Club Bench Show had five entries that same year, with three judges sending Dr Cryer's Roderick out of the ring, disqualifying him for "carrying his tail on the wrong side" (the right-hand side), which was erroneously thought by some to be a fault. First prize was given to Punko, and it seems to have been his one and only success. The following year there were 33 Pug entries at New York.

As in England, the American show scene was fiercely competitive among breeders. 1881 was the first year that champion prizes were offered for pugs in America. And at New York there were two entries in the champion class: Mr Dagget's Dick and young Sooty. For some reason Dick was absent and young Sooty had a walk-over. In the open dog class there were 12 entries, including imported dogs George and Roderick, both of Philadelphia. Roderick won and the woman owner of George was so put out that she presented the judge, Dr Niven, with a beautifully bound volume of Stonehenge's book, containing his version of the breed standard, telling the judge to read up the points of a Pug before he assumed to judge again!

Pictured is TumTum II, another popular winner of the day, note the very black face.

After this promising start, Pugs went into decline after about 1890, losing out to longer coated breeds as the Pomeranian and Japanese Spaniel. Breeder Al Eberhardt of Camp Dennison, Ohio, kept the show flag flying for the breed, and Mrs Howard Gould was one who continued to show black Pugs but, despite the initial great excitement in the US, the blacks never caught on as had been anticipated. In the first two decades of the 20th century, only a handful of breeders were still exhibiting and at some shows, no Pugs at all were entered. In 1915 the AKC registered only 32 Pugs and this had plummeted to five by 1920.

The 1919 American The Book Of Dogs - An Intimate Study Of Mankind's Best Friend states: "The pug was once a great favourite with those who liked pet dogs, but he has long since been supplanted by other and more attractive breeds. Almost obsolete in America, at least, the pug is now most often encountered in his china image, which still graces the mantel in many mid-Victorian home.

"Mastiff colours characterise this curly tailed, stocky, stiff legged little dog, 'apricot fawn' with black face and ears being the invariable rule except for the all-black variety, which was never popular here. On fawn dogs a black 'trace' down the back is very greatly prized. The face is very short and cobby, the chest wide, neck short and loose of skin and the legs straight and well boned, but not too heavy. The eyes are set wide apart and quite low. They are rather full and prominent. The ears are small, thin and soft, and the coat is short, fine and hard. They are clean, companionably dogs with a tendency to get fat, blind, and asthmatic as they get old."

Another writer of the day said: "There is no reason why this breed should be neglected in this way. Compare the pug with any of the popular fancies and it will stand the test. Tastes differ, but to our mind the character and beauty of wrinkle in the head of such a dog as Ding Dong is far ahead of the abnormally developed Japanese spaniel, for instance. Look at the care called for by these long coated dogs, and the impossibility of making a pet and companion of any of the long, silky-coated toys.

"The pug needs no more coddling than a hardy terrier, nor any more care in coat. He is a dog that has always had a reputation for keeping himself clean and tidy and they used to say that he had less doggy perfume than any other house dog. He may not be quite so demonstrative as some of the effervescing little toys, but he is just as intelligent and has a dignity and composure all his own.

Photograph by Davis, Painesville, O.

DING DONG
Property of F. C. Nims, Painesville, O.

"Ere long we fully expect to see the black pugs become popular for they are certainly very attractive in their brilliant coat of black satin. As Mr Mayhew says they are apt to be "tight-skinned" and fail to show the wrinkle such as Ding Dong (pictured) displays, but a few do show improvement in that direction and it is only a matter of careful selection and breeding such as one has to carry out in all breeds to reach success. There is a good field here for those who want to take up something that is bound eventually to become a popular breed."

Slowly, however, the Pug's fortunes began to turn around as more people became interested in the breed. The first pug dog club was formed in 1931, stirred up by breeders on the East coast, and held its first show six years later. It was the forerunner to today's Pug Dog Club of America. The first members of the PDCA were prominent Pug people such as Dr Nancy Riser, Filomena Doherty, Mrs Joseph Rowe, Suzanne Bellinger, Dr James Stubbs, Ralph Adair, Mary Lou Mann, Miriam Dock, Mr And Mrs John Madore and J. Hartley Mellick, Jr.

But it was in the 1950s that the Pug's started to truly regain its popularity - between 1950 and 1960 AKC registrations went from 958 to more than 5,000 and the Pug became the 17th most popular breed in America.

Since then the Pug has remained a popular breed on both sides of the Atlantic. At the time of writing, the Pug is enjoying a huge renaissance in the UK where it is in the top half dozen most popular Kennel Club registrations.

Pugs are frequently seen in the show ring, and these days numbers in classes can rise to many dozens. Although a Pug has yet to win Crufts, in 1981 Ch. Dhandys Favorite Woodchuck, owned by Robert A. Hauslohner, became the first Pug ever to win the famous Westminster Kennel Club Show. To date, "Chucky," as his friends called him, is the only Pug to earn this honour. He was bred by Mrs W. U. Braley and Mrs R. D. Hutchinson and was handled by Robert Barlow.

The most famous Royal Pug lovers of the 20th century were The Duke and Duchess of Windsor (pictured), who owned as many as 11 Pugs. They took their dogs, (along with their Pugs' personal chefs and "pooper scoopers") with them to almost all social activities. Among their most famous ones were Dizzy (short for Mr Disraeli), Davy Crockett, Impy (short for Emperor), Mr Chu, Rufus, Gen Sengh, Winston, Minoru and Trooper. Most were born in America, except for Masberk Disraeli, Goldengleam Trooper and Normpug Black Minoru.

Diamond, one of the Duke's favourites, always slept on his bed. One day, about two weeks before the Duke died, Diamond run away from home and came back on the very night the Duke passed away.

The breed enjoyed another spike in popularity after the 1997 Hollywood movie Men in Black, starring Will Smith and Tommy Lee Jones, which featured a fawn Pug playing the part of Frank the Alien. This character was so popular that it was later expanded in the 2002 sequel Men in Black II.

Celebrity Pug owners include Ted Danson, Paris Hilton, Billy Joel, Mickey Rourke, Kelly Osbourne (pictured), Paula Abdul, Hugh Laurie, Jonathan Ross and a host of others.

With organisations such as the Pug Dog Club of America and the Pug Dog Club in the UK dedicated to promoting and protecting the breed, the future of the Pug is in safe hands.

Numerous references were used in the research of this history, in particular:

- *London Zoological Society,*
- *"Actions in the Low Countries" 1618, Sir Roger Williams*
- *"The Dogs Of The British Islands" 1882, J. H. Walsh (known as ' Stonehenge')*
- *"A History And Description Of The Modern Dogs Of Great Britain And Ireland. (Non-Sporting Division)" 1894, Rawdon Briggs Lee*
- *"British Dogs: Their Varieties, History, Characteristics, Breeding, Management, And Exhibition" 1897, Hugh Dalziel.*
- *"British Dogs, Their Points, Selection, And Show Preparation" 1903, W. D. Drury, also known as 'Stonehenge'*
- *"The Dog Book, A Popular History of the Dog, with Practical Information as to Care and Management of House, Kennel and Exhibition Dogs; and Descriptions of all the Important Breeds" 1905, James Watson*
- *"Every Woman's Encyclopaedia" 1910-1912, various authors*
- *"The Book Of Dogs - An Intimate Study Of Mankind's Best Friend" 1919, Ernest Harold Baynes and Louis Agassiz Fuertes*
- *"The Pug -a Complete Anthology of the Dog 1850-1940" various authors*
- *"Dogs of China and Japan in Nature and Art" 1921, V W F Collier*
- *Chest of Books www.chestofbooks.com*
- *Wikipedia*

A favourite female Pug depicted in 1802 by Henry Bernard Chalon

3. The Breed Standard

The **breed standard** is what makes a Pug a Pug and a Great Dane a Great Dane.

It is a blueprint for not only how each breed of dog should look, but also how the dog moves and what sort of temperament he or she should have.

It is laid down by the breed societies, and the Kennel Club (UK) and American Kennel Club keep the register of purebred (pedigree) dogs. The dogs entered in shows run under Kennel Club and AKC rules are judged against this ideal list of attributes, and breeders approved by the Kennel Clubs agree to breed puppies to the breed standards.

Registration of a purebred or pedigree Pug – or any other breed - encourages breeding from responsible breeders who have gone into the background of their breeding stock. Responsible breeders select only the best dogs for reproduction, based on factors such as the health, looks, temperament and character of the parents and their ancestors. They do not simply take any available male and female and allow them to breed.

They also aim to reduce or eradicate some illnesses which may affect the breed. In the case of Pugs, this may involve breathing, knee, eye, brain and spine problems. The Kennel Clubs in North America, UK and Europe all have lists of assured or accredited breeders. If you have not yet got a puppy, this is the best place to start looking for one.

These breeders have agreed to breed a puppy to the breed standard and maintain certain welfare standards. Visit the Kennel Club in your country to find approved breeders in your area.

Just because your dog is not registered with the Kennel Club does not mean that it is a bad dog. But if your dog is registered, it is more likely that the breeder is experienced and knowledgeable and has spent time considering health and temperament before allowing her dogs to produce puppies.

The breed standard can vary over time and from country to country, and this is true of the Pug, whose physical appearance has changed over the centuries; 200 years ago the breed had a longer neck, nose and legs.

If you are serious about getting a Pug, then study the breed standard before visiting any puppies, so you know what a well-bred Pug should look like. If you've already bought one, these are features he or she should display.

UK Breed Standard

In the UK the Pug is in the Toy Group, along with such breeds as the Bichon Frise, Maltese, Pomeranian, Yorkshire Terrier, Pekingese and Havanese. The Kennel Club says:

"The Toy breeds are small companion or lap dogs. Many of the Toy breeds were bred for this capacity although some have been placed into this category simply due to their size. They should have friendly personalities and love attention. They do not need a large amount of exercise and some can be finicky eaters."

Here is the KC's description of the Pug:

"The Pug arrived in England when William III came to the throne. Until 1877, the breed was seen here only in fawn, but in that year a black pair was introduced from the Orient and the Kennel Club now allows four colourings. Once very popular with royalty and the aristocracy, the Pug now has a following in all walks of life.

"A dignified dog, very intelligent, good-natured and sociable, he is robust and self-reliant, with great character and personality. An adaptable companion for both young and old, and one who integrates himself very closely with family life. He can talk with his eyes, has his mischievous moments, and usually lives to a ripe old age."

General Appearance - Decidedly square and cobby, it is 'multum in parvo' shown in compactness of form, well-knit proportions and hardness of muscle, but never to appear low on legs, nor lean and leggy.

Characteristics - Great charm, dignity and intelligence.

Temperament - Even-tempered, happy and lively disposition.

Head and Skull – Head relatively large and in proportion to body, round, not apple-headed, with no indentation of skull. Muzzle relatively short, blunt, square, not upfaced. Nose black, fairly large with well open nostrils. Wrinkles on forehead clearly defined without exaggeration. Eyes or nose never adversely affected or obscured by over nose wrinkle. Pinched nostrils and heavy over nose wrinkle is unacceptable and should be heavily penalised.

Eyes – Dark, relatively large, round in shape, soft and solicitous in expression, very lustrous, and when excited, full of fire. Never protruding, exaggerated or showing white when looking straight ahead. Free from obvious eye problems.

Ears – Thin, small soft like black velvet. Two kinds – 'Button ear' – ear flap folding forward, tip lying close to skull to cover opening. 'Rose ear' – small drop ear which folds over and back to reveal the burr.

Mouth – Slightly undershot. Wide lower jaw with incisors almost in a straight line. Wry mouths, teeth or tongue showing all highly undesirable and should be heavily penalised.

Neck - Slightly arched to resemble a crest, strong, thick with enough length to carry head proudly.

Forequarters - Legs very strong, straight, of moderate length, and well under body. Shoulders well sloped.

Body - Short and cobby, broad in chest. Ribs well sprung and carried well back. Topline level neither roached nor dipping.

Hindquarters - Legs very strong, of moderate length, with good turn of stifle, well under body, straight and parallel when viewed from rear.

Feet - Neither so long as the foot of the hare, nor so round as that of the cat; well split up toes; the nails black.

Tail - High-set, tightly curled over hip. Double curl highly desirable.

Gait/Movement - Viewed from in front should rise and fall with legs well under shoulder, feet keeping directly to front, not turning in or out. From behind action just as true. Using forelegs strongly putting them well forward with hindlegs moving freely and using stifles well. A slight unexaggerated roll of hindquarters typifies gait. Capable of purposeful and steady movement.

Coat - Fine, smooth, soft, short and glossy, neither harsh, off-standing nor woolly.

Colour - Silver, apricot, fawn or black. Each clearly defined, to make contrast complete between colour, trace (black line extending from occiput to tail) and mask. Markings clearly defined. Muzzle or mask, ears, moles on cheeks, thumb mark or diamond on forehead and trace as black as possible.

Size - Ideal weight 6.3-8.1 kgs (14-18 lbs). Should be hard of muscle but substance must not be confused with overweight.

Faults - Any departure from the foregoing points should be considered a fault and the seriousness with which the fault should be regarded should be in exact proportion to its degree and its effect upon the health and welfare of the dog and on the dog's ability to perform its traditional work.

Note - Male animals should have two apparently normal testicles fully descended into the scrotum.

American Breed Standard

In the US the Pug is also in the Toy Group, alongside such other breeds as the Brussels Griffon, Cavalier King Charles Spaniel, Chihuahua, Havanese, Italian Greyhound, Maltese, Shih Tzu, Pekingese and Yorkshire Terrier.

This is that the AKC has to say about dogs in the Toy Group: "The diminutive size and winsome expressions of Toy dogs illustrate the main function of this Group: to embody sheer delight.

"Don't let their tiny stature fool you, though - - many Toys are tough as nails. If you haven't yet experienced the barking of an angry Chihuahua, for example, well, just wait.

"Toy dogs will always be popular with city dwellers and people without much living space. They make ideal apartment dogs and terrific lap warmers on nippy nights. (Incidentally, small breeds may be found in every Group, not just the Toy Group.

"We advise everyone to seriously consider getting a small breed, when appropriate, if for no other reason than to minimize some of the problems inherent in canines such as shedding, creating messes and cost of care. And training aside, it's still easier to control a ten-pound dog than it is one ten times that size.)"

The AKC describes the Pug as: "Even-tempered, charming, mischievous and loving."

General Appearance: Symmetry and general appearance are decidedly square and cobby. A lean, leggy Pug and a dog with short legs and a long body are equally objectionable.

Size, Proportion, Substance: The Pug should be multum in parvo, and this condensation (if the word may be used) is shown by compactness of form, well-knit proportions, and hardness of developed muscle.

Weight from 14 to 18 pounds (dog or bitch) desirable. Proportion square.

Head: The *head* is large, massive, round - not apple-headed, with no indentation of the *skull*. The *eyes* are dark in color, very large, bold and prominent, globular in shape, soft and solicitous in *expression*, very lustrous, and, when excited, full of fire. The *ears* are thin, small, soft, like black velvet. There are two kinds - the "rose" and the "button." Preference is given to the latter. The wrinkles are large and deep. The muzzle is short, blunt, square, but not upfaced. *Bite* – A Pug's bite should be very slightly undershot.

Neck, Topline, Body: The *neck* is slightly arched. It is strong, thick, and with enough length to carry the head proudly. The short *back* is level from the withers to the high tail set. The *body* is short and cobby, wide in chest and well ribbed up. The *tail* is curled as tightly as possible over the hip. The double curl is perfection.

Forequarters: The legs are very strong, straight, of moderate length, and are set well under. The elbows should be directly under the withers when viewed from the side. The shoulders are moderately laid back. The pasterns are strong, neither steep nor down. The feet are neither so long as the foot of the hare, nor so round as that of the cat; well split-up toes, and the nails black. Dewclaws are generally removed.

Hindquarters: The strong, powerful hindquarters have moderate bend of stifle and short hocks perpendicular to the ground. The legs are parallel when viewed from behind. The hindquarters are in balance with the forequarters. The thighs and buttocks are full and muscular. Feet as in front.

Coat: The coat is fine, smooth, soft, short and glossy, neither hard nor woolly.

Color: The colors are fawn or black. The fawn color should be decided so as to make the contrast complete between the color and the trace and mask.

Markings: The markings are clearly defined. The muzzle or mask, ears, moles on cheeks, thumb mark or diamond on forehead, and the back trace should be as black as possible. The mask should be black. The more intense and well defined it is, the better. The trace is a black line extending from the occiput to the tail.

Gait: Viewed from the front, the forelegs should be carried well forward, showing no weakness in the pasterns, the paws landing squarely with the central toes straight ahead. The rear action should be strong and free through hocks and stifles, with no twisting or turning in or out at the joints. The hind legs should follow in line with the front. There is a slight natural convergence of the limbs both fore and aft. A slight roll of the hindquarters typifies the gait which should be free, self-assured, and jaunty.

Temperament: This is an even-tempered breed, exhibiting stability, playfulness, great charm, dignity, and an outgoing, loving disposition.

Disqualification - *Any color other than fawn or black*

Technical Terms Explained

Cobby: thick set, chunky, stocky

Multum in parvo – a lot in a little

Mask - the black skin pigmentation and hairs on the face

Roach: arched, when referring to the back (a Pug should have a straight, not a roach, back)

Stifle: knee

Pastern: the dog's 'shock absorber' between the knee and the paw

Stop: the degree of angle change between the skull and the nasal bone near the eyes

Withers: top of the shoulders

Dewclaws: a now a functionless digit on the inner side of a dog's leg, often removed in puppies to prevent injury.

---

4. Choosing a Pug Puppy

Are You Ready?

With their wrinkled faces, cute expressions and velvet fur, there are few more appealing sights on this Earth than a litter of Pug puppies. If you go to view a litter the pups are sure to melt your heart and it is extremely difficult – if not downright impossible - to walk away without choosing one.

However, the best way to select a Pug puppy is with your head and not your heart. Do your research before you visit any litters to make sure you select a responsible breeder with healthy pups with good temperaments. After all, apart from getting married or having a baby, getting a puppy is one of the most important, demanding, expensive and life-enriching decisions you will ever make.

Just like babies, puppies will love you unconditionally - but there is a price to pay. In return for their loyalty and devotion, you have to fulfil your part of the bargain. In the beginning you have to be prepared to devote several hours a day to your new puppy. You have to feed and housetrain him every day, give him your attention and start to gently introduce the rules of the house as well as take care of his general health and welfare. You also have to be prepared to part with hard cash for regular healthcare, and even more money in vets' bills in the case of illness.

If you are not prepared, or unable, to devote the time and money to a new arrival – or if you are out at work all day – then now might not be the right time for you to consider getting a puppy. Pugs are above all companion dogs who love being with their people.

If you are out at work all day these are NOT the dogs for you, Pugs have been bred as companions and thrive on interaction with their humans. To leave a Pug alone for long periods is just not fair on this lovable dog that is happiest when he's with you. Nor can you leave them alone outside for hours on end. Like all flat-faced (brachycephalic) breeds, they are very sensitive to temperature changes. Your Pug may well live for over 10 years, so getting a puppy is definitely a long-term commitment. Before committing, ask yourself some questions:

Have I Got Enough Time?

In the first days after leaving his - or her - mother and littermates, your puppy will feel very lonely and maybe even a little afraid. You and your family have to spend time with your new arrival to make him feel safe and sound. Ideally, for the first few days you will be around all of the time to help him settle and to start bonding with him. If you work, book a couple of weeks off, but don't just get a puppy and leave him alone in the house a couple of days later.

As well as housetraining, short sessions of behaviour training are also recommended to curb puppy biting and to teach your new arrival the rules of the house. And although Pugs generally don't need a lot of exercise, it is still a good idea to get into the habit of taking him out of the house and garden or yard (once he is safe to do so after his vaccinations) for a short walk every day –more as he gets older. New surroundings stimulate his interest and help to stop him from becoming bored and stubborn or disengaged.

You'll also have to feed your dog daily, in fact several times a day with a young puppy, and feeding your Pug the right diet and the right amount is of paramount importance. Most Pugs also require regular care in the form of eye, ear and wrinkle cleaning, as well as light grooming. You will also need time to visit the vet's surgery for regular healthcare visits and annual vaccinations.

How Long Can I Leave Him For?

This is a question we get asked all of the time and one which causes a lot of debate among owners and prospective owners. All dogs are pack animals; their natural state is to be with others. Being alone is not normal for them, although many have to get used to it.

Another issue is the toilet; all Pugs have smaller bladders than humans. Forget the emotional side of it, how would you like to be left for eight hours without being able to visit the bathroom?

So how many hours can you leave a dog alone for? Well, a useful guide comes from the canine rescue organisations. In the UK, they will not allow anybody to adopt if they are intending leaving the dog alone for more than four or five hours a day.

Dogs left at home alone all day become bored and, in the case of Pugs and other breeds which are highly dependent on human company for their happiness, they may well become sad or depressed. Separation anxiety is not uncommon among Pugs. Of course, it depends on the character and temperament of your dog, but a lonely Pug may display signs of unhappiness by being destructive, displaying poor behaviour or disengaging when you return home.

A puppy or fully-grown dog must NEVER be left shut in a crate all day. It is OK to leave a puppy or adult dog in a crate if he or she is happy there, but the door should never be closed for more than two or three hours. A crate is a place where a puppy or adult should feel safe, not a prison. Ask yourself why you want a dog – is it for selfish reasons or can you really offer a good home to a young puppy - and then adult dog - for a decade, or if you are lucky, even longer? Would it be more sensible to wait until you are at home more?

Is My Home Suitable?

If you have decided to get a puppy, then choose one which will fit in with your living conditions. The good news is that Pugs are very adaptable, they can live in an apartment or on a farm, much depends on what they get used to as puppies. All dogs, even Pugs with low energy levels, need some time out of doors. However, Pugs do not have high exercise requirements and many people living in apartments find that the breed makes an excellent companion.

Successful apartment living for a canine involves having easy access to the outside and to spend time housetraining. This may mean training the dog to use a pad or a tray as an indoor bathroom. Opinions on how easy Pugs are to housetrain vary widely between breeders - see our section on

Housetraining in **Chapter 5** for more information. If you live in an apartment and don't want your dog eliminate inside, it is very important to take your puppy outside to perform his several times a day. If you can take him out at least three or four times a day to do what he needs to do, there is no need to indoor housetrain him. If you live in a house and have a yard, don't leave your Pug unattended for long periods – they love to sunbathe and can easily overheat. They may also wander off through a gap in the fence and, due to their high price, they are sadly targets for thieves.

Pug-proofing your home should involve moving anything sharp, breakable or chewable - including your shoes! - out of reach to sharp little teeth. Make sure he can't chew electrical cords – lift them off the floor if necessary, and block off any off-limits areas of the house, such as upstairs or your bedroom, with a child gate or barrier, especially as he will probably be following you around the house in the first few days. If you have a yard or garden, make sure there are no poisonous plants or chemicals he could eat or drink. **In Chapter 5. Bringing your Pug Home** there is specific advice from breeders on extra precautions required with Pug puppies, particularly in light of their protruding eyes, tiny size and general delicacy when young.

Family and Children

What about the other members of your family, do they all want the puppy as well? A puppy will grow into a dog which will become a part of your family for many years to come. If you have children they will, of course, be delighted. One of the wonderful things about Pugs is how naturally good they are with children; they usually love to be around them.

But remember that Pug puppies are extremely small and delicate, so robust play is out of the question as your pup may suffer damage to his joints or eyes, and it's always a good idea to supervise any young children with dogs – no matter how well they get along. Small kids lack co-ordination and a young Pug may inadvertently get poked in the eye or trodden on if you don't keep an eye on them.

Dogs are hierarchical – they appreciate the order of the pack -and often puppies regard children as being on their own level, like a playmate, and so they might chase, jump and nip at them with sharp teeth. This is not aggression; this is normal play for puppies. Train yours to be gentle with your children and your children to be gentle with your dog. See **Chapter 8. Training** on how to deal with puppy biting.

Discourage the kids from constantly picking up your gorgeous new puppy. They should learn respect for the dog, which is a living creature with his or her own needs, not a toy. Make sure your puppy gets enough time to sleep – which is most of the time in the beginning - so don't let your children constantly pester him. Sleep is very important to puppies, just as it is for babies. Allow your Pug to eat at his or her own pace uninterrupted, letting youngsters play with the dog while eating is a no-no as it may promote food aggression or gulping of food. One of the reasons some dogs end up in rescue centres is that the owners are unable to cope with the demands of small children AND a dog.

On the other hand, it is also a fantastic opportunity for you to educate your little darlings (both human and canine) on how to get along with each other and set the pattern for a wonderful life-long friendship

Dogs are hierarchical, in other words, there is a pecking order. Although Pugs are not generally regarded as one-person dogs, there is usually one human that the puppy will regard as pack leader (alpha), usually the person who feeds him or who spends most time with him.

Fortunately, most Pugs are not nuisance barkers and they spend much of their life indoors, so they are not likely to cause a problem for your neighbours.

Older People

If you are older or have elderly relatives living with you, the good news is that Pugs are great company. They love to be with people and are affectionate in a laid-back way. Nobody has told the Pug that he is not a lapdog and is happiest when snoozing on a chair, on the bed or on you.

If you are older, make sure you have the energy and patience to deal with a young puppy. And ask yourself if you are fit enough to take your dog for at least one short walk every day.

Dogs can be great for older people. My father is in his 80s, but takes his dog out walking for an hour to 90 minutes every day - a morning and an afternoon walk – even in the rain or snow. It's good for him and it's good for the dog, helping to keep both of them fit and socialised! They get fresh air, exercise and the chance to communicate with other dogs and their humans. Some Pugs survive perfectly well by only going out into the garden or yard, but there is no substitute in most dogs' minds for a walk away from the home at least once a day – even a short one. Take out the lead and see how your dog reacts, you'll soon find out if he'd rather go for a walk or stay at home.

Pugs are also great company at home – you're never alone when you've got a dog. Many older people get a dog after losing a loved one (a husband, wife or previous much-loved dog). A pet gives them something to care for and love, as well as a constant companion. However, it is not uncommon for Pugs to develop health issues at some point in their lives, so it's important for an older person to be able to afford annual pet insurance, veterinary fees or both.

Single People

Many single adults own dogs, but if you live alone, having a puppy will require a lot of dedication on your part. There will be nobody to share the responsibility, so taking on a dog requires a huge commitment and a lot of your time if the dog is to have a decent life. If you are out of the house all day as well, it is not really fair to get a puppy, or even an adult dog. Left alone all day, they will feel isolated, bored and sad. However, if you work from home or are at home all day and you can spend considerable time with the puppy every day, then great; Pugs make excellent companions.

Other Pets

If you already have other pets in your household, they may not be too happy at the arrival of your new addition - although your new Pug will generally get on well with other pets, even small ones. (It might not be a good idea to leave your hamster running loose with your pup initially, as your Pug will probably think the hamster is a toy and may injure him). In the beginning spend time to introduce them to each other gradually and supervise the sessions. Pug puppies are naturally curious and playful and they will sniff and investigate other pets.

If you have a cat, try to avoid a situation where the cat could lash out and scratch your pup's eyes by keeping either your Pug or your cat in a crate or on a lead, allowing them to sniff safely until they get used to each other. If things seem to be going well after one or two supervised sessions with no aggression, then let them loose together. It works the other way round too, a timid cat might need protection from a bold, playful Pug. Take the process slowly, if your cat is stressed and frightened he may decide to leave. Our feline friends are notorious for abandoning home because the food and facilities are better down the road. Until you know that they can get on together, don't leave them alone. Here is a YouTube video link to show different interactions between Pugs and cats: www.youtube.com/watch?v=eXhKKtJ5TRk – note how easy it is for a Pug's eyes to be damaged by a cat's claws.

If you have other dogs, supervised sessions from an early age will help the dogs to get along and chances are they will become the best of friends. Pugs generally get on well with other dogs, and particular other Pugs if properly socialised.

You might become victim to the phenomenon known as "A Pile of Pugs" where you are so enamoured with your first Pug, that you decide to get another, then another...and another...and so on.

If you are thinking of getting more than one Pug, you might consider waiting until your first Pug is an adolescent or adult before getting a second, so your older dog is calmer and can help train the younger one. Coping with, training and housetraining one puppy is hard enough, without having to do it with two.

In terms of gender, much depends on the temperament of the individual dog - the differences WITHIN the sexes is greater than the differences BETWEEN the sexes. For example, two dominant dogs may not get along, regardless of whether they are two males, one male and one female, or two females.

As with all dogs, how well they get on also depends on the temperament of the individuals. With another dog, it is important to introduce the two on neutral territory, rather than in areas one pet deems his own. You don't want one dog to feel he has to protect his territory. Walking the dogs parallel to each other before heading home for the first time is one way of getting them used to each other.

There is also the question of whether to get two puppies from the same litter or not. Some owners have done this very successfully; while some animal psychologists claim that each puppy's first loyalty will always be to the other puppy, rather than you, as that initial bond from birth has never been broken.

Due to its sensitivities and healthcare needs, the Pug is not a breed suitable to be left for long periods. If you do leave a young dog alone for any length of time, you may want to leave a newspaper or wee pad on the floor in case of an accident. If you decide to use a crate, only leave your pup in it for short periods initially and only after he has accepted it and is comfortable there.

The ideal scenario is to leave the pup in his open crate, block off other rooms or areas, so he has a small area he can wander round in, but remember to remove any chewable or sharp objects. If you're still determined to have a Pug when you're out for several hours at a time, here are some useful points:

Top 10 Tips For Working Pug Owners

1. Either come home during your lunch break to let your dog out or employ a dog walker (or neighbour) to take him out for a walk in the middle of the day

2. Do you know anybody you could leave your dog with during the day? Consider leaving the dog with a friend, relative or elderly neighbour who would welcome the companionship of a Pug without the full responsibility of ownership

3. Take him for a walk before you go to work – even if this means getting up at the crack of dawn – and spend time with him as soon as you get home. Exercise generates serotonin in the brain and has a calming effect. A dog that has been exercised will be less anxious and more ready for a good nap. Remember that most Pugs cannot tolerate very strenuous exercise, so don't go jogging with him

4. Leave him in a place of his own where he feels comfortable. If you use a crate, leave the door open, otherwise his favourite dog bed or chair. If possible, leave him in a room with a view of the outside world. This will be more interesting than staring at four blank walls

5. VERY IMPORTANT WITH PUGS: Make sure that it does not get too hot during the day and there are no cold draughts in the place where you leave him. Your dog can die if he overheats, so in very hot weather he needs an air conditioned room

6. Food and drink. Although Pugs love their food, it is still generally a good idea to put food down at specific meal times and remove it after 15 or 20 minutes if uneaten. If food is left all day he may become a fussy eater or 'punish' you for leaving him alone by refusing to eat. Make sure he has access to water at all times. Dogs cannot cool down by sweating; they do not have many sweat glands (which is why they pant, but this is much less efficient than perspiring) and can die without sufficient water

7. Leave toys available to play with to prevent boredom and destructive chewing (a popular occupation of a bored Pug or one suffering from separation anxiety). Stuff a Kong toy with treats to keep him occupied for a while. Choose the right size of Kong, you can even smear the inside with peanut butter or another favourite to keep him occupied for longer

8. Consider getting a companion for your Pug. This will involve even more of your time and twice the expense, and if you have not got time for one dog, you have hardly time for two. A better idea is to find someone you can leave the dog with during the day; there are also dog sitters and doggie day care for those who can afford them

9. Consider leaving a radio or TV on very softly in the background. The 'white noise' can have a soothing effect on some pets. If you do this, select your channel carefully – try and avoid one with lots of bangs and crashes or heavy metal music!

10. Stick to the same routine before you leave your dog home alone. This will help him to feel secure. Before you go to work, get into a daily habit of getting yourself ready, then feeding and exercising your Pug. Dogs love routine. But don't make a huge fuss of him when you leave, this can also stress the dog; just leave the house calmly

Similarly when you come home, your Pug will feel starved of attention and be pleased to see you. Greet him normally, but try not to go overboard by making too much of a fuss as soon as you walk through the door. Give him a pat and a stroke then take off your coat and do a few other things before turning your attention back to him. Lavishing your Pug with too much attention the second you walk through the door may encourage demanding behaviour or separation anxiety.

Puppy Stages

It is important to understand how a puppy develops into a fully grown dog. This knowledge will help you to be a good owner. The first few months and weeks of a puppy's life will have an effect on his behaviour and temperament for the rest of his life. This Puppy Schedule will help you to understand the early stages:

Birth to seven weeks	A puppy needs sleep, food and warmth. He needs his mother for security and discipline and littermates for learning and socialisation. The puppy learns to function within a pack and learns the pack order of dominance. He begins to become aware of his environment. During this period, puppies should be left with their mother.
Eight to 12 weeks	A puppy should NOT leave his mother before eight weeks. At this age the brain is fully developed and **he now needs socialising with the outside world**. He needs to change from being part of a canine pack to being part of a human pack. This period is a fear period for the puppy, avoid causing him fright and pain.
13 to 16 weeks	Training and formal obedience should begin. **This is a critical period for socialising with other humans, places and situations.** This period will pass easily if you remember that this is a puppy's change to adolescence. Be firm and fair. His flight instinct may be prominent. Avoid being too strict or too soft with him during this time and praise his good behaviour.
Four to eight months	Another fear period for a puppy is between seven to eight months of age. It passes quickly, but be cautious of fright or pain which may leave the puppy traumatised. The puppy reaches sexual maturity and dominant traits are established. Your Pug should now understand the following commands: 'sit', 'down', 'come' and 'stay'.

Plan Ahead

Many puppies leave the litter for their new homes when they are eight weeks or older. However, with Pugs, 10 to 12 weeks is more normal. It is important that puppies have time to develop and learn the rules of the pack from their mothers. Toy breeds take a little longer to develop physically and mentally, and a puppy which leaves the litter too early may suffer with issues, for example a lack of confidence throughout his or her life. Breeders who allow their pups to leave before the correct time may be more interested in a quick buck than a long-term puppy placement. If you want a well-bred Pug puppy, it pays to plan ahead as many Kennel Club and AKC-registered breeders have waiting lists. Choosing the right breeder is one of the most important decisions you will make.

Like humans, your puppy will be a product of his or her parents and will inherit many of their characteristics. His temperament and how healthy your puppy will be now and throughout his life

will largely depend on the genes of his parents. It is essential that you select a good, responsible breeder. They will have checked out the health records and temperament of the parents and will only breed from suitable stock. Some Pug breeders have their own websites, particularly in the USA, and many are trustworthy and conscientious. You have to learn to spot the good ones from the bad ones. Our photo shows two healthy male pups bred by Linda and Kim Wright, of Wright's Pugs, Springport, Michigan

The cost of a Pug puppy registered with the Kennel Club in the UK or AKC in America ranges from around £1,000 to £1,500 in the UK (slightly less in Northern Ireland) and $1,000 to $2,000 dollars in North America, but you will pay double or more for a puppy for showing. Good breeding comes at a price and if a puppy is being sold for less, you have to ask why.

Because of these high prices, unscrupulous breeders with little knowledge of the breed have sprung up, tempted by the prospect of making easy cash. A healthy Pug will be your irreplaceable companion for the next decade or more. You wouldn't choose a good friend without screening them first and getting to know them, so why buy an unseen or imported puppy, or one from a pet shop or general advertisement? Good Pug breeders do not sell their dogs on general purpose websites or in pet shops. They usually have a waiting list of prospective owners.

At the very minimum you MUST visit the breeder personally and follow our **Top 10 Tips for Selecting a Good Breeder** to help you make the right decision. Buying a poorly-bred puppy may save you a few hundred pounds or dollars in the short term, but could cost you thousands in extra veterinary bills in the long run; not to mention the terrible heartache of having a sickly dog.

Rescue groups know only too well the dangers of buying a poorly-bred dog. Many years of problems can arise, usually these are health issues with Pugs, but behaviour problems can also result from poor breeding, causing pain and distress for both dog and owner. All rescue groups strongly recommend taking the time to find a good breeder. There's certainly a Pug breeder with the right puppy for you - but how do you find them? Everybody knows you should get your puppy from "a good breeder." But how can you tell the good guys from the bad guys?

The Kennel Club or breed club in your country is a great place to start as they have lists of approved breeders. The list of UK Kennel Club registered breeders can be found here: **www.thekennelclub.org.uk/services/public/acbr/Default.aspx?breed=Pug** - the ones with the rosette symbol are "Assured", which means they have been personally visited and approved by the KC. The UK's Pug Dog Club also has a list of breeders with available puppies at: **http://pugdogclub.org.uk/own-a-pug**

In the USA, the Pug Dog Club of America has an online Breeder Directory which can be found at: **http://pugs.org/breeder-directory** and the AKC has a Breeders Classified section online at: **www.apps.akc.org/apps/classified/search/index.cfm** - search for 'Pug.' For Canada: **www.ckc.ca/Choosing-a-Dog/PuppyList/Breed.aspx?breedname=Pug&breedcode=PUG**

You might have had a personal recommendation, or like the look of a friend's handsome Pug and want one which looks the same. If that's the case, make sure you ask all the right questions of the breeder regarding how they select their breeding stock and ask to see the parents' health certificates, or at the very least what health screening the dam and sire (parents) have had.

If you haven't already taken the plunge and committed to a specific puppy, here is some advice from two breeders, one in the UK and one in America. Carly Firth, Mumandau Pugs, Greater Manchester, UK: "Although a Pug is quite adaptable and able to fit into many different owners' lifestyles, e.g. families etc., it is a dog after all. And if having a dog is manageable for a new owner, Pugs are overall a good choice.

"They're not demanding exercise-wise, but care does need to considered when taking care of them. New owners should be mindful to research and question the health problems and socialisation required to get the best out of their Pug. It is important they select from a reputable breeder. Can they see the dam at least? Question their health. Do they have K.C. paperwork?

"If not why? If they don't I would be suspicious, is it a planned/accidental mating that shouldn't have happened? Or is it in fact full pedigree? Some breeders can over use their bitches for breeding, purely to make money. If this is the case, you should be wary. You should buy from breeders who would over-use their bitch for breeding purposes."

Roberta Kelley-Martin, of HRH Pugs, Chico, California: "Of utmost importance is that make sure no matter what animal you choose to bring in as a member of your family, you are aware that you are responsible for that animal for its life.

"It is extremely important if buying a purebred dog that you buy from a reputable breeder. Make sure they sell only with a contract. This ensures that you know exactly what they expect and what you can expect. Never buy from a breeder that doesn't specifically state that at any time should you not be able to keep your new family member, that the dog can be returned to them, the breeder."

Code of Ethics

The Pug breed clubs all have a code of ethics which their registered breeders must stick to in order to protect the integrity of the breed. Here is the one for the Pug Dog Club of America (PDCA) , reproduced with their kind permission. The UK's Pug Dog Club has a similar code.

> ✓ **Each member shall be familiar with and observe the rules and regulations of the American Kennel Club and the Pug Dog Club of America. No member shall have surgery performed on any Pug to alter cosmetic features (as mentioned in the AKC Policy**

Manual, Section XII Change in Appearance-www.akc.org) to serve the purposes of exhibition.

✓ Each member shall be familiar with the Pug Standard as approved the by PDCA and The American Kennel Club.

✓ Each Member should be aware at all times that the Club exists to protect the breed.

✓ Each Member should know that our Code of Ethics is more than a set of rules. It is a commitment to a high standard of practice in owning and breeding Pugs.

✓ Each member shall at all times display good sportsmanship and conduct. Whether at home, traveling, at shows or motels they will treat all present, including competitors, judges, officials and spectators with respect and courtesy.

✓ No Member shall engage in false advertising. No member shall maliciously malign another member by making false or misleading statements regarding a competitor's dog, breeding practices, or person.

✓ No member shall EVER sell or donate dogs for auctions or raffles, or to pet shops, catalog houses, brokers or for resale purposes.

✓ Breeders shall be familiar with AKC rules concerning record keeping, registration, sale and transfer of dogs, and abide by these rules.

✓ Breeders shall exercise great care when selecting stud dogs or brood bitches.

✓ Breeders shall use stock of characteristic type, exhibit soundness, stable temperament, be in good health and condition and be free of communicable diseases and serious genetic defects.

✓ Breeders do not breed just for the pet market and believe the only justifiable reason to breed is to improve the breed. Pugs sold as pet quality are to be sold with limited registration and spay/neuter requirements.

✓ Breeders shall provide with each Pug sold: diet and care information, immunization, health record, three generation pedigree, registration application or transfer (when applicable), Code of Ethics, and will strive to help with problems and provide information throughout the dog's life.

✓ Breeders shall endeavor to place puppies in good homes but understand they are responsible for puppies they have bred, and are responsible to take these puppies back if the need arises.

✓ Breeders shall at all times consider the lives of their dogs, as this breed is to provide love and companionship. They should be maintained in a clean, comfortable and healthy environment, with proper socialization and exercise of primary importance.

Of course, there are no cast iron guarantees that your puppy will be healthy and have a good temperament, but choosing an approved breeder who conforms to a code of ethics is a very good place to start. (Pictured is PDCA members Donna Shank and Brenda Schuettenberg's Solo, of Rokuciera Pugs, California).

Another way to familiarise yourself with the breed and to get to know good breeders is to visit Pug shows and chat with breeders. Many reputable breeders do not have to advertise, such is the demand for their puppies - so it's up to you to do your research to find a really good breeder.

If, for whatever reason, you're not able to buy a puppy from one of these accredited breeders and you've never bought a Pug puppy before, how do you avoid buying one from a "backstreet breeder" or puppy mill? These are people who just breed puppies for profit and sell them to the first person who turns up with the cash. Unhappily, this can end in heartbreak for a family months or years later when their puppy develops health or temperament problems due to poor breeding.

Where NOT to buy a Pug Puppy From

Due to the relatively high cost of Pug puppies – as well as waiting lists for litters - unscrupulous breeders have sprung up to cash in on this unique little breed's popularity.

While new owners might think they have bagged a "bargain" or "rare colour", this more often than not turns out to be false economy and an emotionally disastrous decision when the puppy develops health problems due to poor breeding, or behavioural problems due to lack of socialisation during the critical early phase of his or her life. As already mentioned, there is no such thing as a "rare colour" in Pugs, if they are not the colours specified in the Breed Standard (see **Chapter 3**) then they are not pure bred Pugs.

In September 2013 The UK's Kennel Club issued a warning of a puppy welfare crisis, with some truly sickening statistics. The situation is no better in America. The Press release stated:

As the popularity of online pups continues to soar:

> - **Almost one in five pups bought on websites or social media die within six months**

> - One in three buy online, in pet stores and via newspaper adverts - outlets often used by puppy farmers – this is an increase from one in five in the previous year

> - The problem is likely to grow as the younger generation favour mail order pups, and breeders of fashionable crossbreeds flout responsible steps

The Kennel Club said: "We are sleepwalking into a dog welfare and consumer crisis as new research shows that more and more people are buying their pups online or through pet shops, outlets often used by cruel puppy farmers, and are paying the price with their pups requiring long-term veterinary treatment or dying before six months old.

"The increasing popularity of online pups is a particular concern. Of those who source their puppies online, half are going on to buy 'mail order pups' directly over the internet."

The KC research found that:

> One third of people who bought their puppy online, over social media or in pet shops failed to experience 'overall good health'

> Almost one in five puppies bought via social media or the internet die before six months old

> Some 12% of puppies bought online or on social media end up with serious health problems that require expensive on-going veterinary treatment from a young age

> Some 94% of puppies bought direct from a breeder were reported as having good overall health

Only half of people who bought their pups online or via social media said their puppy had shown no behavioural problems. This is a big problem in puppy-farmed pups, which can result unsociability around other dogs or people, fear of their surroundings or aggressiveness.

The Kennel Club established the Kennel Club Assured Breeder Scheme in 2004 to ensure that its members always follow responsible steps when breeding and selling puppies. However, the research has revealed that too many people are still going to unscrupulous breeders, with:

> One third of people failing to see the puppy with its mother

> More than half not seeing the breeding environment

> 70% receive no contract of sale

> 82% were not offered post -sales advice

> 69% did not see any relevant health certificates for the puppy's parents, which indicate the likely health of the puppy

These are all steps that Kennel Club Assured Breeders have to follow.

Caroline Kisko, Kennel Club Secretary, said: "More and more people are buying puppies from sources such as the internet, which are often used by puppy farmers.

"Whilst there is nothing wrong with initially finding a puppy online, it is essential to then see the breeder and ensure that they are doing all of the right things.

"This research clearly shows that too many people are failing to do this, and the consequences can be seen in the shocking number of puppies that are becoming sick or dying. We have an extremely serious consumer protection and puppy welfare crisis on our hands.

"We urge people to always buy a puppy from a member of the Kennel Club Assured Breeder Scheme, who are the only breeders in the country whose membership is based upon their ability to show that the health and welfare of their pups comes first and foremost."

The research revealed that the problem was likely to get worse as mail order pups bought over the internet are the second most common way for the younger generation of 18 to 24 year olds to buy a puppy (31%).

Marc Abraham, TV vet and founder of Pup Aid, said: "Sadly, if the 'buy it now' culture persists, then this horrific situation will only get worse. There is nothing wrong with sourcing a puppy online, but people need to be aware of what they should then expect from the breeder.

"For example, you should not buy a car without getting its service history and seeing it at its registered address, so you certainly shouldn't buy a puppy without the correct paperwork and health certificates and without seeing where it was bred. However, too many people are opting to buy directly from third parties such as the internet, pet shops, or from puppy dealers, where you cannot possibly know how or where the puppy was raised.

"Not only are people buying sickly puppies, but many people are being scammed into paying money for puppies that don't exist, as the research showed that 7% of those who buy online were scammed in this way".

———————————

The Kennel Club has launched an online video and has a Find A Puppy app to show the dos and don'ts of buying a puppy. View the video at www.thekennelclub.org.uk/paw

———————————

Caveat Emptor – Buyer Beware

Here are some signs that a puppy may have arrived via a puppy broker (somebody who makes money from buying and selling puppies) or even an importer or is advertised on the website from an unscrupulous breeder. Our strong advice is that if you suspect that this is the case, walk away - unless you want to risk a lot of trouble and heartache in the future.

You can't buy a Rolls Royce motor car for a couple of thousand pounds or dollars - you'd immediately suspect that the "bargain" on offer wasn't the real thing. No matter how lovely it looked, you'd be right - and the same applies to Pugs. Here are some signs to look out for:

- ➤ The person you are buying the puppy from did not breed the dog themselves

- ➤ The place you meet the puppy seller is a car park or place other than the puppies' home

- ➤ "You can't see the parent dogs because......" This is a familiar tale. ALWAYS ask to see the parents and at a minimum, see the mother and how she looks and behaves

- ➤ The seller tells you that the puppy comes from

top, caring breeders from your or another country. Not true. There are reputable, caring breeders all over the world, but not one of them sells their puppies through brokers

➢ Price – if you are offered a "pedigree" or purebred" Pug for just a few hundred pounds or dollars, he or she almost certainly comes from dubious stock. Careful breeding, taking good care of mother and puppies and health screening all add up to one big bill for breeders of Pugs. Anyone selling their puppies at a knock-down price has certainly cut corners – and this involves temperament and health screening and selective breeding

➢ Ignore photographs of so-called "champion" ancestors (unless you are buying from an approved breeder), in all likelihood these are fiction

➢ You are offered two prices - one with registration papers, one without - a sure sign of dubious heritage

➢ Ask to see photos of the puppy from birth to present day. If the seller has none, there is a reason – walk away

➢ You are offered a Pug in a "rare colour" – there is no such thing

➢ The Pug puppy looks a little large - or small – for his or her age

➢ If you get a rescue Pug, make sure it is from a recognised rescue group and not a "puppy flipper" who may be posing as a do-gooder but is in fact getting dogs – including stolen ones - from unscrupulous sources

➢ Websites – buying a puppy from a website does not necessarily mean that the puppy will turn out to have problems. But avoid websites where there are no pictures of the home, environment and owners. If they are only showing close-up photos of cute puppies, click the **X** button

➢ Don't buy a website puppy with a shopping cart symbol next to his picture

➢ Don't commit to a website puppy unless you have seen it face-to-face. If this is not possible at the very least you must speak (on the phone) with the breeder and ask questions, don't deal with an intermediary.

In fact the whole brokering business is just another version of the puppy mill and should be avoided at all costs. Bear in mind that for every cute Pug puppy you see from a broker or importer, other puppies have died.

Good Pug breeders will only breed from dogs which have been carefully selected for health, temperament, physical shape and lineage. There are plenty out there, it's just a question of finding one. The good news is that there are signs to help the savvy buyer spot a good breeder.

Top 10 Tips for Choosing a Good Breeder

1. Good Pug breeders keep the dogs in the home as part of the family - not outside in kennel runs, garages or outbuildings. Check that the area where the puppies are kept is clean and that the puppies themselves look clean

2. Their Pugs appear happy and healthy. The pups are alert, excited to meet new people and don't shy away from visitors

3. A good breeder will encourage you to spend time with the puppy's parents - or at least the mother - when you visit. They want your entire family to meet the puppy and are happy for you to make more than one visit

4. They breed only one, or maximum two, types of dog and are very familiar with the breed standards

5. Pugs can have genetic weaknesses. Check that the puppy has clean eyes, nose and bum (butt) with no discharge and that he breathes easily. A good breeder will explain the extra care a Pug needs. Although not compulsory, many good breeders have health certificates (BVA in the UK or OFA in the US for hip, patellar, CERF for eyes, and there is also a DNA test for PDE), to show that both parents are free from genetic defects

6. Responsible breeders should provide you with a written contract and health guarantee and allow you plenty of time to read it. They will also show you records of the puppy's visits to the vet, vaccinations, worming medication, etc. and explain what other vaccinations your puppy will need

7. They feed their adults and puppies high quality 'premium' dog food or possibly even a raw diet – a good diet is especially important for Pugs. A good breeder will give you guidance on feeding and caring for your puppy and will be available for advice after you take your puppy home

8. They don't always have pups available, but keep a list of interested people for the next available litter

9. They don't over-breed, but do limit the number of litters from their dams. Over-breeding or breeding from older females can be detrimental to the female's health

10. And finally ... good Pug breeders want to know their beloved pups are going to good homes and will ask YOU a lot of questions about your suitability as owners. DON'T buy a puppy from a website or advert where a PayPal or credit card deposit secures you a puppy without any questions

Pug puppies should not be regarded as must-have accessories. They are not objects, they are warm-blooded, living, breathing creatures. A good breeder will, if asked, provide references from other people who have bought their puppies; make sure you call at least one before you commit. They will also agree to take a puppy back within a certain time frame if it does not work out for you, or if there is a health problem.

Healthy, happy puppies and adult dogs are what everybody wants. Taking the time now to find a responsible and committed breeder with well-bred Pugs is time well spent. It could save you a lot of time, money and heartache in the future and help to ensure that you and your chosen puppy are happy together for many years.

The Most Important Questions to Ask a Breeder

Many of these points have been covered in the previous section, but here's a reminder and checklist of the questions you should be asking.

Have the parents been health screened? Ask to see original copies of health certificates. If no certificates are available, ask what guarantees the breeder or seller is offering in terms of genetic illnesses, and how long these guarantees last – 12 weeks, a year, a lifetime? It will vary from breeder to breeder, but good ones will definitely give you some form of guarantee – always ask for this in writing.
They will also want to be informed of any hereditary health problems with your puppy, as they may choose not to breed from the dam or sire (mother or father) again. Some breeders keep a chart documenting the full family health history of the pup – ask if one exists and if you can see it

Can you put me in touch with someone who already has one of your puppies?

Are you a member of one of the Pug associations or clubs, and are you listed as a recommended breeder? (If not, why not?)

How long have you been breeding Pugs? You are looking for someone who has a track record with the breed

How many litters has the mother had? Female Pugs should not have litters until they are two and then only have perhaps three litters in their lifetime. Many more and the breeder may be a "puppy mill", churning out cute pups for a fast buck

Do you breed any other types of dog? Buy from a Pug specialist

What is so special about this litter? You are looking for a breeder who has used good breeding stock and his or her knowledge to produce healthy, handsome dogs with good temperaments, not just cute-looking dogs with flat faces. All Pug puppies look cute, don't buy the first one you see – be patient and pick the right one. If you don't get a satisfactory answer, look elsewhere

What do you feed your adults and puppies? Many Pugs do not do well on cheap feed bulked up with corn. A reputable breeder will feed a top quality dog food and advise that you do the same

What special care do you recommend? Your Pug will probably need all or some of the following: regular eye, ear and wrinkle cleaning

What is the average lifespan of your dogs? Generally, pups bred from healthy stock live longer.

Why aren't you asking me any questions? A responsible breeder will be committed to making a good match between the new owners and their puppies. If the breeder spends more time discussing money than the welfare of the puppy and how you will care for him, you can draw your own conclusions as to what his or her priorities are – and they probably don't include improving the breed. Walk away.

TOP TIPS: Take your puppy to a vet – always try and find one who is familiar with Pugs or at least flat-faced breeds – to have a thorough check-up within 48 hours of purchase. If your vet is not happy with the health of the dog, no matter how painful it may be, return the pup to the breeder. Keeping an unhealthy puppy will only cause more distress and expense in the long run.

When buying a purebred (pedigree) Pug, the puppy will have official AKC or Kennel Club papers (papers from another country do not count, unless it is from a highly reputable breeder with a track record of show success), make sure you are given original copies of these. If they are not available, then the puppy is not a true purebred/pedigree registered with the Kennel Clubs - no matter what the breeder says.

Some top breeders may place restrictions on the sale. For example they may say that you cannot breed from your Pug or that if your female has puppies, they have first pick of the litter.

Puppy Contracts

Ask if the puppy is being sold with a Puppy Contract. These are recommended by breed clubs around the world and protect both buyer and seller by providing information on diet, worming, vaccination and veterinary visits from the birth of the puppy until it leaves the breeder. You should also have a health guarantee for a specified time period.

The UK's The Royal Society for the Prevention of Cruelty to Animals (RSPCA) has a downloadable puppy contract endorsed by vets and animal welfare organisations. You can see a copy here and should be looking for something similar from the breeder or seller of the puppy:

http://puppycontract.rspca.org.uk/webContent/staticImages/Microsites/PuppyContract/Downloads/PuppyContractDownload.pdf

A Puppy Contract will answer such questions as whether the puppy:

> ➢ Is covered by breeder's insurance and can be returned if there is a health issue within a certain period of time
> ➢ Was born by Caesarean section
> ➢ Has been micro-chipped and/or vaccinated and details of worming treatments
> ➢ The puppy has been partially or wholly housetrained
> ➢ And what health issues the pup and parents have been screened for

It should also cover details of the mother and father, what the puppy is currently being fed by the breeder and how much socialisation has taken place. Do your research before you go to see the litter, as once you are there the cute Pug puppies will undoubtedly be irresistible, and you will buy with your heart rather than your head. If you have any doubts at all about the breeder, seller or the puppy, WALK AWAY. Spending the time now to get your Pug from a good breeder with a proven track record will help to reduce the chances of health and behaviour problems with your adult dog.

Top 12 Tips for Choosing a Healthy Pug

1. Pugs are chunky and your puppy should have a well-fed appearance. They should NOT, however, have a distended abdomen (pot belly) as this can be a sign of worms - or other illnesses such as Cushing's disease in adults. The ideal puppy should not be too thin either, you should not be able to see his ribs

2. The puppy's nostrils should be round, not slits. He should breathe normally with no coughing or wheezing. Watch him run around and then listen to his breathing – does it sound normal or laboured?

3. His nose should be cool, damp and clean with no discharge. Avoid choosing a puppy with very heavy skin folds/rolls around his nose; sometimes they will get proportionately smaller as the pup grows, but if they remain large they will need regular cleaning as they become a breeding ground for bacteria

4. The pup's eyes should be bright and clear with no discharge or tear stain. Steer clear of a puppy which blinks a lot, this could be the sign of a problem

5. The pup's ears should be clean with no sign of discharge, soreness or redness

6. His gums should be clean and a healthy pink colour

7. Check the puppy's bottom to make sure it is clean and there are no signs of diarrhoea.

8. A Pug's coat should be clean with no signs of ticks or fleas. Red or irritated skin or bald spots could be a sign of infestation or a skin condition. Also check between the toes of the paws for signs of redness or swelling, some Pugs can suffer from inter-digital cysts

9. Choose a puppy that is solid in build and moves freely without any sign of injury or lameness. It should be a fluid movement, not jerky or stiff, which could be a sign of joint problems

10. When the puppy is distracted, clap or make a noise behind him - not so loud as to frighten him - to make sure he is not deaf

Finally, ask to see veterinary records to confirm your puppy has been wormed and had his first injections. If you are unlucky enough to have a health problem with your pup within the first few months, a reputable breeder will allow you to return the pup

Also, if you get the Pug puppy home and things don't work out for whatever reason, good breeders should also take the puppy back. Make sure this is the case before you commit.

Picking the Right Temperament

If you've decided that a Pug is the ideal dog for you, then here are two important points to bear in mind at the outset:

> ➢ Find a responsible breeder with a good reputation (we can't stress that enough)

> ➢ Secondly, take your time. Choosing a puppy which will share your home and your life for the next decade or so is an important decision. Don't rush it

You've picked a Pug because you really like the way these dogs look, their temperament and adaptability, and maybe because they don't need a huge amount of exercise and are suited to apartment living. Presumably you're planning on spending a lot of time with your new puppy, as Pugs love being with humans.

Individuals - The next thing to remember is that while different Pugs may share many characteristics and temperament traits, each puppy also has his own individual character, just like humans.

The generally pleasant temperament and affectionate nature of the Pug suits most people. However, if you are buying a puppy, visit the breeder more than once to see how your chosen pup interacts and get an idea of his character in comparison to his littermates. If you are rescuing or adopting an adult dog, make sure you are ready to cope with any health or behaviour problems which may arise.

Some Pug puppies will run up to greet you, pull at your shoelaces and playfully bite your fingers. Others will be more content to stay in the basket sleeping. Watch their behaviour and energy levels. Are you an active person who enjoys a daily walk or a couch potato? Choose the puppy which will be most suitable.

Submissive or dominant? - A submissive dog will by nature be more passive, less energetic and also possibly easier to train. A dominant dog will usually be more energetic and lively. They may also be more stubborn and need a firmer hand when training or socialising with other dogs. If you have a dominant dog you have to be careful about introducing new dogs into the household; two dominant Pugs may not live together comfortably

There is no good or bad, it's a question of which type of character will best suit you and your lifestyle. Here are a couple of quick tests to try at the breeder's to see if your puppy has a submissive or dominant personality:

> Roll the puppy gently on to his or her back in the crook of your arm (or on the floor). Then rest a hand on the pup's chest and look into his eyes for a few seconds. If he or she immediately struggles to get free, they are considered to be **dominant**. A puppy that doesn't struggle, but is happy to stay on his or her back has a more **submissive** character

> A similar test is the suspension test. Gently lift the puppy at arm's length under the armpits for a few seconds while allowing his hind legs to dangle free. A dominant pup will kick and struggle to get free. A puppy that is happy to remain dangling is more submissive

---

Useful Tips

Here are some other useful signs to look out for –

> Watch how he interacts with other puppies in the litter. Does he try and dominate them, does he walk away from them or is he happy to play with his littermates? This may give you an idea of how easy it will be to socialise him with other dogs

> After contact, does the pup want to follow you or walk away from you? Not following may mean he has a more independent nature

> If you throw something for the puppy is he happy to retrieve it for you or does he ignore it? This may measure their willingness to work with humans

> If you drop a bunch of keys behind the Pug puppy, does he act normally or does he flinch and jump away? The latter may be an indication of a timid or nervous disposition. Not reacting could also be a sign of deafness

Decide which temperament would fit in with you and your family and the rest is up to you. A Pug that has constant positive interactions with people and other animals during the first three to four months of life will be a happier, more stable dog. In contrast, a puppy plucked from its family too early and/or isolated at home alone for weeks on end will be less happy, less socialised and may display behaviour problems later on.

Puppies are like children. Being properly raised contributes to their confidence, sociability, stability and intellectual development. The bottom line is that a pup raised in a warm, loving environment with people is likely to be more tolerant and accepting and less likely to develop behaviour problems.

For those of you who prefer a scientific approach to choosing the right puppy, we are including the full Volhard Puppy Aptitude Test (PAT). This test has been developed by the highly respected Wendy and Jack Volhard who have built up an international reputation over the last 30 years for

their invaluable contribution to dog training, health and nutrition. Their philosophy is: "We believe that one of life's great joys is living in harmony with your dog."

They have written several books and the Volhard PAT is regarded as the premier method for evaluating the nature of young puppies. Jack and Wendy have also written the excellent Dog Training for Dummies book. Visit their website at **www.volhard.com** for details of their upcoming dog training camps, as well as their training and nutrition groups.

The Volhard Puppy Aptitude Test

Here are the ground rules for performing the test:

The testing is done in a location unfamiliar to the puppies. This does not mean they have to taken away from home. A 10-foot square area is perfectly adequate, such as a room in the house where the puppies have not been.

The puppies are tested one at a time.

There are no other dogs or people, except the scorer and the tester, in the testing area

The puppies do not know the tester.

The scorer is a disinterested third party and not the person interested in selling you a puppy.

The scorer is unobtrusive and positions himself so he can observe the puppies' responses without having to move.

The puppies are tested before they are fed.

The puppies are tested when they are at their liveliest.

Do not try to test a puppy that is not feeling well.

Puppies should not be tested the day of or the day after being vaccinated.

Only the first response counts! Tip: During the test, watch the puppy's tail. It will make a difference in the scoring whether the tail is up or down.

The tests are simple to perform and anyone with some common sense can do them. You can, however, elicit the help of someone who has tested puppies before and knows what they are doing.

Social attraction - the owner or caretaker of the puppies places it in the test area about four feet from the tester and then leaves the test area. The tester kneels down and coaxes the puppy to come to him or her by encouragingly and gently clapping hands and calling. The tester must coax the puppy in the opposite direction from where it entered the test area. Hint: Lean backward, sitting on your heels instead of leaning forward toward the puppy. Keep your hands close to your body encouraging the puppy to come to you instead of trying to reach for the puppy.

Following - the tester stands up and slowly walks away encouraging the puppy to follow. Hint: Make sure the puppy sees you walk away and get the puppy to focus on you by lightly clapping your hands and using verbal encouragement to get the puppy to follow you. Do not lean over the puppy.

Restraint - the tester crouches down and gently rolls the puppy on its back for 30 seconds. Hint: Hold the puppy down without applying too much pressure. The object is not to keep it on its back but to test its response to being placed in that position.

Social Dominance - let the puppy stand up or sit and gently stroke it from the head to the back while you crouch beside it. See if it will lick your face, an indication of a forgiving nature. Continue stroking until you see a behaviour you can score. Hint: When you crouch next to the puppy avoid leaning or hovering over it. Have the puppy at your side, both of you facing in the same direction.

Tip: During testing maintain a positive, upbeat and friendly attitude toward the puppies. Try to get each puppy to interact with you to bring out the best in him or her. Make the test a pleasant experience for the puppy.

Elevation Dominance - the tester cradles the puppy with both hands, supporting the puppy under its chest and gently lifts it two feet off the ground and holds it there for 30 seconds.

Retrieving - the tester crouches beside the puppy and attracts its attention with a crumpled up piece of paper. When the puppy shows some interest, the tester throws the paper no more than four feet in front of the puppy encouraging it to retrieve the paper.

Touch Sensitivity - the tester locates the webbing of one the puppy's front paws and presses it lightly between his index finger and thumb. The tester gradually increases pressure while counting to ten and stops when the puppy pulls away or shows signs of discomfort.

Sound Sensitivity - the puppy is placed in the centre of the testing area and an assistant stationed at the perimeter makes a sharp noise, such as banging a metal spoon on the bottom of a metal pan.

Sight Sensitivity - the puppy is placed in the centre of the testing area. The tester ties a string around a bath towel and jerks it across the floor, two feet away from the puppy.

Stability - an umbrella is opened about five feet from the puppy and gently placed on the ground.

During the testing, make a note of the heart rate of the pup, this is an indication of how it deals with stress, as well as its energy level.

Puppies come with high, medium or low energy levels. You have to decide for yourself, which suits your life style. Dogs with high energy levels need a great deal of exercise, and will get into mischief if this energy is not channelled into the right direction.

Finally, look at the overall structure of the puppy. You see what you get at 49 days age (seven weeks). If the pup has strong and straight front and back legs, with all four feet pointing in the same direction, it will grow up that way, provided you give it the proper diet and environment. If you notice something out of the ordinary at this age, it will stay with puppy for the rest of its life. He will not grow out of it.

Scoring the Results

Following are the responses you will see and the score assigned to each particular response. You will see some variations and will have to make a judgment on what score to give them –

Test	Response	Score
SOCIAL ATTRACTION	Came readily, tail up, jumped, bit at hands	1
	Came readily, tail up, pawed, licked at hands	2
	Came readily, tail up	3
	Came readily, tail down	4
	Came hesitantly, tail down	5
	Didn't come at all	6
FOLLOWING	Followed readily, tail up, got underfoot, bit at feet	1
	Followed readily, tail up, got underfoot	2
	Followed readily, tail up	3
	Followed readily, tail down	4
	Followed hesitantly, tail down	5
	Did not follow or went away	6
RESTRAINT	Struggled fiercely, flailed, bit	1
	Struggled fiercely, flailed	2
	Settled, struggled, settled with some eye contact	3
	Struggled, then settled	4
	No struggle	5
	No struggle, strained to avoid eye contact	6

SOCIAL DOMINANCE	Jumped, pawed, bit, growled	1
	Jumped, pawed	2
	Cuddled up to tester and tried to lick face	3
	Squirmed, licked at hands	4
	Rolled over, licked at hands	5
	Went away and stayed away	6
ELEVATION DOMINANCE	Struggled fiercely, tried to bite	1
	Struggled fiercely	2
	Struggled, settled, struggled, settled	3
	No struggle, relaxed	4
	No struggle, body stiff	5
	No struggle, froze	6
RETRIEVING	Chased object, picked it up and ran away	1
	Chased object, stood over it and did not return	2
	Chased object, picked it up and returned with it to tester	3
	Chased object and returned without it to tester	4
	Started to chase object, lost interest	5
	Does not chase object	6
TOUCH SENSITIVITY	8-10 count before response	1
	6-8 count before response	2
	5-6 count before response	3
	3-5 count before response	4
	2-3 count before response	5
	1-2 count before response	6
SOUND SENSITIVITY	Listened, located sound and ran toward it barking	1
	Listened, located sound and walked slowly toward it	2
	Listened, located sound and showed curiosity	3
	Listened and located sound	4
	Cringed, backed off and hid behind tester 5	5
	Ignored sound and showed no curiosity	6
SIGHT SENSITIVITY	Looked, attacked and bit object	1
	Looked and put feet on object and put mouth on it	2
	Looked with curiosity and attempted to investigate, tail up	3
	Looked with curiosity, tail down	4
	Ran away or hid behind tester	5
	Hid behind tester	6
STABILITY	Looked and ran to the umbrella, mouthing or biting it	1
	Looked and walked to the umbrella, smelling it cautiously	2
	Looked and went to investigate	3
	Sat and looked, but did not move toward the umbrella	4
	Showed little or no interest	5
	Ran away from the umbrella	6

The scores are interpreted as follows:

Mostly 1s - Strong desire to be pack leader and is not shy about bucking for a promotion. Has a predisposition to be aggressive to people and other dogs and will bite.

Should only be placed into a very experienced home where the dog will be trained and worked on a regular basis.

Tip: Stay away from the puppy with a lot of 1's or 2's. It has lots of leadership aspirations and may be difficult to manage. This puppy needs an experienced home. Not good with children.

Mostly 2s - Also has leadership aspirations. May be hard to manage and has the capacity to bite. Has lots of self-confidence. Should not be placed into an inexperienced home. Too unruly to be good with children and elderly people, or other animals. Needs strict schedule, loads of exercise and lots of training. Has the potential to be a great show dog with someone who understands dog behaviour.

Mostly 3s - Can be a high-energy dog and may need lots of exercise. Good with people and other animals. Can be a bit of a handful to live with. Needs training, does very well at it and learns quickly. Great dog for second-time owner.

Mostly 4s - The kind of dog that makes the perfect pet. Best choice for the first time owner. Rarely will buck for a promotion in the family. Easy to train, and rather quiet. Good with elderly people, children, although may need protection from the children. Choose this pup, take it to obedience classes, and you'll be the star, without having to do too much work!

Tip: The puppy with mostly 3's and 4's can be quite a handful, but should be good with children and does well with training. Energy needs to be dispersed with plenty of exercise.

Mostly 5s - Fearful, shy and needs special handling. Will run away at the slightest stress in its life. Strange people, strange places, different floor or surfaces may upset it. Often afraid of loud noises and terrified of thunderstorms. When you greet it upon your return, may submissively urinate. Needs a very special home where the environment doesn't change too much and where there are no children. Best for a quiet, elderly couple. If cornered and cannot get away, has a tendency to bite.

Mostly 6s – So independent that he doesn't need you or other people. Doesn't care if he is trained or not - he is his own person. Unlikely to bond to you, since he doesn't need you. A great guard dog for gas stations! Do not take this puppy and think you can change him into a lovable bundle - you can't, so leave well enough alone.

Tip: Avoid the puppy with several 6's. It is so independent it doesn't need you or anyone. He is his own person and unlikely to bond to you.

The Scores - Few puppies will test with all 2's or all 3's, there'll be a mixture of scores. For that first time, wonderfully easy to train, potential star, look for a puppy that scores with mostly 4's and 3's. Don't worry about the score on Touch Sensitivity - you can compensate for that with the right training equipment.

It's hard not to become emotional when picking a puppy - they are all so cute, soft and cuddly. Remind yourself that this dog is going to be with you for eight to 16 years. Don't hesitate to step back a little to contemplate your decision. Sleep on it and review it in the light of day.

Avoid the puppy with a score of 1 on the Restraint and Elevation tests. This puppy will be too much for the first-time owner. It's a lot more fun to have a good dog, one that is easy to train, one you can live with and one you can be proud of, than one that is a constant struggle.

Getting a Dog From a Shelter - Don't overlook an animal shelter as a source for a good dog. Not all dogs wind up in a shelter because they are bad. After that cute puppy stage, when the dog grows up, it may become too much for its owner. Or, there has been a change in the owner's circumstances forcing him or her into having to give up the dog.

Most of the time these dogs are housetrained and already have some training. If the dog has been properly socialised to people, it will be able to adapt to a new environment. Bonding may take a little longer, but once accomplished, results in a devoted companion.

A Dog or a Bitch (Male or Female)?

When you have decided to get a Pug puppy and know how to find a good breeder, the next decision is whether to get a male or female. Male puppies are sometimes slightly less expensive than females from the same litter. Remember that the differences within the sexes are greater than the differences between the sexes. In other words, you can get a dominant female and a submissive male, or vice versa. There are, however, some general traits which are more common with one sex or another.

Pugs are sociable dogs and, unless they have had a bad experience, they are not normally aggressive. However, un-neutered males – referred to as 'dogs' – may be more likely to display aggression if confronted by aggression from other males. An entire (un-neutered) male is also more likely to go wandering off on the scent of a female.

If you take a male Pug for a walk, you can expect him to stop at every lamp-post, gate and interesting blade of grass to leave his mark by urinating. A female will tend to urinate far less often on a walk. Our male dog can manage at least two dozen 30-40 pit stops on a normal walk - very frustrating when I'm in a hurry - and no, he can't be rushed!

Female dogs, or bitches, generally tend to be less aggressive towards other dogs, except when raising puppies. With some breeds, families consider a female if they have young children as a bitch may be more tolerant towards young creatures. However, virtually all Pugs, regardless of their gender, are generally good with children.

Female Pugs can be a bit messy when they come into heat every six months, due to the blood loss. If your female is not spayed, you will also have the nuisance of becoming a magnet for all the free-wandering male dogs in your neighbourhood.

Unless you bought your Pug specifically for breeding, you should consider having your dog neutered - or spayed if she is a female. If you plan to have two or more Pugs living together, this is even more advisable. One interesting fact is that if you have more than one female Pug, they will often synchronise and come into heat at the same time – nature never ceases to amaze us! See **Chapter 13. The Birds and The Bees** for more information.

Bear in mind that when you select a puppy, you should also be looking out for the right temperament as well as the right sex. In short, spend time to find a good breeder and then arm yourself with the knowledge in this chapter to pick a puppy most likely to have the temperament you are looking for.

5. Bringing Your Puppy Home

As the Boy Scouts say: Be Prepared! Before you bring your precious little bundle of joy home, it's a smart idea to prepare the surroundings before he or she arrives while you still have the chance. All puppies are demanding and once they land, they will swallow up most of your time. Here's a list of things you ought to think about getting beforehand:

Puppy Checklist

- ✓ A dog bed or basket
- ✓ Bedding – old towels or a blanket which can easily be washed
- ✓ If possible, a towel or piece of cloth which has been rubbed on the puppy's mother to put in his bed
- ✓ A collar, or harness, and lead
- ✓ An identification tag for the collar or harness
- ✓ Food and water bowls, preferably stainless steel
- ✓ Lots of newspapers for housetraining
- ✓ Poo(p) bags
- ✓ Puppy food – find out what the breeder is feeding and stick with it initially
- ✓ Puppy treats (preferably healthy ones, not rawhide)
- ✓ Toys and chews suitable for puppies
- ✓ A puppy coat if you live in a cool climate
- ✓ A crate if you decide to use one
- ✓ Old towels for cleaning your puppy and covering the crate.

AND PLENTY OF TIME!

Later on you'll also need a longer lead, a grooming brush and maybe a comb, dog shampoo, flea and worming products and possibly an additional crate for travelling.

Puppy Proofing Your Home

Before your puppy arrives at his or her new home, you may have to make a few adjustments to make your home safe and suitable. Young Pug puppies are small bundles of instinct and energy (when they are awake), with little common sense and even less self-control. They are like babies and it's up to you to set the boundaries – both physically and in terms of behaviour – but one step at a time.

All young Pugs are curious, they love to investigate and have a great sense of fun. Many pups have short, chaotic bursts of energy and you have to ensure that he or she can't come to any harm during these mad five minutes – once you've done that, you can sit back, relax and enjoy the show.

Create an area where the puppy is allowed to go and then keep the rest of the house off-limits until housetraining is complete - this can be anything from a few days to a few months with Pugs, according to the breeders involved in this book. One of the biggest factors influencing the success and speed of housetraining is your commitment - another reason for taking a week or two off work when your puppy arrives home.

Like babies, most puppies are mini chewing machines and so remove anything breakable and/or chewable within the puppy's reach – including wooden furniture. Obviously you cannot remove your kitchen cupboards, doors, skirting boards and other fixtures and fittings, so don't leave him unattended for any length of time where he can chew something which is hard to replace.

A baby gate is a relatively inexpensive method of preventing a puppy from going upstairs and leaving an unwanted gift on your precious bedroom carpets. A puppy's bones are soft and recent studies have shown that if allowed to climb or descend stairs, young pups can develop joint problems later in life. You can also use a baby gate or wire panels, available from pet shops, to keep the puppy enclosed in one room – preferably one with a floor which is easy to wipe clean and not too far away from a door to the garden or yard for housetraining.

In any case, you may also want to remove your expensive oriental rugs to other rooms until he or she is fully housetrained and has stopped chewing everything. Make sure you have some toys suitable for sharp little teeth, soft enough to chew and too big to swallow. Don't give old socks, shoes or slippers or your pup will regard your footwear as fair game. Rawhide chews as they can get stuck in the throat.

The puppy's designated area or room should be not too hot cold or damp, and free from draughts. Pugs, like other brachycephalic (flat faced) breeds are sensitive to temperature fluctuations and cannot tolerate heat or cold. If you live in a hot climate and it's summer, your new puppy will probably need an air conditioned room.

Scientists have proved that the domestic dog is a direct descendant of the wolf, and just like a wolf, your puppy needs a den. This den is a haven where your puppy feels safe for the first few weeks after the traumatic experience of leaving his or her mother and littermates. Young puppies sleep for over 18 hours a day at the beginning, some may sleep for up to 22 hours a day; this is normal.

 If you have young children, you must restrict the time they spend with the puppy to a few short sessions a day. Plenty of sleep is **essential** for the normal development of a young dog. You wouldn't wake a baby up every hour or so to play and shouldn't do that with a puppy. Don't invite friends round to see your new puppy for at least a day or two, preferably longer. However excited you are, he needs a few days to get over the stress of leaving his mother and siblings and then to start bonding with you.

You have a couple of options with the den; you can get a dog bed or basket, or you can use a crate. Crates have long been popular in America and are becoming increasingly used in the UK, particularly as it is often quicker to train a puppy using a crate.

The idea of keeping a dog in a cage like a rabbit or hamster is abhorrent to many animal-loving Brits. And using the crate as a prison to contain the dog for hours on end certainly is cruel. But the crate has its place as a sanctuary for your dog, a place where he or she can go; it is their own space and they know no harm will come to them in there. See the section later in this chapter on **Crate Training** for getting your Pug used to - and even enjoy - being in his crate.

Most puppies' natural instinct is not to soil the area where they sleep. Put plenty of newspapers down in the area next to the den and your puppy should choose to go to the toilet here if you are not quick enough to take him or her outside. Of course, they may also decide to trash their designated area by chewing their blankets and shredding the newspaper – patience is the key in this situation!

If you have a garden or yard that you intend letting your puppy roam in, make sure that every little gap has been plugged. You'd be amazed at the tiny holes they can escape through. Also, don't leave your Pug unattended as they can come to harm and dogs are increasingly being targeted by thieves, who are even stealing from gardens.

Make sure there are no poisonous plants which your pup might chew. There are over 700 plants which are toxic to animals, some of the more common include azalea, begonia, carnation, chrysanthemum, cyclamen, daffodil, foxglove, holly berries, hosta, ivy, lily, mistletoe, oleander, poinsettia, tomato plant, tulip and yew.

Another very important point to bear in mind is that the Pug has bulbous eyes and a flat face, resulting in little or no protection for the eyes. Owners have to take extra special care to ensure there are no low plants or branches with sharp edges or thorns which could injure your puppy.

In order for puppies to grow into well-adjusted dogs, they have to feel comfortable and relaxed in their new surroundings and they need a great deal of sleep. They are leaving the warmth and protection of their mother and littermates and so for the first few days at least, your puppy will feel very sad. It is important to make the transition from the birth home to your home as easy as possible.

His life is in your hands. How you react and interact with him in the first few days and weeks will shape your relationship and his character for the years ahead.

What the Breeders Say

We asked a number of breeders in the UK and America what essential advice they would give to new owners of Pug puppies and this is what they said:

Robert and Holly Hitchcock, Bobitch Pugs, Derbyshire, UK: "We always furnish our buyers with endless advice sheets, but the one thing we always say is: 'Watch their eyes.' Puppies are fearless and a combination of short muzzle and fairly large eyes may lead to the eye getting knocked."

Linda Guy, Londonderry Pugs, Northern Ireland: "Avoid blows to the head as this can dislodge the eyeball - rough play should be limited for this reason. Ensure nails are cut regularly as they can curl into the pad of the foot and cause pain and infection, and be aware that chocolate, macadamia nuts, etc. cause gastroenteritis."

Holly Attwood, Taftazini, Sheffield, UK: "Essential advice would be not to be fooled into thinking that because they are a small toy breed that Pugs are minimal effort. This is a high maintenance breed that requires a lot of care and attention. They may be small but they love their walks and do need exercise.

"The most important things for new owners to be aware of is the high risk of eye injury. They don't have a long nose to act as a bumper as with other breeds, therefore their eyes are at an increased risk of injuries. Owners must be very vigilant when the pup is playing and running around and interacting with other dogs.

"I would also strongly advise owners of the signs of an eye problem. They should be checked daily for squinting, excessive blinking, redness and general soreness and if there are any concerns, they must seek veterinary attention immediately, as things can change very quickly with a Pug eye and there is a risk of losing it altogether.

"Another key care requirement is the nose wrinkle; this must be kept clean and dry, using appropriate products. I use and highly recommend Malacetic Wipes. These are antibacterial and antifungal and effectively clean the wrinkle. Again, the owner should check for redness, swelling, a horrible odour or a yellow crust or if the Pug is scratching or rubbing it on furniture; all of which are indicative of infection or a yeast problem which require veterinary attention."

(Our photo shows champion Ch. Tsuselena Jimmy Dean JW, known as 'Dennis', owned by Holly and bred by Sue Lee, Sheffield, reproduced by kind permission of photographer Pauline Oliver).

Sue Wragg, Glammarags Pugs, Cheshire, UK: "Pug puppies love people so want to be near them at all times. As they are quite small they can get stepped on - or they can trip you up. Take care of the eyes - Pugs aren't afraid of anything and will rush into rose bushes or other thorny plants, or will tackle a snarling cat with no thought for their eyesight. At the first sign of any type of eye injury take the pup to the vets immediately to try and avoid the dreaded eye ulcer."

Sandra Mayoh, Drumlinfold Pugs, North Yorkshire, UK: "Be very careful not to leave a Pug unattended in the garden due to theft. They are like all normal puppies; inclined to get into mischief. They also eat anything."

Melanie Clark breeder of Pugginpugs, UK: "The main thing as a new puppy owner is to make sure that the puppy is kept safe, as you would do a small child; a puppy is just as adventurous.

"Wrinkles need to be cleaned at least once a week to prevent bacteria from harbouring. They're also very susceptible to climate change and can pick up a cold or overheat easily. It's vital that when walking they are wrapped up warm in colder weather and taken for walks at the coolest part of the day in the summer - a paddling pool is also great for helping them maintain their body temperature throughout the summer days. I also advise against collars and suggest a harness for walks, as breathing is already very restricted."

Saran Evans, Sephina Pugs, Carmarthenshire, Wales, UK: "Always be vigilant regarding eyes, Pugs are the most curious of breeds and put their little faces where they shouldn't. Eye injury is very common and requires immediate treatment to avoid ulceration and the potential loss of an eye. Also, give your puppy plenty of rest to allow immature limbs to grow."

Linda and Kim Wright, Wright's Pugs, Springport, Michigan, USA: "New owners must be made aware that care of a Pug includes precautions against extreme heat and cold. I also let them know that they shed a lot all year long and that they require a lot of attention and love. They will eat until they are as wide as they are long and try to convince you they are starving. It is very important to monitor their weight and prevent them from becoming fat or obese."

J. Candy Schlieper, CandyLand Pugs, Tipp City, Ohio, USA: "I always stress to new owners about how heat can be very harmful to this breed and how they need to closely watch all Pugs when it is hot and humid.

"I also try to tell all new puppy owners to be aware of allowing them to climb and jump off of furniture while they are still growing and their growth plates are still open. I have seen puppies get really bad injuries when allowed to do this. Pugs carry so much of their weight on their front that we need to protect them from injuries by keep them off of furniture and not allowing them to run and jump stairs."

Donna Shank and Brenda Schuettenberg, Rokiciera Pugs, California, USA: "Heat can and does kill flat faced animals, if it is over 80 degrees Fahrenheit, watch for heat stress. If it's humid start watching at 75 degrees and above. Know the signs and what steps to take. Just because the dog has access to shade does not mean it will not suffer heatstroke, as Pugs will follow their people everywhere, even if it is dangerous to their health."

Catherine Jones-Kyle, of Dixie Darlings, Leipers Fork, Tennessee: "Do not take them out around other dogs until they are at least 12 weeks old to avoid any contagions - you may be a responsible dog owner, don't assume everyone is. Keep their nose rolls clean, a quick wipe every night before bed is all it needs, don't let them talk you into a bite of human food, one bite leads to more and then you have an overweight Pug. Watch for rough play around the eyes, they can be easily damaged."

Erin Ford, Fur-N-Feathers, Florida: "As any new puppy the most important thing to do is remember they will put any and everything in their mouth, Be very mindful and watch them very closely, especially while outside." (Pictured is Erin's Lady Pug).

Laura Libner: "The biggest thing I would caution new owners to be aware of is risk of eye injury. Because of the Pug's innate curiosity and the proximity of the nose and eye, they are inevitably more prone to eye injuries than many other breeds, and this can be extremely expensive very quickly if not taken care of expeditiously. Also, this is not a breed that can be left outside - period. They cannot tolerate extreme heat or humidity and must be protected as they are more vulnerable than other breeds due to their flat faces."

The First Few Days

Before you collect your puppy, let the breeder know what time you will be arriving and ask her not to feed the pup for three or four hours beforehand (unless you have a very long journey, in which case the puppy will need to eat something). He will be less likely to be car sick and should be hungry when he arrives in his new home. The same applies to an adult dog moving to a new home.

When you arrive, ask the breeder for an old towel which has been with the dam – you can leave one on an earlier visit to collect with the pup. Or take one with you and rub the mother with it to collect her scent and put this with the puppy for the first few days. It may help him to settle in.

Make sure you get copies of any health certificates relating to the parents. A good breeder will also have a Contract of Sale or Puppy Contract – **see Chapter 4** - which outlines your and the their rights and responsibilities.

It should also state that you can return the puppy if there are health issues within a certain time frame – although if you have picked your breeder carefully, it should hopefully not come to this. The breeder should also give you details of worming and any vaccinations. Most good breeders supply an information sheet for new owners.

You should also find out exactly what the breeder is feeding and how much. You cannot suddenly switch a dog's diet; their digestive systems cannot cope with a sudden change, so you should stick to whatever the puppy is used to initially.

The Journey Home

Bringing a new puppy or home in the car can be a traumatic experience, your puppy will be devastated at leaving his or her mother, brothers and sisters and a familiar environment. Everything will be strange and frightening and he will probably whimper and whine - or even howl or bark - on the way to his or her new home.

If you can, take somebody with you to take care of him on that first journey. Under no circumstances have the puppy on your lap when driving. It is simply too dangerous, a little Pug puppy is cute, lively and far too distracting.

The best and safest way is to transport the pup in a crate – either a purpose-made travel crate or a wire crate which he will use at home. Put a comfortable blanket in the bottom - preferably rubbed with the scent of the mother. See if you can get a familiar toy from the breeder as well. Ask your travel companion to sit next to the crate and talk softly to the frightened little bundle of nerves.

(Pictured relaxing at home is one of J. Candy Schlieper's puppies, of CandyLand Pugs, Ohio.)

If you don't have a crate, your passenger may wish to hold the puppy. If so, have an old towel between the person and the pup as he may quite possibly urinate (the puppy, not the passenger!)

If you have a journey of more than a couple of hours, make sure that you take water and offer the puppy a drink en route. He may need to eliminate or have diarrhoea (hopefully, only due to nerves), but don't let him outside on to the ground in a strange place, as he is not yet fully inoculated. If you have a long journey, cover the bottom of the crate with a waterproof material and put newspapers in half of it so the pup can eliminate without staining the car seats.

Arriving Home

As soon as you arrive home, let your puppy into the garden or yard and when he 'performs,' praise him for his efforts.

These first few days are critical in getting your puppy to feel safe and confident in his new surroundings. Spend time with your new arrival, talk to him often in a reassuring manner. Introduce him to his den and toys, slowly allow him to explore and show him around the house. Pug puppies are extremely curious - and amusing, you might be surprised at his reactions to everyday objects. Remember that puppies and babies explore with their mouths, so don't scold for chewing. Instead, remove objects you don't want chewed out of reach and replace them with toys he can chew.

If you have other animals, introduce them slowly and in supervised sessions, preferably once the pup has got used to his new surroundings, not as soon as you walk through the door. Gentleness and patience are the keys to these first few days, so don't over-face your puppy. Have a special, gentle puppy voice with which to talk to him and use his name often in a pleasant, encouraging manner. Never use his name to scold or he will associate it with bad things. The sound of his name should always make him want to pay attention to you as something good is going to happen - praise, food, play time and so on.

Resist the urge to pick the puppy up all the time. Let him explore on his own legs, encouraging a little independence. One of the most important things at this stage is to ensure that your puppy has enough sleep – which is nearly all the time - no matter how much you want to watch his antics when awake or play with him.

If you haven't decided what to call your little Pug yet, 'Shadow' might be a good suggestion, as he or she will follow you everywhere! Many puppies from different breeds do this, but Pugs are "Velcro dogs," they like to stick close to their owners – both as puppies and adults.

Our website receives many emails from worried new owners. Here are some of the most common concerns:

➢ My puppy sleeps all the time, is this normal?
➢ My puppy won't stop crying or whining
➢ My puppy is shivering
➢ My puppy won't eat

> My puppy is very timid
> My puppy follows me everywhere, she won't let me out of her sight

Most of the above are quite common. They are just a young pup's reaction to leaving his mother and littermates and entering into a strange new world. It is normal for puppies to sleep most of the time, just like babies. It is also normal for some puppies to whine a lot during the first few days. Make your new pup as comfortable as possible, ensuring he has a warm (but not too hot), quiet den away from draughts, where he is not pestered by children or other pets. Handle him gently, while giving him plenty of time to sleep. During the first few nights your puppy will whine, try your best to ignore the pitiful cries.

Unless they are especially dominant, most puppies will be nervous and timid for the first few days. They will think of you as their new mother and follow you around the house. This is also quite natural, but after a few days start to leave your puppy for a few minutes at a time, gradually building up the time. Pugs, like other breeds selectively bred for companionship, can be prone to separation anxiety, particularly if they are used to being with you virtually 24/7. See **Chapter 8. Behaviour** for more information.

If your routine means you are normally out of the house for a few hours during the day, get your puppy on a Friday or Saturday so he has at least a couple of days to adjust to his new surroundings. A far better idea is to book at least a week or two off work to help your puppy settle in. If you don't work, leave your diary free for the first couple of weeks. Helping a new pup to settle in is virtually a full-time job.

This is a frightening time for your puppy. Is your puppy shivering with cold or is it nerves? Avoid placing your puppy under stress by making too many demands on him. If you have children they have to learn that the puppy needs to sleep most of the time. Don't allow them to pester and, until they have learned how to handle a dog, don't allow them to pick up the puppy unsupervised, as they could inadvertently damage the Pug puppy's tiny little body.

If your puppy won't eat, spend time gently coaxing him. If he leaves his food, take it away and try it later, don't leave it down all of the time or he may get used to turning his nose up at it. Then the next time you put something down for him, he is more likely to be hungry.

If your puppy is crying, it is probably for one of the following reasons:

> He is lonely
> He is hungry
> He wants attention from you
> He needs to go to the toilet

If it is none of these, then check his body and eyes to make sure he hasn't picked up an injury. Try not to fuss over him. If he whimpers, just reassure him with a quiet word. If he cries loudly and tries to get out of his allotted area, he probably needs to go to the toilet. Even if it is the middle of the night, get up (yes, sorry, this is best) and take him outside. Praise him if he goes to the toilet.

The strongest bonding period for a puppy is between eight and 12 weeks of age. The most important factors in bonding with your puppy are TIME spent with him and PATIENCE, even when he or she makes a mess in the house or chews something he shouldn't.

Remember, your Pug pup is just a baby dog and it takes time to learn not to do these things. Spend time with your pup and you will have a loyal friend for life. Pugs are not known for their unwavering loyalty to one particular person but, like all companion dogs, they have a very strong instinct to bond with humans. That emotional attachment between you and your Pug may grow to become one of the most important aspects of your - and his - life.

Where Should the Puppy Sleep?

Where do you want your new puppy to sleep? You cannot simply allow him or her to wander freely around the house. Ideally your puppy will be in a contained area, a playpen or a crate, at night. While it is not acceptable to shut a dog in a cage all day, you can keep your puppy in a crate at night until he or she is housetrained.

You also have to consider whether you want the pup to sleep in your bedroom or elsewhere. If your puppy is in the bedroom, don't let him climb up or downstairs until he has stopped growing, as he can damage his joints.

If he is to sleep outside your bedroom, put him in a comfortable bed of his own, or a crate – and then block your ears for the first couple of nights. He will almost certainly whine and whimper, but this won't last long and he will soon get used to sleeping on his own, without his littermates or you.

We don't recommend letting your new pup sleep on the bed. He will not be housetrained and also a puppy needs to learn his place in the household – and this should be below you in the pecking order if you don't want him to rule your life. If you decide to let him on the bed later, that's up to you, but lift him on and off so he doesn't injure himself jumping.

Another point to consider is that while it is not good to leave a dog alone all day, it is also not healthy to spend 24 hours a day with him. He becomes too reliant on you and will almost certainly develop separation anxiety when you do have to leave him. A puppy used to being on his own every night is less likely to develop attachment issues, so consider this when deciding where your pup should sleep.

Many owners prefer to bite the bullet in the beginning by leaving leave the pup in a safe place downstairs or in a different room to the bedroom so he gets used to being on his own right from the beginning. If you do this, you might find a set of earplugs very useful for helping (you) to survive the first few nights! In a moment of weakness you might consider letting the puppy sleep

in the bedroom for a couple of nights until he gets used to your home, but then it is even harder to turf him out later.

Pictured is Catherine Jones-Kyle's Ivan, showing just how hard it is to resist the appeal of a cute Pug puppy – BE FIRM!

If you decide you definitely do want your Pug to sleep in the bedroom from Day One, initially put him in a crate with a soft blanket covering part of the crate or in a high-sided cardboard box he can't climb out of. Put newspapers underneath as he will not be able to last the night without urinating.

Once your dog has been housetrained and can access other areas of the house, you may reconsider where he sleeps. Some people will continue to keep him in the place where he started out; others will want the dog to sleep in the bedroom. But before you immediately choose the bedroom, bear in mind that most Pugs snuffle, snore, fart, scratch and wander about in the night!

Vaccinations and Worming

It is **always** a good idea to have your Pug checked out by a vet within a few days of picking him up. Keep him away from other dogs in the waiting room as he will not be fully protected against canine diseases until the vaccination schedule is complete.

He will also have to complete his vaccinations. All puppies need these injections; very occasionally a puppy has a reaction, but this is very rare and the advantages of immunisation far outweigh the disadvantages.

An unimmunised puppy is at risk every time he meets other dogs as he has no protection against potentially fatal diseases – another point is that is unlikely a pet insurer will cover an unimmunised dog. It should be stressed that vaccinations are generally quite safe and side effects are uncommon. (There is some anecdotal evidence that a small minority of Pugs have suffered a reaction to a rabies injection, speak to your vet for more information). If your Pug is unlucky enough to be one of the very few that suffers an adverse reaction, here are the signs to look out for; a pup may exhibit one or more of these:

Mild Reaction - Sleepiness, irritability and not wanting to be touched. Sore or a small lump at the place where he was injected. Nasal discharge or sneezing. Puffy face and ears.

Severe Reaction - Anaphylactic shock. A sudden and quick reaction, usually before leaving the vet's, which causes breathing difficulties. Vomiting, diarrhoea, staggering and seizures.

A severe reaction is extremely rare. There is a far, far greater risk of your Pug either being ill and/or spreading disease if he does not have the injections.

The usual schedule is for the pup to have his first vaccination at six to eight weeks of age. This will protect him from a number of diseases in one shot. In the UK these are Distemper, Canine Parvovirus (Parvo), Infectious Canine Hepatitis (Adenovirus), Leptospirosis and Kennel Cough (Bordetella). In the USA this is known as DHPP. Puppies in the US also need vaccinating separately against Rabies, and optional vaccinations for Coronavirus and, depending on where you

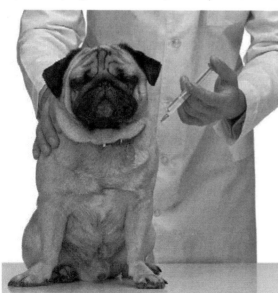

live and if your dog is regularly in or near woods or forests, Lyme Disease.

The puppy requires a second vaccination around four weeks later and then maybe a third to complete his immunity, which is often from 10 to 12 weeks of age. Seven days after that he is safe to mix with other dogs. When you take your Pug for an initial check up within a few days of bringing him home, ask your vet exactly what injections are needed.

Diseases such as Parvo and Kennel Cough are highly contagious and you should not let your puppy mix with other dogs - unless they are your own and have already been vaccinated - until a week after he has completed his vaccinations, otherwise he will not be fully immunised. Parvovirus can also be transmitted by fox faeces.

You shouldn't take your new puppy to places where unvaccinated dogs might have been, like the local park. This does not mean that your puppy should be isolated - far from it; this is an important time for socialisation. It is OK for the puppy to mix with another dog which you 100% know has been vaccinated and is up to date with its annual boosters. Perhaps invite a friend's dog round to play in your garden to begin the socialisation process.

Once your puppy is fully immunised, you have a window of a few weeks to introduce him to as many new experiences, dogs, people, traffic, noises, other animals, etc. during that critical period when he is most receptive, before he gets to five months old. Socialisation should not stop at that age, but continue for the rest of your Pug's life, but it is particularly important to socialise young puppies. Your dog will need a booster injection every year of his life. The vet should give you a record card or send you a reminder, but it's a good idea to keep a note of the date in your diary.

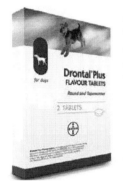 All puppies need worming. A good breeder will give the puppies their first dose of worming medication at around two weeks old, then probably again at five and eight weeks before they leave the litter. Get the details and inform your vet exactly what treatment, if any, your pup has already had. The main types of worms affecting puppies are roundworm and tapeworm.

Roundworm can also be transmitted from a puppy to humans – most often children - and can in severe cases cause blindness, or miscarriage in women, so it's important to keep up to date with worming. Puppies can be quite susceptible to worms, most commonly picking them up through their mother's milk. If you have children, get them into the habit of washing their hands after they have been in contact with the puppy – lack of hygiene is the reason why children are most susceptible. Most vets recommend worming a puppy once a month until he is six months old, and then around every two or three months.

Fleas can pass on tapeworms to dogs, but a puppy would not normally be treated unless it is known for certain he has fleas. And then only with caution. You need to know the weight of your pet and then speak to your vet about the safest treatment to rid your puppy of the parasites. It is not usually worth buying a cheap worming or flea treatment from a supermarket, as they are often far less effective than more expensive vet-recommended preparations, such as Drontal. Many people living in the US have contacted our website claiming the parasite treatment Trifexis has caused severe side effects and even death to their dogs. Although this evidence is only anecdotal, to be on the safe side you might want consider avoiding Trifexis - even if your vet recommends it.

6. How to Crate Train

If you are unfamiliar with them, crates may seem like a cruel punishment for a lovable Pug puppy. They are, however, becoming increasingly popular to help with housetraining and to keep the dog safe at night or when you are not there. Many breeders, trainers, behaviourists, and people who show dogs use them.

If you decide to use a crate, then remember that it is not a prison to restrain the dog. It should only be used in a humane manner and time should be spent to make the puppy or adult dog feel like the crate is his own safe little haven. If the door is closed on the crate, your puppy must ALWAYS have access to water while inside. If used correctly and if time is spent getting the puppy used to the crate, it can be a valuable tool.

We tried our dog Max with a crate when he was a young puppy and he howled and whined every time he went in. In the end, we couldn't bear to hear the noise and so we abandoned it. It is now in the porch at our house and makes a very useful storage place for Wellington boots and running shoes. Now, several years later, having heard from so many of our American readers about how much their dogs love their crates, I think perhaps we gave up too easily.

But crates are not for every Pug and they should never be used as a means of imprisonment because you are out of the house all day. Pugs are companion creatures; they are not like hamsters or pet mice which can adapt to life in a cage. They are dogs which thrive on physically being close to their humans – they want to be WITH YOU. Being caged all day is a miserable existence.

If you do decide to use a crate perhaps to put your dog in for short periods while you leave the house, or at night, the best place for it is in the corner of a room away from cold draughts or too much heat. Pugs like to be near their family - which is you.

It is only natural for a Pug, or any other dog, to whine in the beginning. He is not crying because he is in a cage, he would cry if he had the freedom of the room and he was alone - he is crying because he is separated from you. However, with patience and the right training he will get used to it and come to regard his crate as a favourite place. Leave him where he can hear you. Some owners make the crate their dog's only bed, so he feels comfortable and safe in there.

Pugs overheat easily, so when you buy a crate get a wire one which allows the air to pass through, not a plastic one which may get very hot. If you cover the crate, don't cover it 100% or you will restrict the flow of air. The crate should be large enough to allow your dog to stretch out flat on his side without being cramped, be able to turn round easily, and to sit up without hitting his head on the top. Bear in mind that a Pug is chunky, rather than flexible, and needs enough room to turn round comfortably.

Crates aren't for every owner or every Pug. But used correctly they:

> Create a canine den
> Are useful for housetraining
> Limit access to the rest of the house while your dog learns the household rules
> Are a safe way to transport your dog in a car

If you use a crate right from Day One, cover half of it with a blanket to help your puppy regard it as a den. He also needs bedding and it's a good idea to put a chew in as well. A large crate may allow your dog to eliminate at one end and sleep at the other, but this may slow down his housetraining. So, if you are buying a crate which will last for a fully-grown Pug, get adjustable crate dividers – or make them yourself - to block part of it off while he is small, so that he feels safe and secure.

Once you've got your crate, you'll need to learn how to use it properly so that it becomes a safe, comfortable den for your dog and not a prison. Here is a tried-and-tested method of getting your dog firstly to accept it, and then to actually want to spend time in there. Initially a pup might not be too happy about going inside, but he will be a lot easier to crate train than an adult dog, which may have got used to having the run of your house. These are the first steps:

1. Drop a few tasty puppy treats around and then inside the crate

2. Put your puppy's favourite bedding or toy in there

3. Keep the door open

4. Feed all of your puppy's meals inside the crate. Again, keep the door open.

Place a chew or treat INSIDE the crate and close the door while your puppy is OUTSIDE the crate. He will be desperate to get in there! Open the door, let him in and praise him for going in. Fasten a long-lasting chew inside the crate and leave the door open. Let your puppy go inside to spend some time eating the chew.

IMPORTANT: Always remove your dog's collar before leaving him unattended in a crate. A collar can get caught in the wire mesh.

After a while, close the crate door and feed him some treats through the mesh while he is in there. At first just do it for a few seconds at a time, then gradually increase the time. If you do it too fast, he will become distressed. Slowly build up the amount of time he is in the crate. For the first few days, stay in the room, then gradually leave for a short time, first one minute, then three, then 10, 30 and so on.

Next Steps

5. Put your dog in his crate at regular intervals during the day - maximum two hours

6. Don't crate only when you are leaving the house. Place the dog in the crate while you are home as well. Use it as a "safe" zone

7. By using the crate both when you are home and while you are gone, your dog becomes comfortable there and not worried that you won't come back, or that you are leaving him alone. This helps to prevent separation anxiety later in life

8. Give him a chew and remove his collar, tags and anything else which could become caught in an opening or between the bars

9. Make it very clear to any children that the crate is NOT a playhouse for them, but a "special room" for the dog

10. Although the crate is your dog's haven and safe place, it must not be off-limits to humans. You should be able to reach inside at any time

The next point is important if crate training is to succeed:

11. Do not let your dog immediately out of the crate if he barks or whines, or he will think that this is the key to opening the door. Wait until the barking or whining has stopped for at least 10 seconds before letting him out

A puppy should not be left in a crate for long periods except at night time, and even then he has to get used to it first. Whether or not you decide to use a crate, the important thing to remember is that those first few days and weeks are a critical time for your puppy. Try and make him feel as safe and comfortable as you can. Bond with him, while at the same time gently and gradually introducing him to new experiences and other animals and humans.

A crate is, however, a good way of transporting your Pug in the car. Put the crate on the shady side of the interior and make sure it can't move around inside the car, put the seatbelt around it if

necessary. If it's very sunny and the top of the crate is wire mesh, cover part of it so your dog has some shade and put the windows up and the air conditioning on. Never leave your Pug unattended in a vehicle, he can quickly overheat - or be targeted by thieves

Allowing your dog to roam freely inside the car is not a safe option, particularly if you - like me – are a bit of a 'leadfoot' on the brake and accelerator! Don't let him put his head out of the window either, he can slip and hurt himself and the wind pressure can cause an ear infection or bits of dust, insects, etc. to fly into your Pug's eyes.

Special travel crates are useful for the car, or for taking your dog to the vet's or a show. Try and pick one with holes or mesh in the side (like the one pictured), to allow free movement of air, rather than a solid plastic one, in which your Pug can become overheated.

What Our Breeders Think of Crates

Traditionally crates have been more popular in America than in the UK and the rest of Europe, but opinion is slowly changing and more owners are starting to use crates on both sides of the Atlantic. This is perhaps because people's perception of a crate is shifting from regarding it as a prison to thinking of it, if used correctly, as a safe haven as well as a useful tool to help with housetraining and transportation.

Without exception, the breeders we contacted believed that the crate should not be used as a means of imprisoning a dog for hours on end while you are away from the house. This is cruel for any dog, but particularly a Pug, whose greatest desire (after food!) is to be with his humans. This is what our breeders said, starting with the USA:

Donna Shank and Brenda Schuettenberg, RoKuCiera Pugs, California: "Yes we have crates and use them daily. Everyone sleeps in a crate because Mom is 79+ and gets around using a walker - that means no sleeping Pugs to trip over on her way to the bathroom in the middle of the night!

"We also insist on crating in the van or RV, think of it like a car seat for your fur-kid....safer for you and the dog in the event of emergency. Adult dogs shouldn't be confined more than eight or nine hours at a time unless they can be taken for a walk and some play/cuddle time frequently.... 20 minutes every two hours. Exercise pens are a better confinement option for extended periods. The longer Pugs are crated the more likely they will bark from boredom and bother the neighbors."

Catherine Jones-Kyle, Dixie Darlings, Tennessee: "We do not crate train our dogs, but I have had families that have opted to crate train and I recommend that they don't confine the dog in the crate longer than about six hours overnight. During the day if they have to be crated I recommend that someone is able to let the dog out every few hours. Pugs want to be with their humans, so crating them for extended periods can lead to depression." Pictured outside the playpen is Catherine's Sissi.

Laura Libner, Loralar Pugs, Michigan: "At night I crate some of mine, not all. I wouldn't want a Pug left in a crate for more than four hours."

Linda and Kim Wright, Wright's Pugs, Michigan: "A crate is necessary to quickly and safely train a puppy. The Pug should only be in it while you are gone and for sleeping at night until past the puppy stage (particularly chewing) and fully house-trained."

Roberta Kelley-Martin, HRH Pugs, California: "The use of a crate is highly recommended, no matter the breed. It allows the puppy/dog to have a safe area in which they can relax and be safe. At an early age all my dogs are crate trained. Puppies, when I cannot physically pay attention to them, are in their crate. At a young age they sleep in crates at night next to my bed so I can hear them when they need to go out during the night. As they age, and no longer need those extra potty trips during the night, I will still have them in crates at night until they are 100% sure about their potty habits during the day.

"With the exception of my very first Pug, which had my Rottweilers to sleep with and use as a pillow, I allow the Pugs (when completely trained) to sleep together in their 'Pug piles,' they tend to choose to sleep next to and on each other. I have an assortment of Pug beds that each one can choose to use, which also lets them choose who they sleep with - every Pug has their favourite pack member that they always choose to sleep with!"

Erin Ford, Fur-N-Feathers, Florida: "I understand a lot of breeders and owners do use crates, although I do not. If someone does want to crate, I think no more than three hours as a puppy then as they get older more time can be added - but no more than eight hours at night. A nice alternative to crating is an inside dog pen, as it give more room but still keeps them confined."

J. Candy Schlieper, CandyLand Pugs, Ohio: "We don't crate our dogs here at CandyLand. Only when we travel with them do they reside in a crate for their safety. I don't think any dog should be crated for long periods of time."

This is what our UK breeders said: Deborah Beecham Fizzlewick Pugs, South Wales: "I only use a crate to ensure rest if convalescence is needed following illness or surgery, or at dog shows. I'm not a fan of them to be honest and don't think you should have dogs to lock them up. I had a bitch back from rescue who had been shut in a crate for hours on end; the first thing she did on coming to us was to put herself in my crate, the sadness on her face was enough to break your heart. She had issues for a long time after. Crates are good in some circumstances, but many people abuse their use."

Saran Evans, Sephina Pugs, Carmarthenshire: "I only use crates to travel in the car. I use puppy playpens in the first few months to put them in to get the rest necessary when they are babies. Given the chance they will run themselves until they are exhausted as they don't want to miss anything, but this is not good for puppies, so a place to rest is essential. My Pugs are also used to my dog show trolley when we go to shows."

Carly Firth, Mumandau Pugs, Greater Manchester: "I do crate my dogs. They are crated overnight generally, and may be crated when left throughout the day (for a maximum of two to three hours). By using a crate, it gives the dogs a den area. This makes a dog feel secure and they learn to understand when it is 'bed time', whilst also understanding to be independent from their humans for a little while. Admittedly though, my lot will often take themselves off to their crate when it's left open, as it's their place to sleep... unless the fire is on! With the exception of overnight, I believe no dog should be left for longer than a maximum of four hours."

Robert and Holly Hitchcock, Bobitch Pugs, Derbyshire: "Ours are penned at night, although some girls live in the kitchen un-penned. Used sensibly, a pen or crate is perfect, we'd say, for three or four hours maximum. Pugs tend to sleep when left."

Linda Guy, Londonderry Pugs: "I used a crate for house training one Pug and for box rest for an injured Pug, but generally my Pugs do not like them and will get depressed if forced into one. I would say two hours is the maximum. Pugs are social dogs and would rather be on your knee."

Holly Attwood, Taftazini, Sheffield: "I always crate train puppies for their own safety and so they become accepting of it for show purposes, and it also aids toilet training. How long to crate them depends on size of crate; if it is a puppy pen, my Pugs are quite comfortable in it for up to three to four hours. If it is small crate, where they can just lie down, then two hours is the maximum."

Sandra Mayoh, Drumlinfold Pugs, North Yorkshire: "My Pugs like their crate, especially with door open. Mine are happy in it with the door shut for an hour or two during day, and all night."

Sue Wragg, Glammarags Pugs: "We have used crates at night in the past, but nowadays only use them for transporting in the car. I think it's OK to leave a Pug in a crate overnight, provided they have not been confined all day, but I think its unwise to leave any dog crated all day."

Melanie Clark, Pugginpugs: "All of my Pugs use a crate as I believe that they like to have their own little space. They will only use them throughout the night. For puppies, I would suggest to use a crate while he or she is left on his or her own to prevent any danger of them getting into wires or any other household items, toys etc. that they could possibly choke on. A puppy usually has bursts of energy, after which I would place them into their crate for a sleep. I would also suggest regular toilet breaks."

And Deborah Hayman, of Fawnydawn Pugs, Malta, says: "I do not use crates at all, I only use them for shows. My Pugs are free to run outside all day and they have their beds at night. (Pictured here is Deborah's Fannydawn Galaxy.)

Top 10 Tips for Housetraining

How easy are Pugs to housetrain?

That's a simple question, yet if you think there were differing views from breeders on the use of crates, there's even more variation when it comes to housetraining -or potty training, as it's often referred to in America.

It's true to say that the breed can have a reputation for being hard to housetrain - although some Pug breeders will strongly disagree with this, as you'll read later in this chapter. The speed and success of housetraining depends largely on two factors:

1. The first, and by far the most important, is the time and effort you are prepared to put into housetraining your Pug at the beginning. The more vigilant you are during the early days, the quicker your dog will be housetrained. It's as simple as that. Taking the advice in this chapter and being consistent with your routines and repetitions is the quickest way to toilet train your Pug.

2. Some Pugs can take a little longer to housetrain, and this often runs in bloodlines. Ask your breeder how long it took her to housetrain the parents and earlier siblings – and get as many tips as you can.

Although they can have a stubborn streak, you have two huge factors in your favour when it comes to housetraining:

1. Pugs are desperate to please their owner

2. They would sell their own mothers for a treat

A further piece of good news is that a puppy's instinct is not to soil his own den. From about the age of three weeks, a pup will leave his sleeping area to go to the toilet.

The bad news is that when you bring your little pup home, he doesn't realise that the whole house or apartment is, in effect, his den and not the place to eliminate. Therefore you need to teach him that it is unacceptable to make a mess anywhere inside the house. How long this takes depends on how quickly your puppy learns and how persistent and patient you are. It could take from a few days to several months if neither of you are vigilant.

Pugs, like all dogs, are creatures of routine - not only do they like the same things happening at the same times every day, but establishing a regular routine with your dog also helps to speed up training and housebreaking. Dogs are also very tactile creatures, so they will pick a toilet area which feels good under their paws. Many dogs like to go on grass - but this will do nothing to improve your lawn, so you should think carefully about what area to encourage your Pug to use.

You may want to consider a small patch of gravel crushed into tiny pieces in your garden, or a dog litter tray if you live in an apartment. Most, but not all, of our breeders, advise against using puppy pads for any length of time as puppies like the softness of the pads, which can encourage them to eliminate on other soft areas - such as your carpets or bed.

Follow these tips to speed up housetraining:

1. **Constant supervision** is essential for the first week or two if you are to housetrain your puppy quickly. This is why it is important to book the week or so off work when you bring him home. Make sure you are there to take him outside regularly. If nobody is there, he will learn to urinate or poo(p) inside the house.

2. **Take your pup outside at the following times:**
   ❖ As soon as he wakes – every time
   ❖ Shortly after each feed
   ❖ After a drink
   ❖ When he gets excited
   ❖ After exercise or play
   ❖ Last thing at night
   ❖ Initially every hour – whether or not he looks like he wants to go

   You may think that the above list is an exaggeration, but it isn't. Housetraining a pup is almost a full-time job for the first few days. If you are serious about housetraining your puppy quickly, then clear your diary for a few days and keep your eyes firmly glued on your pup…Learn to spot that expression or circling motion just before he eliminates all over your floor! Most puppies learn quickly once they know what is expected of them.

3. Take your Pug to **the same place** every time, you may need to use a lead in the beginning - or tempt him there with a treat if he is not yet lead-trained. Only pick him up and dump him there in an emergency, it is better if he learns to take himself to the chosen toilet spot. Dogs naturally develop a preference for going in the same place or on the same surface - often grass or dirt. Take him to the same patch every time so he learns this is his bathroom - preferably an area in a corner of your yard or garden.

4. **No pressure – be patient.** You must allow your distracted little pup time to wander around and have a good sniff before performing his duties – but do not leave him, stay around a short distance away. Sadly, puppies are not known for their powers of concentration; it may take a while for them to select that perfect restroom!

5. **Housetraining is reward-based.** Praise him or give him a treat immediately when he performs his duties in the chosen spot. Pugs love praise and they love treats even more – a powerful combination if used correctly. Reward-based training is the most successful method for Pugs.

6. **Share the responsibility.** It doesn't have to be the same person that takes the dog outside all the time. In fact it's easier if there are a couple of you, as housetraining is a very time-consuming business. Just make sure you stick to the same principles and patch of ground.

7. **Stick to the same routine.** Dogs understand and like routine. Sticking to the same one for mealtimes, short exercise sessions, play time, sleeping and toilet breaks will help to not only housetrain him quicker, but help him settle into his new home.

8. **Use your voice if you catch him in the act indoors.** A short sharp negative sound is best - **NO! ACK! EH!** - it doesn't matter so long as it is loud enough to make him stop. Then start running enthusiastically towards your door, calling him into the garden and the chosen place and patiently wait until he has finished what he started indoors. It is no good scolding your dog if you find a puddle or unwanted gift in the house but don't see him do it, he won't know why you are cross with him. Only scold if you catch him in the act.

9. **No punishment.** Accidents will happen at the beginning, do not punish your Pug for them. He is a baby with a tiny bladder and bowels, and housetraining takes time - it is perfectly natural to have accidents early on. Remain calm and clean up the mess with a good strong-smelling cleaner to remove the odour, so he won't be tempted to use that spot again.

   Dogs have a very strong sense of smell and to make 100% sure there is no trace of what they left behind, you can use a special spray from your vet or a hot solution of washing powder to completely eliminate the odour. Smacking or rubbing his nose in it can have the opposite effect: he will become afraid to do his business in your presence and may start going behind the couch or under the bed, rather than outside

10. **Look for the signs.** These may be whining, sniffing the floor in a determined manner, circling and looking for a place to go or walking uncomfortably, particularly at the rear end! Take him outside straight away. **Do not pick him up if you can help it,** he has to learn to walk to the door himself when he needs to go outside.

If you use puppy pads, only do so for a short time or your puppy will get used to them. You can also separate a larger crate into two areas and put a pad in one area to help housetrain your baby Pug. He will eliminate on the pad and keep his bed clean.

If you decide to keep your puppy in a crate overnight and you want him to learn not to soil the crate right from the very beginning, you need to have the crate in the bedroom so you can hear him whine when he needs to go. Initially this might be once or twice a night. By the age of four or five months a Pug pup should be able to last all night without needing the toilet – provided you let him out last thing at night and first thing in the morning.

With a crate, remember that the door should not be closed until your Pug is happy with being inside. He needs to believe that this is a safe place and not a trap or prison. Rather than use a crate, many people prefer to section off an area inside one room or use a puppy playpen to confine their puppy. Inside this area is a bed and another area with pads or newspapers which the puppy can use as a toilet area.

Apartment Living

If you live on the 11th floor of an apartment, housetraining can be a little trickier as you don't have easy access to the outdoors. One suggestion is to indoor housetrain your puppy. Pugs spend much of their time indoors and indoor dogs can be housetrained fairly easily - especially if you start early. Stick to the same principles already outlined - the only difference is that you will be placing your Pug on training pads or newspaper instead of taking him outside.

Start by blocking off a section of the apartment for your new puppy, you can use a baby gate or make your own barrier - pick a chew-proof material, or use a puppy pen. You will be able to keep a better eye on him than if he has free run of the whole place. It will also be easier to monitor his "accidents."

Select a corner away from his eating and sleeping area that will become his permanent bathroom area – carpets are to be avoided if at all possible. At first, cover a larger area than is actually needed - about three to four square feet - with newspaper (or training pads.) You can reduce the area as training progresses. Take your puppy there as indicated in our Housebreaking Tips.

Praise him enthusiastically when he eliminates on the allotted area. If you catch him doing his business out of the toilet area, pick him up and take him back there. Correct with a firm voice - never a hand. With positive reinforcement and a strict schedule, he will soon be walking to the area on his own.

Owners attempting indoor housetraining should be aware that it will generally take longer than outdoor training; some Pugs may resist. Also, once a dog learns to go indoors, it can be difficult to train him to eliminate outdoors. Any laziness on your part by not monitoring your puppy carefully enough - especially in the beginning – will make indoor housetraining a lot longer and more difficult process. The first week is crucial to your puppy learning what is expected of him.

GENERAL HOUSETRAINING TIP: You may also want to use a trigger to encourage your dog to perform his duties; this can be very effective. Some people use a clicker or a bell - we used a word; well two actually. Within a week or so I trained our puppy to urinate on the command of "wee wee." Think very carefully before choosing the word or phrase, as I often feel an idiot wandering around our garden last thing at night shouting "Max, WEE WEE!" in an encouraging manner - although I'm not sure that the American expression "GO POTTY" sounds much better!

Breeders on Housetraining

Ask 100 breeders whether Pugs are easy to housetrain and what tips they have and you'll get 100 different answers. Some dogs are and some aren't - success may depend on the character of the individual dog – but more often it's down to you and how vigilant you are.

Roberta Kelley-Martin, HRH Pugs, has some interesting findings : "Having lived with large dogs for well over 20 years prior to bringing home my first Pug, I found it completely different than my usual experience. Pugs will voluntarily piddle and poo anywhere they care to. Crate training is essential to successfully potty training a Pug.

"My theory on this is that a majority of Pug breeders employ the use of soft, warm, bedding throughout the Pugs' whelping box and play pen/space. Potty training is a tactile experience for dogs. If their feet are used to the feel of plush, warm carpet or similar to potty on, then that's what they will use.

I start raising my Pugs with soft bedding, but also at a very early age had a hard surface space with a potty mat that uses a synthetic grass. The grass has an attractant in it to encourage it to be used as a potty space. I've found that the litters that I use this synthetic grass with are more easily potty trained."

Our photo shows two of Roberta's Pugs: Millpond's Satin Sheets, "Sassy" and Ch. Pocket's Petal Pusher, "Posey" - nicknamed Yin and Yang in this photo - not wanting to venture out.

This is what other breeders said: J. Candy Schlieper, Candyland: "I think most are easy to train because a Pug truly does want to please their owner. I tell people to put them on a schedule and stick to it and they tend to learn more quickly. I find using a special treat that they love to reward them when they potty helps. Use this treat for only this behaviour and they learn to potty and come running for this treat. It must be something they really love. Most Pugs are very food-oriented and, of course, give them tons of praise."

Sue Wragg, Glammarags Pugs: "It can take a long time to housetrain a Pug, much longer than larger dogs, for example, and even as adults they HATE going outside in the rain. I always advise new puppy owners to stay outside with the pup until he/she performs so that you can praise them and they start to realise why they've come outside."

Sandra Mayoh, Drumlinfold Pugs: "They are tricky to housetrain as they always want to be with you. They hate rain and cold weather. Use puppy pads for toilet training and watch for circle sniffing."

Linda and Kim Wright, Wright's Pugs, agree about the crate: "We find them harder to housetrain than a lot of other breeds. A crate is an absolute necessity for training any puppy. It's for sleeping at night and for anytime you are not at home to be with them. We take puppies outside to potty immediately when removed from the crate, and give them lots and lots of praise when they do. You have to watch them continuously when loose In the house. If you catch them pottying in the house, say a strong "NO" and then take them outside immediately."

Linda Guy, Londonderry Pugs: "Housetraining can take one to two months with occasional accidents up to two years. Food treats are especially helpful for Pugs as they love their food. They understand words and if you say "Go pee" as they urinate, they will remember this and you can use it for training.

"If you use puppy pads to train they will pee on your rugs and other soft things for the rest of their lives - so avoid them. They are very stubborn, so once they are trained they are usually faithful to their housetraining, as long as they aren't left too long – they only have small tummies so can't hold it in for more than eight to 10 hours.

Laura Libner, Loralar Pugs: "Pugs are average to quick to housetrain, depending on your methods and set up. It's best to keep a pup in a smaller confined area until you can completely trust them because Pugs are small and quick to squat somewhere and have an accident unnoticed unless you are on your toes...."

Holly Attwood, Taftazini: " Pugs are really variable; generally I wouldn't be alarmed if it took six to seven months. My first Pug was still having accidents at seven months, but my other Pug was housetrained by about 18 weeks. You definitely have to be actively training them all the time, consistency is key!"

Here's an interesting tip from Deborah Hayman, Fannydawn Pugs: "I start my puppies on newspapers as soon as they start to relieve by themselves and they have always followed the newspapers. Eventually I change the place of the newspapers, always getting closer to the outdoors and I do put newspapers outside. They soon realise that outside is the place! I give the new owners the same tip."

Deborah Beecham, Fizzlewick Pugs: "I think toilet training is much the same as in children, some pick it up very quickly, others take longer. Perseverance is the key. Pugs are certainly not stupid, but maybe a little too laid-back sometimes."

Donna Shank and Brenda Schuettenberg, RoKuCiera Pugs: "It is harder to potty train when it rains, as Pugs prefer warm and dry potty time. My pups have a potty pad they start crawling out of the whelping bed to use as soon as they have bladder control, at about 14 to 18 days old. If the pads continue to be available they will continue to use them all their life, even if they learn to go outside.

"Teach your pup a word for 'Go potty,' so they know what you want them to do when you take them out into the cold rain. If you use it frequently as they are going and treat lavishly after they are done, even the little ones get the idea pretty quickly. Also, have the youngsters sleep in a crate so you know when they wake up and can take them immediately out to the potty spot."

Carly Firth, Mumandau Pugs: "Housetraining Pugs is not the easiest by far! But again I feel this is due to their first few months. If the breeder is consistent with the training it can be mastered, but the same technique must be followed when transferred to their new homes. My pups always leave to relieving themselves on newspaper only (first placed in the whelping box, and then around it when they are more mobile).

"The best tip is, from the day those pups can hear and are mobile, put it on command (whilst on newspaper) and reward. The dog will associate this behaviour with the command, and will look forward to their reward. To this day I have problems with my adult Pugs and feel it's down to their dominant pack behaviour and being unneutered. However, I have had lots of positive feedback on all the puppies I have bred on to how well housetrained they are, and many of the owners have been new to dogs.

"I would expect accidents to naturally take place due to their new environment and owners, However, by giving the command repeatedly, it becomes familiar to the puppies, resulting in them naturally repeating the behaviour. The only downside to housetraining Pugs - and I'm sure every Pug owner will agree with this one - is... rain! They do not like to nip out for their business if it's raining. Staying warm and dry in their beds is far more appealing."

Melanie Clark, Pugginpugs: "They really are not the easiest of breed to toilet train. However, my advice would be to look for the signs that he/she maybe wanting to go i.e. sniffing the floor walking in circles and crouching, normally around 20 minutes after a feed. In these instances, I would take them straight outside and give them praise once they have emptied themselves in order to encourage this behaviour further."

Saran Evans, Sephina Pugs: "They take a little longer than some breeds to housetrain. Pugs hate cold/wet weather and this hampers housetraining, as they are so reluctant to venture out in these conditions. Be consistent, and keep taking them outside to toilet, they do eventually get there!"

"How can you tell the dogs need to go out?"

7. Feeding A Pug

Your Pug may appear stocky, but that tough exterior is covering a delicately balanced interior. And to keep his or her whole biological machine in good working order, your dog needs the right fuel, just like a finely-tuned sports car.

Feeding the correct diet is an essential part of keeping your Pug fit and healthy.

However, the topic of feeding your dog the right diet is something of a minefield. Owners are bombarded with endless choices as well as countless adverts from dog food companies, all claiming that theirs is best.

There is not one food that will give every single dog the brightest eyes, the shiniest coat, the most energy, the best digestion, the longest life and stop him from scratching or having skin problems. Dogs are individuals just like people, which means that you could feed a premium food to a group of dogs and find that most of them do great on it, some not so well, while a few may get an upset stomach or even an allergic reaction. The question is: "Which food is best for my Pug?"

If you have been given a recommended food from a breeder, rescue centre or previous owner, it is best to stick to this as long as your dog is doing well on it. A good breeder will know which food their Pugs thrive on. If you do decide - for whatever reason - to change diet, then this must be done gradually. There are a few things to be aware of when it comes to feeding a Pug:

1. Most Pugs LOVE their food. Add to this their eagerness to please and you have a powerful training tool. You can use feeding time to reinforce a simple command on a daily basis

2. Some dogs have food sensitivities or allergies - more on this topic later

3. Many Pugs do not do well on diets with a high wheat or corn content

4. There is anecdotal evidence from breeders on both sides of the Atlantic that many Pugs do well on a raw diet - if you have the time and money to stick to it – however, others disagree

5. Sometimes elderly dogs may just get bored with their diet and go off their food. This does not necessarily mean that they are ill, simply that they have lost interest and a new food should be gradually introduced

6. Pugs are prone to obesity, so controlling their intake is important, as obesity can trigger or worsen numerous health conditions

There are many different food options on the market. The most popular manufactured foods include dry complete diets, tinned food (with or without a biscuit mixer), and semi-moist. Some dog foods contain only natural ingredients. Then there is the option of feeding your dog a home-made diet; some owners swear by a raw diet, while others feed their dogs vegetarian food.

Within the manufactured options, there are many different qualities of food, and some which are specifically formulated for Pugs. Usually you get what you pay for, so a more expensive food is more likely to provide better nutrition for your dog - in terms of minerals, nutrients and high quality meats – rather than a cheap one, which will most likely contain a lot of grain.

Dried foods (also called kibble in the US) tend to be less expensive than other foods. They have improved a lot over the last few years and some of the more expensive ones are now a good choice for a healthy, complete diet. Dried foods also contain the least fat and the most preservatives.

Our dog Max, who has inhalant allergies, is on a quality dried food called James Wellbeloved. It contains natural ingredients and the manufacturers claim it is "hypoallergenic," i.e. good for dogs with allergies. Max seems to do well on it, but not all dogs thrive on dried food. We tried several other foods first; it is a question of each owner finding the best food for their dog. If you got your dog from a good breeder, they should be able to advise you on this.

TIP: Beware of buying a food just because it is described as 'premium', many manufacturers blithely use this word, but there are no official guidelines as to what premium means. Always check the ingredients on any food sack, packet or tin to see which ingredients are listed first, and it should be meat or poultry, not corn or grain. If you are in the US, look for a dog food which has been endorsed by AAFCO (Association of American Feed Control Officials). In general, tinned foods are 60-70% water. Often semi-moist foods contain a lot of artificial substances and sugar, which is maybe why some dogs love them!

Choosing the right food for your Pug is important; it will certainly influence his health, coat and even temperament. There are also three stages of your dog's life to consider when feeding: puppy, adult and senior (also called veteran). Some manufacturers also produce a Junior feed for adolescent dogs. Each represents a different physical stage of his life and you need to choose the right food to cope with his body during each particular phase. Also, a pregnant female will require a special diet to cope with the extra demands on her body, this is especially important as she nears the latter stages of pregnancy.

Most owners feed their Pugs twice a day and some feed two different meals each day to provide variety. One meal could be dried kibble, while the other might be home-made, with fresh meat, poultry and vegetables. If you do this, speak with your vet to make sure the two separate meals provide a balanced diet and that they are not too rich in protein.

This book will not recommend one brand of dog food over another, but we do have some general tips to help you choose what to feed. There is also some advice for owners of Pugs with food allergies. Sufferers may itch, lick or chew their paws and/or legs, or rub their face. They may also get frequent ear infections as well as redness and swelling on their face. Switching to a grain-free diet can help to alleviate the symptoms, as your dog's digestive system does not have to work as hard. In the wild, a dog or wolf's staple diet would be meat with some vegetable matter from the stomach and intestines of the herbivores (plant eating animals) he ate – but no grains. Dogs do not digest corn or wheat (which are often staples of cheap commercial dog food) very efficiently. Grain-free diets still provide carbohydrates through fruits and vegetables, so your dog still gets all his nutrients.

16 Top Tips for Feeding your Pug

1. If you choose a manufactured food, **don't pick one where meat or poultry content is NOT the first item listed on the bag.** Foods with lots of cheap cereals or sugar are not the best choice for many dogs, particularly finely balanced ones

2. Some Pugs suffer from sensitive skin, 'hot spots' or allergies. A cheap dog food, often bulked up with grain, will only make this worse. If this is the case, bite the bullet and **choose a high quality – usually more expensive – food or consider a raw diet.** You'll probably save money in vets' bills in the long run and your dog will be happier. A food may be described as "hypoallergenic" on the sack, this means "less likely to cause allergies" and is a good place to start

3. **Feed your Pug twice a day**, rather than once. Pugs are gassy dogs and two smaller feeds will reduce flatulence and be easier to digest. Puppies need to be fed more often, discuss exactly how often with your breeder

4. **Establish a feeding regime and stick to it.** Dogs like routine. If you are feeding twice a day, feed once in the morning and then again at tea-time. Stick to the same times of day. Do not give the last feed too late, or your dog's body will not have chance to process or burn off the food before sleeping. He will also need a walk or letting out in the garden or yard after his second feed to allow him to go to empty his bowels. Feeding at the same times each day helps your dog establish a toilet regime

5. **Take away any uneaten food between meals.** Most Pugs love their food, but any dog can become a fussy eater if it is available all day. Imagine if your dinner was left on the table for hours until you finished it. Returning to the table two or three hours later would not be such a tempting prospect, but coming back for a fresh meal would be far more appetising

Also when food is left down all day, some dogs seem to take the food for granted and lose their appetite. Then they begin to leave the food and you are at your wits' end trying to find a food that they will actually eat. Put the food bowl down twice a day and then take it up after 20 minutes – even if he has left some. If he is healthy and hungry, he will look forward to his next meal and soon stop leaving food. If your dog does not eat anything for days, it could well be a sign that he is not well

6. **Do not feed too many titbits and treats between meals.** Pugs are often greedy and prone to obesity, which is a dangerous condition. Already a chunky breed, your Pug cannot afford to carry extra weight as it will place extra strain on his organs and joints, have a detrimental effect on his health and even his lifespan. It also throws his balanced diet out of the window. Try to avoid feeding your dog from the table or your plate, as this encourages attention-seeking behaviour and drooling

7. **NEVER feed the following items to your dog**: grapes, raisins, chocolate, onions, Macadamia nuts, any fruits with seeds or stones, tomatoes, avocadoes, rhubarb, tea, coffee or alcohol. ALL of these are poisonous to dogs.

8. **If you switch to a new food, do the transition gradually.** Unlike humans, dogs' digestive systems cannot handle sudden changes in diet. Begin by gradually mixing some of the new food in with the old and increase the proportion so that after seven to eight days, all the food is the new one. The following ratios are recommended by Doctors Foster & Smith Inc: Days 1-3 add 25% of the new food, Days 4-6 add 50%, Days 7-9 add 75%, Day 10 feed 100% of the new food. By the way, if you stick to the identical brand, you can change flavours in one go

9. **Check your dog's faeces** (aka stools, poo or poop!) If his diet is suitable, the food should be easily digested and produce dark brown, firm stools. If your dog produces soft or light stools, or has gas (even more than usual!) or diarrhoea, then the diet may not suit him, so consult your vet or breeder for advice

10. **Pugs are prone to overheating**, so a good idea is to get him used to frozen yoghurt or ice pops (popsicles) while he is young, as these will help him to keep cool throughout the rest of his life. Most dogs like ice cubes – and love popsicles. Just make some beef or chicken broth from a stock cube - low sodium is best - mixed with water and freeze it in ice cube trays. You can also freeze vegetables. Yoghurt is particularly good for gassy dogs and helps with general digestion, some Pug owners add a spoonful of (unfrozen) natural yoghurt to one of their pet's daily feeds

11. **Never give your dog cooked bones,** as these can splinter and cause him to choke or suffer intestinal problems. It's also a good idea to avoid giving him rawhide, as dogs who gulp their food have a tendency to chew and then swallow rawhide, without first bothering to nibble it down into smaller pieces

12. **Feed your dog in stainless steel dishes.** Plastic bowls don't last as long and, more importantly, a Pug has a sensitive face and they can trigger a reaction in some. Ceramic bowls are best for keeping water cold

13. **If you have more than one dog, consider feeding them separately**. Pugs usually get on fine with other pets, especially if introduced at an early age. But they are also greedy and feeding dogs together can lead to dog food aggression from your Pug, either protecting his own food or trying to eat the food designated for another pet

14. **If you do feed leftovers, feed them INSTEAD of a balanced meal,** not as well as (unless you are feeding a raw diet). High quality dog foods already provide all the nutrients, vitamins, minerals and calories that your dog needs. Feeding titbits or leftovers may be too rich for your Pug in addition to his regular diet and cause him to scratch or have other problems, as well as get fat. You can feed your dog vegetables such as carrots as a healthy low-calorie treat, most dogs love 'em.

15. **Check your dog's weight regularly.** Obesity in Pugs, as well as being generally unhealthy, can lead to the development of some serious health issues, such as diabetes, high blood pressure and heart disease. Although the weight will vary from one dog to another, a good rule of thumb is that your Pug's tummy should be level with, or higher than, his rib cage. If his belly hangs down below it, he is overweight

16. And finally, **always make sure that your Pug has access to clean, fresh water.** Change the water and clean the bowl regularly – it gets slimy!

Types of Dog Food

We are what we eat. The right food is a very important part of a healthy lifestyle - and this is especially true for Pugs. There are several different types of food you can feed your dog: dry, semi-moist, canned, frozen or freeze-dried are just some of the options. Or you might decide to feed a home-made or raw diet; this is an option increasingly being considered by Pug owners for a number of reasons.

Dry dog food

Called kibble in the US, this is a popular choice and one of the less expensive ways of providing a balanced diet. It comes in a variety of flavours and with differing ingredients to suit the different stages of a dog's life. It's worth paying for a high quality dry food as cheaper ones may contain a lot of grain. Cheap foods are often false economy, particularly if your Pug does not tolerate grain/cereal very well. It may also mean that you have to feed larger quantities to ensure he gets sufficient nutrients.

Manufacturer Royal Canin has dried foods specially formulated for Pug puppies and adults. The company says of its adult Pug food: "The Pug Adult diet combines specially shaped and textured kibbles to suit the breed's broad head and short muzzle, making them easier to grip and chew. The kibble contains a balance of ingredients, tailored to the maintenance of the breed's muscle tone and weight, and a blend of key vitamins and polyphenols (grape and green tea)." There are also many other high quality manufactured foods popular with Pug owners.

Canned food

This is another popular choice – and it's often very popular with dogs too. They love the taste and it generally comes in a variety of flavours. Canned food is often mixed with dry kibble, and a small amount may be added to a dog on a dry food diet if he has lost interest in food. It tends to be more expensive than dried food and many owners don't like the mess.

A part-opened tin may have to be kept in the refrigerator between meals and it can have a strong smell when you open the fridge door. As with dry food, read the label closely. Generally, you get what you pay for and the origins of cheap canned dog food are often somewhat dubious. If you choose canned food, you may decide to feed this once daily and then kibble or other food for the second meal.

Semi-Moist

These are commercial dog foods shaped like pork chops, salamis, burgers or other meaty foods and they are the least nutritional of all dog foods. They are full of sugars, artificial flavourings and colourings to help make them visually appealing. Pugs don't care what their food looks like, they only care how it smells and tastes; the shapes are designed to appeal to us humans. While you may give your dog one as an occasional treat, they are not a diet in themselves and do not provide the nutrition that your dog needs. Steer clear of them for regular feeding.

Freeze-Dried

This is made by frozen food manufacturers for owners who like the convenience – this type of food keeps for six months to a year - or for those going on a trip with their dog. It says 'freeze-dried' on the packet and is highly palatable, but the freeze-drying process bumps up the cost.

Home-Cooked

Some dog owners want the ability to be in complete control of their dog's diet, know exactly what their dog is eating and to be absolutely sure that his nutritional needs are being met. Feeding your dog a home-cooked diet is time consuming and expensive, and the difficult thing – as with the raw diet - is sticking to it once you have started out with the best of intentions. But many owners think the extra effort is worth the peace of mind. If you decide to go ahead, you should spend the time to become proficient and learn about canine nutrition to ensure your dog gets all his vital nutrients.

The Raw Diet

There is a quiet revolution going on in the world of dog food. After years of feeding dry or tinned dog food, increasing numbers of dog owners –and many breeders of Pugs - are now feeding a raw diet to their beloved pets. There is anecdotal evidence that many dogs thrive on a raw diet, although scientific proof is lagging behind. There are a number of claims made by fans of the raw diet, including:

❖ Reduced symptoms of - or less likelihood of – allergies, and less scratching

❖ Better skin and coats

❖ Easier weight management

❖ Improved digestion

❖ Less doggie odour and flatulence

❖ Fresher breath and improved dental health

❖ Helps fussy eaters

❖ Drier and less smelly stools, more like pellets

❖ Reduced risk of bloat

❖ Overall improvement in general health and less disease

❖ Higher energy levels

❖ Most dogs love a raw diet

If your dog is not doing well on a commercially-prepared dog food, you might consider a raw diet, which emulates the way dogs ate before the existence of commercial dog foods. Some of these may contain artificial preservatives and excessive protein and fillers – causing a reaction in some Pugs. Dry, canned and other styles of processed food were mainly created as a means of convenience, but unfortunately this convenience sometimes can affect a dog's health. Some nutritionists believe that dogs fed raw whole foods tend to be healthier than those on other diets. They say there are inherent beneficial enzymes, vitamins, minerals and other qualities in meats, fruits, vegetables and grains in their natural forms that are denatured or destroyed when cooked. Many also believe dogs are less likely to have allergic reactions to the ingredients on this diet.

Unsurprisingly, the topic is not without controversy. Critics of a raw diet say that the risks of nutritional imbalance, intestinal problems and food-borne illnesses caused by handling and feeding raw meat outweigh any benefits. It is true that owners must pay strict attention to hygiene when preparing a raw diet and it may not be a suitable option if there are children in the household. The dog may also be more likely to ingest bacteria or parasites such as Salmonella, E.coli and Ecchinococcus.

Frozen food can be a valuable aid to the raw diet. The food is highly palatable, made from high quality ingredients and dogs usually wolf it down. The downsides are that not all pet food stores stock it and it is expensive.

There are two main types of raw diet, one involves feeding raw, meaty bones and the other is known as the BARF diet (*Biologically Appropriate Raw Food* or *Bones And Raw Food*), created by Dr Ian Billinghurst.

Raw Meaty Bones

This diet is:

❖ Raw meaty bones or carcasses, if available, should form the bulk of the diet

❖ Table scraps both cooked and raw, such as vegetables, can be fed

❖ As with any diet, fresh water should be constantly available. **NOTE: Do NOT feed cooked bones, they can splinter**

Australian veterinarian Dr Tom Lonsdale is a leading proponent of the raw meaty bones diet. He believes the following foods are suitable:

- ❖ Chicken and turkey carcasses, after the meat has been removed for human consumption
- ❖ Poultry by-products, including heads, feet, necks and wings
- ❖ Whole fish and fish heads
- ❖ Sheep, calf, goat, and deer carcasses sawn into large pieces of meat and bone
- ❖ Other by-products, e.g. pigs' trotters, pigs' heads, sheep heads, brisket, tail and rib bones
- ❖ A certain amount of offal can be included in the diet, e.g. liver, lungs, trachea, hearts, tripe

He says that low-fat game animals, fish and poultry provide the best source of food for pet carnivores. If you feed meat from farm animals (cattle, sheep and pigs), avoid excessive fat and bones that are too large to be eaten.

Some of it will depend on what's available locally and how expensive it is. If you shop around you should be able to source a regular supply of suitable raw meaty bones at a reasonable price. Start with your local butcher or farm shop. When deciding what type of bones to feed your Pug, one point to bear in mind is that dogs are more likely to break their teeth when eating large knuckle bones and bones sawn lengthwise than when eating meat and bone together.

You'll also need to think about WHERE you are going to feed your dog. A dog takes some time to eat a raw bone and will push it around the floor, so the kitchen may not be the most suitable or hygienic place. Outside is one option, but what do you do when it's raining?

Establishing the right quantity to feed your Pug is a matter of trial an error. You will reach a decision based on your dog's activity levels, appetite and body condition. High activity and a big appetite show a need for increased food, and vice versa. A very approximate guide, based on raw meaty bones, for the average dog is 15%-20% of body weight in one week, or 2%-3% a day. So, if your Pug weights 22lbs (10 kilos), he or she will require 4lb-4.4lb (1.5-2 kilos) of carcasses or raw meaty bones weekly. Table scraps should be fed as an extra component of the diet. These figures are only a rough guide and relate to adult pets in a domestic environment. Pregnant or lactating females and growing puppies may need much more food than adult animals of similar body weight.

Dr Lonsdale says: "Wherever possible, feed the meat and bone ration in one large piece requiring much ripping, tearing and gnawing. This makes for contented pets with clean teeth. Wild carnivores feed at irregular intervals, in a domestic setting regularity works best and accordingly I suggest that you feed adult dogs and cats once daily. If you live in a hot climate I recommend that you feed pets in the evening to avoid attracting flies.

"I suggest that on one or two days each week your dog may be fasted — just like animals in the wild. On occasions you may run out of natural food. Don't be tempted to buy artificial food, fast your dog and stock up with natural food the next day. Puppies...sick or underweight dogs should not be fasted (unless on veterinary advice)."

Table scraps and some fruit and vegetable peelings can also be fed, but should not make up more than one-third of the diet. Liquidising cooked and uncooked scraps in a food mixer can make them easier to digest.

Things to Avoid

- ❖ Excessive meat off the bone — not balanced
- ❖ Excessive vegetables — not balanced
- ❖ Small pieces of bone — can be swallowed whole and get stuck
- ❖ Cooked bones — get stuck
- ❖ Mineral and vitamin additives — create imbalance
- ❖ Processed food — leads to dental and other diseases
- ❖ Excessive starchy food — associated with bloat
- ❖ Onions, garlic and chocolate, grapes, raisins, sultanas, currants — toxic to pets
- ❖ Fruit stones (pips) and corn cobs — get stuck
- ❖ Milk — associated with diarrhoea. Animals drink it whether thirsty or not and consequently get fat

Points of Concern

- ❖ Old dogs used to processed food may experience initial difficulty when changed on to a natural diet. Discuss the change with your vet first and then, if he or she agrees, switch your dog's diet over a period of a week to 10 days

- ❖ Raw meaty bones are not suitable for dogs with dental or jaw problems

- ❖ This diet may not be suitable if your dog gulps his food, as the bones can become lodged inside him, larger bones may prevent gulping

- ❖ The diet should be varied, any nutrients fed to excess can be harmful

- ❖ Liver is an excellent foodstuff, but should not be fed more than once weekly

- ❖ Other offal, e.g. ox stomachs, should not make up more than half of the diet

- ❖ Whole fish are an excellent source of food, but avoid feeding one species of fish constantly. Some species, e.g. carp, contain an enzyme which destroys thiamine (vitamin B1)

- ❖ If you have more than one dog, do not allow them to fight over the food, feed them separately if necessary

- ❖ Be prepared to monitor your dog while he eats the bones, especially in the beginning, and do not feed bones with sharp points. Take the bone off your dog before it becomes small enough to swallow

- ❖ Make sure that children do not disturb the dog when he is feeding or try to take the bone away

- ❖ Hygiene: Make sure the raw meaty bones are kept separate from human food and clean thoroughly any surface the uncooked meat or bones have touched. This is especially important if you have children. Feeding bowls are unnecessary, your dog will drag the bones across the floor, so feed them outside if you can, or on a floor which is easy to clean

- ❖ Puppies can and do eat diets of raw meaty bones, but you should consult the breeder or a vet before embarking on this diet with a young dog

You will need a regular supply of meaty bones – either locally or online - and you should buy in bulk to ensure a consistency of supply. For this you will need a large freezer. You can then parcel up the bones into daily portions. You can also feed frozen bones, some dogs will gnaw them straight away, others will wait for them to thaw.

More information is available from the website www.rawmeatybones.com and I would strongly recommend discussing the matter with your breeder or vet first before switching to raw meaty bones.

The BARF diet

A variation if the raw meaty bones diet is the BARF created by Dr Ian Billinghurst, who owns the registered trademark 'Barf Diet'. A typical BARF diet is made up of 60%-75% of raw meaty bones (bones with about 50% meat, such as chicken neck, back and wings) and 25%-40% of fruit and vegetables, offal, meat, eggs or dairy foods. Bones must not be cooked or they can splinter inside the dog.

There is a great deal of information on the BARF diet on the internet.

One point to consider is that a raw diet is not always suitable for the jaws and teeth conditions of brachycephalic breeds - dogs with short, broad skulls – like the Pug. You could consider a gradual shift and see how your Pug copes with the raw bones. You might also consider feeding two different daily meals to your dog - one dry kibble and one raw diet, for example. If you do, then research the subject, and consult your veterinarian to make sure that the two combined meals provide a balanced diet.

NOTE: Only start a raw diet if you have done your research and are sure you have the time and money to keep it going. There are numerous websites and canine forums with information on switching to a raw diet and everything it involves.

What The Breeders Say

In the research for this book we contacted a large number of Pug breeders in the UK and US and asked their opinion on a whole range of subjects. One which generated a lot of interest was the subject of feeding a raw diet to Pugs.

While some breeders did not think that a raw diet was a good idea, the majority were in favour of a raw diet in our entirely unscientific survey. At the end of the day, if your Pug is thriving on a manufactured duet, there is no need to change. If you have concerns regarding flatulence, energy levels, allergies or intolerances, skin or health issues, then a raw diet may be worth considering – provided you have the time to research it thoroughly and then the money to continue following the diet. This is what our breeders said, starting with those that were anti-raw.

Linda Guy, Londonderry Pugs, Northern Ireland, said: "Pugs respond well to commercial dog food and it provides a balanced diet. Raw feeding in my opinion is unnecessary."

Catherine Jones-Kyle, Dixie Darlings, Tennessee, USA: "We do not use a raw diet as raw meat is very difficult for Pugs to digest."

Sandra Mayoh, Drumlinfold Pugs, North Yorkshire, UK said that she had no experience of feeding a raw diet, but was not an advocate, as she believed it to be mineral and vitamin deficient.

Erin Ford, Fur N Feathers, Florida, USA: "I was feeding a raw diet for a few months and found it didn't do well with my Pugs. They had very runny stools and the uncooked food caused too much bad bacteria in their stomachs. I don't believe dogs should be given uncooked food."

The following breeders were all pro-raw diet.

Carly Firth, Mumandau Pugs, Greater Manchester, UK, had a lot of good advice for anyone thinking of feeding raw: "For many years I have fed my dogs the 'barf' diet. Not all dogs will take to this straight away. If this is the case, they are required to be weaned onto it very steadily.

"This can be done with perhaps introducing a chicken wing/neck every other day initially. Then gradually introduce with their main meal. I used 'Nature's Menu', which is already prepared, and packaged frozen in the form of ice cubes, easy enough to begin to measure out to be weaned. My Pugs and the Griffon Bruxellois appeared to wean perfectly. As opposed to other breeds, they can take a while to eat this (wings, necks, trachea, etc.), due to a lack of a pronounced muzzle." (Our photo shows Carly's five-week old litter).

"I found many benefits such as a massive difference in the condition of their coats e.g. shiny and silky to touch with less moult, even more so when fed pigeon and black pudding. Their breath and teeth seem less demanding for us humans to get involved to maintain. Their need to relieve faeces is less, and the consistency of it is smaller and harder (I suspect due to a lack of bulking agents in complete foods). And I would say overall that the dogs do appear healthier.

"I am also aware of other colleagues' dogs (Labradors) that are known to be atopic, and have been fed this diet which has resulted in their condition being considerably improved. The downside to the barf diet is that your vets seem to give you a lecture every time you go for a visit, and inform you of complications they've experienced due to it (bones becoming lodged).

"The diet is raw, so bones should be soft, easy to chew and digestible for your dog. I can imagine issues could occur if bones were cooked! When feeding a Pug a raw diet, cost-wise it works out reasonable. However, I can image if you had many dogs, or fed a larger breed of dog, the cost would be considerable. You also have to make sure you have plenty of room in your freezer. I would often get some bargains buying in bulk, and then fail to remember 'is there room for this?' Meat, especially pork, does have to go through a freezing process to kill off any unwanted bacteria. If not, this can result in your dog suffering from diarrhoea.

"Another benefit of feeding Pugs the barf diet is that it's a highly stimulating activity for them. They can take a good hour to eat something, and afterwards are ready for a sleep. As for puppies, I tend to feed them and supply the buyer with a complete diet (James Wellbeloved ocean fresh fish and rice, with a dash of salmon oil). This is done as I am aware that the raw diet isn't for everyone. By providing new owners with a diet that is readily available and easy to use, I am less likely to worry about my babies going off to their new homes. It's important the owners keep to the diet provided, and if they choose to change, they may do so later on in the dog's life. I think some new owners would be mortified if I'd hand them over a bag of duck necks, etc., so this is the best way for the puppy to be cared for effectively."

Roberta Kelley-Martin, HRH Pugs, California, USA: "I personally have experience with changing to a raw, balanced diet and having allergies disappear with feeding raw. It isn't easy, but it's so worth it for everyone involved."

Holly Attwood, Taftazini, Sheffield, UK: "I am a strong believer in feeding raw and believe Pugs thrive on a raw diet. I feed Natural Instinct, mostly raw tripe. Their coat and skin looks fantastic, they seem to shed less and their weight is more manageable and easy to control. They pass fewer faeces and they are significantly firmer, indicating a healthy gastrointestinal tract. Plus the dogs love it!"

J. Candy Schlieper, CandyLand Pugs, Ohio, USA: "I do occasionally feed some of my Pugs and all of my cats a raw diet. It can be cost prohibitive to feed as many dogs as I currently have, but I have seen wonderful benefits from it. Better teeth, coats and overall general health. I tend to feed dogs that may appear to have an allergy to a commercial food and they do very well on the raw diet. I use a commercially prepared frozen raw diet and that makes it easy for me and safer for my dogs."

Sue Wragg, Glammarags Pugs, UK: All my dogs are fed the raw diet and they absolutely thrive on it. They are fit and healthy, have clean teeth, shiny coats etc., and produce tiny poos - making the picking-up easier."

Laura Libner, Loralar Pugs, Michigan, USA: I think a raw diet is fabulous- I've fed my dogs raw before and the benefits are wide and reaching. However, I found it was quite costly, so cannot maintain this for multiple dogs on-going."

Deborah Beecham, Fizzlewick Pugs, South Wales, UK: "Raw diets are the only way to go in my opinion. All my dogs were all switched several years ago after my oldest fawn bitch became ill with heart problems. After doing some research into kibble and what goes into it, we made the change and I'm glad we did, the change in the health and vitality of my Pugs is amazing. Their teeth are cleaner, their coats softer, eyes brighter and poop – well, that's amazing too; small, firm and non-smelly." Our photo shows Deborah's Sinjari li'l miss Addams with Fizzlewick.

Donna Shank and Brenda Schuettenberg, RoKuCiera Pugs, California, USA: "Raw is a BIG commitment, not a bad thing but you must be willing to see it through all the time. There are less allergies, better stools (less of them also), better teeth and gums. It's a good feeding option if you can stick to it consistently."

Robert and Holly Hitchcock, Bobitch Pugs, Derbyshire, UK: "We feed raw, the coats, muscle tone and teeth improve, they seem content for longer and far less hyper."

Saran Evans, Sephina Pugs, Carmarthenshire, UK:" I feed raw minced chicken and tripe, my Pugs LOVE it and their coats are beautiful. I show my Pugs at Championship Show level with success, so this proves how good they look on this diet."

Linda and Kim Wright, Wright's Pugs, Michigan, USA, do not feed a raw diet, but they do home cook for their Pugs. This is what Linda said: "I have several friends who feed a raw diet. I'm not opposed to it if done right, but I do not. I do cook every night for my dogs though. I order both ground meat and turkey hearts in bulk with those friends who feed raw.

"I feed a high quality kibble, but also boil ground meat and turkey hearts and pour the broth and a little meat over every bowl of kibble. Each dog gets a turkey heart every night. The first thing they do is look for and gobble up the heart. If I run out, I get that look 'Are you kidding me mom – where's my heart?'"

Pugs and Food Allergies

Symptoms

Dog food allergies affect about one in 10 dogs. They are the third most common canine allergy for dogs after atopy (inhaled or contact allergies) and flea bite allergies. While there's no scientific evidence of links between specific breeds and food allergies, there is anecdotal evidence from owners that some bloodlines do suffer from food allergies or intolerances.

Food allergies affect males and females in equal measures as well as neutered and intact pets. They can start when your dog is five months or 12 years old - although the vast majority start when the dog is between two and six years old. It is not uncommon for dogs with food allergies to also have other types of allergies.

If your Pug is not well, how do you know if the problem lies with his food or not? Here are some common symptoms of food allergies to look out for:

❖ Itchy skin (this is the most common). Your Pug may lick or chew his paws or legs and rub his face with his paws or on the furniture, carpet, etc.
❖ Excessive scratching
❖ Ear infections
❖ Hot patches of skin
❖ Hair loss
❖ Redness and inflammation on the chin and face
❖ Recurring skin infections
❖ Increased bowel movements (maybe twice as often as usual)
❖ Skin infections that clear up with antibiotics but recur when the antibiotics run out

Allergies or Intolerance?

There's a difference between dog food **allergies** and dog food **intolerance**:

Typical reactions to allergies are skin problems and/or itching

Typical reactions to intolerance are diarrhoea and/or vomiting

Dog food intolerance can be compared to people who get diarrhoea or an upset stomach from eating spicy food. Both can be cured by a change to a diet specifically suited to your dog, although a food allergy may be harder to get to the root cause of. As they say in the canine world: "One dog's meat is another dog's poison".

With dogs, certain ingredients are more likely to cause allergies than others. In order of the most common triggers they are: **Beef, dairy products, chicken, wheat, eggs, corn, soy.** There is also anecdotal evidence that some Pugs are sensitive to wheat or grain.

Unfortunately, these most common offenders are also the most common ingredients in dog foods! By the way, don't think if you put your dog on a rice and lamb kibble diet that it will automatically cure the problem. It might, but then again there's a fair chance it won't. The reason lamb and rice were thought to be less likely to cause allergies is simply because they have not traditionally been included in dog food recipes - therefore less dogs had reactions to them.

It is also worth noting that a dog is allergic or sensitive to an **ingredient**, not to a particular brand of dog food, so it is very important to read the label on the sack or tin. If your Pug has a reaction to beef, for example, he will react to any food containing beef, regardless of how expensive it is or how well it has been prepared.

Symptoms of food allergies are well documented. Unfortunately, the problem is that these conditions may also be symptoms of other issues such as environmental or flea bite allergies, intestinal problems, mange and yeast or bacterial infections. You can have a blood test on your dog for food allergies, but many veterinarians now believe that this is not accurate enough.

The only way to completely cure a food allergy or intolerance is complete avoidance. This is not as easy as it sounds. First you have to be sure that your dog does have a food allergy, and then you have to discover which food is causing the reaction. Blood tests are not thought to be reliable and, as far as I am aware, the only true way to determine exactly what your dog is allergic to, is to start a food trial. If you don't or can't do this for the whole 12 weeks, then you could try a more amateurish approach, which is eliminating ingredients from your dog's diet one at a time by switching diets – remember to do this over a period of a week to 10 days.

A food trial is usually the option of last resort, due to the amount of time and attention that it requires. It is also called '*an exclusion diet*' and is the only truly accurate way of finding out if your dog has a food allergy and what is causing it. Before embarking on one, try switching dog food. A hypoallergenic dog food, either commercial or home-made, is a good place to start. There are a number of these on the market and they all have the word '*hypoallergenic*' in the name.

Although usually more expensive, hypoallergenic dog food ingredients do not include common allergens such as wheat protein or soya, thereby minimising the risk of an allergic reaction. Many may have less common ingredients, such as venison, duck or types of fish. Here are some things to look for in a high quality food: meat or poultry as the first ingredient, vegetables, natural herbs such as rosemary or parsley, oils such as rapeseed (canola) or salmon.

Here's what to avoid: corn, corn meal, corn gluten meal, meat or poultry by-products (as you don't know exactly what these are or how they have been handled), artificial preservatives (including BHA, BHT, Propyl Gallate, Ethoxyquin, Sodium Nitrite/Nitrate and TBHQBHA), artificial colours, sugars and sweeteners like corn syrup, sucrose and ammoniated glycyrrhizin, powdered cellulose, propylene glycol. If you can rule out all of the above, and you have tried switching diet without much success, then a food trial may be the only option left.

Food Trials

Before you embark on one of these, you need to know that they are a real pain-in-the-you-know-what to monitor. You have to be incredibly vigilant and determined, so only start one if you 100% know you can see it through to the end, or you are wasting your time. It is important to keep a diary during a food trial to record any changes in your dog's symptoms, behaviour or habits.

A food trial involves feeding one specific food for 12 weeks, something the dog has never eaten before, such as rabbit and rice or venison and potato. Surprisingly, dogs are typically NOT allergic to foods they have never eaten before. The food should contain no added colouring, preservatives or flavourings.

There are a number of these commercial diets on the market, as well as specialised diets that have proteins and carbohydrates broken down into such small molecular sizes that they no longer trigger an allergic reaction. These are called **'limited antigen'** or **'hydrolysed protein'** diets.

Home-made diets are another option as you can strictly control the ingredients. The difficult thing is that this must be the **only thing** the dog eats during the trial. Any treats or snacks make the whole thing a waste of time. During the trial, you shouldn't allow your dog to roam freely, as you cannot control what he is eating or drinking when he is out of sight outdoors. Only the recommended diet must be fed. Do NOT give:

- ❖ Treats
- ❖ Rawhide (you shouldn't feed these to a Pug, anyway)
- ❖ Pigs' ears
- ❖ Cows' hooves
- ❖ Flavoured medications (including heartworm treatments) or supplements
- ❖ Flavoured toothpastes
- ❖ Flavoured plastic toys

If you want to give a treat, use the recommended diet. (Tinned diets can be frozen in chunks or baked and then used as treats.) If you have other dogs, either feed them all on the trial diet or feed the others in an entirely different location.

If you have a cat, don't let the dog near the cat litter tray. And keep your pet out of the room when you are eating. Even small amounts of food dropped on the floor or licked off of a plate can ruin an elimination trial, meaning you'll have to start all over again.

Pugs and Grain

Although beef is the food most likely to cause allergies in the general dog population, there is evidence to suggest that the ingredient most likely to cause a problem in many Pugs is grain. Grain is wheat or any other cultivated cereal crop.

Pugs - as well as Bully breeds such as Bulldogs, Boxers, Bull Terriers and Boston Terriers - are prone to a build-up of yeast in the digestive system. Foods that are high in grains and sugar can cause an increase in unhealthy bacteria and yeast in the stomach. This crowds out the good bacteria in the stomach and can cause toxins to occur that affect the immune system.

When the immune system is not functioning properly the itchiness related to food allergies can cause secondary bacterial and yeast infections, which often show as ear infections, skin disorders, bladder infections and reddish or dark brown tear stains. Symptoms of a yeast infection also include:

- ❖ Itchiness
- ❖ A musty smell
- ❖ Skin lesions or redness on the underside of the neck, the belly or paws

Although drugs such as antihistamines and steroids will temporarily help, they do not address the cause. Switching to a grain-free diet may help your dog get rid of the yeast and toxins. Some owners also feed their Pugs a daily spoonful of natural or live yoghurt, as this contains healthy bacteria and helps to balance the bacteria in your dog's digestive system (By the way, it works for humans too!) Others have switched their dogs to a raw diet.

Switching to a grain-free diet may help to get rid of yeast and bad bacteria in the digestive system. Introduce the new food over a week to 10 days and be patient, it may take two to three months for symptoms to subside – but you will definitely know if it has worked after 12 weeks.

Wheat products are also known to produce flatulence in some Pugs, while corn products and feed fillers may cause skin rashes or irritations. It is also worth noting that some of the symptoms of food allergies - particularly the scratching, licking, chewing and redness - can also be a sign of inhalant or contact (environmental) allergies, which are caused by a reaction to such triggers as pollen, grass or dust. Some dogs are also allergic to flea bites. See **Chapter 11. Pug Skin and Allergies** for more details.

If you suspect your Pug has a food allergy, the first port of call should be to the vet to discuss the best course of action. However, many vets' practices promote specific brands of dog food, which may or may not be the best for your dog. Don't buy anything without first checking every ingredient on the label. The website www.dogfoodadvisor.com provides useful information with star ratings for grain-free and hypoallergenic dogs foods. We have no vested interest in this website, but have found it to be a good source of independent advice.

How Much Food?

This is another question I am often asked. The answer is … there is no easy answer! The correct amount of food for your dog depends on a number of factors:

- ❖ Breed
- ❖ Gender
- ❖ Age
- ❖ Energy levels

- ❖ Amount of daily exercise
- ❖ Health
- ❖ Environment
- ❖ Number of dogs in house
- ❖ Quality of the food

Some breeds have a higher metabolic rate than others. Pugs are generally regarded as dogs with medium to low activity levels – often with short bursts of energy - but this is a bit misleading, as energy levels vary tremendously from individual dog to dog. Some Pugs, especially young ones and those used to more exercise, are full of energy. (Our photo shows Catherine Jones-Kyle's Harry enjoying the spring sunshine).

Generally smaller dogs have faster metabolisms so require a higher amount of food per pound of body weight. Female dogs are slightly more prone to putting on weight than male dogs. Some people say that dogs which have been spayed or neutered are more likely to put on weight, although this is disputed by others. Growing puppies and young dogs need more food than senior dogs with a slower lifestyle.

Every dog is different; you can have two Pugs with different temperaments. The energetic dog will burn off more calories. Maintaining a healthy body weight for dogs – and humans – is all about balancing what you take in with how much you burn off. If your dog is exercised a couple of times a day and has play sessions with humans or other dogs, he will need more calories than a couch potato Pug. And certain health conditions such as an underactive thyroid, diabetes, arthritis or heart disease can lead to dogs putting on weight, so their food has to be adjusted accordingly.

Just like us, a dog kept in a very cold environment will need more calories to keep warm than a dog in a warm climate. They burn extra calories in keeping themselves warm. Here's an interesting fact: a dog kept on his own is more likely to be overweight than a dog kept with other dogs, as he receives all of the food-based attention. Manufacturers of cheaper foods usually recommend feeding more to your dog, as much of the food is made up of cereals, which are not doing much except bulking up the weight of the food – and possibly triggering allergies in your Pug.

The daily recommended amount listed on the dog food sacks or tins are generally too high – after all, the more your dog eats, they more they sell! Because there are so many factors involved, there is no simple answer. However, below we have listed a broad guideline of the average number of **calories** a Pug with medium energy and activity levels needs.

We feed our dog a dried hypoallergenic dog food made by James Wellbeloved in England. Max has seasonal allergies which make him scratch, but he seems to do pretty well on this food. On the next page are James Wellbeloved's recommended feeding amounts for dogs, listed in kilograms and grams. (28.3 grams=1 ounce. 1kg=2.2 pounds). The number on the left is the dog's **adult weight** in kilograms. The numbers on the right are the amount of daily food in grams that an average dog with average energy levels requires, measured in grams (divide this by 28.3 to get the amount in ounces). For example, a three-month-old Pug puppy which will grow into a 10kg (22lb) adult would require around 190 grams of food per day (6.73 ounces).

NOTE: These are only very general guidelines, your dog may need more or less than this. Use the chart as a guideline only and if your dog appears to lose or gain weight, adjust his or her feeds accordingly.

Canine Feeding Chart

PUPPY

Size type	Expected adult body weight (kg)	Daily serving (g)					
		2 mths	3 mths	4 mths	5 mths	6 mths	> 6 mths
Toy	2	50	60	60	60	55	Change to Adult or Small Breed Adult
	5	95	110	115	115	110	
Small	10	155	185	195	190	185	
Medium	17	215	265	285	285	280	Change to Junior
	25	270	350	375	375	370	
	32	300	400	445	450	450	
	40	355	475	525	530	530	
	50	405	545	610	625		
	60	450	605	685			
	70	485	670				
Large	90	580					Change to Large Breed Junior

JUNIOR

Size type	Expected adult body weight (kg)	Daily serving (g)						
		6 mths	7 mths	8 mths	10 mths	12 mths	14 mths	16 mths
	10	195	185	175	160			
Medium	17	290	285	270	245	Change to Adult		
	25	390	380	365	330	320		
	32	445	435	415	380	365		Change to Large Breed Adult
Large	40	555	545	530	500	460	460	

ADULT

Size type	Bodyweight (kg)	Daily serving (g)		
		High activity	Normal activity	Low activity
Toy	2-5	60-115	55-100	45-85

Small	5-10	115-190	100-170	85-145
	10-15	190-255	170-225	145-195
Medium	15-25	255-380	225-330	195-285
	25-40	380-535	330-475	285-410
	40-55	535-680	475-600	410-520
	55-70	680-820	600-720	520-620
Large	70-90	820-985	720-870	620-750

SENIOR

Size type	Bodyweight (kg)	Daily serving (g)	
		Active	Normal
Toy	2-5	50-105	45-90
Small	5-10	105-175	90-150
Medium	10-15	175-235	150-205
	15-25	235-345	205-300
	25-40	345-495	300-425
	40-55	495-625	425-540
	55-70	625-750	540-650
Large	70-90	750-905	650-780

Overweight Dogs

It is far easier to regulate your Pug's weight and keep it at a healthy level than to try and slim down a voraciously hungry Pug when he becomes overweight. Pugs are, however, prone to putting on weight and, sadly, overweight and obese dogs are susceptible to a range of illnesses. According to James Howie, Veterinary Advisor to Lintbells, some of the main ones are:

Joint disease – excessive body weight may increase joint stress which is a risk factor in joint degeneration (arthrosis), as is cruciate disease (knee ligament rupture). Joint disease tends to lead to a reduction in exercise which then increases the likelihood of weight gain which reduces exercise further. A vicious cycle is created. Overfeeding Pugs while they are growing can lead to various problems, including the worsening of hip dysplasia. Weight management may be the only measure required to control clinical signs in some cases.

Heart and lung problems – fatty deposits within the chest cavity and excessive circulating fat play important roles in the development of cardio-respiratory and cardiovascular disease.

Diabetes – resistance to insulin has been shown to occur in overweight dogs, leading to a greater risk of diabetes mellitus.

Tumours – obesity increases the risk of mammary tumours in female dogs.

Liver disease – fat degeneration may result in liver insufficiency.

Reduced Lifespan - one of the most serious proven findings in obesity studies is that obesity in both humans and dogs reduces lifespan.

Exercise intolerance – this is also a common finding with overweight dogs, which can compound an obesity problem as fewer calories are burned off and are therefore stored, leading to further weight gain.

Obesity also puts greater strain on the delicate respiratory system of Pugs, making breathing even more difficult for them.

Most Pugs are very attached to their humans. However, beware of going too far in regarding your dog as a member of the family. It has been shown that dogs regarded as 'family members' (i.e. anthropomorphosis) by the owner are at greater risk of becoming overweight. This is because attention given to the dog often results in food being given as well.

The important thing to remember is that many of the problems associated with being overweight are reversible. Increasing exercise increases the calories burned, which in turn reduces weight. If you do put your dog on a diet, the reduced amount of food will also mean reduced nutrients, so he may need a supplement during this time.

Feeding Puppies

Puppy foods

Feeding your Pug puppy the right diet is important to help his young body and bones grow strong and healthy. Puppyhood is a time of rapid growth and development, and puppies require different levels of nutrients to adult dogs.

For the first six weeks, puppies need milk about five to seven times a day, which they take from their mother. Generally they make some sound if they want to feed. The frequency is reduced when the pup reaches six to eight weeks old.

Pug puppies should stay with their mothers and littermates until **at least** eight weeks old. During this time, the mother is still teaching her offspring some important rules about life. For the first few days after that, it's a good idea to continue feeding the same puppy food and at the same times as the breeder. Dogs do not adapt to changes in their diet or feeding habits as easily as humans.

You can then slowly change his food based on information from the breeder and your vet. This should be done very gradually by mixing in a little more of the new food each day over a period of seven to 10 days. If at any time your puppy starts being sick, has loose stools or is constipated, slow the rate at which you are switching him over. If he continues vomiting, seek veterinary advice as he may have a problem with the food you have chosen. Puppies who are vomiting or who have diarrhoea quickly dehydrate.

Because of their special nutritional needs, you should only give your puppy a food that is approved either just for puppies or for all life stages. If a feed is recommended for adult dogs only, it won't have enough protein, and the balance of calcium and other nutrients will not be right for a pup.

Puppy food is very high in calories and nutritional supplements, so you want to switch to a junior or adult food once he leaves puppyhood. Feeding puppy food too long can result in obesity and orthopaedic problems – check with your vet on the right time to switch.

Getting the amount and type of food right for your pup is important. Feeding too much will cause him to put on excess pounds, and overweight puppies are more likely to grow into overweight adults. As a very broad guideline, dogs normally mature into fully developed adults at around two years old.

DON'T:

❖ Feed table scraps from the table. Your Pug will get used to begging for food, it will also affect a puppy's carefully balanced diet

❖ Feed food or uncooked meat which has gone off. Puppies have sensitive stomachs, stick to a prepared puppy food suitable for Pug, preferably one recommended by your breeder

DO:

❖ Regularly check the weight of your growing puppy to make sure he is within normal limits for his age. There are charts available on numerous websites, just type "puppy weight chart" into Google – you'll need to know the exact age and current weight of your puppy

❖ Take your puppy to the vet if he has diarrhoea or is vomiting for two days or more

❖ Remove his food after it has been down for 15 to 20 minutes. Food available 24/7 encourages fussy eaters

How often?

Puppies have small stomachs but large appetites, so feed them small amounts on a frequent basis. Establishing a regular feeding routine with your puppy is a good idea, as this will also help to toilet train him. Get him used to regular mealtimes and then let him outside to do his business straight away when he has finished. Puppies have fast metabolisms, so the results may be pretty quick!

Don't leave food out for the puppy so that he can eat it whenever he wants. You need to be there for the feeds because you want him and his body on a set schedule. Smaller meals are easier for him to digest and energy levels don't peak and fall so much with frequent feeds. There is some variation between recommendations, but as a general rule of thumb:

- ❖ Up to the age of three or four months, feed your puppy four times a day
- ❖ Feed him three times a day until he is six months old
- ❖ Then twice a day for the rest of his life

Pugs are known for their healthy appetites and will eat most things put in front of them, it's up to you to control their intake and manage their diet. Stick to the correct amount, you're doing your pup no favours by overfeeding him. Unless your puppy is particularly thin (which is highly unlikely), don't give in - no matter how much your cute Pug pup pleads with his big brown eyes. You must be firm and resist the temptation to give him extra food or treats.

A very broad rule of thumb is to feed puppy food for a year, but some owners start earlier on adult food, while others delay switching until their Pug is 18 months or even two years old. If you are not sure, consult your breeder or your vet.

Cupboard Love

Pugs are very loving companions, but they are not always fiercely loyal to one person. If your dog is not responding well to a particular family member, a useful tactic is to get that person to feed the dog every day. The way to a Pug's heart is often through his or her stomach!

Something else to bear in mind is that if your mealtimes coincide with those of your puppy or adult dog, you should eat something from your plate before feeding your dog. Dogs are very hierarchical; they respect the pecking order and in the wild the top dogs eat first. If you feed your puppy first, he may think that he is higher up the pecking order than you.

If allowed, some Pugs can develop a "cocksure" attitude and think that they rule the roost. So feeding your dog **after** yourself and your family is a normal part of training and discipline.

Your dog will not love you any less because you are the boss. In fact, just the opposite.

Feeding Seniors

Once your adolescent dog has switched to an adult diet he will be on this for several years. As a dog moves towards old age, his body has different requirements to those of a young dog. This is the time to consider switching to a senior diet. Dogs are living to a much older age than they did 30 years ago. There are many factors contributing to this, including better vaccines and veterinary care, but one of the most important factors is better nutrition. Generally a dog is considered to be 'older' or senior if he is in the last third of his normal life expectancy.

Some owners of large breeds, such as Great Danes with a lifespan of nine years, switch their dogs from an adult to a senior diet when they are only six or seven years old. A Pug's lifespan is from 10 years upwards and when you switch depends on your individual Pug, his or her size, energy levels and general health.

Look for signs of your dog slowing down or having joint problems. That may be the time to talk to your vet about moving to a senior diet. You can describe any changes at your dog's annual vaccination appointment, rather than having the expense of a separate consultation.

As a dog grows older, his metabolism slows down, his joints may stiffen, his energy levels decrease and he needs less exercise, just like with humans. You may notice in middle or old age that your dog starts to put weight on. The adult diet he is on may be too rich and have too many calories, so it may be the time to consider switching.

Even though he is older, keep his weight in check, as obesity in old age only puts more strain on his body - especially joints and organs - and makes any health problems even worse. Because of lower activity levels, many older dogs will gain weight and getting an older dog to slim down can be very difficult. It is much better not to let your Pug get too chunky than to put him on a diet. But if he is overweight, put in the effort to shed the extra pounds. This is one of the single most important things you can do to increase your Pug's quality AND length of life.

Other changes in canines are again similar to those in older humans and might include stiff joints or arthritis, moving more slowly and sleeping more. His hearing and vision may not be so sharp and organs don't all work as efficiently as they used to, his teeth may have become worn down.

When this starts to happen, it is time to feed your old friend a senior diet, which will take these changes into account. Specially formulated senior diets are lower in protein and calories but help to create a feeling of fullness. Older dogs are more prone to develop constipation, so senior diets are often higher in fibre - at around 3% to 5%. Wheat bran can also be added to regular dog food to increase the amount of fibre - but do not try this if your Pug has a low tolerance or intolerance to grain. If your dog has poor kidney function, then a low phosphorus diet will help to lower the workload for the kidneys.

Aging dogs have special dietary needs, some of which can be provided in the form of supplements, such as glucosamine and chondroitin, which help joints. If your dog is not eating a complete balanced diet, then a vitamin/mineral supplement is recommended to prevent any deficiencies. Some owners also feed extra antioxidants to an older dog – ask your vet's advice on your next visit. Antioxidants are also found naturally in fruit and vegetables.

While many older Pugs suffer from obesity, others have the opposite problem – they lose weight and are disinterested in food. If your old dog is losing weight and not eating well, firstly get him checked out by the vet to rule out any possible disease problems. If he gets the all-clear, your next challenge is to tempt him to eat. He may be having trouble with his teeth, so if he's on a dry food, try smaller kibble or moistening it with water.

Our dog loved his twice daily feeds until he recently got to the age of 10 when he suddenly lost interest in his food, which is a hypoallergenic kibble. We tried switching flavours within the same brand, but that didn't work. After a short while we mixed his daily feeds with a little gravy and a spoonful of tinned dog food – Bingo! He's wolfing it down again and lively as ever.

Some dogs can tolerate a small amount of milk or eggs added to their food, and home-made diets of boiled rice, potatoes, vegetables and chicken or meat with the right vitamin and mineral supplements can also work well. See **Chapter 15. Caring for Older Dogs** for more information on looking after a senior.

Reading Dog Food Labels

A NASA scientist would have a hard job understanding some dog food manufacturers' labels, so it's no easy task for us lowly dog owners. Here are some things to look out for on the manufacturers' labels:

❖ The ingredients are listed by weight and the top one should always be the main content, such as chicken or lamb. Don't pick one where grain is the first ingredient, it is a poor quality feed and some Pugs can develop grain intolerances or allergies, often it is specifically wheat they have a reaction to

❖ High up the list should be meat or poultry by-products, these are clean parts of slaughtered animals, not including meat. They include organs, blood and bone, but not hair, horns, teeth or hooves

❖ Guaranteed Analysis – This guarantees that your dog's food contains the labelled percentages of crude protein, fat, fibre and moisture. Keep in mind that wet and dry dog foods use different standards. (It does not list the digestibility of protein and fat and this can vary widely depending on their sources).

Crude Protein (min)	32.25%
Lysine (min)	0.43%
Methionine (min)	0.49%
Crude Fat (min)	10.67%
Crude Fiber (max)	7.3%
Calcium (min)	0.50%
Calcium (max)	1.00%
Phosphorus (min)	0.44%
Salt (min)	0.01%
Salt (max)	0.51%

While the guaranteed analysis is a start in understanding the food quality, be wary about relying on it too much. One pet food manufacturer made a mock product with a guaranteed analysis of 10% protein, 6.5% fat, 2.4% fibre, and 68% moisture (similar to what's on many canned pet food labels) – the only problem was that the ingredients were old leather boots, used motor oil, crushed coal and water!

❖ Chicken meal (dehydrated chicken) has more protein than fresh chicken, which is 80% water. The same goes for beef, fish and lamb. So, if any of these meals are number one on the ingredient list, the food should contain enough protein

❖ A certain amount of flavourings can make a food more appetising for your dog. Chose a food with a specific flavouring, like *'beef flavouring'* rather than a general *'meat flavouring'*, where the origins are not so clear

❖ Find a food that fits your dog's age, breed and size. Talk to your vet or visit an online Pug forum and ask other owners what they are feeding their dogs

❖ If your Pug has a food allergy or intolerance to wheat, check whether the food is gluten free. All wheat contains gluten

❖ Natural is best. Food labelled *'natural'* means that the ingredients have not been chemically altered, according to the FDA in the USA. However, there are no such guidelines governing foods labelled "holistic" – so check the ingredients and how it has been prepared

❖ In the USA, dog food that meets minimum nutrition requirements has a label that confirms this. It states: **"[food name] is formulated to meet the nutritional levels established by the AAFCO Dog Food Nutrient Profiles for [life stage(s)]"**

Even better, look for a food that meets the minimum nutritional requirements *'as fed'* to real pets in an AAFCO-defined feeding trial, then you know the food really delivers the nutrients that it is *'formulated'* to AAFCO feeding trials on real dogs are the gold standard. Brands that do costly feeding trials (including Nestle and Hill's) indicate so on the package

NOTE: Dog food labelled *'supplemental'* isn't complete and balanced. Unless you have a specific, vet-approved need for it, it's not something you want to feed your dog for an extended period of time. Check with your vet if in doubt.

If it all still looks a bit baffling, you might find the following website, mentioned earlier, very useful: www.dogfoodadvisor.com run by Mike Sagman. He has a medical background and analyses and rates hundreds of brands of dog food based on the listed ingredients and meat content. You might be surprised at some of his findings.

To recap: no one food is right for every dog; you must decide on the best for yours. If you have a puppy, initially stick to the same food that the breeder has been feeding the litter, and only change diet later and gradually. Once you have decided on a food, monitor your puppy or adult. The best test of a food is how well your dog is doing on it.

If your Pug is happy and healthy, interested in life, has enough energy, is not too fat and not too thin, doesn't scratch a lot and has healthy-looking stools, then…

Congratulations, you've got it right!

8. Behaviour and Training

Writing about the behaviour of Pugs is challenging, as no two Pugs are the same and no two Pugs behave the same. There are, however, some generalisations which are true, and there is also cause and effect - understanding how your actions might affect your Pug's behaviour. Here are some statements about Pugs which are largely true, Of course, there are always exceptions.

Typical Pug Traits

1. Pugs were bred as companions and most have a naturally sweet and gentle temperament. They make wonderful companions and are known for being good with children. However, any dog can become badly behaved if spoiled rotten, and this is especially true of Pugs. Give them too much attention, allow them to rule the roost and they can become demanding and jealous - particularly of other animals or people to whom you show affection. Food jealousy can also become an issue. Pictured is Saran Evans' perfectly-behaved Percy, of Sephina Pugs, Carmarthenshire, UK, trying out his most appealing look.

2. Despite what you may have read about Pugs being couch potatoes, puppies are most definitely NOT. They are balls of fire with high energy levels, erratic behaviour and usually short, mad bursts of high octane activity until they get older. Be prepared to devote time to your young puppy to keep him entertained and stimulated. He will dash round, maybe crash into things, and chew for Europe - or America – if left to his own devices. You also need to ensure he can't come to any harm during his lunatic phase (which may last up to two years). See **Chapter 5. Bringing Your Puppy Home** for more information.

3. Anecdotally, blacks tend to have higher energy levels than fawns, and even a streak of mischief. Some may be dominant with big personalities, which can result in them being harder to obedience train or housetrain. However, owners of blacks generally think they are well worth the effort - even if they do sometimes need a little extra time and patience. Other owners say that there is no difference between fawns and blacks - ask the breeder what she thinks.

4. Some owners say that males (fawn and black) are naturally more easy-going than females, who can be more 'in your face' or demanding than males. However, one of the biggest factors affecting your dog's behaviour, whether male or female, is how you treat them.

5. Most Pugs HATE going out in the rain. This can make housetraining harder if you live in a wet climate or you get your Pug during the rainy season - bear it in mind when deciding what time of year to get your puppy; they are easier to housetrain in dry conditions. And Pugs still need exercise, regardless of weather; you just have to pick your times more carefully. Again, there is anecdotal evidence that **some** blacks are less averse to bad weather conditions as they are keener for exercise.

6. Pugs are not German Shepherd Dogs and cannot be trained as such. They were bred as companion dogs and are happiest just being with you. Many have a slightly stubborn or independent streak, which means you need perseverance when obedience training - unless you want to be twisted around their little paws.

7. The upside of this is that your Pug will keep you amused with his antics; they are attention seekers. You can never be 100% sure just what is going on in his or her head and they will do the daftest things for no good reason at all.

8. Pugs are incredibly greedy. On the one hand they will do anything for a treat or food, which is great when training, but on the other hand they put on weight very easily, which is detrimental to their health. Keeping a Pug at an ideal weight is a constant challenge for owners. Beware that Pugs, especially young ones, may eat anything - including coins, tissues, sticks and plastic. True story: a two-year-old Pug called Stella was taken to the vet in Albuquerque, New Mexico, after she continuously vomited one night. The vet operated and found one quarter and 104 cents in the dog's stomach (total $1.29!) Stella made a full recovery.

9. Pugs make funny noises. They may snuffle, snort, snore, wheeze, bark, howl, moan and even 'scream.' Gas regularly comes out of both ends, so don't get a Pug if you are easily embarrassed! However, they generally do not bark a lot and their voice is surprisingly deep for such a small dog. Bear in mind that most are snorers if you are thinking of allowing yours to sleep in the bedroom.

10. Pugs want to be with you 24/7, but factor in some time apart, otherwise your dog is a candidate for separation anxiety - which is stressful for both dog and owner.

11. Pugs love to lick you. They are tactile and this is one of the ways they show affection. Get used to "Puggy kisses." They may also use their paws like hands to communicate by 'batting' or high-fiving you to get your attention. Pictured receiving adoring Puggy kisses is the grandson of Candy Schlieper, CandyLand Pugs, Ohio.

12. Pugs will not generally start a fight but, due to their stubborn streak, many will not back down from one either. They are unaware of their size and lack of fighting ability, so don't let your precious Pug get into a confrontation with an aggressive dog or he or she may get seriously injured.

13. They generally don't have any road sense and this is not something easily taught to Pugs, so keep yours on a lead (leash) near roads and traffic.

14. Don't presume that all Pugs are couch potatoes, they aren't. Energy levels vary widely from one bloodline to another. It also depends on how much exercise the puppy gets used to. They don't have major exercise requirements, but Pugs still do need some form of daily exercise – particularly as obesity is a problem within the breed.

15. Some can be difficult to housetrain. They don't like bad weather and are reluctant to go outside to do their business unless you are with them offering encouragement every step of the way - Pugs love company and praise almost as much as food. Some will even 'fake it'

by pretending to eliminate outside and then making a mess as soon as they come back indoors! Patience and persistence are needed for these frustrating little critters.

16. Pugs will steal your heart. OK, so that's not very scientific - but ask anyone who owns one and they'll tell you the same.

Cause and Effect

Treated well and taught the rules of the household, Pugs make incomparable canine companions. They are extremely sociable, love being around people, forming close bonds and entertaining their humans - which is why once you've had one, no other dog seems quite the same. But sometimes Pugs, just like other breeds, can develop behaviour problems. There are numerous reasons for this; every dog is an individual with his or her own character, temperament and environment, all of which influence the way he or she interacts with you and the world.

Poor behaviour may result from a number of factors, including:

❖ Poor breeding
❖ Being badly treated
❖ Boredom, due to lack of exercise or stimulation
❖ Being left alone too long
❖ A change in living conditions
❖ Anxiety or insecurity
❖ Lack of socialisation
❖ Fear
❖ Being spoiled (particularly true with Pugs)

Bad behaviour may show itself in a number of different ways, such as:

❖ Chewing or destructive behaviour
❖ Jumping up
❖ Pestering
❖ Soiling or urinating inside the house
❖ Growling – perhaps due to jealousy if you pet another animal
❖ Excessive barking
❖ Nipping or biting
❖ Aggression towards other dogs- perhaps where food is concerned

This chapter looks at some of the more familiar behaviour problems. Although every dog is different, some common causes of bad behaviour are discussed and general pointers given to help improve the situation. The best way to avoid poor behaviour is to put in the time early on to teach your dog good manners and nip any potential problems in the bud. This isn't always possible if, for example, you are rehoming a dog, when more time and patience will be needed. Another important tip for Pug owners is: DON'T SPOIL YOUR DOG. Treat him like a dog, not a baby, and teach him in a fun and patient way to respect the rules of the household.

In the most extreme cases when a dog exhibits persistent bad behaviour that the owner is unable to correct, a canine professional may be called in, but this is not cheap. It's far better to spend time acting quickly as soon as you spot the early signs of poor behaviour.

Personality

Just like humans, your Pug's personality is made up of a combination of temperament and character.

Temperament is the nature the dog is born with and it is inherited. This is why getting your puppy from a good breeder is so important. Not only will a responsible breeder produce puppies from physically healthy dams and sires, but they will also look at the temperament of their dogs and only breed from those with good traits.

Character is what develops through the dog's life and is formed by a combination of temperament and environment. How you treat your Pug will have a great effect on his or her personality and behaviour. Starting off on the right foot with good routines for your puppy is very important. Treat your dog well, spend time with him and give him the exercise he needs. A short walk once a day is enough for some, but all dogs need different environments, scents and experiences to keep them well-balanced and stimulated. Praise good behaviour and be firm when discipline is required. Set guidelines for your Pug. These measures will all help your dog grow into a happy, well-adjusted and well-behaved adult who is a delight to be with.

If you adopt a Pug from a rescue centre, you may need a little extra patience. These comical, eager-to-please people-loving dogs may also arrive with some baggage. They have been abandoned by their previous owners for a variety of reasons - or perhaps tied up and forced to produce puppies in a puppy mill - and may very well still carry the scars of that trauma. They may feel insecure or fearful, they may not know how to properly interact with a loving owner. Your time and patience is needed to teach these poor creatures to trust again and to become happy in their new forever homes.

Understanding Canine Emotions

Pugs are a law unto themselves, you might never know exactly what goes on in that quirky Puggy mind. But it helps to have an idea of how the canine mind works to better understand why your dog behaves like he or she does.

As pet lovers, we are all too keen to ascribe human traits to our dogs, this is called **anthropomorphism** – "the attribution of human characteristics to anything other than a human being." Most of us dog lovers are guilty of that as we come to regard our pets as members of the family - and Pugs certainly regard themselves as members of the family. In fact many are convinced that they are the centre of it and we belong to them!

An example of anthropomorphism might be that the owner of a male dog might not want to have him neutered because he will "miss sex," as a human might if he or she were no longer able to have sex. This is simply not true. A male dog's impulse to mate is entirely governed by his hormones, not emotions. If he gets the scent of a bitch on heat, his hormones (which are just chemicals) tell him he has to mate with her. He does not stop to consider how attractive she is or whether she is 'the one' to produce his puppies. No, his reaction is entirely physical, he just wants to dive in there and get on with it!

It's the same with females. When they are on heat, a chemical impulse is triggered in their brain making them want to mate – with any male, they aren't at all fussy. So don't expect your little princess to be all coy when she is on heat, she is not waiting for Prince Charming to come along, the tramp down the road or any other scruffy pooch will do! It is entirely physical, not emotional. Food is another issue. A Pug will not stop to count the calories of that lovely treat (you have to do that). No, he or she is driven by food and just thinks they want the treat. They will eat as long as you will feed them.

Treating Pugs like babies or children is all too easy for some owners – and a trap to be avoided. The Pug is a unique dog with appealing eyes, a squashed face and wrinkles. And the same can be said of his personality; he is very loving, eager to please you, and if he doesn't make you laugh, you must have had a humour by-pass. All of these characteristics add up to one thing: an extremely endearing and loving family member that it's all too easy to reward - or spoil.

It's fine to treat your Pug like a member of the family -as long as you keep in mind that he is a canine and not a human. Understand his mind, patiently train him to understand that you are above him in the pecking order and that there are some house rules he needs to learn and you will be rewarded with a companion who is second to none and fits in beautifully with your family and lifestyle.

Dr Stanley Coren is a psychologist, well known for his work on canine psychology and behaviour. He and other researchers believe that in many ways a dog's emotional development is equivalent to that of a young child. Dr Coren says: "Researchers have now come to believe that the mind of a dog is roughly equivalent to that of a human who is two to two-and-a-half years old. This conclusion holds for most mental abilities as well as emotions.

"Thus, we can look to the human research to see what we might expect of our dogs. Just like a two-year-old child, our dogs clearly have emotions, but many fewer kinds of emotions than found in adult humans. At birth, a human infant only has an emotion that we might call excitement. This indicates how excited he is, ranging from very calm up to a state of frenzy. Within the first weeks of life the excitement state comes to take on a varying positive or a negative flavour, so we can now detect the general emotions of contentment and distress.

"In the next couple of months, disgust, fear, and anger become detectable in the infant. Joy often does not appear until the infant is nearly six months of age and it is followed by the emergence of shyness or suspicion. True affection, the sort that it makes sense to use the label "love" for, does not fully emerge until nine or ten months of age."

So, our Pugs can truly love us – but we knew that already!

According to Dr Coren, dogs can't feel shame, so if you are housetraining your puppy, don't expect him to be ashamed if he makes a mess in the house, he can't; he simply isn't capable of feeling shame. But he will not like it when you tell him off in a firm voice for making the mess, and he will love it when you praise him for eliminating outdoors. He is simply responding to your reaction with his simplified range of emotions.

Dr Coren also believes that dogs cannot experience guilt, contempt or pride. I'm not sure I agree. Take a Pug to a show, watch him or her parade in front of the judges and then win a rosette-surely the dog's delight is something akin to pride? And Pugs can certainly experience joy. They love to be the centre of attention, and when they are showing off and lapping up your attention, their reaction can only be described as a mixture of pure joy and pride.

Dogs can certainly show empathy - "the ability to understand and share the feelings of another" - and this is certainly true of Pugs. Like many companion breeds, after a while they get into tune with the rhythms of the household and pick up on the mood and emotions of the owner. This may not be scientifically proven, but there are numerous stories from owners of how their dogs have stayed with an ill or dying relative, of how they have comforted a person showing distress - by licking, staying close, crying or even shedding tears.

One canine emotion which Pugs can certainly experience is jealousy. An interesting article was published in the PLOS (Public Library of Science) Journal in summer 2014 following an experiment into whether dogs get jealous. Building on research that shows that six-month old infants display jealousy, the scientists studied 36 dogs in their homes and video recorded their actions when their owners displayed affection to a realistic-looking stuffed canine!

Over three-quarters of the dogs were likely to push or touch the owner when they interacted with the decoy (pictured left). The envious mutts were more than three times as likely to do this for interactions with the stuffed dog compared to when their owners gave their attention to other objects, including a book. Around a third tried to get between the owner and the plush toy, while a quarter of the put-upon pooches snapped at the dummy dog.

"Our study suggests not only that dogs do engage in what appear to be jealous behaviours, but also that they were seeking to break up the connection between the owner and a seeming rival," said Professor Christine Harris from University of California in San Diego. The researchers believe that the dogs understood that the stuffed dog was real. The authors cite the fact that 86% of the dogs sniffed the toy's rear end, during and after the experiment!

"We can't really speak of the dogs' subjective experiences, of course, but it looks as though they were motivated to protect an important social relationship. Many people have assumed that jealousy is a social construction of human beings - or that it's an emotion specifically tied to sexual and romantic relationships," said Professor Harris: "Our results challenge these ideas, showing that animals besides ourselves display strong distress whenever a rival usurps a loved one's affection."

Ten Ways to Avoid Bad Behaviour

Different dogs have different reasons for exhibiting bad behaviour. There is no simple cure for everything. Your best chance of ensuring your Pug does not become badly behaved is to start out on the right foot and follow these simple guidelines:

1. **Buy from a good breeder**. A good breeder will only breed Pugs (or maybe one other breed). They use their expertise to match suitable breeding couples, taking into account factors such as good temperament and health

2. **Start training early** - you can't start too soon. Like babies, Pug puppies have incredibly enquiring minds which can quickly absorb a lot of new information. You can start teaching your puppy to learn his own name as well as some simple commands from as early as two months old.

3. **Basic training should cover several areas:** housetraining, chew prevention, puppy biting, simple commands like sit, come, stay and familiarising him with a collar or harness and lead. Adopt a gentle approach when your dog is young. He will lose attention and get frightened if you are too harsh, Pugs are sensitive to you and your mood and they do not respond well to harsh words or treatment. Start with five or 10 minutes a day and build up. Often the way a dog responds to his or her environment is a result of owner training and management – or lack of it.

4. **Take the time to learn what sort of temperament your dog has.** Is he by nature a nervous type or a confident chap? What was he like as a puppy, did he rush forward or hang back? Did he fight to get upright when you turned him on his back or was he happy to lie there? Is he a couch potato or more energetic? Your puppy's temperament will affect his behaviour and how he reacts to the world around him. A timid Pug will not respond well to a loud approach on your part, whereas a dominant, strong-willed one will need more effort as well as more patience and exercise.

5. **Socialise your dog with other dogs and people.** Pugs are often regarded as indoor dogs. This isn't necessarily true of all, some enjoy regular walks, even long ones. But for those Pugs who do spend most of their time indoors with you, it's important to expose them to other people, places, animals and experiences. Lack of interaction with other people and canines is one of the major causes of bad behaviour. Puppy classes or adult dog obedience classes

are a great way to start, but make sure you do your homework afterwards. Spend a few minutes each day reinforcing what you have both learned in class. Owners need training as well as Pugs!

IMPORTANT: Socialisation does not end at puppyhood. Dogs are social creatures that thrive on seeing, smelling and even licking their fellow canines. While the foundation for good behaviour is laid down during the first few months, good owners will reinforce social skills and training throughout a dog's life. Exposing your Pug to different people, animals and environments - from visits to the vet and friends' houses to walks in the park - goes a long way in helping a dog become a more stable, happy and trustworthy companion and reduces his chances of developing unwanted behaviour traits.

Pugs love to be the centre of attention and it is important that they learn when young that they are not the centre of the universe. Socialisation helps them to learn their place in that universe and to become comfortable with it.

6. **Enough exercise and stimulation.** A lack of exercise or stimulation is another main reason why dogs behave badly. Most Pugs do not need great amounts of exercise, but a at least one short daily walk away from the home is recommended, not only for keeping them from becoming obese, but also for mental and physical stimulation. Indoor or outdoor

games and toys are a good way of stimulating your dog and stopping him from becoming bored or frustrated.

7. Reward your Pug for good behaviour. All behaviour training should be based on positive reinforcement; praising and rewarding your dog when he does something good. Generally Pugs are very keen to please their owners, although they will not hang on your every word and jump to attention when you demand it. They are Pugs, not Collies! They also have a stubborn streak and do not respond well to shouting; training should never become a battle between you and the dog.

The main aims of training are to build a better relationship between your dog and you. Pugs may become stubborn and stop obeying commands if there is not much interaction between them and their owners, or they may switch off because they think they are top dog. Make sure you tell him what a good boy/girl (s)he is when he behaves well, and speak firmly if (s)he misbehaves. If your dog ignores you, stick with it and offer treats – most Pugs will do almost anything for a treat.

8. **Ignore bad behaviour**, no matter how hard this may be. If, for example, he is chewing his way through your shoes, couch or toilet rolls, remove him from the situation and then ignore him. For some dogs even negative attention, such as shouting, is some attention. Or if he is constantly pestering you demanding your attention, ignore him. Even remove yourself from the room so he learns that you give attention when YOU want to give it, not when he demands it.

The more time you spend praising and rewarding good behaviour while ignoring bad behaviour, the more likely he is to respond to you. If your pup is a chewer –and most are - make sure he has plenty of durable toys to keep him occupied. Pugs can chew their way through flimsy toys in no time.

9. **Learn to leave your dog.** Just as leaving your dog alone for too long can lead to behaviour problems, so can being with him 100% of the time. The dog becomes over-reliant on you and then gets stressed when left. This is known as **separation anxiety** and is something Pugs – like many breeds which thrive on human contact - are susceptible to. When your dog is a puppy, or when he arrives at your house as an adult, start by leaving him for a few minutes every day and gradually build it up so that after a few weeks or months you can leave him for up to four hours.

10. **Love your Pug – but don't spoil him,** however difficult that might be. Pug pups are adorable and almost impossible not to spoil. Their wrinkled faces, squashed-in features and chunky body resemble that of a plump little baby. But remember that they will grow into larger adults and can be independent-minded. This strength of character can turn to stubbornness, making them hard to control if they are allowed to rule the roost. You also don't do your Pug any favours by giving him too many treats for good behaviour. Obesity

can be a contributory factor to a number of health problems, including diabetes, organ problems and bladder stones.

Dogs don't just suddenly start behaving badly for no reason. As with humans, there's usually a trigger - often a bad experience or a pattern of poor behaviour you and your Pug get into. Get to know the temperament of Pugs in general and your own dog's individual personality and build up a loving, trusting relationship.

Separation Anxiety

It's not just Pugs that experience separation anxiety - people do too. About 7% of adults and 4% of children suffer from this disorder. Typical symptoms for humans are:

- ❖ Distress at being separated from a loved one
- ❖ Fear of being left alone

Our canine companions aren't much different to us. When a dog leaves the litter, his owners become his new family or pack. It's estimated that as many as 10% to 15% of dogs suffer from separation anxiety. Both male and female Pugs are susceptible because they are companion dogs and thrive on being with people; they generally do not do well if left alone for long periods. It is an exaggerated fear response caused by separation from their owner.

Separation anxiety is on the increase and recognised by behaviourists as the most common form of stress for dogs. Millions of dogs suffer from separation anxiety.

It can be equally distressing for the owner - I know because our dog, Max, suffers from this. He howls whenever we leave home without him. Fortunately his problem is only a mild one. If we return after only a short while, he's usually quiet. Although if we silently sneak back home and peek in through the letterbox, he's never asleep. Instead he's waiting by the door looking and listening for our return.

It can be embarrassing. Whenever I go to the Post Office, I tie him up outside and even though he can see me through the glass door, he still barks his head off - so loud that the people inside can't make themselves heard. Luckily the lady behind the counter is a dog lover and, despite the large **'GUIDE DOGS ONLY'** sign outside, she lets Max in. He promptly dashes through the door, sits down beside me and stays quiet as a mouse!

Tell-Tale Signs

Does your Pug do any of the following?

- ❖ Dig, chew, or scratch at doors and windows trying to join you?
- ❖ Tear up paper or chew cushions, couches or other things?
- ❖ Howl, whine or bark in an attempt to get you to return?

- ❖ Grunt, growl or make other noises when you leave?
- ❖ Foul or urinate inside the house, even though he is housetrained? (This **only** occurs when left alone)
- ❖ Follow you from room to room whenever you're home?
- ❖ Exhibit restlessness - such as licking his coat excessively, pacing or circling?
- ❖ Greet you ecstatically every time you come home – even if you've only been out to empty the bins?
- ❖ Get anxious or stressed when you're getting ready to leave the house?
- ❖ Wait by the window or door until you return?
- ❖ Dislike spending time alone in the garden or yard?
- ❖ Howl or whine when one family member leaves -even though others are still in the room or car?

If so, he or she may suffer from separation anxiety. Fortunately, in many cases this can be cured.

Canine Separation Anxiety in Puppies

This is fairly common, as dogs are pack animals and it is not natural for them to be alone. Puppies need to be patiently taught to get used to isolation slowly and in a structured way if they are to be comfortable with it.

A puppy will emotionally latch on to his new owner who has taken the place of his mother and siblings. He will want to follow you everywhere initially and although you want to shower him with love and attention, it's important to leave your new puppy alone for short periods in the beginning and then later on to avoid him becoming totally dependent on you.

Adopted dogs may be particularly susceptible to separation anxiety. They may have been abandoned once already and fear it happening again.

I was working from home when we got Max. With hindsight, it would have been better if we'd regularly left him alone for a couple of hours more often in the first few months.

Symptoms are not commonly seen in middle-aged dogs, although dogs that develop symptoms when young may be at risk later on. Separation anxiety is, however, common in elderly dogs. Pets age and - like humans - their senses, such as hearing and sight, deteriorate. They become more dependent on their owners and may then become more anxious when they are separated from them - or even out of view.

It may be very flattering and cute that your dog wants to be with you all the time, but insecurity and separation anxiety are forms of panic, which is distressing for your Pug. If he shows any signs, help him to become more self-reliant and confident; he will be a happier dog. So what can you do if your dog is showing signs of canine separation anxiety? Every dog is different, but here are tried and tested techniques which have proved effective for some dogs.

Ten Tips to Reduce Separation Anxiety

1. Practice leaving your dog for short periods, starting with a minute or two and gradually lengthening the time you are out of sight

2. Exercise. Tire your Pug out before you leave him alone. Take him for a walk or play a game until he runs out of steam. When you leave the house he'll be too tired to make a big fuss

3. Keep arrivals and departures low key. Don't make a big fuss when you go out or when you come home. For example when I come home, Max is hysterically happy and runs round whimpering with a toy in his mouth. I make him sit and stay and then let him out into the garden without patting or acknowledging him. I pat him several minutes later

4. Leave your dog a "security blanket" such as an old piece of clothing you have recently worn which still has your scent on it, or leave a radio on - not too loud - in the room with the dog. Avoid a heavy rock station! If it will be dark when you return, leave a lamp on a timer

5. Associate your departure with something good. As you leave, give your dog a rubber toy like a Kong filled with a tasty treat. This may take his mind off of your departure. (We've tried this with Max, but he "punishes" us by refusing to touch the treat until we return home - and then he wolfs it down)

6. If your dog is used to a crate, try crating him when you go out. Many dogs feel safe there, and being in a crate can also help to reduce destructiveness. Always take the collar off first. Pretend to leave the house, but listen for a few minutes. Warning: if your dog starts to show major signs of distress, remove him from the crate immediately as he may injure himself

7. Structure and routine can help to reduce anxiety in your Pug. Carry out regular activities such as feeding and exercising at the same time every day

8. Dogs read body language very well and many Pugs are intuitive. They may start to fret when they think you are going to leave them. One technique is to mimic your departure routine when you have no intention of leaving. So put your coat on, grab your car keys, go out of the door and return a few seconds later. Do this randomly and regularly and it may help to reduce your dog's stress levels when you do them for real

9. Some dogs show anxiety in new places, get him used to different environments and people

10. Get another Pug to keep the first one company. But first ask yourself whether you have the time and money for two or more Pugs. What if one or more needs veterinary attention, can you afford the fees or will yours be one of those who ends up in a rescue centre when something goes wrong? It's all too easy to fall victim to the 'pile of Pugs' syndrome, but make sure you can afford it.

Sit-Stay-Down

Another technique for reducing separation anxiety in dogs is to practice the common "sit-stay" or "down-stay" exercises using positive reinforcement. The goal is to be able to move briefly out of your dog's sight while he is in the "stay" position. Through this your dog learns that he can remain calmly and happily in one place while you go about your normal daily life.

You have to progress extremely slowly with this and much patience is needed, it may take weeks or even months. Get your dog to sit and stay and then walk away from him for five seconds, then 10, 15 and so on, gradually increase the distance you move away from your dog. Reward your dog with a treat every time he stays calm.

Then move out of sight or out of the room for a few seconds, return and give him the treat if he is calm, gradually lengthen the time you are out of sight. If you're watching TV with your Pug snuggled up at your side and you get up for a snack, say 'stay' and leave the room. When you come back, give him a treat or praise him quietly. It is a good idea to practice these techniques after exercise or when your dog is sleepy, as he is likely to be more relaxed.

What You Must Never Do

Canine Separation Anxiety is NOT the result of disobedience or lack of training. It's a psychological condition; your dog feels anxious and insecure.

NEVER punish your Pug for showing signs of separation anxiety – even if he has chewed your best shoes. This will only make him worse.

NEVER leave your dog in a crate if he's frantic to get out, it can cause physical or mental harm.

Excessive Barking

Pugs, especially youngsters, will push the envelope to see what they can "train" their owners to do. While Pugs make excellent, loving companions, they can have a bit of a stubborn streak. However, while most Pugs, snuffle, snort and make a unique array of Puggy sounds, they are not normally prone to excessive barking. Some puppies start off by being noisy from the outset, while others hardly bark at all until they reach adolescence or adulthood. On our website we get emails from dog owners worried that their young dogs are not barking enough. However, we get many more from owners whose canines are barking too much!

Some Pugs will bark if someone comes to the door – and then welcome them like old friends - while others remain quiet. The fact that they are not generally noisy is another reason why Pugs make good apartment dogs. However, they do not make good guard dogs, as they want to be friends with everyone.

There can be a number of reasons a Pug barks too much. He may be lonely, bored or demanding your attention. He may be possessive and over-protective and so barks (or howls) his head off when others are near you. Excessive, habitual barking is a problem which should be corrected early on before it gets out of hand and drives you and your neighbours nuts. The problem often develops during adolescence or early adulthood as your dog becomes more confident. If your barking dog is an adolescent, he is probably still teething, so get him a good selection of hardy chews, and stuff a Kong Toy with a treat or peanut butter to keep him occupied and gnawing. But

give him these when he is quiet, not when he is barking. Your behaviour can also encourage excessive barking. If your dog barks non-stop for several minutes and then you give him a treat to quieten him, he associates his barking with getting a nice treat. A better way to deal with it is to say in a firm voice **"Quiet"** after he has made a few barks. When he stops, praise him and he will get the idea that what you want him to do is stop. The trick is to nip the bad behaviour in the bud before it becomes ingrained.

If he's barking to get your attention, ignore him. If that doesn't work, leave the room and don't allow him to follow you, so you deprive him of your attention. Do this as well if his barking and attention-seeking turns to nipping. Tell him to **Stop!** in a firm voice - not shouting - remove your hand or leg and, if necessary, leave the room.

As humans, we can use our voice in many different ways: to express happiness or anger, to scold, to shout a warning, and so on. Dogs are the same; different barks and noises give out different messages, and Pugs are known for making lots of different noises. They have a relatively deep bark; a very high pitched bark may indicate fear. **Listen** to your dog and try and get an understanding of his Pug language. Learn to recognise the difference between an alert bark, an excited bark, a demanding bark, an aggressive bark or a plain "I'm barking 'coz I can bark" bark. Some Pugs emit a high pitched howl and other weird noises, you'll have to work those out for yourself!

If your Pug is barking at other dogs, arm yourselves with lots of treats and spend time calming your dog down. When he or she starts to bark wildly at another dog - usually this happens when your Pug is on a lead – distract your dog by letting them sniff a treat in your hand. Make your dog sit down and give him or her a treat. Talk in a gentle manner and keep showing and giving your dog a treat for remaining calm and not barking. There are several videos on YouTube which show how to deal with this problem in the manner described here.

Speak and Shush!

Pugs are not good guard dogs, they couldn't care less if somebody breaks in and walks off with the family silver – they might even approach them for a pat or a treat. But if you do have a problem with excessive barking when somebody visits your home, the Speak and Shush technique is one way of getting him to quieten down. If your Pug doesn't bark and you want him to, a slight variation of this method can also be used to get him to bark as a way of alerting you that someone is at the door.

When your dog barks at an arrival at your house, gently praise him after the first few barks. If he persists, gently tell him that that is enough. Like humans, some dogs can get carried away with the sound of their own voice, so try and discourage too much barking from the outset. The Speak and Shush technique teaches your dog or puppy to bark and be quiet on command. Get a friend to stand outside your front door and say "Speak" - or "Woof" or "Alert." This is the cue for your accomplice to knock or ring the bell –don't worry if you both feel like idiots, it will be worth the embarrassment!

When your Pug barks, praise him profusely. You can even bark yourself in encouragement…. After a few good barks, say "Shush" and then dangle a tasty treat in front of his nose. He will stop barking as soon as he sniffs the treat, because it is physically impossible for a dog to sniff and woof at the same time.

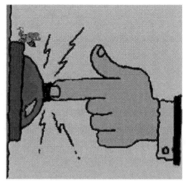

Praise your dog again as he sniffs quietly and then give him the treat. Repeat this routine a few times a day and your Pug will learn to bark whenever the doorbell rings and you ask him to speak. Eventually your dog will bark after your request but BEFORE the doorbell rings, meaning he has learned to bark on command. Even better, he will learn to anticipate the likelihood of getting a treat following your "Shush" request and will also be quiet on command.

With Speak and Shush training, progressively increase the length of required shush time before offering a treat - at first just a couple of seconds, then three, five, 10, 20, and so on. By alternating instructions to speak and shush, the dog is praised and rewarded for barking on request and also for stopping barking on request.

To get your Pug to bark on command, you need to have some treats at the ready, waiting for that rare bark. Wait until he barks - for whatever reason - then say "Speak" or whatever word you want to use, praise him and give him a treat. At this stage, he won't know why he is receiving the treat. Keep praising him every time he barks and give him a treat.

After you've done this for several days, hold a treat in your hand in front of his face and say "Speak." Your Pug will probably still not know what to do, but will eventually get so frustrated at not getting the treat that he will bark. At which point, praise him and give him the treat.

Always use your favourite 'teacher voice' when training, speak softly when instructing your dog to shush, and reinforce the shush with whisper-praise. The more softly you speak, the more your dog will be likely to pay attention. Pugs often respond well to training if it is kept fun and short.

Aggression

Some breeds are more prone to aggression than others. Fortunately, this is a problem not often seen in Pugs, as they are usually non-aggressive by nature. However, given a certain set of circumstances, any dog can growl, bark or even bite. And if a Pug does get involved in a fight – beware. He will not back down. As well as snarling, charging, barking and biting, you should also look out for other physical signs of aggression which are, in a Pug, raised hackles, ears up and tail raised. Here are a number of possible scenarios involving aggressive behaviour:

- ❖ Growling at you or other people
- ❖ Snarling or charging if you come in or out of the door
- ❖ Growling or biting if you go near his food
- ❖ Bullying other dogs near food
- ❖ Growling if you pet or show attention to another animal
- ❖ Being possessive with toys
- ❖ Marking territory by urinating inside the house
- ❖ Growling and chasing other small animals
- ❖ Growling and chasing cars, joggers or strangers
- ❖ Standing in your way, blocking your path
- ❖ Pulling and growling on the lead

Pugs love to be the centre of attention, but they can also become possessive of you, their food or their toys, which can lead to aggression. They are obsessed with food and giving a treat to stop bad behaviour is the worst thing you can do, as they learn that being bad equals nice treat.

Aggression may be caused by a number of factors: a lack of socialisation when young, an adolescent dog trying to see how far he can push the boundaries, a particularly dominant dog, being spoiled by the owner, jealousy or even fear. This fear often comes from a bad experience the dog has suffered or from lack of proper socialisation. Another form of fear-aggression is when a Pug becomes over-protective of his owner, which can lead to barking and lunging at other dogs or humans.

An owner's treatment of a dog can be a further reason. If the owner has been too harsh with the dog, such as shouting, using physical violence or reprimanding the dog too often, this in turn causes poor behaviour. Aggression breeds aggression. Dogs can also become aggressive if they are consistently left alone, cooped up, under-fed or under-exercised. A bad experience with another dog or dogs can be a further cause.

Many dogs are more combative on the lead (leash). This is because once on a lead, they cannot run away and escape. They therefore become more aggressive, barking or growling to warn off the other dog or person. The dog knows he can't run off, so tries to make himself as frightening as possible. Socialising your Pug when young is very important. The first five months or so of a puppy's life is the critical time for socialisation and during that early period they should be introduced to as many different situations, people and dogs as possible.

If your Pug suddenly shows a change of behaviour and becomes aggressive, have him checked out by a vet to rule out any underlying medical reason for the crankiness, such as toothache or earache. Raging hormones can be another reason for aggressive actions. Consider having your Pug spayed or neutered if he or she has not already been done. A levelling-off of hormones can lead to a more laid-back dog.

One of the main reasons Pugs display aggression is because they have been spoiled by their owners and have come to believe that the world revolves around them. Not spoiling your Pug and teaching him or her what is unacceptable behaviour in the first place is the best preventative measure. Early training, especially during puppyhood and before he or she develops selfish habits, can save a lot of trouble in the future. Professional dog trainers employ a variety of techniques with a dog which has become aggressive. Firstly they will look at the causes and then they almost always use reward-based methods to try and cure aggressive or fearful dogs.

Counter conditioning is a positive training technique used by many professional trainers to help change a dog's aggressive behaviour towards other dogs. A typical example would be a dog which snarls, barks and lunges at other dogs while on the lead. It is the presence of other dogs which is triggering the dog to act in a fearful or anxious manner. Every time the dog sees another dog, he or she is given a tasty treat to counter the aggression. With enough steady repetition, the dog starts to associate the presence of other dogs with a tasty treat. Properly and patiently done (it won't happen overnight), the final result is a dog which calmly looks to the owner for the treat whenever he or she sees another dog while on the lead.

Whenever you encounter a potentially aggressive situation, divert your Pug's attention by turning his head away from the other dog and towards you, so that he cannot make eye contact with the other dog.

Aggression Towards People

Desensitisation is the most common method of treating aggression. It starts by breaking down the triggers for the behaviour one small step at a time. The aim is to get the dog to associate pleasant things with the trigger, i.e. people or a specific person which he previously feared or regarded as a threat. This is done through using positive reinforcement, such as praise or treats. Successful desensitisation takes time, patience and knowledge. If your dog is starting to growl or snarl at people, there are a couple of techniques you can try to break him of this bad habit before it develops into full-blown biting.

One method is to arrange for some friends to come round, one at a time. When they arrive at your house, get them to scatter kibble on the floor in front of them so that your dog associates the arrival of people with tasty treats. As they move into the house, and your dog eats the kibble, praise your canine for being a good boy. Manage your dog's environment. Don't over-face him.

Most Pugs love children but if he's at all anxious or aggressive around them, separate them or manage him carefully around them. Children typically react to dogs enthusiastically and some dogs may regard this as an invasion of their space.

Some canines, particularly spoiled companion dogs, become aggressive towards the partner of the owner. Several people have written to our website on this topic and it usually involves a male partner or husband! Often the dog is jealous of the attention his owner is giving to the man, or it could be that the dog feels threatened by him. This is not uncommon with Toy breeds such as Pugs. If this does arise, the key here is for the partner to gradually gain the trust of the dog. He or she should show that they are not a threat by speaking gently to him and giving treats for good behaviour. Avoid eye contact, as the dog may see this as a challenge. If the subject of the aggression lives in the house, then try letting this person give the dog his daily feeds. The way to a Pug's heart is through his stomach.

A crate is also a useful tool for removing an aggressive dog from the situation for short periods of time, allowing him out gradually and praising good behaviour. As with any form of aggression, the key is to take steps to deal with it immediately.

Coprophagia (Eating Faeces)

It is hard for us to understand why a dog would want to eat his or any other animal's faeces (stools, poop or poo, call it what you will), but it does happen. There is plenty of anecdotal evidence that some Pugs love the stuff. Nobody fully understands why dogs do this, it may simply be an unpleasant behaviour trait or there could be an underlying reason.

If your dog eats faeces from the cat litter tray - a problem several owners have contacted us about - the first thing to do is to place the litter tray somewhere where your dog can't get to it – but the cat can. Perhaps on a shelf or put a guard around it, small enough for the cat to get through but not your Pug.

Our dog sometimes eats cow or horse manure when out in the countryside. He usually stops when we tell him to and he hasn't suffered any after effects – so far. But again, this is a very unpleasant habit as the offending material sticks to the fur around his mouth and has to be cleaned off.

Sometimes he rolls in the stuff and then has to be washed down. You may find that your Pug will roll in fox poo to cover the fox's scent. It's a good idea to avoid areas you know are frequented by foxes if you can, as their faeces can transmit several diseases, including Canine Parvovirus or lungworm – neither of these should pose a serious health risk if your dog is up to date with vaccinations and worming medication.

Vets have found that canine diets with low levels of fibre and high levels of starch increase the likelihood of coprophagia. If your dog is exhibiting this behaviour, first check that the diet you are feeding is nutritionally complete. Look at the first ingredient on the dog food packet or tin - is it corn or meat? Does he look underweight? Check that you are feeding the right amount. If there is no underlying medical reason, you will have to try and modify your dog's behaviour. Remove cat litter trays, clean up after your dog and do not allow him to eat his own faeces. If it's not there, he can't eat it. Don't reprimand the dog for this behaviour. A better technique is to distract him while he is in the act and then remove the offending material.

Coprophagia is often seen in pups aged between six months to a year and often disappears after this age.

Important: This chapter provides just a general overview of canine behaviour. If your Pug exhibits persistent behavioural problems, particularly if he or she is aggressive towards people or other dogs, you should consider seeking help from a reputable canine behaviourist.

9. Exercise and Training

One of the reasons that you have chosen a Pug is probably because you've read that the breed doesn't need much exercise. And while it's true that Pugs are predominantly indoor dogs, the breed as a whole has got a somewhat unfair couch potato reputation. Some people have confused the easy-going temperament and Pugs' love of being indoors with their families as meaning they doesn't want or need any exercise.

This is far from the truth. All dogs require exercise – even Pugs, particularly as they are prone to putting on weight.

The truth is that, while the breed as a whole does not need masses of exercise, energy levels vary tremendously from one Pug to another. The Kennel Club in the UK states that the breed requires less than 30 minutes as day (although the KC also says that Pugs only need grooming once a week which, if you have a heavy shedder, you might disagree with). The American Kennel Club gives them an energy and exercise level of three out of five and says: "Somewhat Active; Pugs are not exactly natural athletes, but they do have strong legs and endless curiosity - exercise both."

But let's be realistic, most Pugs are not athletic and are quite happy sitting at home, snoozing in a comfortable chair surrounded by their human family. Although puppies and adolescents are often playful and full of energy, most slow down as they mature, and the Pug is regarded as a breed which does well indoors, and in apartments, with medium to low exercise requirements.

The Pug is primarily a companion dog. If you have an active lifestyle and are looking for a canine jogging or cycling partner, choose a more athletic breed with more stamina. The Pug loves playing games and typically has short, mad bursts of energy, but not much staying power. Due to their physical make-up, they soon run out of breath.

Don't expect your Pug automatically to plunge into lakes or the ocean to retrieve that ball or stick. While some do enjoy it, many swim like stones. With most breeds you can say that the dogs swim or they don't; with Pugs it depends. Their relatively heavy, barrel-shaped bodies make swimming an extremely strenuous exercise, so even if your dog loves water, swim time should be limited to a few short minutes so he or she doesn't get exhausted.

Even those that swim do not cope well with water which is cold or too warm, or chemicals in swimming pools. Consider using chlorine substitutes if you have a pool, and if your dog does jump in, make sure you wash him or her thoroughly in clean water afterwards and clean the eyes. Always dry ears and wrinkles after swimming. As drowning can be a cause for concern, some owners who regularly visit water buy a lifejacket for their dog. No matter how good a swimmer your dog is, never let him or her out of your sight when in water.

The Pug is not suited to very hot or very cold conditions either, so if you live in a warm climate, exercise in the cool of the morning or evening.

Benefits of Regular Exercise

One thing all dogs – including every Pug ever born - have in common is that they need daily exercise and the best way to give them this is by regular walks. Exercise helps to keep you and your dog healthy, happy and free from disease. It:

❖ Strengthens respiratory and circulatory systems
❖ Helps get oxygen to tissue cells
❖ Wards off obesity – very important with Pugs
❖ Keeps muscles toned and joints flexible
❖ Helps digestion
❖ Keeps your dog mentally stimulated - regularly exercised dogs are less likely to have behaviour problems

Dogs, unlike humans, do not suffer from hardening of the arteries, but all dogs can be susceptible to heart problems. One way of staving off the ill effects is a daily walk or two which keeps the heart muscles exercised. Regular exercise which raises the heartbeat can help to prolong your Pug's life. Whether you live in an apartment or on a farm, establish regular exercise and feeding patterns early so your dog gets used to and adapts to the daily routine. When you are out on a walk, keep your Pug within sight or on a lead (leash). The breed generally has no road sense and may also be tempted to wander off with a stranger.

How Much Exercise?

There is no one-rule-fits-all solution, the amount of exercise that each individual dog needs varies tremendously. It depends on a number of issues, including temperament and natural energy levels (which are largely genetic), whether the dog is kept with other dogs, your living conditions and, importantly, what your dog gets used to. Ask the breeder how much exercise she gives the parents.

I know of Pugs who spend nearly all of their day indoors, and another which has up to two or more hours a day walking around the hills of Yorkshire – and both the owner and the Pug are fit and healthy. It's important to note that they have gradually built up to this amount of exercise, you can't take an unfit, overweight or young Pug and expect him or her suddenly to walk for an hour or two.

This is what our breeders said regarding exercise and, as you will read, there is a wide variation, with UK breeders tending to physically take their dogs on walks more often than American ones, who often have large plots of land their dogs can access. We start with comments from the UK: Saran Evans, of Sephina Pugs, Carmarthenshire: "Half an hour twice a day. They also have continual access to our large garden." Pictured is Saran's George enjoying a jog on the beach.

Robert and Holly Hitchcock, Bobitch Pugs, Derbyshire: "On a fine day they're outside playing, with a couple of 20-minute walks and some free running." Note the 'on a fine day' comment. Many Pugs HATE rain, so rather than not exercise your Pugs, pick your times carefully if you live in a damp climate – like rainy Britain!

Carly Firth, Mumandau Pugs, Greater Manchester: "Throughout the week they may generally get their quick 20-minute run around the field in the evening, but I think they are quite content slobbing around on the sofa with their humans. However, on a weekend they get to run around in the woods and on the moors for a good couple of hours, and seem to be able to adapt the change of stamina required for this. Consideration is required regarding hot weather conditions. Due to their breathing they can struggle more so than other breeds (with a more pronounced muzzle), and if pushed they may well collapse."

Deborah Beecham Fizzlewick Pugs South Wales: "We usually go out for about half an hour every day." Melanie Clark of Pugginpugs takes hers out for at least 45 minutes daily and Holly Attwood, Taftazini, Sheffield, exercises her Pugs for at least an hour a day. For Sandra Mayoh, Drumlinfold Pugs, North Yorkshire, it's 20 minutes two or three times a day and more at weekends, while Linda Guy, Londonderry Pugs, says: "I exercise my dogs for 10 minutes. Over-exercising will cause damage to the joints. My Pugs are content with this amount of exercise, but if they did show signs of wanting to go out more, I'd probably do ten minutes in the morning and ten in the evening."

Sue Wragg - Glammarags Pugs: "They have two long walks per day, but if the weather's fine and we are outside in the garden, they run about playing all day." And Deborah Hayman, Fawnydawn Pugs, Malta, adds: "I do not exercise mine that much, as they are free to run around all day, but I do take the ones I show for a half an hour walk daily. Our photo shows Deborah's Pugs contemplating climbing a tree.

Erin Ford, Fur-N-Feathers, Florida: "I am on nine acres, so for me I don't have the average day. My Pugs go outside five to seven times a day and up to 15 minute per time." Catherine Jones-Kyle Dixie Darlings, Tennessee, adds: "Our Pugs are out in the yard running around for about 15 minutes four or five times a day and they play a lot inside with our kids."

Linda and Kim Wright, Wright's Pugs, Michigan, say: "We live in the country on 15 acres on a dirt road. Everyone goes outside to romp and play (and potty) several times a day. When showing a Pug, they also take a one-mile walk every day (weather permitting). I might put them on the treadmill if needed for about half a mile or 15 minutes. The Pugs who are not being shown also alternate during the week for those walks."

Donna Shank and Brenda Schuettenberg, RoKuCiera Pugs, California, also use a treadmill on bad weather days: "We all go for a one mile walk every morning, the seat of Mom's rollator walker is perfect for the oldster or the youngest if they tire out part way through the walk. When the weather is just awful, we all use the treadmill to cover the same distance and the young ones may get on for short trots to use up all their energy that can't be expended outside due to rain and cold."

J. Candy Schlieper, CandyLand Pugs, Ohio: "My dogs have an acre of fenced yard to run and play in depending, of course, on the weather. This allows them to exercise at their own pace and builds up muscle naturally." Laura Libner, Loralar Pugs, Michigan says: "It depends on the day- usually about 15 to 20 minutes...they aren't a breed that requires extensive exercise. However, that isn't to say they don't require attention... they do."

Roberta Kelley-Martin, of HRH Pugs, California comments: "Pugs don't truly require exercise. Just following you around the yard and house will give them the required amount of exercise they need. They have a tendency to follow you no matter where you are going. I haven't closed the loo door in ages!

"They can benefit from a leisurely stroll if you are watchful that they are not becoming over-heated. Their minds will be exercised by the new surroundings and meeting new people. I've walked with mine with a friend that uses a baby pram to 'walk' her older pug. People gravitate to the oldsters while being taken out for their 'walk.'"

So, some owners prefer to take their dogs for one longer daily walk, while others split the time into short walks. And For some Pugs, 15 to 20 minutes a day is enough, while others enjoy longer daily walks more often. A walk is a stimulating experience for a dog. Much depends on what they get used to when they are young as dogs get used to your daily routine, so start out as you mean to go on.

As well as the physical exercise, there are new scents, people, places, sounds, dogs and experiences, all of which help to keep them mentally stimulated. Boredom is one of the main causes of poor behaviour – and chewing - in dogs.

The Pug has been bred to accentuate certain features, such as the distinctive short-nosed wrinkled head, and stocky or 'cobby' physique. The knock-on effect of this and short necks mean that the Pug's air passages are very small for its size, restricting the flow of oxygen. Excessive exercise, or exercising in heat, can lead to serious respiratory problems and even death - see the section on **Overheating** in **Chapter 10. Health** for signs of distress. It's also a reason why many owners prefer to use a harness and lead rather than a collar and lead on walks.

A fenced garden or yard is an advantage, but should not be seen as a total replacement for daily walks. You shouldn't think about getting a Pug - or any other type of dog - if you cannot commit to at least one walk every day. Exercise also plays an important role in socialising your dog, giving him new experiences away from the cosy home environment.

It is important not to over-exercise puppies when they are small; their bones and joints are developing and cannot tolerate a great deal of stress, so playing Frisbee or rough-housing for hours on end with your puppy or adolescent dog is not a sensible option. Neither is letting them run up and down stairs or jump on and off beds or sofas. You'll end up with a damaged dog and a pile of vets' bills.

Establish a Routine

What is a good idea, however, is to get your dog used to exercise at the same time every day at a time that fits in with your daily routine - and stick to it as much as you can. If you begin by taking your Pug out once or twice a day and then suddenly stop, he may start chewing, become attention-seeking or simply switch off because he has been used to having more exercise.

Conversely, don't expect a Pug used to very little exercise to suddenly go on long walks, he will probably struggle.

Test your dog's temperament, show him his lead and see how he reacts. Is he is excited at the prospect of leaving the home and going for a walk or would he rather snooze? Adjust the level of exercise to suit your dog – but try and commit to at least one short daily walk. Remember that Pugs generally love playing games - and all of this adds up to exercise. Factor in some regular play time to keep your Pug happy and stimulated, allow him to have fun and let off steam.

If your dog's behaviour deteriorates or he suddenly starts chewing things he's not supposed to, the first question you should ask yourself is: "Is he getting enough exercise?" (and the next question is whether a physical problem has developed, such as toothache). Boredom through lack of exercise or stimulation - such as being alone or staring at four walls - leads to bad behaviour and it's why some Pugs end up in rescue centres through no fault of their own. On the other hand, a Pug at the heart of the family getting daily exercise and mental stimulation is a happy, affectionate dog and a companion second to none.

Don't think that as your dog gets older, he won't need exercising. Senior dogs need gentle exercise to keep their bodies, organs, joints and systems functioning properly. They need a less strenuous regime than younger dogs, but still enough to keep them alert and healthy as well as mentally stimulated. If they get too stiff for walks, take them out in a pram (baby stroller), they still enjoy the smells, sights and sounds of different places.

Exercising Puppies

We are often asked how much to exercise a pup. It does, of course, vary depending on the factors already discussed. Pug puppies, like babies, have different temperaments and some will be livelier and need more exercise than others. All puppies require much less exercise than fully-grown dogs. If you over-exercise a growing puppy you can overtire him and damage his developing joints, causing early arthritis or other issues. The golden rule is to start slowly and build it up. The worst danger is a combination of over exercise and overweight when the puppy is growing.

Do not take him out of the yard or garden until he has completed his vaccinations and it is safe to do so. Then start with short walks on the lead every day. A good guideline is a maximum of:

Five minutes of exercise per day per month of age

until the puppy is fully grown. That means no more than 15 minutes when he is three months (13 weeks old), or 20 minutes when four months old (17 weeks), and so on. (Pugs are on the low side of this scale in terms of minutes per day). Slowly increase the time as he gets used to being exercised and this will gradually build up his muscles and stamina. Once he is fully grown, he can go out for longer.

Remember: a long, healthy life is best started slowly

Many of our breeders have strongly recommended blocking off the stairs and not allowing young Pugs to jump up and down on to furniture as this can lead to joint damage which shows later in life. If your dog is to be allowed upstairs, carry him up and down, and one option is to get or make a ramp to allow your Pug to safely get on and off the sofa or in and out of the car.

Pug puppies have extremely enquiring minds. They should be allowed to exercise every day in a safe and secure area, such an enclosed garden or yard, or they may become frustrated. If you live in an apartment, make the effort to take yours out every day after the all-clear on the vaccinations. Get your pup used to being outside the home environment and experiencing new situations as soon as possible; socialising young Pugs is an important part of their development into well-rounded adults.

If you have two or more dogs, they will naturally get more exercise than a single dog living with humans. If you are thinking of getting two Pugs, many believe it is a good idea to wait until the first pup has grown so it can teach the new arrival some good manners. Another point to consider is that if you keep two puppies from the same litter, their first loyalty may be the one with them since birth – i.e. their loyalty to each other, rather than to you as their owner. It may also be harder to housetrain train two dogs at the same time. Having said that, some people do prefer to get two dogs within a short space of each other so the first one has company and they get all the training and housebreaking over in one go.

Under no circumstances leave a puppy imprisoned in a crate for hours on end.

Exercise Tips

- ❖ Avoid exercising Pugs in hot conditions, wait until later in the day when it cools down. On warm days, always carry water on your walk. Dogs can't sweat and most Pugs have restricted airways compared with non-brachycephalic (non-flat-faced) breeds

- ❖ Do not throw a ball, toy or stick repeatedly for a puppy, as he may run and run to fetch it in order to please you - or because he thinks it is a great game. He can become over-tired, strain his heart, damage his joints, pull a muscle or otherwise damage himself

- ❖ Some Pugs have a stubborn streak, if your Pug stares at you and tries to pull you in another direction, ignore him. Do not return his stare as he is challenging you. Just continue along the way YOU want to go, not him!

- ❖ Train your Pug not to pull on the lead

- ❖ Many Pugs do not have much stamina – don't over-exert your dog. Keep play sessions and walks within your dog's capabilities

- ❖ If your Pug seems to be panting excessively, foaming or struggling for breath, stop the exercise immediately and make sure he has access to water

- ❖ Be vigilant near water. Pugs have short legs and dense, heavy bodies which makes them poor swimmers or complete non-swimmers. Some Pugs enjoy swimming and a life vest keeps them fully afloat, but only use this in shallow water until your dog gets used to it

- ❖ Vary your exercise route – it will be more interesting for you and the dog

❖ Avoid confrontational situations with aggressive dogs, Pugs are not good fighters, but they don't like backing down if challenged

❖ Never leave a Pug unattended in a car. Not only are temperatures likely to be high inside the vehicle – and it doesn't have to be hot for a Pug to suffer from heatstroke – but add to this the stress of being separated from his or her owner and the result could be devastating

For many owners, the fact that Pugs have relatively low exercise requirements is a bonus – but don't become a complete couch potato just because you and your Pug love lounging about on the sofa together - we all do! It's all too tempting NOT to take the dog out when you are both comfortably settled inside, but Pugs DO benefit physically and mentally from daily exercise away from the home.

Regular exercise is one of the best ways of prolonging your dog's life. It also helps the two of you to bond, it helps keep you both fit and healthy, you experience different scenery and mix with other companions – both canine and human. Trust me, if you make the effort it will enhance both of your lives – even if you are one of Nature's couch potatoes!

Obedience Training

"How easy do you find Pugs to obedience train?" It was a simple enough question, but it brought a smile to some of our breeders' lips. "Pugs? Trainable? Hummm?" was one response! It's fair to say there was again a wide range of opinions on the trainability of Pugs by those who know them best.

Another said: "Obedience training and Pugs, haha don't make me laugh! It's us that get trained by them; you don't own a Pug, the Pug owns you. Have you ever heard the saying 'Most dogs have owners, Pugs have staff?' Well I suppose that's true." However, she did add: "On a serious note, I know lots of people who have trained agility Pugs and companion Pugs - so it can be done." Here are other comments from breeders:

➢ "Very easy to train!! They are an intelligent, food-driven breed that loves to learn. My Pugs have a whole repertoire of party tricks. I find clicker training is very effective with them."
➢ "They are clever but stubborn. They will perform on their own terms - generally when food is offered."
➢ "I think again it's what we expect from our dogs. If you are enthusiastic to teach your dog obedience, tricks, etc. then the key is patience. To get the best of any dog, I would look at their natural ability. Pugs offer the capabilities to learn some basic obedience and tricks.... which, of course, must contain food for optimum results."
➢ "I've had other breeds that are easier to train."
➢ "They're a very stubborn breed but if you can get their full attention then you will do well"
➢ "Not too hard, though I can't say I've fully obedience trained any!"
➢ "I never tried obedience, maybe mine are too spoiled."
➢ "They are easy for basic commands as they are quite bright dogs. They wouldn't see the point in advanced skills like a Collie or German Shepherd Dog."

- "Most are quite stubborn, but with time and patience it is possible to train Pugs to an amazing standard - there are agility and obedience Pugs in the ring these days. Most can manage the average sit, wait, here, etc. fairly easily."
- "This is a breed that loves to please their owners, so I find them fairly easy to train. Again, they are very food and praise-oriented, so this helps with the training."

One UK breeder summed up the opinion of many when she said: "Pugs can be obedience trained, although they can be somewhat stubborn. Plenty of treats (as Pugs are obsessed with food) are necessary, as well as lots of praise."

An American breeder stressed the importance of starting training early: "You have to be smarter than the dog. You have to make the dog think that the behaviour you're trying to get them to learn is their idea. Motivational training is a sure way to make certain you get your message across and that you maintain a happy working dog. It also helps immensely if you start teaching behaviours to your dogs very early. Letting them learn to learn is a sure way to promote continued learning."

Training a Pug is like bringing up a child. Put in the effort early on and you will be rewarded with a sociable, amusing individual who will be a joy to spend time with for years to come. The breed makes a make great companion for us humans, but let your Pug do what he wants, allow him to think he's the boss and you may well finish up with a wilful, attention-seeking adult. Often people at most risk of spoiling their Pugs are people who live alone. Pugs make such natural companion for humans - after all, that is what they are bred for – that it becomes all too easy to treat them like a human and spoil them.

The secret of training Pugs can be summed up in four words: **FOOD,** praise, patience and persistence - with the emphasis on food as the prime motivator.

Most Pugs are naturally easy going, they love to please their owners and keep them entertained with their amusing antics. However, this can be combined with a streak of stubbornness, they can be independent thinkers – which may mean that he or she may be slow to respond to your command. You are not going have your Pug jump to attention every time you click your fingers. Nope.

He might or he might not, but he will want to weigh everything up first before he decides IF he is going to do what you ask. This is not a lack of intelligence, this is the dog thinking for himself; a trait which makes the Pug more quirky and interesting, but can mean that a certain amount of patience is required when training. Some of this might be down to the dog's individual nature, some of it may be that he can't be bothered and some if it is down to the breed itself.

The trick when training a Pug is to persuade him that he really wants to do what you are asking him to do - without stopping to consider all the options. And this is best achieved by rewards, in the shape of treats and praise, and patience.

Psychologist and canine expert Dr Stanley Coren has written a book called **"The Intelligence of Dogs"** in which he ranks 140 breeds of dog. He used "understanding of new commands" and "obey first command" as his standards of intelligence, surveying dog trainers to compile the list. He says there are three types of dog intelligence:

- ❖ Adaptive Intelligence (learning and problem-solving ability). This is specific to the individual animal and is measured by canine IQ tests.
- ❖ Instinctive Intelligence. This is specific to the individual animal and is measured by canine IQ tests.
- ❖ Working/Obedience Intelligence. This is breed-dependent.

Pug lovers will be disappointed to hear that their beloved breed is joint 57th, which equates to number 111 on the list, one place above French Bulldogs. They are in the fifth lowest of the six sections; in the Fair Working/Obedience Intelligence section, with only the Lowest Degree of Working/Obedience Intelligence below. According to Dr Coren, the Pug and similarly rated canine companions:

- ❖ Understand new commands after 40 to 80 repetitions
- ❖ Obey first command: 30% of the time or better

So you see, you have your work cut out! To be fair, the Pug is not a breed which is particularly unintelligent, this is far from the truth - Pugs can be empathetic, picking up on your mood and dream up antics to amuse you. Indeed, the list did not take account of genetic intelligence, which can be measured by ingenuity and a dog's understanding of a common situation. The drawback of this rating scale, by the author's own admission, is that it is heavily weighted towards obedience-related behavioural traits, which are often found in working or guard dogs, rather than understanding or creativity (e.g. hunting dogs).

As a result, some breeds including the Pug and all the Bully breeds - appear lower on the list due to their stubborn or independent nature, but this certainly does not make them dumb or impossible to train. Incidentally, the top three dogs were, in order: Border Collie, Poodle and German Shepherd.

OK, so we all know that the Pug is not a Border Collie, nor would we want him to be, so how do we go about training him? Well, for a start, training should always be positive, not punitive, and most Pugs really want to please their owners and are highly motivated by treats. They also love to be the centre of attention and enjoy showing off – and these traits can be harnessed.

Three golden rules when training a Pug are:

1. Training must be reward-based, not punishment based – treats not threats
2. Keep sessions short or your dog will get bored
3. Keep sessions fun, give your Pug a chance to shine

You might also consider enlisting the help of a professional trainer, but that option may not be practical or within the budget of most new owners. One excellent option is to join a puppy training/behaviour class in your town. Check out any local organisations which might run them - or ask at your vet's. These days some veterinary practices even run their own puppy classes. This way the pup or adolescent learns with his peers and is socialised with other dogs at the same time. You could also think about getting a dog training DVD - the beauty of this is that it brings training techniques right into your home – but it doesn't replace classes with other dogs.

When you train your Pug, remember it is not a battle of wills between you and your dog, it should be a positive learning experience for both. As well as being stubborn, Pugs are sensitive little flowers and bawling at the top of your voice or smacking should play no part in training.

Dogs are pack animals and very hierarchical. They - and you – need to learn their place in the pack - and yours is as pack leader (alpha). This is not something forced on a dog through shouting or violence, it is the establishment of the natural order of things by mutual consent and brought about by good training.

Like most dogs, Pugs are happiest and behave well when they know and are comfortable with their place in the household. They may push the boundaries, especially when they are lively youngsters, but stick to your guns and establish yourself - or a family member - as pack leader and the household will run much smoother. Again, this is done with positive techniques, not threats.

Sometimes your dog's concentration will lapse during training, particularly with a pup or young dog. Keep training short and fun, especially at the beginning. If you have adopted an older dog, you can still train him, but it will take a little longer to get rid of bad habits and instil good manners. Patience and persistence are the keys here.

Common Training Questions

1. **At what age can I start training my puppy?**
   As soon as he arrives home. Begin with a couple of minutes a day. Some may try to establish dominance over their human housemates, or become too territorial, so lay down the household rules from the beginning. Pugs make companions second-to-none when they are relaxed and know their place in the household.

2. **How important is socialisation for Pugs?**
   Extremely. It should begin as soon as your dog is safe to go out after his vaccinations. Your puppy's breeder will begin this process for you with the litter and then it's up to you to keep it going when your new pup arrives home. A critical time for your puppy's learning is before he is 16-20 weeks old. During this time, puppies can absorb a great deal of information, but they are also vulnerable to bad experiences. Pups who are not properly exposed to different people and other animals can find them very frightening when they do finally encounter them at an older age.

   They may react by barking, growling, cowering, lunging or biting. Food possession can also become an issue with some Pugs. But if they have positive experiences with people and animals before they turn 16-20 weeks of age, they are less likely to be afraid or try to establish dominance later. Don't just leave your dog at home in the early days, take him out and about with you, get him used to new people, places and noises. Pugs that miss out on being socialised can become territorial, over-protective or jealous. A puppy class is a great place to help develop these socialisation skills.

3. **What challenges does training involve?**
   Chewing can be an issue, train your young Pug only to chew the things you give him – so don't give him your footwear, an old piece of carpet nor anything that resembles anything you don't want him to chew. Instead get purpose-made long-lasting chew toys.

Socialisation

Socialisation means learning to be part of society, or integration. When we talk about socialising puppies, it means helping them learn to be comfortable within a human society that includes many different types of people, environments, buildings, sights, noises, smells, animals and other dogs. Even if your Pug is a house dog, he still needs socialising when young to avoid him thinking that the world is tiny and it revolves around him.

Most young animals, including dogs, are naturally able to get used to the everyday things they encounter in their environment—until they reach a certain age. When they reach that age they naturally become much more suspicious of things they haven't yet experienced, which is why it often takes longer to train an older dog.

This age-specific natural development lets a young puppy get comfortable with the everyday sights, sounds, people and animals that will be a part of his life. It ensures that he doesn't spend his life jumping in fright at every blowing leaf or bird in song. The suspicion they develop in later puppyhood – after the age of about four and a half or five months - also ensures that they do react with a healthy dose of caution to new things that could really be dangerous - Mother Nature is smart!

Developing the Well-Rounded Adult Dog

Well-socialised puppies usually develop into safer, more relaxed and enjoyable adult dogs. This is because they're more comfortable in a wider variety of situations than poorly socialised canines. They're less likely to behave fearfully or aggressively when faced with something new. Dogs which have not been properly integrated are much more likely to react with fear or aggression to unfamiliar people, dogs and experiences.

Pugs who are relaxed about other dogs, honking horns, cats, cyclists, veterinary examinations, crowds and noise are easier and safer to live with than dogs who find these situations threatening. Well socialised dogs also live more relaxed, peaceful and happy lives than canines which are unintegrated and constantly stressed by their environment. Socialisation isn't an "all or nothing" project. You can socialise a puppy a bit, a lot, or a whole lot. The wider the range of experiences you expose him to, the better his chances are of being comfortable in a wide variety of situations as an adult. Socialising is not just for pups, it should continue throughout your dog's life.

Don't over-face your little Pug in the beginning, socialisation should never be forced, but approached systematically and in a manner that builds confidence and curious interaction. If your pup finds a new experience frightening, take a step back, introduce him to the scary situation much more gradually, and make a big effort to do something he loves during the situation or right afterwards. For example, if your puppy seems to be frightened by traffic at a busy intersection, take him further away from the action and offer him a treat each time a huge noisy vehicle goes past. Another solution is to go to a much quieter road, use praise and treats to help convince him it's a great place to be, and then over days or even weeks, gradually approach the busy junction again once he's started to get used to the sound of noisy traffic.

Meeting Other Dogs

When you take your gorgeous and vulnerable little pup out with other dogs for the first few times, you are bound to be a little nervous. To start with, introduce your puppy to just one other dog – one which you know to be friendly, rather than taking him straight to the park where there are lots of dogs of all sizes, which may frighten more timid dogs. Always make the initial introductions on neutral ground, so as not to trigger territorial behaviour. You want your Pug to approach other dogs with confidence, not fear. Fear can turn to aggression. Anecdotally, some dogs have been known to act suspiciously around brachycephalic (flat-faced) breeds.

From the first meeting, help both dogs experience good things when they're in each other's presence. Let them sniff each other briefly, which is normal canine greeting behaviour. As they do, talk to them in a happy, friendly tone of voice; never use a threatening tone. Don't allow them to sniff each other for too long as this may escalate to an aggressive response. After a short time get the attention of both dogs and give each a treat in return for obeying a simple command, such as "sit" or "stay." Continue with the "happy talk," food rewards, and simple commands. So here are some signs of fear to look out for when your dog interacts with other canines.

- ❖ Running away
- ❖ Freezing on the spot
- ❖ Frantic/nervous behaviour, such as excessive sniffing, drinking or playing with a toy frenetically
- ❖ A lowered body stance or crouching
- ❖ Lying on his back with his paws in the air – this is a submissive gesture
- ❖ Lowering of the head, or turning the head away
- ❖ Lips pulled back baring teeth and/or growling
- ❖ Hair raised on his back (hackles)
- ❖ Tail lifted in the air
- ❖ Ears high on the head

Some of these responses are normal. A pup may well crouch on the ground or roll on to his back to show other dogs he is not a threat. Try not to be over-protective, your Pug has to learn how to interact with other dogs, but if the situation looks like escalating into something more aggressive, calmly distract the dogs or remove your puppy – don't shout or shriek. The dogs will pick up on your fear and this in itself could trigger an unpleasant situation.

Another sign to look out for is eyeballing. In the canine world, staring a dog in the eyes is a challenge and may trigger an aggressive response. This is more relevant to adult dogs, as a young pup will soon be put in his place by bigger or older dogs; it is how they learn. Pugs will usually not start a fight, but they will not back down either so don't allow a situation where that can happen. The rule of thumb with puppy socialisation is to keep a close eye on your pup's reaction to whatever you expose him to so that you can tone things down if he seems at all frightened. Always follow up a socialisation experience with praise, petting, a fun game or a special treat. A typical Pug posture when things are going well is a 'play-bow' - your Pug will crouch with his front legs on the ground and his rear end in the air. This is an invitation to play, and a posture that usually gets a friendly response from the other dog.

13 Tips for Training Your Pug

1. **Start training and socialising early.** Like babies, puppies learn quickly and it's this learned behaviour which stays with them through adult life. Old dogs can be taught new tricks, but it's a lot harder to unlearn bad habits. It's best to start training with a clean slate. Puppy training should start with a few minutes a day from Day One when you bring him home, even if he's only a few weeks old.

2. **Your voice is a very important training tool.** Your dog has to learn to understand your language and you have to understand him. Commands should be issued in a calm, authoritative voice - not shouted. Praise should be given in a happy, encouraging voice, accompanied by stroking or patting. If your dog has done something wrong, use a stern voice, not a harsh shriek. This applies even if your Pug is unresponsive at the beginning.

3. **Avoid giving your dog commands you know you can't enforce.** Every time you give a command that you don't enforce, he learns that commands are optional.

4. **Train your dog gently and humanely.** Pugs can be sensitive dogs and do not respond well to being shouted at or hit. Do not get into a battle of wills, instead teach him using friendly, motivational methods. Keep training sessions short and upbeat so the whole experience is enjoyable for you and him. If obedience training is a bit of a bore, pep things up a bit by 'play training'. Use constructive, non-adversarial games such as Go Find, Hide and Seek or Fetch. The game Tug Of War is not recommended as it can promote dominance and aggression. The dog may also – either accidentally or on purpose – grip your hand in his jaws in an attempt to get the toy. It's OK to play it with an older, well-trained Pug who has already learned your house rules and knows his boundaries so will stop or let go when you tell him to do so.

5. **Begin your training around the house and garden or yard**. How well your dog responds to you at home affects his behaviour away from the home as well. If he doesn't respond well at home, he certainly won't respond any better when he's out and about where there are 101 distractions, such as food scraps, other dogs, people, cats, interesting scents, etc.

6. **One command equals one response.** Give your dog only one command - twice maximum - then gently enforce it. Repeating commands or nagging will make your Pug tune out. They also teach him that the first few commands are a bluff. Telling your dog to **"SIT, SIT, SIT, SIT!!!"** is neither efficient nor effective. Give your dog a single "SIT" command, gently place him in the sitting position and then praise him.

7. **Use your dog's name often and in a positive manner.** When you bring your pup or new dog home, start using his name often so he gets used to the sound of it. He won't know what it means in the beginning, but it won't take him long to realise you're talking to him. DON'T use his name when reprimanding, warning or punishing. He should trust that when he hears his name, good things happen. His name should always be a word he responds to with enthusiasm, never hesitancy or fear. Use the words "NO" or "BAD BOY/GIRL" in a stern - not shouted - voice instead. Some people with children, prefer not to use the word "NO" with their dog, as they often use it around the human youngsters and

is likely to confuse the young canine! You can make a sound like "ACK!" instead. Say it sharply and the dog should stop whatever it is he is doing wrong – it works for us.

8. **Don't give your dog lots of attention (even negative attention) when he misbehaves.** Pugs love attention. If he gets lots of attention when he jumps up on you, his bad behaviour is being reinforced. If he jumps up, push him away, use the command "NO" or "DOWN" and then ignore him.

9. **Timing is critical to successful training.** When your puppy does something right, praise him immediately. Similarly, when he does something wrong, like peeing in the house, correct him straight away. If you don't praise or scold your puppy immediately for something he has done, you cannot do it at all as he will have no idea what he has done right or wrong.

10. **Have a "NO" sound.** When a puppy is corrected by his mother – for example if he bites her with his sharp baby teeth – she growls at him to warn him not to do it again. When your puppy makes a mistake, make a short sharp sound like **"ACK!"** to tell the puppy not to do that again. This works surprisingly well.

11. **Give your dog attention when YOU want to** – not when he wants it. Pugs are sociable creatures, they love being with you and around the family. When you are training, give your puppy lots of positive attention when he is good. But if he starts jumping up, nudging you constantly or barking to demand your attention, ignore him. If you give in to his every demand, he will start to think he is the boss. Wait a while and pat him when you want and when he has stopped demanding your attention.

12. **Be patient.** Rome wasn't built in a day and a Pug won't be trained in a week either. But you'll reap the rewards of a few weeks of short, regular training sessions for the rest of the dog's life when you have a happy, well-behaved friend and loving companion.

13. **Start as you mean to go on.** In other words, in terms of rules and training, treat your cute little Pug as though he were fully grown: make him abide by the rules you want him to live by as an adult. If you don't want him to take over your couch or jump up at people when he is an adult, don't allow him to do it when he is small. You can't have one set of rules for a pup and one set for a fully grown dog, he won't understand.

This simple phrase holds the key: TREATS, NOT THREATS.

Teaching Basic Commands

Sit - Teaching the Sit command to your Pug is relatively easy. Teaching a young pup to sit still is a bit more difficult! In the beginning you may want to put your protégé on a lead to hold his attention.

1. Stand facing each other and hold a treat between your thumb and fingers just an inch or so above his head. Don't let your fingers and the treat get any further away or you might have trouble getting him to move his body into a sitting position. In fact, if your dog jumps up when you try to guide him into the Sit, you're probably holding your hand too far away from his nose. If your dog backs up, you can practice with a wall behind him.

NOTE: It's rather pointless paying for a high quality, possibly hypoallergenic dog food and then filling him with trashy treats. Buy premium treats with natural ingredients which won't cause allergies, or use natural meat, fish or poultry titbits.

2. As he reaches up to sniff it, move the treat upwards and back over the dog towards his tail at the same time as saying "Sit". Most dogs will track the treat with their eyes and follow it with their noses, causing their snouts to point straight up.

3. As his head moves up toward the treat, his rear end should automatically go down towards the floor. TaDa! (drum roll!)

4. As soon as he sits, say "Yes!" give him the treat and tell your dog (s)he's a good boy or girl. Stroke and praise him for as long as he stays in the sitting position. If he jumps up on his back legs and paws you while you are moving the treat, be patient and start all over again. Another method is to put one hand on his chest and with your other hand, gently push down on his rear end until he is sitting, while saying "Sit". Give him a treat and praise, even though you have made him do it, he will eventually associate the position with the word 'sit'.

5. Once your dog catches on, leave the treat in your pocket (or have it in your other hand). Repeat the sequence, but this time your dog will just follow your empty hand. Say "Sit" and bring your empty hand in front of your dog's nose, holding your fingers as if you had a treat. Move your hand exactly as you did when you held the treat.

6. When your dog sits, say "Yes!" and then give him a treat from your other hand or your pocket.

7. Gradually lessen the amount of movement with your hand. First, say "Sit" then hold your hand eight to 10 inches above your dog's face and wait a moment. Most likely, he will sit. If he doesn't, help him by moving your hand back over his head, like you did before, but make a smaller movement this time. Then try again. Your goal is to eventually just say "Sit" without having to move or extend your hand at all.

Once your dog reliably sits on cue, you can ask him to sit whenever you meet and talk to people (admittedly, it may not work, but it might calm him down a bit). The key is anticipation. Give your Pug the cue before he gets too excited to hear you and before he starts jumping up on the person just arrived. Generously reward your dog the instant he sits. Say "Yes" and give him treats every few seconds while he holds the Sit. Whenever possible, ask the person you're greeting to help you out by walking away if your dog gets up from the sit and lunges or jumps towards him or her. With many consistent repetitions of this exercise, your dog will learn that lunging or jumping makes people go away, and polite sitting makes them stay and give him attention.

'Sit' is a useful command and can be used in a number of different situations. For example when you are putting his lead on, while you are preparing his meal, when he returned the ball you have just thrown, when he is jumping up, demanding attention or getting over-excited.

Come - This is another basic command which you can teach right from the beginning. Teaching your dog to come to you when you call (also known as the recall) is an important lesson. A dog who responds quickly and consistently can enjoy freedoms that other dogs cannot. Although you might spend more time teaching this command to your Pug than any other, the benefits make it well worth the investment.

No matter how much effort you put into training, no dog is ever going to be 100% reliable at coming when called and especially not an independent-minded Pug. Dogs are not machines. They're like people in that they have their good days and their bad days. Sometimes they don't hear you call, sometimes they're paying attention to something else, sometimes they misunderstand what you want, and sometimes a Pug simply decides that he would rather do something else.

Whether you're teaching a young puppy or an older Pug, the first step is always to establish that coming to you is the best thing he can do. Any time your dog comes to you whether you've called him or not, acknowledge that you appreciate it. You can do this with smiles, praise, affection, play or treats. This consistent reinforcement ensures that your dog will continue to "check in" with you frequently.

1. Say your dog's name followed by the command **"Come!"** in an enthusiastic voice. You'll usually be more successful if you walk or run away from him while you call. Dogs find it hard to resist chasing after a running person, especially their owner.

2. He should run towards you. NOTE: Dogs tend to tune us out if we talk to them all the time. Whether you're training or out for an off-lead walk, refrain from constantly chattering to your dog - no matter how much of a brilliant conversationalist you are! If you're quiet much of the time, he is more likely to pay attention when you call him. When he does, praise him and give him a treat.

3. Often, especially outdoors, a dog will start off running towards you but then get distracted and head off in another direction. Pre-empt this situation by praising your dog and cheering him on when he starts to come to you and before he has a chance to get distracted. Your praise will keep him focused so that he'll be more likely to come all the way to you. If he

stops or turns away, you can give him feedback by saying "Uh-uh!" or "Hey!" in a different tone of voice (displeased or unpleasantly surprised). When he looks at you again, smile, call him and praise him as he approaches you.

Progress your dog's training in baby steps. If he's learned to come when called in your kitchen, you can't expect him to be able to do it straight away at the park when he's surrounded by distractions. When you try this outdoors, make sure there's no one around to distract your dog when you first test his recall. It's a good idea to consider using a long training lead - or to do the training within a safe, fenced area. Only when your dog has mastered the recall in a number of locations and in the face of numerous distractions can you expect that he'll come to you.

***

Down - There are a number of different ways to teach this command. It is one which does not come naturally to a young pup, so it may take a little while for him to master. Don't make it a battle of wills and, although you may gently push him down, don't physically force him down against his will. This will be seen as you asserting dominance in an aggressive manner and your Pug will not respond well.

1. Give the **Sit** command.

2. When your dog sits, don't give him the treat immediately, but keep it in your closed hand. Slowly move your hand straight down toward the floor, between his front legs. As your dog's nose follows the treat, just like a magnet, his head will bend all the way down to the floor.

3. When the treat is on the floor between your dog's paws, start to move it away from him, like you're drawing a line along the floor. (The entire luring motion forms an L-shape).

4. At the same time say "Down!" in a firm manner.

5. To continue to follow the treat, your dog will probably ease himself into the Down position. The instant his elbows touch the floor, say "Yes!" and immediately let him eat the treat. If your dog doesn't automatically stand up after eating the treat, just move a step or two away to encourage him to move out of the Down position. Then repeat the sequence above several times. Aim for two short sessions of five minutes or so per day.

If it doesn't work, try using a different treat. And if your dog's back end pops up when you try to lure him into a Down, quickly snatch the treat away. Then immediately ask your dog to sit and try again. It may help to let your dog nibble on the treat as you move it toward the floor. If you've tried to lure your dog into a Down but he still seems confused or reluctant, try this trick:

❖ Sit down on the floor with your legs straight out in front of you. Your dog should be at your side. Keeping your legs together and your feet on the floor, bend your knees to make a "tent" shape
❖ Hold a treat right in front of your dog's nose. As he licks and sniffs the treat, slowly move it down to the floor and then underneath your legs. Continue to lure him until he has to crouch down to keep following the treat
❖ The instant his belly touches the floor, say "Yes!" and let him eat the treat. If your dog seems nervous about following the treat under your legs, make a trail of treats for him to eat along the way

Some dogs find it easier to follow a treat into the Down from a standing position.

- Hold the treat right in front of your dog's nose, and then slowly move it straight down to the floor, right between his front paws. His nose will follow the treat
- If you let him lick the treat as you continue to hold it still on the floor, your dog will probably plop into the Down position
- The moment he does, say "Yes!" and let him eat the treat

Many dogs are reluctant to lie on a cold floor. It may be easier to teach yours to lie down on a carpet. The next step is to introduce a hand signal. You'll still reward him with treats, though, so keep them nearby or hidden behind your back.

- Start with your dog in a Sit
- Say "Down!"
- Without a treat in your fingers, use the same hand motion you did before
- As soon as your dog's elbows touch the floor, say "Yes!" and immediately get a treat to give him. Important: Even though you're not using a treat to lure your dog into position, you must still give him a reward when he lies down. You want your dog to learn that he doesn't have to see a treat to get one.

Clap your hands or take a few steps away to encourage him to stand up. Then repeat the sequence from the beginning several times for a week or two. When your dog readily lies down as soon as you say the cue and then use your new hand signal, you're ready for the next step. You probably don't want to keep bending all the way down to the floor to make your Pug lie down. To make things more convenient, you can gradually shrink the signal so that it becomes a smaller movement. To make sure your dog continues to understand what you want him to do, you'll need to progress slowly.

Repeat the hand signal, but instead of guiding your dog into the Down by moving your hand all the way to the floor, move it almost all the way down. Stop moving your hand when it's an inch or two above the floor. Practice the Down exercise for a day or two, using this slightly smaller hand signal. Then you can make your movement an inch or two smaller, stopping your hand three or four inches above the floor.

After practising for another couple of days, you can shrink the signal again. As you continue to gradually stop your hand signal farther and farther away from the floor, you'll bend over less and less. Eventually, you won't have to bend over at all. You'll be able to stand up straight, say "Down," and then just point to the floor.

Your next job is a bit harder - it's to practise your dog's new skill in many different situations and locations so that he can lie down whenever and wherever you ask him to. Slowly increase the level of distraction, for example, first practise in calm places like different rooms in your house or in your backyard when there's no one else around. Then increase the distractions, practise at home when family members are moving around, on walks and then at friends' houses, too.

Stay - This is a very useful command, but it's not so easy to teach a lively and distracted young Pug pup to stay still for any length of time. Here is a simple method to get your dog to stay, but if you are training a young dog, don't ask him to stay for more than a few seconds at the beginning.

1. As this requires some concentration from your dog, pick a time when he's relaxed and well exercised or has just finished playing a game, especially if training a youngster. Start with your dog in the position you want him to hold, either the Sit or Down position.

2. Command your dog to sit or lie down, but instead of giving a treat as soon as he hits the floor, hold off for one second. Then say "Yes!" in an enthusiastic voice and give him a treat. If your dog tends to bounce up again instantly, have two treats ready. Feed one right away, before he has time to move; then say "Yes!" and feed the second treat.

3. You need a release word or phrase. It might be "Free!" or "Here!" or a word which you only use to release your dog from this command. Once you've given the treat, immediately give your release cue and encourage your dog to get up. Then repeat the exercise, perhaps up to a dozen times in one training session, gradually wait a tiny bit longer before releasing the treat. (You can delay the first treat for a moment if your dog bounces up.)

4. A common mistake is to hold the treat high up and then give the reward slowly. As your dog doesn't know the command yet, he sees the treat coming and gets up to meet the food. Solve this problem by bringing the treat toward your dog quickly - the best place to deliver it is right between his front paws. If you're working on a Sit-Stay, give the treat at chest height.

5. When your dog can stay for several seconds, start to add a little distance. At first, you'll walk backwards, because your Pug is more likely to get up to follow you if you turn away from him. Take one single step away, then step back towards your dog and say "Yes!" and give the treat. Give him the signal to get up immediately, even if five seconds haven't passed.

   The stay gets harder for your dog depending on how long it is, how far away you are, and what else is going on around him. Trainer shorthand is "distance, duration, distraction." For best success in teaching a stay, work on one factor at a time. Whenever you make one factor more difficult, such as distance, ease up on the others at first, then build them back up. That's why, when you take that first step back from your dog, adding **distance,** you should cut the **duration** of the stay.

6. Now your dog has mastered the Stay with you alone, move the training on so that he learns to do the same with distractions. Have someone walk into the room, or squeak a toy or bounce a ball once. A rock-solid stay is mostly a matter of working slowly and patiently to start with. Don't go too fast, the ideal scenario is that your Pug never breaks out of the Stay position until you release him. If he does get up, take a breather and then give him a short refresher, starting at a point easier than whatever you were working on when he cracked. If you think he's tired or had enough, leave it for the day and come back later – just finish off on a positive note by giving one very easy command you know he will obey, followed by a treat reward.

Don't use the "Stay" command in situations where it is unpleasant for your Pug. For instance, avoid telling him to stay as you close the door behind you on your way to work. Finally, don't use Stay to keep a dog in a scary situation.

Clicker Training

Clicker training is a method of training that uses a sound - a click - to tell an animal when he does something right. The clicker is a tiny plastic box held in the palm of your hand, with a metal tongue that you push quickly to make the sound.

 The clicker creates an efficient language between a human trainer and a trainee. First, a trainer teaches a dog that every time he hears the clicking sound, he gets a treat. Once the dog understands that clicks are always followed by treats, the click becomes a powerful reward.

When this happens, the trainer can use the click to mark the instant the animal performs the right behaviour. For example, if a trainer wants to teach a dog to sit, she'll click the instant his rump hits the floor and then deliver a tasty treat. With repetition, the dog learns that sitting earns rewards.

So the 'click' takes on huge meaning. To the animal it means: "What I was doing the moment my trainer clicked, **that's** what she wants me to do!" The clicker in animal training is like the winning buzzer on a game show that tells a contestant she's just won the money! Through the clicker, the trainer communicates precisely with the dog, and that speeds up training.

Although the clicker is ideal because it makes a unique, consistent sound, you do need a spare hand to hold it. For that reason, some trainers prefer to keep both hands free and instead use a one-syllable word like "Yes!" or "Good!" to mark the desired behaviour. In the steps below, you can substitute the word in place of the click to teach your pet what the sound means.

It's easy to introduce the clicker to your Pug. Spend half an hour or so teaching him that the sound of the click means "Treat!" Here's how:

1. Sit and watch TV or read a book with your dog in the room. Have a container of treats within reach.

2. Place one treat in your hand and the clicker in the other. (If your dog smells the treat and tries to get it by pawing, sniffing, mouthing or barking at you, just close your hand around the treat and wait until he gives up and leaves you alone.)

3. Click once and immediately open your hand to give your dog the treat. Put another treat in your closed hand and resume watching TV or reading. Ignore your dog.

4. Several minutes later, click again and offer another treat.

5. Continue to repeat the click-and-treat combination at varying intervals, sometimes after one minute, sometimes after five minutes. Make sure you vary the time so that your dog doesn't know exactly when the next click is coming. Eventually, he'll start to turn toward you and look expectant when he hears the click—which means he understands that the sound of the clicker means a treat is coming his way.

If your dog runs away when he hears the click, you can make the sound softer by putting it in your pocket or wrapping a towel around your hand that's holding the clicker. You can also try using a different sound, like the click of a retractable pen or the word "Yes."

Clicker Training Basics

Once your dog seems to understand the connection between the click and the treat, you're ready to get started.

1. Click just once, right when your pet does what you want him to do. Think of it like pressing the shutter of a camera to take a picture of the behaviour.

2. Remember to follow every click with a treat. After you click, deliver the treat to your pet's mouth **as quickly as possible.**

3. It's fine to switch between practising two or three behaviours within a session, but work on one behaviour at a time. For example, say you're teaching your Pug to sit, lie down and raise his paw. You can do 10 repetitions of sit and take a quick play break. Then do 10 repetitions of down, and take another quick break. Then do 10 repetitions of stay, and so on. Keep training sessions short and stop before you or your dog gets tired of the game.

4. End training sessions on a good note, when your dog has succeeded with what you're working on. If necessary, ask him to do something you know he can do well at the end of a session.

Collar and Lead Training

Your Pug has to be trained to get used to a collar or harness and lead (leash) and then he has to be taught to walk nicely on the lead. Teaching these manners can be challenging because Pugs can be stubborn and they don't necessarily want to walk at the same pace as you.

Firstly, you have to get him used to the collar and/or harness and lead – some dogs don't mind them, some will try to fight it, while others will slump to the floor like you have hung a two-ton weight around their necks! You need to be patient and calm and proceed at a pace comfortable to him; don't fight him and force the collar on.

1. The secret to getting a collar is to buy one that fits your puppy now - not one he is going to grow into - so choose a small lightweight one that he will hardly notice. A big collar like the one pictured may be too heavy and frightening for him. You can buy one with clips to start with, just put it on and clip it together, rather than fiddling with buckles, which can be scary when he's wearing a collar for the first time. Stick to the principle of positive reward-based training - treats not threats - and give him a treat once the collar is on, not after you have taken it off. Then gradually increase the length of time you leave the collar on.

    IMPORTANT: If you leave your dog in a crate, or leave him alone in the house, take off the collar. He is not used to it and it may get caught on something, causing panic or injury to your dog.

    So put the collar on when there are other things that will occupy him, like when he is going outside to be with you, or in the home when you are interacting with him. Or put it on at mealtimes or when you are doing some basic training. Don't put the collar on too tight, you want him to forget it's there. If he scratches the collar, get his attention by encouraging him to follow you or play with a toy - Pugs love to play - so he forgets the irritation.

2. Once your puppy is happy wearing the collar, introduce the lead. An extending or retractable one is not particularly suitable for starting off with, as they are not very strong and no good for training him to walk close. Buy a fixed-length lead. Start off in the house, don't try to go out and about straight away. Think of the lead as a safety device to stop him running off, not something to drag him around with. You want a Pug that doesn't pull, so don't start by pulling him around. You definitely don't want to get into a tug of war contest.

3. Attach the lead to the collar and give him a treat while you put it on. The minute it is attached, use the treats (instead of pulling on the lead) to lure him beside you, so that he gets used to walking with the collar and lead. As well as using treats you can also make good use of toys to do exactly the same thing - especially if your dog has a favourite. Walk around the house with the lead on and lure him forwards with the toy. It might feel a bit odd but it's a good way for your pup to develop a positive relationship with the collar and lead with the minimum of fuss. Act as though it's the most natural thing in the world for you to walk around the house or apartment with your dog on a lead – and just hope that the neighbours aren't watching!

Some dogs react the moment you attach the lead and they feel some tension on it – a bit like when a horse is being broken in for the first time. Drop the lead and allow him to run round the house or yard, dragging it after him, but be careful he doesn't get tangled and hurt himself. Try to make him forget about it by playing or starting a short fun training routine with treats. Treats are a huge distraction for most Pugs. While he is concentrating on the new task, occasionally pick up the lead and call him to you. Do it gently and in an encouraging tone.

4. The most important thing is to never pull on the lead. If it is gets tight, just lure him back beside you with a treat or a toy while walking. All you're doing is getting him to move around beside you. Remember to keep your hand down (the one holding the treat or toy) so your dog doesn't get the habit of jumping up at you. If you feel he is getting stressed when walking outside on a lead, try putting treats along the route you'll be taking to turn this into a rewarding game: good times are ahead... That way he learns to focus on what's ahead of him with curiosity and not fear.

Take collar and lead training slowly, give your Pug time to process all this new information about what the lead is and does. Let him gain confidence in you, and then in the lead and himself. Some dogs can sit and decide not to move. If this happens, walk a few steps away, go down on one knee and encourage him to come to you using a treat, then walk off again.

For some pups, the collar and lead can be restricting and they will react with resistance. Some dogs are perfectly happy to walk alongside you off-lead, but behave differently when they have one on. Proceed in tiny steps if that is what your puppy is happy with, don't over face him, but stick at it if you are met with resistance. With training, your puppy **will** learn to walk nicely on a lead, it is just a question of when, not if.

Walking on a Lead

Some Pugs can pull like steam trains and if you don't want to get dragged round your neighbourhood, it is essential yours is trained to walk nicely - the sooner the better. If you live in an apartment, you may have to put your dog on a lead every time he leaves home. When you are both ready, pick up the lead, but don't try and get him to walk to heel straight away – it's one step at a time, literally.

A training collar can be very useful in getting a dog to walk to heel in a short space of time, although some Pug owners are happy using one due to the breed's short necks and restricted airways. The training collar is half chain, half leather or nylon (pictured), so that when you pull the lead sharply, it tightens around the dog's neck, but only to a point. It is much less severe than a choke collar.

There are different methods, but we have found the following one to be successful for quick results. Initially the lead should be kept fairly loose. Have a treat in your hand as you walk, it will encourage your dog to sniff the treat as he walks alongside. He will not pull ahead, as he will want to remain near the treat. Give him the command **Walk** or **Heel** and then proceed with the treat in your hand, keep giving him a treat every few steps initially, then gradually extend the time between treats. Eventually, you should be able to walk with your hand comfortably at your side, periodically (every minute or so) reaching into your pocket to grab a treat to reward your dog.

If your dog starts pulling ahead, first give him a warning, by saying **No** or **Easy,** or a similar command. If he slows down, give him a treat. But if he continues to pull ahead so that your arm becomes fully extended, give the lead a sharp jerk by pulling swiftly backwards and upwards. You need to move your arm forward a few inches to give yourself the slack on the lead to jerk back. (Make sure your action is a sharp jab and not a slower pull.) You may need to do this a couple of times before the dog slows down. Your Pug will not like the sensation, but soon realises that this is what happens when he pulls ahead. How much pressure you apply depends on the individual dog. If your Pug is sensitive, you will need only slight force, if he's a bit more single minded or stubborn, he'll need a sharper jab. Be sure to quickly reward him with treats and praise any time he doesn't pull and walks with you with the lead slack. If you have a lively young pup who is dashing all over the place on the lead, try starting training when he is already tired - after a play or exercise session.

If you are worried about pulling on your Pug's collar, there are a couple of other options. Many Pug owners prefer a body harness instead of a collar, but bear in mind that harnesses are pretty useless for training a dog to walk to heel. You might consider using a training collar for a short space of time and then switching to a harness.

Another option is the 'suitcase leash' in which a leash is wrapped around the dog like a harness, it exerts some pressure on the body to encourage the dog to stop pulling. Instructions on how to use the suitcase leash can be found at the Pug Village online forum at http://bit.ly/1DcUoco

Puppy Biting

Pug puppies spend a great deal of time chewing, playing, and investigating objects. All of these normal activities involve them using their mouths and their needle-sharp teeth. Like babies, this is how they investigate the world. When puppies play with people, they often bite, chew and mouth on people's hands, limbs and clothing. Play biting is normal for puppies, they do it all the time with their littermates. They bite moving targets with their sharp teeth; it's a great game. But when

they arrive in your home, they have to be taught that human skin is sensitive and body parts are not suitable material for biting. Biting is never acceptable, not even from a small dog or puppy.

As a puppy grows and feels more confident in his surroundings, he may become slightly more aggressive and his bites may hurt someone – especially if you have children or elderly people at home. Make sure every time you have a play session, you have a soft toy nearby and when he starts to chew your hand or feet, clench your fingers (or toes!) to make it more difficult and distract him with a soft toy in your other hand. Keep the game interesting by moving the toy around or rolling it around in front of him. (He may be too young to fetch it back if you throw it.) He may continue to chew you, but will eventually realize that the toy is far more interesting and lively than your boring hand.

If he becomes over-excited and too aggressive with the toy, if he growls a lot, stop playing with him and **walk away**. Although it might be quite cute and funny now, you don't want your Pug doing this as an adult. Remember, if not checked, any unwanted behaviour traits will continue into adulthood, when you certainly don't want him to bite a child's hand – even accidentally.

When you walk away, don't say anything or make eye or physical contact with your puppy. Simply ignore him, this is extremely effective and often works within a few days. If your pup is more persistent and tries to bite your legs as you walk away, thinking this is another fantastic game, stand still and ignore him. If he still persists, tell him "**No!**" in a very stern voice, then praise him when he lets go. If you have to physically remove him from your trouser leg or shoe, leave him alone in the room for a while and ignore his demands for attention if he starts barking.

Many Pugs are very sensitive and another method which can be very successful is to make a sharp cry of **"Ouch!"** when your pup bites your hand – even when it doesn't hurt. This worked very well for us. Your pup may well jump back in amazement, surprised that he has hurt you.

Divert your attention from your puppy to your hand. He will probably try to get your attention or lick you as a way of saying sorry. Praise him for stopping biting and continue with the game. If he bites you again, repeat the process. A sensitive Pug will soon stop biting you. You may also think about keeping the toys you use to play with your puppy separate from other toys. That way he will associate certain toys with having fun with you and will work harder to please you.

Pugs love playing with toys and you can use this to your advantage by teaching your dog how to play nicely with you and the toy and then by using play time as a reward for good behaviour.

GENERAL NOTE: Wait until your puppy or young dog is tired before starting any form of training, it will be much more effective.

CREDIT: With thanks to the American Society for the Prevention of Cruelty to Animals for assistance with parts of this chapter. The ASPCA has a great deal of good advice and training tips on its website at: http://www.aspca.org/pet-care/virtual-pet- behaviourist/dog- behaviour/training-your-dog

10. Pug Health

There is not a single breed of dog without a genetic weakness. Most breeds have not just one, but several ailments that they are more likely to inherit than other breeds.

For example, German Shepherds are more prone to hip problems than some other breeds, and 30% of Dalmatians have problems with their hearing. If you get a German Shepherd or a Dalmatian, your dog will not automatically suffer from these issues, but he or she will statistically be more likely to have them than a breed with no genetic history of the complaint.

Although many live long and healthy lives, for a small dog the Pug is generally regarded as an expensive breed when it comes to pet insurance and veterinary bills. This is not uncommon for

flat-faced breeds, and is a factor which should be taken into account.

The health of individual Pugs varies tremendously, some poor Pugs are destined to be plagued with health problems throughout their lives, while others enjoy long, fit and active lives lasting well over a decade.

Even though the Pug's flat face gives the breed an extremely appealing look, it is often the Pugs with the longer noses and legs and lighter, more athletic bodies which can avoid some of the more common health issues, such as breathing, eye and joint problems.

You can't see inside your Pug to know if he or she has inherited any internal defects or dispositions, but you can reduce this risk by buying from a good breeder, seeing the parents (or at least the mother) and asking to see all of their and the puppy's health certificates.

In the US the Orthopedic Foundation for Animals (OFA) carried out a Pug health survey, more than 800 owners responded and the results are most interesting. In answer to the question: "What do you consider the top health problems facing Pugs?" 47% of owners answered brachycephalic syndrome/trouble breathing.

The next concern for owners was rear end ataxia weakness (25%), followed by pigmentary keratitis - now called pigmentary keratopathy (23.6%), PDE (Pug Dog Encephalitis)/NME (19%), dental disease (15%) and cancer (13.4%). Other health issues were, in order: other diseases, hip dysplasia, patellar luxation, vaccine reactions, autoimmune disease, liver shunts and heart disease.

What the Breeders Say

The New Pug Handbook conducted its own survey among breeders and this is what some of them said. **Linda Wright**, Wright's Pugs, Michigan, USA: "PDE is a large threat. Also, while I can see that it's very popular to breed the flattest face and the shortest nose, breathing difficulties are common (pinched nostrils, elongated pallet). I'd like to see the trend reverse some to create a little more muzzle."

Saran Evans, Sephina Pugs, Carmarthenshire, UK: "Hemivertebrae is a problem within the breed, I X-ray all my Pugs for this condition, but sadly the majority do not. In its most severe form it causes paralysis in hind limbs and incontinence, and ultimately the Pug is euthanized. Many Pugs have a mild form of Hemivertebrae but do not exhibit clinical symptoms, therefore X-raying prior to breeding is absolutely essential to prevent this condition affecting future generations. Patella Sub-Luxation is a problem not only affecting Pugs, but many Toy breeds. My Pugs are screened for this using the Putnam Patella scoring system.

"Pugs are also susceptible to PDE (Pug Dog Encephalitis). This nasty condition causes Pugs to have repeated seizures and display other neurological symptoms (head banging etc.). Although research into this condition is relatively in its infancy, there is a test available which shows whether your Pug is more or less likely to develop or pass this condition on."

Catherine Jones-Kyle, Dixie Darlings, Tennessee, USA: "PDE - it's a horrible ugly disease, it strikes hard and fast. The sad thing is that it can be prevented if breeders do their research and get the genetic tests done, and above all else breed with the correct knowledge, it's widely available, so not running the test is just irresponsible." She added that keeping a dog trim helps to reduce breathing problems.

Deborah Beecham, Fizzlewick Pugs, South Wales, UK: "There are many health issues with Pugs, I think we are seeing these problems today because of the limited gene pool several decades ago where the same stud dogs produced huge quantities of litters. They can be prone to Hemivertebrae and joint problems, such as luxation of the patella and hip dysplasia. They can also develop neurological problems like PDE."

Holly Attwood, Taftazini, Sheffield, UK, endorsed this view of the importance of health testing: "There are various hereditary conditions that are still early on in their research. However, all Pugs that are being bred from should most certainly be X-rayed clear of Hemivertebrae and tested for Pug Dog Encephalitis (PDE). Additional health concerns that can be a problem include luxating patellas, eye and breathing problems."

Melanie Clark, Pugginpugs, UK: "The most common issues with Pugs are their eyes and breathing. Protruding eyes can scratch easily or get dust particles trapped within the lids and cause eye ulcers, so eyes should be checked on a daily basis, also their breathing can be restricted by stenotic nares, where the nostrils are almost closed.

"Another condition related to breathing is elongated pallet. This can cause backward sneezing in which rubbing the throat can sometimes help - backward (or reverse) sneezing usually comes on when they get over-excited. The most common threat to the breed is PDE, inflammation of the nervous system, which is fatal."

Roberta Kelley-Martin, of HRH Pugs, California, believes that rear end ataxia (the loss of full control of bodily movements) is a distressing and major issue, particularly with older dogs: "It's extremely heart-breaking to have a dog that is fully cognisant of their surroundings and wants to interact normally, but is unable to walk and has lost the ability to control their bladder and bowels.

"Their eyes are a major concern as well as their nose roll. Keeping a Pug from injuring an eye is of utmost importance. I've removed the temptation of my Pugs of rummaging around the base of my roses by fencing off the garden. I keep other plants trimmed up and safe for them, too. I've had eye injuries from Pugs playing together. So, even with being very careful with things that could poke their eyes, their housemates have caused injuries.

"Some Pugs need their nose roll cleaned daily, while others can go every other day or more. It's best to get in the habit of cleaning every one every day. They get used to being handled and their nose roll cleaned and you get in the habit of cleaning.

"Pug Dog Encephalitis is something to be aware of. When I first came to the breed, there was no genetic testing for PDE. Now, with the advent of the genetic marker being identified, and with the DNA test kits so easily acquired and used, we can safely breed knowing the outcome of the puppies."

Sue Wragg, Glammarags Pugs, UK: "Allegedly the main threat is Hemivertibrae, but it is not seen so much these days as most responsible breeders try and do as many health tests as possible for it. Sadly it occurs now and again even using two health tested parents, so much research is being done to identify the genetic identifiers for this disease. Pugs' eyes have been problematical in the past, but as the Kennel Club has recently changed the standard, Pugs' eyes are no longer so bulbous."

J. Candy Schlieper, Candyland Pugs, Ohio: "I think the biggest threat to the health of the breed is the fact that we have bred them so flat-faced that we are now seeing more breathing issues, as well as eye issues from the nose roll pushing on the lower lids of the eyes. I also think we need to find out what is causing lung lobe torsions in some of these dogs and get the word out to all vets and owners as to what to look for, how to diagnose and how surgery can save their lives."

One of the concerns raised by many breeders was the Pug's intolerance to heat, which is covered later in this chapter. Roberta Kelley-Martin added: "Obviously the issue of being a brachycephalic breed is a major concern here in sunny California. It actually is a concern anywhere that a Pug is mismanaged while out-of-doors or allowed to play too hard for too long and becomes over exerted. Pugs do not know when enough is enough. They will play until they become too hot to dissipate the heat naturally themselves. Owners must be the play police and halt too much play."

The other issue mentioned by most breeders was the care that owners should take to avoid Pugs damaging their prominent eyes. Rough play with children, adults or larger dogs should be avoided and houses and yards or gardens should be Pug-proofed. Fence off any areas containing sharp, low plants or other potential hazards. See more in **Chapter 5 Bringing Your Pup Home.**

Deborah Beecham added: "One of the biggest day-to-day problems with Pugs is risk of injury to the eyes, which are large and round, so care must be taken around the garden with any bushes and shrubs that are sharp or prickly, and it helps to keep their nails nice and short if you have more than one, as they like to use their front paws to wrestle and play with each other."

This invaluable input from breeders who between them have hundreds of years of experience with the breed will give potential owners an idea of what potential health issues to look out for when selecting a puppy and new owners an insight into the extra care which needs to be taken with the breed to avoid injury or illness. Hopefully your Pug will be happy, healthy and long-lived. The aim is this chapter is not to scare you, but to give easy to understand information on some of the illnesses which can affect Pugs, explain why they occur and what to do if your dog is unlucky enough to have one.

All dogs have one of three shapes of head:

❖ Long and narrow (dolichocephalic), like a Borzoi, Afghan Hound, Saluki and Dachshund

❖ Wolf–like (mesaticephalic), or equally proportioned, in which the width of the dog's skull is similar to the length of the nasal cavity, like a Beagle, Border Collie, Cocker Spaniel or Labrador Retriever

❖ Short and broad (brachycephalic), like the Pug, all the Bulldog breeds and Dogue de Bordeaux

Pugs, along with other breeds including Bulldogs, Boxers, Boston Terriers, Cavalier King Charles Spaniels, Pekingese, Pugs, Lhasa Apsos, Shih Tzus and Bull Mastiffs, are all regarded as **brachycephalic** breeds of dog. "Brachy" means shortened and "cephalic" means head.

Over the years, successive breeding has led to the skull bones of these dogs being shortened to give the face and nose a "pushed in" appearance. This skull shape gives the dogs the characteristic cute flat face and short nose. Although this makes them appear attractive – and fans of the breed claim that the Pug is the most visually appealing of all dogs - it can also cause some major health issues. The shortened cranium means there is often not enough room inside for the soft, pink tissue and the breathing passages.

A brachycephalic head can lead to respiration, skin, eye, mating and birthing problems, as well as an intolerance to heat.

Points of Concern

Health problems with the brachycephalic dog breeds were highlighted in the BBC documentary **Pedigree Dogs Exposed** which investigated health and welfare issues caused by the breeding of some purebred dogs. It was aired on TV in the UK in 2008 and caused a stir around the world.

In it the Kennel Club (the UK's governing body for pedigree dogs which runs the prestigious dog show Crufts) was criticised for allowing breed standards, judging standards and breeding practices to compromise the health of pedigree (purebred) dogs. The BBC had previously broadcast the highly popular Crufts show for 42 years, but withdrew its coverage and has still not renewed it in an effort to persuade breeders to place more emphasis on the health of their puppies, rather than on just their physical appearance.

The Kennel Club lodged a complaint with broadcasting regulator, claiming unfair treatment and editing. However, due to strong public opinion, the KC later rolled out new health plans and reviewed standards for every breed. Three separate health reports were commissioned as a result of the programme. They concluded that current breeding practices were detrimental to the welfare of pedigree dogs and made various recommendations to the KC and UK breeders to improve pedigree dog health.

I was at Crufts this year and it is apparent that responsible breeders of the 200-and-odd breeds listed with the Kennel Club are making serious efforts to improve the health of pedigree dogs. At the show there was lots of information on each breed regarding potential inherited problems and the recommended health tests.

The change in the shape of the Pug has been less pronounced than with some other breeds, such as the Bulldog.

But even so, a modern Pug looks very different from his ancestor of two or even one hundred years ago when the breed had a longer muzzle and more open nostrils, longer legs and tail and a lighter body – as this painting of a female Pug from 1802 shows.

Following **Pedigree Dogs Exposed**, the Kennel Club set up its Breed Watch programme. The KC describes it as "*an 'early warning system' to identify points of concern for individual breeds. Its primary purpose is to enable anyone involved in the world of dogs, but in particular dog show judges, to find out about any breed specific conformational issues which may lead to health problems. These conditions are known as a 'point(s) of concern.'*"

All breeds are in one of three categories:

1 Breeds with no current points of concern reported

2 Breeds with Breed Watch points of concern

3 Breeds where some dogs have visible conditions or exaggerations that can cause pain or discomfort (previously known as High Profile)

The following breeds are listed in Category Three: Pug, Basset Hound, Bloodhound, Bulldog, Chow Chow, Clumber Spaniel, Dogue de Bordeaux, German Shepherd, Mastiff, Neapolitan Mastiff, Pekingese, Shar-Pei, and Saint Bernard. The KC states: "The Kennel Club works closely with the clubs for these breeds in identifying key issues to be addressed within the breed, obtaining the opinion of breed experts on the issues identified, advising on how breed clubs can effectively address health and conformational issues and investigating how the Kennel Club can assist."

The points of concern listed below for the Pug are derived from a combination of health surveys, veterinary advice, a meeting of Kennel Club Group judges, feedback from judges at shows or consultation with individual breed club(s)/councils via the breed health coordinators.

* ❖ Difficulty breathing
* ❖ Excessive nasal folds
* ❖ Excessively prominent eyes
* ❖ Hair loss or scarring from previous dermatitis
* ❖ Incomplete blink
* ❖ Pinched nostrils
* ❖ Significantly overweight
* ❖ Signs of dermatitis in skin folds
* ❖ Sore eyes due to damage or poor eyelid conformation
* ❖ Unsound movement

These are features you should be on the lookout for when selecting a Pug puppy or an adult dog. Bear in mind that all Pug puppies should be roly-poly and excessive weight does not develop until later, when obesity becomes one of the main triggers for poor health in Pugs. All of the breeders we contact stressed the importance of good breeding and health testing. There is more information on how to select a healthy Pug in **Chapter 4 Getting a Pug Puppy.**

Pug Insurance

The best time to get pet insurance is BEFORE you bring your dog home and before any health issues develop. Don't wait until you need to seek veterinary help – bite the bullet and take out annual insurance. If you can afford it take out life cover. This may be more expensive, but will cover your dog throughout his or her lifetime - including for recurring problems such as respiratory, eye, back or joint issues.

Insuring a healthy puppy or adult dog is the only sure fire way to ensure vets' bills are covered before anything unforeseen happens - and you'd be a rare owner indeed if you didn't use your policy several times during your dog's lifetime. In the UK, pet insurers Petplan has teamed up with Bought By Many to launch a pet insurance policy designed specifically for Pugs. Owners first have to join the company's Pug Group, which currently has more than 1,000 members. With a puppy costing anywhere between £1,200-£2,000, ($1,800-$3,000), they have enhanced the Covered for Life Classic plan to help with key issues such as theft.

Petplan says: "There are three key reasons why pug owners - or pug parents - can benefit from joining this group to buy pet insurance for their pug. Firstly, there are several breed-specific pug health problems which some insurers exclude from pet insurance cover.

"Secondly, owing to a combination of their sociable and inquisitive temperament, their diminutive size, and their financial value, regrettably pug puppies are a popular target for thieves. And thirdly, the growing number of pugs means there is an opportunity for you to club together with other pug owners and use your combined buying-power to get a better deal on pet insurance."

Steven Mendel, CEO and Co-Founder of Bought By Many added: "In the UK, more people search online for 'pug insurance' than for any other breed of dog – and insurance that covers the risk of theft is a must". https://boughtbymany.com/offers/pug-insurance

Increasingly, Pugs are at risk theft from criminals, including organised gangs. With the cost of pedigree dogs rising, dognapping more than quadrupled in the UK between 2010 and 2015, with some 50 dogs a day being stolen. Some 49% of dogs are snatched from owners' gardens and 13% from peoples' homes. If you take out a policy, check that theft is included. Although nothing can ever replace your beloved Pug, a good insurance policy will ensure you are not out of pocket.

In the US, Consumers' Advocate listed the top 10 pet insurance companies taking into account reimbursement policies, coverage and customers' reviews. Here is their league table: Healthy Pets, 2. PetPlan, 3. Trupanion, 4. Embrace, 5. PetFirst, 6. Pets Best, 7. VPI Pet Insurance, 8. Pet Partners, 9. ASPCA Pet Health Insurance, 10. Pet Premium.

We hope that the information in this chapter will help you to recognise symptoms of the main conditions affecting Pugs and enable you to take prompt action should the need arise. There are also a number of measures you can take to prevent or reduce the chances of certain problems developing, including keeping your dog's weight in check, giving him at least one or more daily walks, face cleaning, and not leaving him or her in very hot or very cold places.

Three Golden Tips for New Pug Owners

There are three golden tips for anybody thinking of getting a Pug which will in all likelihood save you a lot of money and heartache.

Tip Number 1: Buy a well-bred puppy

Scientists have come to realise the important role that genetics play in determining a person's long-term health. Well, the same is true of dogs. This means ensuring you get your puppy from a reputable breeder who selects the parent dogs based on a number of factors, the main ones of which are health and temperament. A good breeder selects their breeding stock based on:

- **health history**
- **bloodline**
- **conformation**
- **temperament**

If you talk to owners who have healthy, happy Pugs, the one factor that most of them have in common is that they did their homework, spent a lot of time researching the breed and specifically breeders before taking the plunge.

Although puppies are expensive, many good, responsible breeders do not make a lot of money on the sale of their puppies, often incurring high bills for health checks and veterinary fees. Breeding Pugs is a specialised art and the main concern of a good breeder is to improve the breed through producing healthy puppies with good temperaments.

It's better to spend time beforehand choosing a puppy which has been properly bred than to spend a great deal of time and money later as your wonderful pet bought from an online advert or pet shop develops health problems due to poor breeding, not to mention the heartache that causes. As the English upper classes say (in a very posh accent): *"There is no substitute for good breeding, darling!"*

So spend some time to find a reputable breeder and read **Chapter 4. Getting a Pug Puppy** for information on finding a good breeder and knowing the right questions to ask.

- Don't buy a puppy from a pet shop. No reputable breeder allows their pups to end up in pet shops. You will in all probability be buying a Pug with questionable heritage and breeding – and you'll be extremely lucky if this does not result in problems at some point in the dog's life.

- Never buy a puppy from a small ad on the internet unless you can personally visit the owners and get the full details of the pup's background, parents and health history.

- Never buy a pup or adult Pug unseen with a credit card deposit – you are storing up trouble and expense for yourself.

Tip Number 2: Get pet insurance as soon as you get your dog

Don't wait until he or she has a health issue and needs to see a veterinarian. Most insurers will exclude all pre-existing conditions on their policies. For example, if your Pug needs soft palate surgery (see the section on 'Elongated Soft Palate' later in this chapter) this could cost you anything from £500 to £1,600 in the UK or $750 to around $2,500 in the US. Surgery to correct breathing problems can be even more expensive.

When choosing insurance check the small print to make sure that any condition which might occur is covered, and that if the problem is a chronic (long term) or recurring one, then it will continue to be covered year after year. When you are working out costs for getting a Pug, factor in the annual or monthly cost of good pet insurance and trips to a vet for check-ups, annual vaccinations, etc.

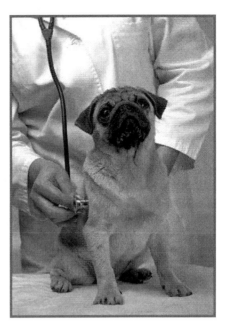

Tip Number 3: Find a vet that understands the Pug

This is a breed which requires specialist veterinary care. Like all brachycephalic breeds, Pugs - particularly young ones - can have an adverse reaction to anaesthesia and surgery should not be undertaken lightly. You could waste a lot of time and money by visiting a vet who is not familiar with Pugs and their specialist healthcare requirements. If you already have a vet, check if he or she is experienced with Toy and brachycephalic breeds, if not you'd be advised to switch to one who is.

We all want our dogs to be healthy -so how can you tell if yours is? Well, our **Top Signs** are a good start. Here are some positive things to look for in a healthy Pug**.**

Top 13 Signs of a Healthy Pug

1. **Breathing** – many Pugs snuffle, snore and make other strange sounds - but they should not pant excessively, nor should their breathing be excessively noisy or laboured when excited or exercising. Regular, quiet breathing is a good sign.

2. **Coats** – these are easy-to-monitor indicators of a healthy dog. A Pug has a fine, short and smooth coat which should be glossy. It sheds right throughout the year. A dull, lifeless coat, a discoloured one or a coat which loses excessive hair can be a sign that something is amiss.

3. **Skin** – This should be smooth without redness. (Normal Pug skin pigment can be pink or black). If your dog is scratching, licking or biting himself a lot, he may have a condition which needs addressing before he makes it worse. Open sores, scales, scabs or growths can be a sign of a problem. Signs of fleas, ticks and other external parasites should be treated immediately.

4. **Ears** – If you are choosing a puppy, gently clap your hands behind the pup (not so loud as to frighten him) to see if he reacts. If not, this may be a sign of deafness. Ear infections are a problem with many breeds of dog and the Pug is no different. The folded ear flaps can hide dirt and dust and should be inspected regularly for infection or ear mites as part of your normal grooming process. An unpleasant smell, redness or inflammation are signs of infection.

5. **Mouth** – Gums should be a healthy pink or with black pigmentation. A change in colour can be an indicator of a health issue. Paleness or whiteness can be a sign of anaemia or lack of oxygen due to heart or breathing problems. Blue gums or tongue area sign that your Pug is not breathing properly. Red, inflamed gums can be a sign of gingivitis or other tooth disease. Again, your dog's breath should smell OK. Young dogs will have sparkling white teeth, whereas older dogs will have darker teeth, but they should not have any hard white, yellow, green or brown bits.

6. **Weight** – Pugs are chunky dogs with the Kennel Clubs giving the ideal weight as 14 to 18lbs. However the sturdiness does not excuse obesity, which is bad for any dog as it causes strain on joints and organs. Dogs may have weight problems due to factors such as diet, lack of exercise, allergies, diabetes, thyroid or other problems. A Pug has a deep chest and a general rule of thumb is that your dog's stomach should be above his rib cage when standing. If his stomach hangs below, he is overweight or he may have a pot belly, which can also be a symptom of other conditions.

7. **Nose** – a dog's nose is an indicator of health symptoms. It should normally be moist and cold to the touch as well as free from clear, watery secretions. Any yellow, green or foul smelling discharge is not normal - in younger dogs this can be a sign of canine distemper. The Kennel Clubs state that a Pug's nose should be black.

8. **Eyes** – a healthy Pug's eyes are dark and shiny (not blue) with no yellowish tint. The area around the eyeball (the conjunctiva) should be a healthy pink; paleness could be a sign of underlying problems. A red swelling in the corner of one or both eyes could by a sign of cherry eye. There should be no thick, green or yellow discharge from the eyes. A cloudy eye could well be a sign of cataracts.

9. **Temperature** – The normal temperature of a dog is 101°F. Excited or exercising dogs may run a slightly higher temperature. Anything above 103°F or below 100°F should be checked out. The exceptions are female dogs about to give birth that will often have a temperature of 99°F. If you take your dog's temperature, make sure he or she is relaxed and **_always_** use a purpose-made canine thermometer.

10. **Attitude** – a generally positive attitude and personality is the sign of good health. Pugs are perky, enthusiastic dogs, so symptoms of illness may include one or all of the following: not eating food, a general lack of interest in his or her surroundings, lethargy and sleeping a lot (even more than normal). The important thing is to look out for any behaviour which is out of the ordinary for your individual dog.

11. **Energy** – The Pug is generally regarded as a dog with low to medium energy levels, although some are more active in short bursts – especially puppies and adolescents. Your dog should have good energy levels with fluid and pain-free movements. Lethargy or lack of energy – if it is not the dog's normal character – could be a sign of an underlying problem.

12. **Stools** –poo, poop, business, faeces – call it what you will - it's the stuff that comes out of the less appealing end of your Pug on a daily basis! It should be firm and brown, not runny, with no signs of worms or parasites. Watery stools or a dog not eliminating regularly are both signs of an upset stomach or other ailments. If it continues for a day or two, consult your vet. If puppies have diarrhoea they need checking out much quicker as they can soon dehydrate.

13. **Smell** – your dog should have a pleasant "doggie" smell. If there is a musty, "off" or generally unpleasant odour coming from his body, it could be a sign of yeast infection. There can be a number of reasons for this, such as his ears or wrinkles not being cleaned properly or an allergy to a certain type of food. You need to get to the root of the problem.

So now you know some of the signs of a healthy dog – what are the signs of an unhealthy one? There are many different symptoms that can indicate that your beloved canine companion isn't feeling great. If you don't yet know your dog, his habits, temperament and behaviour patterns, then we recommend spending some time getting acquainted with him.

What are his normal character and temperament? Lively or sedate, playful or serious, a joker or an introvert, happy to be left alone or loves to be with people, a keen appetite or a fussy eater? How often does he empty his bowels, does he ever vomit? (Dogs will often eat grass to make themselves sick, this is perfectly normal and a canine's natural way of cleansing his digestive system.)

You may think your Pug can't talk, **but he can!** If you really know your dog, his character and habits, then he CAN tell you when he's not well. He does this by changing his patterns. Some symptoms are physical, some emotional and others are behavioural. It's important for you to be able to recognise these changes as soon as possible. Early treatment can be the key to keeping a simple problem from snowballing into a serious illness. If you think your Pug is unwell, it is useful to keep an accurate and detailed account of his symptoms to give to the vet. This will help him or her correctly diagnose and effectively treat your dog. Most canine illnesses are detected through a combination of signs and symptoms.

Five Vital Signs of Illness

1. Temperature

A new-born puppy will have a temperature of 94-97ºF. This will reach the normal adult body temperature of 101ºF at about four weeks old. Anything between 100ºF and 102ºF-103ºF is normal. A dog's temperature is normally taken via the rectum. If you do this, be very careful. It's easier if you get someone to hold your dog while you do this.

Digital thermometers are a good choice, but **only use one specifically made for rectal use,** as normal glass thermometers can easily break off in the rectum. Ear thermometers are now available, making the task much easier, although they can be expensive and don't suit all dogs' ears. (Walmart has started stocking them). Remember that exercise or excitement can cause the temperature to rise by 2ºF to 3ºF when your dog is actually in good health, so better to wait until he is relaxed and calm before taking his temperature. If it is above or below the norms, give your vet a call.

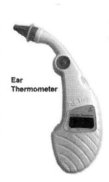
Ear Thermometer

2. Respiratory Rate

Another symptom of canine illness is a change in breathing patterns. This varies a lot depending on the size and weight of the dog. An adult dog will have a respiratory rate of 15-25 breaths per minute when resting. You can easily check this by counting your dog's breaths for a minute with a stopwatch handy. Don't do this if he is panting – it doesn't count.

3. Heart Rate
You can feel your Pug's heartbeat by placing your hand on his lower ribcage – just behind the elbow. Don't be alarmed if the heartbeat seems irregular compared to a human.

It IS irregular in some dogs. Your Pug will probably love the attention, so it should be quite easy to check his heartbeat. Just lay him on his side and bend his left front leg at the elbow, bring the elbow in to his chest and place your fingers or a stethoscope on this area and count the beats.

> ➤ **Small dogs like Pugs have a normal rate of 90 to 140 beats per minute**
> ➤ **Medium-sized dogs have a normal rate of 80 to 120 beats per minute**
> ➤ **Big dogs have a normal rate of 70 to 120 beats per minute**
> ➤ **A young puppy has a heartbeat of around 220 beats per minute**
> ➤ **An older dog has a slower heartbeat**

4. Behaviour Changes

Classic symptoms of illness are any inexplicable behaviour changes. If there has NOT been a change in the household atmosphere, such as another new pet, a new baby, moving home or the absence of a family member, then the following symptoms may well be a sign that all is not well:

- ❖ Depression
- ❖ Anxiety and/or trembling
- ❖ Falling or stumbling
- ❖ Loss of appetite
- ❖ Walking in circles
- ❖ Being more vocal - grunting, whining and whimpering
- ❖ Aggression – Pugs are normally extremely friendly, so this can be a sign of ill health
- ❖ Tiredness - sleeping more than normal and/or not wanting to exercise
- ❖ Abnormal posture

5. Breathing Patterns

Pugs are particularly susceptible to breathing problems due to their anatomy. Here are some signs to look out for:

- ❖ The belly and chest move when breathing
- ❖ Nostrils may flare open when breathing
- ❖ Breathing with an open mouth
- ❖ Breathing with the elbows sticking out from the body
- ❖ Neck and head are held low and out in front of the body
- ❖ Noisy breathing
- ❖ Fast breathing and shallow breaths
- ❖ Excessive panting

Your Pug may normally show some of these signs, but if any of them appear for the first time or worse than usual, you need to keep him under close watch for a few hours or even days. Quite often he will return to normal of his own accord. Like humans, dogs have off-days too.

If he is showing any of the above symptoms, then don't over-exercise him, and avoid stressful situations and hot or cold places. Make sure he has access to clean water. There are many other signals of ill health, but these are five of the most important. Keep a record for your vet. If your dog does need professional medical attention, most vets will want to know:

WHEN the symptoms first appeared in your dog

WHETHER they are getting better or worse, and

HOW FREQUENT the symptoms are. Are they intermittent, continuous or increasing?

We have highlighted some of the indicators of good and poor health to help you monitor your dog's wellbeing. Getting to know his or her character, habits and temperament will go a long way towards spotting the early signs of ill health. The next section looks in detail at some of the most common ailments affecting Pugs, with complicated medical terminology explained in simple terms. We also cover the symptoms and treatments of various conditions.

The Pug Dog Club of America supports the CHIC registry (Canine Health Information Center) and recommends all dogs used for breeding and exhibition be screened for the following health issues: Hip Dysplasia, Patellar Luxation, CERF Eye Examination (annually), Pug Dog Encephalitis (PDE). in stark contrast to the Kennel Club or UK breed club which lists no health tests for pugs.

While there are currently no recommended tests in the UK, The Pug Dog Club says: "We are committed to ensuring the health of our breed, which includes monitoring the breed's health, putting in place health programmes, supporting research and in providing education for breeders, owners and others involved with the breed."

Brachycephalic Upper Airway Obstruction Syndrome (BUAOS)

Brachycephalic breeds include Pugs, Bulldogs, French Bulldogs, Boxers, Boston Terriers, Pekingese, Lhasa Apsos, Shih Tzus and Bull Mastiffs.

The Pug's head has been successively bred shorter so that it is a lot less pointed than it was a century or two ago. However, the amount of soft tissue inside has remained the same. This includes the soft palate, the cartilage inside the nose and the tongue, which are all now crammed into a smaller space. In some cases, there is simply too much Pug on the inside. There is also a lack of nasal bone which causes the nostrils to become very narrow, like small slits instead of open holes.

The term BUAOS - also called Brachycephalic Airway Syndrome - is used to describe the range of abnormalities which result from this and includes an **elongated soft palate, stenotic nares, a hypoplastic trachea** and **everted laryngeal saccules**. A dog with this syndrome may have one or a combination of these conditions, with variable effects on his respiration.

An elongated soft palate (the soft part of the roof of the mouth) is too long for the short mouth and so partially blocks the entrance to the trachea (windpipe) at the back of the throat. Dogs with **stenotic nares** have nostrils which are too narrow, restricting the amount of air that can be inhaled. A

hypoplastic trachea (or **tracheal stenosis**) means that the windpipe is narrower than normal.

The knock-on effect of a dog struggling to breathe can create another problem. Unfortunately the increased effort creates a suction effect in the back of the throat at the opening to the windpipe. This opening into the windpipe is called the larynx (or voice box in people) and it has a tough cartilage frame which keeps it open wide.

However, constant suction in this area over a period of months or years can cause it to fold inwards, which narrows the airway even further and really does cause serious breathing difficulty. This secondary problem is called **laryngeal collapse**. The **laryngeal saccules** are small pouches just inside the larynx. They evert (turn outwards) causing a further obstruction of the airways.

Symptoms of BUOAS

- ❖ Loud snoring
- ❖ Noisy breathing – especially during excitement or exercise
- ❖ Panting
- ❖ Poor ability to exercise
- ❖ Intolerance to heat
- ❖ Choking on food
- ❖ Regurgitating
- ❖ Laboured breathing
- ❖ Blue gums or tongue
- ❖ Fainting

Affected dogs may also suffer from:

- ❖ Difficulty swallowing
- ❖ Strange body posture as the dog tries to breathe more efficiently
- ❖ Tooth or gum disease
- ❖ Increased eye problems
- ❖ Infections in the facial skin folds

The problem is that a large number of brachycephalic dogs may show a mild form of some of these symptoms in their daily lives. Some vets believe that our tolerance of what is acceptable in Pugs has shifted to think that the above signs are normal, which they are not. They are, however, all signs that the respiratory system is not functioning efficiently. Another problem for the stoic Pug is that, like his cousin the Bulldog, he has a high tolerance to pain. That, coupled with his good humour may hide the fact that he is in distress. So it's up to you to monitor him or her.

Veterinarians are keen to get the message out that **these symptoms are not normal** and if your Pug is displaying some of them then he needs help. If you are thinking of getting a puppy, do not choose one exhibiting any of the above symptoms.

Treatment -Fortunately there are things that can be done to reduce the breathing problems associated with this syndrome. Various forms of surgery can be carried out to help brachycephalic dogs breathe better. Although these treatments will not produce a normal airway, they improve the flow of air, helping dogs to breathe more easily and improving their quality of life and ability to exercise. Exercise is important to avoid obesity, which makes things much worse.

One of the most important factors in deciding outcomes is how early the problem(s) are diagnosed. Tackling breathing issues early in the Pug's life helps to reduce the amount of suction at the back of the throat and to prevent or delay the development of the dreaded laryngeal (voice box) collapse, for which there are only limited options.

The vet may have a good idea that BUAOS is the problem, based on symptoms, age and the fact that Pugs are prone to the condition. But before he or she can make a proper diagnosis, the dog will have to be examined under general anaesthetic – which is also not without risk for brachycephalic breeds. The vet may also take a biopsy (small tissue sample) and blood sample to check carbon dioxide and alkaline levels.

 A small flexible camera called an **endoscope** (pictured) may be used to examine the throat, larynx and possibly the windpipe. Many vets prefer to perform corrective surgery to remodel some of the soft tissue at the same time, so that the dog is only knocked out once. Dogs which still have excessive soft tissue have a higher risk of problems with anaesthesia. Your vet will discuss all of this with you.

Here are some of the options your vet may discuss with you:

An **elongated soft palate** can be surgically shortened so it no longer protrudes into the back of the throat.

Everted laryngeal saccules can be surgically removed to increase the size of the laryngeal airway.

Stenotic nares (pinched or narrow nostrils, pictured) can be surgically opened by removing a wedge of tissue from the nares allowing better airflow through the nose.

With today's laser technology some of these procedures can be performed with a minimal amount of bleeding and no need for stitches. The level of success depends on the age of the animal and when these procedures are performed. The earlier BUAOS is diagnosed and treated, the better, as the condition can worsen with time and cause other abnormalities.

Everted laryngeal saccules and a weakening of the windpipe can result when the dog has to breathe through a restrictive airway for a long time. If the veterinary surgeon can increase the size of the airway and decrease the inspiratory (breathing in) pressure before the airway is damaged, then the dog can breathe much easier.

The key here is to keep a lookout for the tell-tale signs and if you are at all worried that your dog is showing one or several of the symptoms, then consult a vet. The earlier BUOAS is diagnosed and treated, the better the outlook for your dog.

Eye Problems

Due to the extremely flat face and round, bulging eyes, a Pug's eyes have very little protection and are prone to injuries. Pugs are also prone to eye disease, and responsible breeders in the US have their breeding stock annually certified clear of eye problems by the Canine Eye Registry Foundation (CERF).

Common eye diseases are keratoconjunctivitis sicca (dry eye), pigmentary keratopathy, cataracts, entropion, progressive retinal atrophy (PRA) and trichiasis. Keratoconjunctivitis sicca and pigmentary keratopathy are the main health concerns of Pug Dog Club of America (PDCA) members.

Entropion

This is a condition in which the edge of the lower eyelid rolls inward, causing the dog's fur to rub the surface of the eyeball, or cornea. In rare cases the upper lid can also be affected, and one or both eyes may be involved. This painful condition is thought to be hereditary and is more commonly found in dog breeds with a wrinkled face, like the Pug and the Bulldog. Other affected breeds include the Chow Chow, Bloodhound, French Bulldog, Bull Mastiff, Great Dane, Rottweiler, Akita, Shar Pei, Spaniel, Poodle and Labrador.

The affected dog will scratch at his painful eye with his paws and this can lead to further injury. If your Pug is to suffer from entropion, he will usually show signs at or before his first birthday. You will notice that his eyes are red and inflamed and they will produce tears. He will probably squint.

The tears typically start off clear and can progress to a thick yellow or green mucus. If the entropion causes corneal ulcers, you might also notice a milky-white colour develop. This is caused by increased fluid which affects the clarity of the cornea. For your poor dog, the irritation is constant. Imagine how painful and uncomfortable it would be if you had permanent hairs touching your eyes. It makes my eyes water just thinking about it.

It's important to get your Pug to the vet as soon as you suspect entropion before he scratches his cornea and worsens the problem. The condition can cause scarring around the eyes or other issues which can jeopardise vision if left untreated. A vet will make the diagnosis after a painless and relatively simple inspection of your dog's eyes. But before he or she can diagnose entropion, they will have to rule out other issues, such as allergies, which might also be making your dog's eyes red and itchy. Some vets may delay surgery for young Pugs and treat the condition with medication until the dog's face is fully formed to avoid having to repeat the procedure later.

In mild cases, the vet may successfully prescribe eye drops, ointment or other medication. However, the most common treatment for more severe cases is a fairly straightforward surgical procedure to pin back the lower eyelid. Discuss the severity of the condition and all possible options with your vet before proceeding to surgery, as anaesthetic is not without risk for Pugs.

Dry Eye (Keratoconjunctivitis sicca)

KCS is the technical term for a condition also known as 'dry eye' caused by not enough tears being produced - and Pugs are particularly susceptible to it. With insufficient tears, a Pug's eyes can become irritated and the conjunctiva appears to be red. The eyes typically develop a thick, yellowy discharge. Infections are common as tears also have anti-bacterial and cleansing properties, and inadequate lubrication allows dust, pollen, etc. to accumulate. The nerves of these glands may also become damaged.

In many cases the reason for dry eye is not known, other times it may be caused by injuries to the tear glands - such as infections or trauma - eye infections, reactions to drugs such as sulphonamides, an immune reaction or even the gland of the third eyelid being surgically removed by mistake. Left untreated, the dog will suffer painful and chronic eye infections. Repeated irritation of the cornea results in severe scarring, ulcers may develop which can lead to blindness.

Treatment usually involves drugs: cyclosporine ophthalmic ointment or drops being the most common. In some cases another eye preparation – tacrolimus - is also used and may be effective when cyclosporine is not. In some cases, artificial tear solutions are also prescribed. In very severe cases, an operation can be performed to transplant a salivary duct into the upper eyelid, causing saliva to drain into and lubricate the eye. . This procedure is rarely used, but is an option.

Pigmentary Keratopathy (PK)

This inflammation of the cornea is characterised by the spread of dark pigmentation (colour) across the surface of the eye. The cause is unknown, although it's often associated with dry eye, entropion, or environmental irritants such as dust or wind. It usually develops in young to middle-aged dogs.

PK is a serious condition that progresses to blindness unless it's diagnosed and treated early. It begins as a red patch, supplied with blood vessels, and sometimes mixed with darker pigment. The pigment can spread across the cornea until the dog is no longer able to see. Fortunately, medications such as cyclosporine and surgery to remove the pigmented layers of the eye have made PK more treatable. With surgery and cyclosporin, a Pug can almost totally regain of his eyesight, although the success of treatment varies from one dog to the next.

Check your pug's eyes regularly for cloudy or dark spots that may indicate a problem. The earlier PK is caught, the more successful treatment will be.

PRA (Progressive Retinal Atrophy)

PRA is the name for several progressive diseases which lead to blindness. First recognised at the beginning of the 20th century in Gordon Setters, this inherited condition has been documented in over 100 breeds, including Pugs, and some mixed breeds.

PRA causes cells in the retina at the back of the eye to degenerate and die, even though the cells seem to develop normally early in life. The 'rod' cells operate in low light levels and are the first to lose normal function, resulting in night blindness for the dog.

As their vision deteriorates, affected dogs will adapt to their handicap as long as their environment remains constant, and they are not faced with situations requiring excellent vision. At the same time the pupils of their eyes become increasingly dilated, in a vain attempt to gather more light, causing a noticeable 'shine' to their eyes; and the lens of their eyes may become cloudy, or opaque, resulting in a cataract.

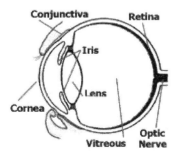

The 'cone' cells gradually lose their normal function in full light situations. Most affected dogs will eventually go blind. Typically, the disease is recognised first in early adolescence or early adulthood. PRA is normally diagnosed by an eye examination by the vet using an instrument called an indirect ophthalmoscope, and requires dilatation of the dog's pupil by application of eye drops.

Conditions that might look like PRA could be another disease and might not be inherited. It's important to remember that not all retinal disease is PRA. Annual eye exams by a veterinary ophthalmologist will build a history of eye health that will help to diagnose disease.

PRA is inherited as a recessive trait. This means that the faulty gene must be inherited **from both parents** in order to cause disease in an offspring. In other words, each parent was either a carrier or a sufferer. It's been proven that all breeds tested for PRA have the same mutated gene, even though the disease may develop at different ages or severities from one breed to another.

Sadly, there is no cure, but PRA can be avoided in future generations by testing dogs before breeding. If your dog is affected it may be helpful to read other owners' experiences living with blind dogs at www.eyevet.org and www.blinddogs.com.

Cherry Eye

Cherry eye is most common in young dogs, especially breeds such as Bulldog, Cavalier King Charles Spaniel, Lhasa Apso, Shih Tzu, West Highland White Terrier, Bloodhound, American Cocker Spaniel, Boston Terrier and Pug.

Humans have two eyelids, but dogs have a third eyelid, called a nictating membrane. This third eyelid is a thin, opaque tissue with a tear gland which rests in the inner corner of the eye. Its purpose is to provide additional protection for the eye and to spread tears over the eyeball. Usually it is retracted and therefore you can't see it, although you may notice it when your dog is relaxed and falling asleep. When the third eyelid becomes visible it may be a sign of illness or a painful eye.

Cherry Eye is a medical condition, officially known as **nictitans gland prolapse**, or prolapse of the gland of the third eyelid. Pugs are one breed with a susceptibility to this, although it is not known whether the condition is inherited.

Causes - The exact cause of cherry eye is not known, but it is thought to be due to a weakness of the fibrous tissue which attaches the gland to the surrounding eye. This weakness allows the gland to fall down, or prolapse. Once this has happened and the gland is exposed to the dry air and irritants, it can become infected and/or begin to swell.

The gland often becomes irritated, red and swollen. There is sometimes a mucous discharge and if the dog rubs or scratches it, he can further damage the gland and even possibly create an ulcer on the surface of the eye.

Symptoms -The main visible symptom in a red, often swollen, mass in the corner of one or both eyes, which is often first seen in young dogs up to the age of two years. It can occur in one or both eyes and may be accompanied by swelling and/or irritation. Although it may look sore, it is not a painful condition for your dog.

Treatment - At one time, it was popular to surgically remove the gland to correct this condition. While this was often effective, it could create problems later on. The gland of the third eyelid is very important for producing tears, without which dogs could suffer from 'dry eye', also known as keratoconjunctivitis sicca (KCS). These days, removing the gland is not considered a good idea.

A far better and straightforward option is to surgically reposition the gland by tacking it back into place with a single stitch that attaches the gland to the deeper structures of the eye socket. There is also another type of operation during which the wedge of tissue is removed from directly over the gland. Tiny dissolving stitches are used to close the gap so that the gland is pushed back into place. After surgery the dog may be placed on antibiotic ointment for a few days.

Mostly surgery is performed quickly and for most dogs that's the end of the matter. However, a few dogs do have a recurrence of cherry eye. The eye should return to normal after about seven days, during which time there may be some redness or swelling. If the affected eye suddenly seems uncomfortable or painful for your dog, or you can see protruding stitches, then take him back to the vet to get checked out. Other options include anti-inflammatory eye drops to reduce the swelling and manually manipulating the gland back into place.

Tip - Sometimes a Pug will develop cherry eye in one eye and then the condition will appear some time later in the other eye. If you have a young dog diagnosed with cherry eye, discuss waiting a few weeks or months before having any surgery to see if the second eye is affected. This will save the dog being anesthetised twice and will also save you money. discuss this with your vet.

Hereditary Cataracts

A cataract is an opaque spot on the lens of the eye that can be a result of the aging process or inherited. Early onset hereditary cataract (EHC), sometimes also referred to as juvenile hereditary cataract (JHC), is a condition that is known to affect the Pug. Hereditary cataracts are found most often in dogs that are five years of age or younger, and they may occur in both eyes (bilateral cataracts).

The purpose of the lens is to focus the rays of light form an image on the retina. If the lens becomes cloudy, less light can enter the eye and the dog's sight will slowly diminish as the cataract becomes larger. One or both eyes may be affected and the cataracts may not appear in both eyes at the same time.

The UK's Animal Health Trust test not only diagnoses dogs affected with the disease, but can also detect those which are carriers, displaying no symptoms of the disease but able to produce affected pups. The disorder is caused by a recessive gene called HSF4 which has to be inherited from **both parents**, so ask either to see both the father's and the mother's eye certificate . If no health certificates are available, ask the breeder for a guarantee that neither parent is a sufferer or a carrier.

A certificate will say whether the parent is CLEAR, CARRIER or AFFECTED. A 'carrier' dog can be bred with a 'clear' dog and the puppies will be clear. However, if this pup is later to be used for breeding, it will have to be DNA tested to see if it is clear or a carrier. Although there are no published scientific reports describing EHC in Pugs, anecdotal evidence indicates the cataracts usually develop within the first year of the dog's life. EHC is different from LHC – late onset cataract, which affects dogs of all breeds in later life.

Diagnosis - Hereditary cataracts are usually first diagnosed when the owner sees their dog bumping into furniture, or when his pupils have changed colour. You may also see that the middle of the pupil has a white spot or area. Try shining a flashlight at your dog's eyes or taking a picture with a flash. You should see a coloured reflection in his eye, if you see something grey or dull white, your puppy may have a cataract.

The vet will refer the pet to the specialist who will carry out the same eye exam that is done for breeding stock. The process is painless and simple, drops are put into the eyes and after a few minutes the dog is taken into a dark room for examination and diagnosis.

Treatment - If you think your Pug may have cataracts, it is important to get him to a vet **as soon as possible.** Sometimes, if the puppy's cataracts are small, they can be watched and may not need treatment. They won't go away, but they may not get bigger quickly. Discuss this with your vet and if you choose this option, you have to be vigilant and monitor your puppy's eyes for any signs of change.

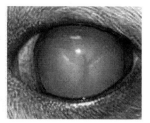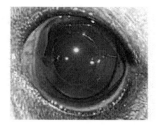

Left: eye with cataracts. Right: same eye with artificial lens

Puppies born with congenital cataracts can improve as they mature. That's because the lens inside the puppy's eye grows along with the dog. When the area of cloudiness on the lens remains the same size, by the time the puppy becomes an adult, the affected portion of the lens is relatively small. By adulthood, many dogs born with cataracts are able to compensate and see "around" the cloudiness.

Early removal of more serious cataracts can restore vision and provide a dramatic improvement in the quality of your dog's life. The only treatment for severe canine cataracts is surgery (unless they are caused by another condition like diabetes). Despite what you may have heard, laser surgery does not exist for canine cataracts, neither is there any proven medical treatment other than surgery.

Surgery is not cheap, but the good news is that it is almost always (85-90%) successful. The dog has to have a general anaesthetic (again, this needs discussion with your vet), but the operation is often performed on an outpatient basis. The procedure is similar to small incision cataract surgery in people. An artificial lens is often implanted in the dog's eye to replace the cataract lens. Dogs can see without an artificial lens, but the image will not be in focus. Discuss with the vet or ophthalmologist whether your dog would benefit from an artificial lens.

Even better news is that once the cataract is removed, it does not recur. However before your Pug can undergo this procedure, he has to be fit and healthy and a suitable candidate for surgery.

After the operation, he will probably have to stay at the surgery overnight so that the professionals can keep an eye on him. Once back home, he will have to wear a protective Elizabethan collar, or E collar, for about one to two weeks while his eye is healing. The next part is important: you have to keep him quiet and calm (not always easy!) You'll also have to give him eye drops, perhaps four times a day for the first week and then less frequently after that.

The success of cataract surgery depends very much on the owner doing all the right things. But all the effort will be worth it when your Pug regains his sight.

Distichiasis and Trichiasis

Distichiasis is the medical term for eyelashes irritating a dog's eyes. (Trichiasis is backwards-growing eyelashes). With this condition small eyelashes abnormally grow on the inner surface or the very edge of the eyelid, and both upper and lower eyelids may be affected. Some breeds are affected more than others, suggesting that it is an inherited trait. Pugs, Cocker Spaniels, Golden Retrievers, Boxers and Pekingese are among those most commonly affected.

The affected eye becomes red, inflamed, and may develop a discharge. The dog will typically squint or blink a lot, just like a human with a hair or other foreign matter in the eye. The dog will often rub his eye against furniture, other objects or the carpet. In severe cases, the cornea can become ulcerated and it looks a blue colour.

If left, the condition usually worsens and severe ulcerations and infections develop which can lead to blindness. The dog can make the condition worse by scratching or rubbing his eyes.

Treatment usually involves surgery or electro- or cryo-epilation, where a needle is inserted into the hair follicle and an ultra-fast electric current is emitted. This current produces heat which destroys the stem cells responsible for hair growth. This procedure may need to be repeated after several months because all of the abnormal hairs may not have developed at the time of the first treatment -although this is not common with dogs older than three years.

If surgery is performed, the lid is actually split and the areas where the abnormal hairs grow are removed. Both treatments require anaesthesia and usually result in a full recovery. After surgery, the eyelids are swollen for four to five days and the eyelid margins turn pink. Usually they return to their normal colour within four months. Antibiotic eye drops are often used following surgery to prevent infections.

Pugs with distichiasis should not be used for breeding, as it is thought that a predisposition to the condition can be inherited

Eye Testing

There are various ways of testing for hereditary eye conditions. In the US there is the OptiGen PRA Test and the Canine Eye Registration Foundation (CERF), which works in conjunction with the Orthopedic Foundation for Animals (OFA). The aim of the OFA is to promote the health and welfare of companion animals through a reduction in the incidence of genetic disease.

In the UK there is the British Veterinary Association (BVA) Eye Test, an annual test, carried out due to the fact some diseases have a late onset. If you are buying a puppy, it is highly advisable to check if the parents have been tested and given the all-clear.

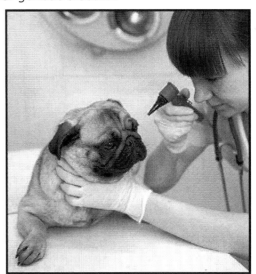

If so, always ensure the breeder lets you see the original certificate (which is white in the UK) and not a photocopy. Identification of dogs that do not carry diseased genes is the key to eradicating the problem.

When you take your Pug in for his annual inoculations, you can also ask him or her to test your dog's tear production. If there is a potential problem with dry eye, you will catch it right at the beginning.

Eye Care for Pugs

Some eye conditions affecting Pugs may be inherited, but there are other issues, such as dirt or pollen in the eye, which are environmental. Pugs love to root around in all sorts of places and can easily finish up with irritating material in their eyes, which will cause them to rub or scratch. Also, some Pugs may suffer from allergies which will also cause their eyes to become irritated.

Whatever the reason, it is a good idea to get into the habit of checking your dog's eyes and the surrounding skin folds (wrinkles) at least once a week. This also enables you to monitor any changes in the eyes and, if a problem such as infection or cherry eye does occur, you can get on top of it right away.

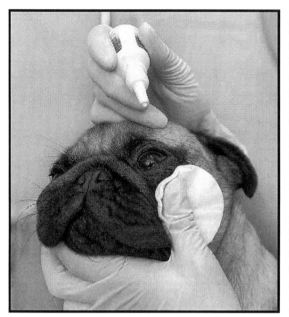

Tear staining is not uncommon with Pugs, especially lighter coloured ones. These brownish, wet stains are also a breeding ground for bacteria and yeast. The most common is Red Yeast, which is usually associated with reddish-brown facial stains, and which may emit an odour. Tear staining can be related to health and diet as well as genetics. Most vets agree that face staining results from excessive tear production and a damp face. In addition, the wrinkles or folds around the eyes and nose attract dirt, so keeping them clean should be a regular part of your PMP (Pug Maintenance Programme!)

Cleaning your dog's tear stains will also help to avoid infection. To do this, wet a cotton ball with a sterile eye wash, or use eye wipes, to gently rub the folds around your dog's eyes, clearing them of any dried discharge. Repeat the action with clean cotton balls or wipes until the area is clean. There are videos on YouTube which demonstrate how to clean your dog's eyes and facial skin folds. Remember to dry the wrinkles after cleaning to deter yeast infections.

There are many canine tear stain removers on the market. One product which some owners have found useful is Angel Eyes for Dogs. It's quite expensive, but if it saves you having to visit the vet's with eye infections, it will be worth it in the long run. Other owners have tried home remedies or holistic with some success, but be extremely careful regarding the substances you put near to your Pug's eyes. If in any doubt at all about a product or remedy, check with your vet.

Pug Dog Encephalitis

Pug Dog Encephalitis, or PDE, is a brain disease that affects only Pugs and is every owner's worst fear. Encephalitis is an inflammation of the brain and brain membranes, and the technical term for the illness is necrotising meningoencephalitis (NME). Fortunately, this is a rare disease affecting just over 1% of Pugs.

Females are more likely to have it than males. PDE usually strikes when the dog is two to three years of age, but it has been seen in dogs as young as six months as well as middle-aged Pugs.

There is also some (unconfirmed) research which shows that fawn females might be slightly more prone to getting PDE than non-fawns.

Vets think that this condition is genetic, as it often affects dogs who are closely related or puppies in the same litter. The causes are not yet known, but latest research is pointing towards an autoimmune disease. Sadly the illness progresses quickly and cannot be cured; it is always fatal.

Symptoms – when the symptoms appear the dog usually only has weeks or months to live:

❖ Seizures
❖ Staggering, and/or Lack of Co-ordination and/or Falling to the Ground
❖ Confusion or Disorientation, Circling
❖ Lethargy
❖ Depression
❖ Blindness

Diagnosis and Treatment - Your vet will need a complete medical history and physical exam to diagnose PDE. If you know that other dogs in your Pug's immediate family have succumbed to this disease, you should tell your vet. MRIs and spinal taps can help him or her to make a diagnosis. Because so little is known about this disease, the vet may ask you to donate your dog's remains to veterinary science.

While PDE is always fatal, treatment can help manage your dog's symptoms during the final weeks of his life. Anti-convulsants can help control the seizures and anti-inflammatory drugs can help to reduce the inflammation in your dog's brain, making him more comfortable. Many owners choose to put their dogs to sleep when they receive a diagnosis of PDE. It is not usually until death that a definite diagnosis can be made through examination of the brain tissue by a veterinary neuropathologist.

You cannot prevent PDE as it is probably genetic in origin. Dogs with this disease should never be bred. If your dog does develop the disease, inform the breeder and, if possible, inform the other owners who may have purchased puppies from the same litter.

Veterinary researchers are working to discover how the disease is passed on. Once that mystery is solved, it will be easier to identify carriers, analyse pedigrees to select breeding stock and develop a test for the disease. Researchers also hope to develop a vaccine against PDE. There is currently a genetic DNA test. It does not tell you if your dog has PDE, it only determines **the risk** of developing PDE and "for selecting matings that will produce puppies that are at decreased risk."

Spine Problems

Hemivertebrae

Hemivertebrae is the name given to a genetic abnormality of the spine which occurs when the puppy is still a foetus in the mother's womb. 'Hemi' means half and 'vertebrae' are the series of small bones which link to make up the backbone or spine. It occurs when one side of the vertebrae does not develop properly. The vertebrae can be fused or they are wedge-shaped, causing a twisting of the spine.

The condition is not uncommon in Pugs and other brachycephalic breeds like the Bulldog, French Bulldog and Boston Terrier. It is a consequence of the breeds having a screw tail. How it affects each individual Pug varies. If the deformity is restricted to the tail, it is not a problem. But when it affects the rest of the spine it can cause serious problems, as the deformed vertebrae create a wedging effect that twists the spine which can cause compression (squashing) of the spinal cord.

Signs usually first appear in puppies and often progressively get worse, until they level off at about nine months, once the spine stops growing. Symptoms include weakness in the hind limbs, pain, and incontinence –both of urine and faeces. It can be a very painful condition and in extreme cases when no more treatment is available, it is tragic for owner and the dog when is kinder to have the dog put to sleep (euthanized).

Diagnosis is relatively straightforward. Your vet will take X-rays to see if the condition is present in the spine. He or she may then use more advanced technologies like myelograms, CT scans or MRIs to see if there is any compression of the spinal cord. Because hemivertebrae is a condition the dog is born with, it cannot be cured. The best way to ensure that your Pug does not have it is to get the dog from a good, responsible breeder who has screened his or her dogs for the problem.

With thanks to the Universities Federation for Animal Welfare (UFAW) for this more detailed explanation of Hemivertebrae, which the technically-minded among you may find useful:

"Pugs commonly have deformities of the bones of the spine. These can lead to pressure on the spinal cord resulting in progressive pain and loss of hind limb function and incontinence.

"Hemivertebrae are bones of the spine that are abnormally shaped. Because of their abnormal shape, these bones tend not to align correctly with their neighbouring bones in the spine. This can lead to instability and deformity of the spinal column, which in turn can lead to the spinal cord or the nerves arising from it becoming squashed and damaged.

"This causes pain – which can be severe - wobbliness (ataxia) on the hind legs and can also cause loss of hind leg function and incontinence (inability to control passing urine or faeces). It appears that the disease is a consequence of selecting for the screw (curly) tail conformation of this breed. The screw-tail shape is due to abnormal shape of tail bones but this abnormality can also affect other parts of the spine with serious consequences as outlined above.

"Pain from spinal cord compression (squashing) can be severe. Affected dogs can also lose function in their hind limbs and sometimes lose bladder and bowel control. Not all animals with hemivertebrae develop these signs; some have milder signs of ataxia or no signs at all. Dogs with severe signs may need major surgical interventions, which have their own welfare impacts, and, despite this, some may not recover and need to be euthanized on humane grounds.

"Young dogs are most commonly affected when problems associated with skeletal deformities develop as their skeleton grows. The skeletal deformity is permanent without surgery. The clinical signs associated with the condition can develop rapidly over days, or gradually over weeks and months. Severely affected individuals would, without surgery, have permanent major disability. Even where surgery is possible, some animals may have unacceptable levels of disability necessitating euthanasia. Thus this condition can severely limit both the quality and length of life.

"The exact numbers affected are not known, but it is considered a common problem in Pugs and other brachycephalic (short-nosed) breeds that have screw-tails. Selection for screw tails, which are caused by deformed vertebrae, has the unintended consequence of causing deformity higher up the spine also.

"Screw tail describes a tail which, in its relaxed position, is coiled, usually to one side. The most severely affected tails cannot be straightened at all, others can be manually straightened but relax back into the coiled position. The exact genetics of this condition have yet to be worked out; however, Pugs are considered to be predisposed to hemivertebrae because of the breed characteristic of a screw-tail. The gene(s) causing the screw-tail deformity (which involves hemivertebrae in the tail) are thought also to be involved in producing hemivertebrae elsewhere in the spine.

"Methods and prospects for elimination of the problem are not known, though whilst the breed standard includes a screw-tail the condition seems likely to persist. It seems likely, since the screw tail is caused by hemivertebrae in the tail, that out-breeding to dogs with straight tails, then selection for a straight tail might be a way forward to eliminate this welfare problem."

Intervertebral Disc Disease (IVDD)

Also called a slipped disc, this can occur in breeds of dogs with relatively long backs, such as Dachshunds, Basset Hounds, Beagles, Pekingese and some Pugs. It is not common in Pugs, but does occur within the breed and is something to be aware of.

The vertebrae (discussed in the last section on Hemivertebrae) are connected by flexible discs made of a cartilage-like material called intervertebral discs. These discs provide cushioning, like a shock absorber, between each bone (vertebra) and allow the dog's neck, spine and tail to bend, so he can change his position and posture. Each vertebra has a tunnel running downwards through its middle and in here is the spinal cord.

The spinal cord is a mass of nerve fibres that transmit messages backwards and forwards between the brain and the rest of the body. It is protected by the surrounding bone, except for the gaps in between the vertebrae where it runs over the top of the discs.

As a dog (or human) gets older, there is natural wear and tear – or degeneration - on the vertebrae; there might also be some trauma. In certain breeds of dog this process occurs early age, and if a Pug is to experience the problem, it may start from are early as three years old.

Degeneration involves the loss of water from the jelly-like centre of the disc, which causes it to lose much of its shock-absorbing ability. When the spine squashes a degenerated disc, the force is transferred to the outer ring of the disc which eventually causes small tears to occur in the outside of the disc. When the outer ring is torn, the inner part of the disc **herniates** or bulges out through the fibres. This is also called a 'slipped disc' and a 'ruptured disc' and it may happen suddenly (acutely) or over a longer period of time (chronically). Sometimes it can be triggered suddenly in Pugs and other small dogs when they jump off the couch, bed or chair.

The symptoms vary according to how serious the problem is. When a disc first ruptures, it usually causes intense pain. If it is in the middle of the back, the dog will arch his back up in pain. If it's in the neck, your dog may be unwilling to turn his head and may not even want to lower it to eat and drink.

Some dogs shiver from the pain and walk very carefully and slowly. In severe cases the back legs may be partially or completely paralysed – this could be temporary or permanent. The nerves affecting the bladder and colon can also be affected, making it difficult for the dog to wee or poo(p) on his own. This is very serious and you should seek veterinary care immediately.

Diagnosis is similar to hemivertebrae and usually starts with your vet watching the dog move, asking about his history and then taking an X-ray. Other tests may follow to assess the extent of the damage.

If this is the first time it has happened or if the symptoms are mild, then non-surgical (medical) treatment may be recommended by your vet. This involves temporarily confining your Pug to a crate. This is one reason why you might want to consider crate training him as a puppy, so that he is used to a crate if it is ever needed for a medical condition. A crate prevents him from jumping, running, twisting or moving in a way which might cause further injury to his back.

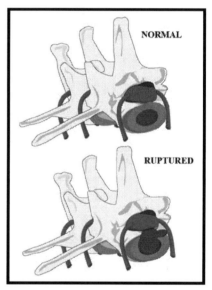

Unfortunately, confinement will generally need to last from four to six weeks. Usually your vet will also prescribe a nonsteroidal anti-inflammatory drug (NSAID) to help reduce swelling around the spinal cord. Pain medication may also be prescribed, but you should never give your Pug pain relievers which have not been prescribed by your vet.

After multiple episodes, or if there is severe pain or more serious nervous system symptoms, your vet may recommend surgery to either remove the protruding disc material and/or to remove a part of the bone that surrounds the spinal cord in order to help relieve the pressure.

However to be effective, the procedure should be done a day or so after the damage occurred. Owners should also be aware that anaesthetic is always a risk with brachycephalic dogs like the Pug and so suitable precautions should be taken, including finding a vet or specialist who is familiar with anaesthetising Bulldogs, Pugs and other brachycephalic breeds.

In some ways, it is a good sign if your dog is experiencing some pain in his limbs. In these situations the prognosis (outlook) for your dog is generally good. However, if the dog is paralysed AND has lost deep pain sensation - or if treatment is delayed – the outlook is not so good.

Whether treatment is medical, surgical or a combination of the two, it may well be weeks or even months before the dog has healed as much as possible. It is essential to get him to the vet as soon as you suspect a spinal problem. The earlier it is diagnosed, the better chance your dog has of a positive outcome.

Luxating Patella

Luxating patella, also called 'floating kneecap,' 'slipped stifle' or 'trick knee' is a painful condition akin to a dislocated knee cap. It is often congenital (present from birth) and typically affects small and miniature breeds. Pugs are listed as susceptible to luxating patella.

Symptoms - A typical sign would be if your dog is running across the park when he suddenly pulls up short and yelps with pain. He might limp on three legs and then after a period of about 10 minutes, drop the affected leg and start to walk normally again.

If the condition is severe, he may hold up the affected leg up for a few days. Dogs that have a luxating patella on both hind legs may change their gait completely, dropping their hindquarters and holding the rear legs further out from the body as they walk.

In the most extreme cases they might not even use their rear legs, but walk like a circus act by balancing on their front legs so their hindquarters don't touch the ground.

Genetics, injury and malformation during development can all cause this problem. Because the most common cause is genetics, a Pug with luxating patella should never be used for breeding. If you are buying a puppy, ask if there is any history in either parent. Typically most sufferers are middle-aged dogs with a history of intermittent lameness in the affected rear leg or legs, although the condition may appear as early as four to six months old.

A groove in the end of the femur (thigh bone) allows the knee cap to glide up and down when the knee joint is bent, while keeping it in place at the same time.

If this groove is too shallow, the knee cap may luxate – or dislocate. It can only return to its natural position when the quadriceps muscle relaxes and increases in length, which is why a dog may have to hold his leg up for some time after the dislocation. Sometimes the problem can be caused by obesity, the excess weight putting too much strain on the joint – another good reason to keep your Pug's weight in check.

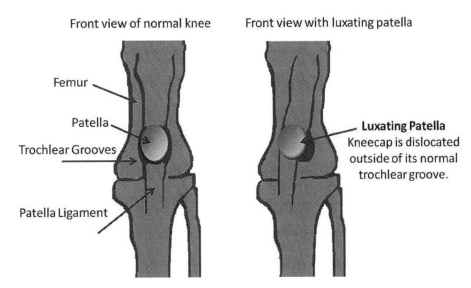

Front view of normal knee   Front view with luxating patella

Femur

Patella

Trochlear Grooves

Patella Ligament

Luxating Patella
Kneecap is dislocated outside of its normal trochlear groove.

Treatment - There are four grades of patellar luxation, ranging from Grade I, which causes a temporary lameness in the joint and may even correct itself, to Grade IV, in which the patella cannot be realigned manually. This gives the dog a bow-legged appearance. If left untreated, the groove will become even shallower and the dog will become progressively lamer, with arthritis prematurely affecting the joint. This will cause a permanently swollen knee and reduce your Pug's mobility. It is therefore important to get your dog in for a veterinary check-up ASAP if you suspect he may have a luxating patella.

In severe cases one option is surgery, although this should not be undertaken lightly, due to potential breathing problems under anaesthetic. The groove at the base of the femur may be surgically deepened to better hold the knee cap in place. This operation is known as a **trochlear modification**. The good news is that dogs generally respond well, whatever the type of surgery, and are usually completely recovered within one to two months.

Hip Dysplasia

Canine Hip Dysplasia (CHD) is the most common cause of hind leg lameness in dogs. It is a hereditary condition which occurs mainly in large breeds, but many Pugs are also affected. Several factors contribute to the development of the disease and some breeds are genetically predisposed to the disease, including Labrador Retrievers, Golden Retrievers, German Shepherds, Rottweilers and Giant Schnauzers.

In tests carried out by the Orthopedic Foundation for Animals (OFA) between 1974 and 2014, the Pug was ranked **second** (behind the Bulldog) out of 172 breeds tested for hip dysplasia

Out of the 565 Pugs tested, a massive 68.7% of them were found to be dysplastic. The figures for earlier years were even higher, which indicates that breeders are making some inroads into the problem. However, not a single Pug tested was rated as "Excellent." You can see the full list here: www.offa.org/stats_hip.html

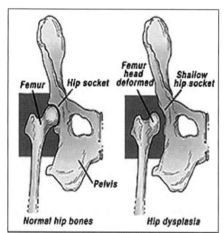

Normal hip bones   Hip dysplasia

The hip is a ball and socket joint. Hip dysplasia is caused when the head of the femur (thigh bone) fits loosely into a shallow and poorly-developed socket in the pelvis. The right hand side of the diagram shows a shallow hip socket and a deformed femur head, causing hip dysplasia. The healthy joint is on the left.

Most dogs with dysplasia are born with normal hips, but due to their genetic make-up – and possibly other factors such as diet – the soft tissues that surround the joint develop abnormally.

The joint carrying the weight of the dog becomes loose and unstable, muscle growth lags behind normal development and is often followed by degenerative joint disease or osteoarthritis, which is the body's attempt to stabilise the loose hip joint. Early diagnosis gives your vet the best chance to tackle the problem as soon as possible, minimising the chance of arthritis developing.

Symptoms range from mild discomfort to extreme pain. A puppy with hip dysplasia usually starts to show signs between five and 13 months old.

Symptoms

- ❖ Lameness in the hind legs, particularly after exercise
- ❖ Difficulty or stiffness when getting up or climbing uphill
- ❖ A 'bunny hop' gait
- ❖ Dragging the rear end when getting up
- ❖ Waddling rear leg gait
- ❖ A painful reaction to stretching the hind legs, resulting in a short stride
- ❖ A side-to-side sway of the croup (area above the tail) with a tendency to tilt the hips down if you push down on the croup
- ❖ A reluctance to jump, exercise or climb stairs
- ❖ Sitting like a frog with legs splayed behind (although this can be normal for some dogs)

Hip evaluations should not be delayed until two years of age (especially in susceptible breeds), but should be performed as young as five to six months old. Using a technique called palpation and hip manipulation, veterinarians can often detect hip dysplasia before symptoms become evident and when radiographs fail to identify malformations. Moving the knee towards the centre causes the hip to fall out of its socket and moving the knee away from the centre causes the hip to return to the socket.

Causes and Triggers

Canine hip dysplasia is usually an inherited condition. But there are also factors which can trigger or worsen the condition, including:

1. Overfeeding, especially on a diet high in protein and calories
2. Excess calcium, also usually due to overfeeding
3. Extended periods without exercise – or too much vigorous exercise – especially when your young Pug and his bones are growing
4. Obesity – this is a major problem with Pugs

Advances in nutritional research have shown that diet plays an important role in the development of hip dysplasia. It's important for owners to realise that, no matter how cutely your Pug stares at you pleading for food with those beautiful big dark eyes, excess pounds will place a strain on your dog and eventually take their toll.

Feeding a high-calorie or high calcium diet to growing dogs can trigger a predisposition to hip dysplasia, as the rapid weight gain places increased stress on the hips. Make sure your dog is on the right diet for his age. When you take your puppy to the vet's for his injections, ask for advice on the best diet. Also speak to your breeder, a good breeder will remain at the end of a phone line to give advice throughout your Pug's life.

Exercise may be another risk factor. Dogs that have a predisposition to hip dysplasia may have an increased chance of getting it if they are over-exercised at a young age. The key here is moderate, low impact exercise for fast-growing young dogs. High impact activities which apply a lot of force to the joint, such and jumping and catching Frisbees, is not recommended with young dogs.

Treatment

As with most conditions, early detection leads to a better outcome. Your vet will take X-rays to make a diagnosis. Treatment is geared towards preventing the hip joint getting worse and decreasing pain. Various medical and surgical treatments are now available to ease the dog's discomfort and restore some mobility.

Treatment depends upon several factors, such as the dog's age, how bad the problem is and, sadly, how much money you can afford to spend on treatment. Management of the condition usually consists of restricting exercise, keeping body weight down and then managing pain with analgesics and anti-inflammatory drugs.

As with humans, cortisone injections may sometimes be used to reduce inflammation and swelling. Cortisone can be injected directly into the affected hip to provide almost immediate relief for a tender, swollen joint. In severe cases, surgery may be an option, especially with older dogs.

Hip Testing

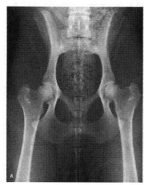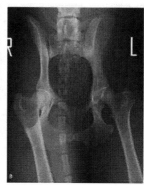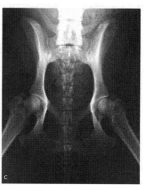

Figure A is the healthy hip, B shows lateral tilting, C shows outward rotation

The Penn Hip system was developed to provide a reliable method for predicting the development of Canine Hip Dysplasia and can be used on dogs as young as 16 weeks old. It is recommended that Pugs to be used for breeding are tested. The Penn Hip method uses three separate radiographs taken under deep sedation or general anaesthesia. Thirty years ago the British Veterinary Association (BVA) and Kennel Club in the UK set up a hip screening program for dogs, which tests them using radiology and gives them a rating or 'hip score'. The KC is responsible for publishing hip dysplasia results for all pedigree dogs in the Kennel Club Breed Records.

Veterinary MRI and radiology specialist Ruth Dennis, of the Animal Health Trust, states: *"For dogs intended for breeding, it is essential that the hips are assessed before mating to ensure that they are free of dysplastic changes or only minimally affected."*

Reverse Sneezing

Some Pugs may display a condition known as backwards or reverse sneezing - the medical name is a pharyngeal gag reflex. It's called a reverse sneeze, because it sounds like the dog is pulling air **into** his nose, whereas in a normal sneeze, the air is pushed **out** through the nose.

A Pug will make rapid and long intakes of breath, stand still and stretch his head forwards. He'll make a loud snorting sound, which may make you think he has something stuck in his nose.

The most common cause is irritation of the soft palate, which results in a spasm. This narrows the airway and makes it temporarily more difficult for the dog to take in air. Factors that may trigger reverse sneezing include excitement, eating or drinking, exercise, physical irritation of the throat such as from pulling on a lead, respiratory tract mites, allergies, irritating chemicals like perfumes or household cleaners, viral infections or foreign bodies caught in the throat.

An episode can last for several seconds to a minute. Some owners claim that a spasm can be shortened by closing the dog's nostrils for several seconds with your hand or massaging the throat. While it may seem alarming, in most cases reverse sneezing is not a harmful condition, there are no ill after-effects, and treatment is unnecessary. Usually the dog is completely normal before and after the episode.

However, in some brachycephalic breeds (like the Pug), noises similar to a reverse sneeze may sometimes be a sign of a respiratory problem, such as an elongated soft palate. In these cases there are usually other respiratory symptoms as well, so when it happens for the first time, you should mention it to your vet on your next visit – or make a new appointment if you are concerned.

Legg-Calve-Perthes Disease

The medical term for this disease is Avascular Necrosis of the Femoral Head. It is a disorder of small breeds such as Poodles, and especially Yorkshire Terriers and West Highland White Terriers, and affects some Pugs.

With this condition, a puppy will grow normally until about three months of age and then the ball (femoral head) of the hip joint begins to degenerate. Vets believe that the blood supply decreases, causing the bone to deteriorate and actually die. (A similar condition occurs in humans). The condition can be diagnosed with X rays, and the end result is a malformed hip joint and secondary arthritis, causing pain and lameness.

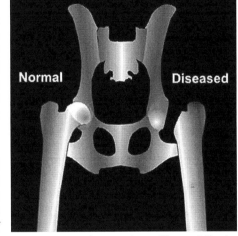

Even though the hip joint deterioration begins at around three months old, it's not until the puppy is six to 10 months old that he starts limping. One or both hip joints may be involved. As well as limping, an affected puppy may be irritable and constantly chew at the affected flank. If untreated, lameness is usually progressive until the dog stops putting weight on the affected limb, which becomes stiff and the surrounding muscles begin to waste away. The hip joint will never be normal and some lameness will always be present. Arthritis will be the result in the affected joint.

There are cases where rest combined with pain killers and cold packing help in treating the dog's lameness. More often surgery to remove the diseased bone is required – and if often successful, but expensive. The hip joint will not return to its full normal function, but the destructive arthritic process is greatly slowed. Surgery is followed by vigorous exercise and physical therapy to rehabilitate the affected limb(s). Otherwise, it may result in delayed recovery and poor response to treatment. In some dogs, small lead weights are attached as ankle bracelets above hock joint to encourage early weight bearing.

The vet will probably recommend a follow-up check every two weeks to make sure the physiotherapy and exercises are working. Overall recovery may take three to six months, so patience and diligence are essential. Obesity is a factor that can slow down recovery, so a vet may recommend a restricted diet for you Pug.

Hypothyroidism

Hypothyroidism is a common hormonal disorder that can affect all breeds of dog and is caused by an under-active thyroid gland. This gland (located on either side of the windpipe in the dog's throat) does not produce enough of the hormone thyroid, which controls the speed of the metabolism.

Dogs with very low thyroid levels have a slow metabolic rate. It occurs mainly in dogs over the age of five. Pugs may be more prone to hypothyroidism than some other breeds, with some vets recording around 8% to 10% in older Pugs, generally over the age of five or six. It occurs in dogs of either gender. The symptoms are often non-specific and quite gradual in onset, and they may vary depending on breed and age. Most forms of hypothyroidism are diagnosed with a blood test.

Common Symptoms - The following symptoms have been listed in order, with the most common ones being at the top of the list:

- ❖ **High blood cholesterol**
- ❖ **Lethargy**
- ❖ **Hair Loss**
- ❖ **Weight gain or obesity**
- ❖ **Dry coat or excessive shedding**
- ❖ **Hyper pigmentation or darkening of the skin, seen in 25% of cases**
- ❖ **Intolerance to cold, seen in 15% of dogs with the condition**

Treatment

Although hypothyroidism is a type of auto-immune disease and cannot be prevented, the good news is that symptoms can usually be easily diagnosed and treated. Most dogs suffering from hypothyroidism can be well-managed on oral thyroid hormone replacement therapy (tablets). The dog is normally placed on a daily dose of a synthetic thyroid hormone called thyroxine (levothyroxine). The dose and frequency of administration of the drug varies depending on the severity of the disease and the response of the individual dog to the drug.

A dog is usually given a standard dose for his weight and then blood samples are taken periodically to check his response and the dose is adjusted accordingly. Depending upon your dog's preferences and needs, the medication can be given in different forms, such as a solid tablet, in liquid form, or a gel that can be rubbed into your Pug's ears. Once treatment has started, he will have to be on it for the rest of his life.

In some less common situations, surgery may be required to remove part or all of the thyroid gland. Another treatment is radioiodine, where radioactive iodine is used to kill the overactive cells of the thyroid. While this is considered one of the most effective treatments, not all animals are suitable for the procedure and a lengthy hospitalisation is often required. Happily, once the diagnosis has been made and treatment has started, whichever treatment your dog undergoes, the majority of symptoms disappear.

NOTE: **Hyper**thyroidism (as opposed to **hypo**thyroidism) is caused by the thyroid gland producing too much thyroid hormone. It is quite rare in dogs, being more commonly seen in cats. A common symptom is the dog being ravenously hungry all the time, but actually losing weight.

Epilepsy

Thanks to **www.canineepilepsy.co.uk** for assistance with this article. If your Pug has epilepsy, we recommend reading this excellent website to gain a greater understanding of the illness.

Pugs are no more or less likely to have epilepsy than other breeds, but if you have witnessed your dog having a seizure (convulsion), you will know how frightening it can be. Seizures are not uncommon in dogs, but many dogs have only a single seizure. If your dog has had more than one seizure it may be that he or she is epileptic. Just as in people, there are medications for dogs to control seizures, allowing your dog to live a more normal life.

Epilepsy means repeated seizures due to abnormal activity in the brain and is caused by an abnormality in the brain itself. It can affect any breed of dog and in fact affects around four or five dogs in every 100, and in some breeds it can be hereditary. If seizures happen because of a problem somewhere else in the body, such as heart disease (which stops oxygen reaching the brain), this is not epilepsy. Your vet may do tests to try to find the reason for the epilepsy but in many cases no cause can be identified.

Symptoms

Some dogs seem to know when they are about to have a seizure and may behave in a certain way. You will come to recognise these signs as meaning that a seizure is likely. Often dogs just seek out their owner's company and come to sit beside them when a seizure is about to start.

Once the seizure starts, the dog is unconscious – he cannot hear or respond to you (unlike with head tremors). Most dogs become stiff, fall onto their side and make running movements with their legs. Sometimes they will cry out and may lose control of their bowels or bladder.

Most seizures last between one and three minutes - **it is worth making a note of the time the seizure starts and ends** because it often seems that a seizure goes on for a lot longer than it actually does.

After a seizure, dogs behave in different ways. Some dogs just get up and carry on with what they were doing, while others appear dazed and confused for up to 24 hours afterwards. Most commonly, dogs will be disoriented for only 10 to 15 minutes before returning to their old self. They often have a set pattern of behaviour that they follow - for example going for a drink of water or asking to go outside to the toilet. If your dog has had more than one seizure, you may well start to notice a pattern of behaviour which is typically repeated.

Most seizures occur while the dog is relaxed and resting quietly. It is very rare for a seizure to occur while exercising. Often seizures occur in the evening or at night. In a few dogs, seizures seem to be triggered by particular events or stress. It is common for a pattern to develop and, should your dog suffer from epilepsy, you will gradually recognize this as specific to your dog.

The most important thing is to **stay calm**. Remember that your dog is unconscious during the seizure and is not in pain or distressed. It is likely to be more distressing for you than for him. Make sure that he is not in a position to injure himself, for example by falling down the stairs, but otherwise do not try to interfere with him. Never try to put your hand inside his mouth during a seizure or you are very likely to get bitten. Seizures can cause damage to the brain and if your dog has repeated occurrences, it is likely that further seizures will occur in the future. The damage caused is cumulative and after a lot of seizures there may be enough brain damage to cause early senility (with loss of learned behaviour and housetraining or behavioural changes).

It is very rare for dogs to injure themselves during a seizure. Occasionally they may bite their tongue and there may appear to be a lot of blood, but is unlikely to be serious; your dog will not swallow his tongue. If a seizure goes on for a very long time (more than 10 minutes), his body temperature will rise and this can cause damage to other organs such as the liver and kidneys as well as the brain. In very extreme cases, some dogs may be left in a coma after severe seizures. If you are able to record your dog's seizure on a mobile phone or video recorder, this will be most useful to show the veterinarian.

When Should I Contact the Vet?

Generally, if your dog has a seizure lasting more than five minutes, or is having more than two or three a day, you should contact your vet. When your dog starts a seizure, make a note of the time. If he comes out of it within five minutes, allow him time to recover quietly before contacting your vet. It is far better for him to recover quietly at home rather than be bundled into the car and carted off to the vet right away.

However, if your dog does not come out of the seizure within five minutes, or has repeated seizures close together, contact your vet immediately, as he or she will want to see your dog as soon as possible. If this is his first seizure, your vet may ask you to bring him in for a check and some routine blood tests. Always call your vet's practice before setting off to be sure that there is someone there who can help your dog.

There are many things other than epilepsy which cause seizures in dogs. When your vet first examines your dog, he or she will not know whether your dog has epilepsy or another illness. It's unlikely that the vet will see your dog during a seizure, so it is **vital** that you're able to describe in some detail just what happens. You might want to make notes or record it on your mobile phone. Epilepsy usually starts when the dog is aged between one and five. So if your dog is older or younger, it's more likely he has a different problem.

Your vet may need to run a range of tests to ensure that there is no other cause of the seizures. These may include blood tests, possibly X-rays, and maybe even a scan (MRI) of your dog's brain. If no other cause can be found, then a diagnosis of epilepsy may be made. If your Pug already has epilepsy, remember these key points:

❖ **Don't change or stop any medication without consulting your vet**
❖ **See your vet at least once a year for follow-up visits**
❖ **Be sceptical of "magic cure" treatments**

Remember, live **with** epilepsy not **for** epilepsy. With the proper medical treatment, most epileptic dogs have far more good days than bad ones. Enjoy all those good days.

Treatment

It is not usually possible to remove the cause of the seizures, so your vet will use medication to control them. Treatment will not cure the disease, but it will manage the signs – even a well-controlled epileptic will have occasional seizures.

Sadly, as yet there is no miracle cure for epilepsy, so don't be tempted with "instant cures" from the internet.

There are many drugs used in the control of epilepsy in people, but very few of these are suitable for long-term use in a dog. Two of the most common are Phenobarbital and Potassium Bromide (check that these drugs are suitable for Pugs, some dogs can have negative results with Phenobarbitol).

Many epileptic dogs require a combination of one or more types of drug to achieve the most effective control of their seizures. Treatment is decided on an individual basis and it may take some time to find the best combination and dose of drugs for your pet. You need patience when managing an epileptic pet. It is important that medication is given at the same time each day.

Once your dog has been on treatment for a while, he will become dependent on the levels of drug in his blood at all times to control seizures. If you miss a dose of treatment, blood levels can drop and this may be enough to trigger a seizure. Each epileptic dog is an individual and a treatment plan will be designed specifically for him. It will be based on the severity and frequency of the seizures and how they respond to different medications.

Keep a record of events in your dog's life, note down dates and times of seizures and record when you have given medication. Each time you visit your vet, take this diary along with you so he or she can see how your dog has been since his last check-up. If seizures are becoming more frequent, it may be necessary to change the medication. The success or otherwise of treatment may depend on YOU keeping a close eye on your Pug to see if there are any physical or behavioural changes.

It is rare for epileptic dogs to stop having seizures altogether. However, provided your dog is checked regularly by your vet to make sure that the drugs are not causing any side-effects, there is a good chance that he will live a full and happy life. Visit www.canineepilepsy.co.uk for more information.

Heart Problems

Pugs are not particularly prone to heart problems, but they are relatively common among the canine population in general. **Heart failure, or congestive heart failure (CHF),** occurs when the heart is not able to pump enough blood around the dog's body.

The heart is a mechanical pump. It receives blood in one half and forces it through the lungs, then the other half pumps the blood through the entire body. The two most common forms of heart failure in dogs are Degenerative Valvular Disease (DVD) and Dilated Cardiomyopathy (DCM), also known as an enlarged heart.

In people, heart disease usually involves the arteries that supply blood to the heart muscle becoming hardened over time, causing the heart muscles to receive less blood than they need. Starved of oxygen, the result is often a heart attack. In dogs, hardening of the arteries (arteriosclerosis) and heart attacks are very rare. However, heart disease is very common. In dogs, heart disease is often seen as heart failure, which means that the muscles 'give out.' This is usually caused by one chamber or side of the heart being required to do more than it is physically able to do. It may be that excessive force is required to pump the blood through an area and over time the muscles fail.

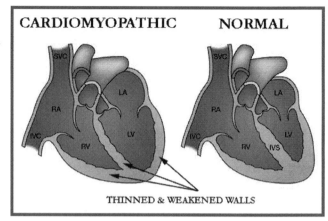

Unlike a heart attack in humans, heart failure in the dog is a slow insidious process that occurs over months or years. In these cases, once symptoms are noted, they will usually worsen over time until the animal is placed on treatment. Heart failure in older dogs is usually due to problems with the mitral valve of the heart, and occurs most commonly in smaller breeds, including small Poodles, Yorkies, Pugs, Lhasa Apsos and Pomeranians.

Symptoms

- ❖ **Tiredness**
- ❖ **Decreased activity levels**
- ❖ **Restlessness,** pacing around instead of settling down to sleep
- ❖ **Intermittent coughing -** especially during exertion or excitement. This tends to occur at night, sometimes about two hours after the dog goes to bed or when he wakes up in the morning. This coughing is an attempt to clear fluid in the lungs and is often the first clinical sign of a mitral valve disorder.

As the condition worsens, other symptoms may appear:

- ❖ **Lack of appetite**
- ❖ **Rapid breathing**
- ❖ **Abdominal swelling (due to fluid)**
- ❖ **Noticeable loss of weight**
- ❖ **Fainting (syncope)**
- ❖ **Paleness**

Diagnosis - If your dog is exhibiting a range of the above symptoms, the veterinarian may suspect congestive heart failure. He will carry out tests to make sure. These may include listening to the heart, chest X-rays, blood tests, electrocardiogram (a record of your dog's heartbeat) or an echocardiogram (ultrasound of the heart).

Treatment - If the heart problem is due to an enlarged heart (DCM) or valve disease, the condition cannot be reversed. Instead, treatment focuses on manages the symptoms with various medications, which may change over time as the condition worsens. The vet may also prescribe a special low salt diet for your dog, as sodium (found in salt) determines the amount of water in the blood, and the amount of exercise your dog has will have to be controlled. There is some evidence that vitamin and other supplements may be beneficial, discuss this with your veterinarian.

The prognosis (outlook) for dogs with congestive heart failure depends on the cause and severity, as well as their response to treatment. Sadly, CHF is progressive, so your dog can never recover from the condition. But once diagnosed, he can live a longer, more comfortable life with the right medication and regular check-ups.

Heart Murmurs - Heart murmurs are not uncommon in dogs. Our dog was diagnosed with a Grade 2 murmur a few years ago and, of course, your heart sinks when the vet gives you the terrible news. But once the shock is over, it's important to realise that there are several different severities of the condition and, at its mildest, it is no great cause for concern.

Literally, a heart murmur is a specific sound heard through a stethoscope, it results from the blood flowing faster than normal within the heart itself or in one of the two major arteries. Instead of the normal 'lubb dupp' noise, an additional sound can be heard that can vary from a mild 'pshhh' to a loud 'whoosh'. The different grades are:

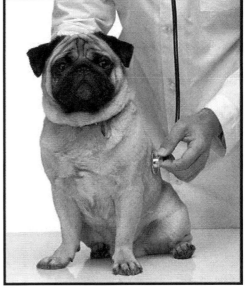

- ♦ **Grade 1**—barely audible
- ♦ **Grade 2**—soft, but easily heard with a stethoscope
- ♦ **Grade 3**—intermediate loudness; most murmurs which are related to the mechanics of blood circulation are at least grade III
- ♦ **Grade 4**—loud murmur that radiates widely, often including opposite side of chest
- ♦ **Grades 5 and Grade 6**—very loud, audible with stethoscope barely touching the chest; the vibration is also strong enough to be felt through the animal's chest wall

Murmurs are caused by a number of factors; it may be a problem with the heart valves or could be due to some other condition, such as hyperthyroidism (see the previous section on this), anaemia, or heartworm.

In puppies, there are two major types of heart murmurs, and they will probably be detected by your vet at the first or second vaccinations. The most common type is called an innocent "flow murmur." This type of murmur is soft - typically Grade 2 or less - and is not caused by underlying heart disease. An innocent flow murmur typically disappears by four to five months of age. However if a puppy has a loud murmur - Grade 3 or louder - or if the heart murmur is still easily heard with a stethoscope after four or five months of age, the likelihood of the puppy having an underlying congenital (from birth) heart problem becomes much higher. The thought of a puppy having congenital heart disease is extremely worrying, but it is important to remember that the disease will not affect all puppies' life expectancy or quality of life.

A heart murmur can also develop suddenly in an adult dog with no prior history of the problem. This is typically due to heart disease that develops with age. In Toy and small breeds, a heart murmur may develop in middle-aged to older dogs due to an age-related thickening and degeneration of one of the valves in the heart, the mitral valve. (This is the type our dog has.)

This thickening of the valve prevents it from closing properly and as a result it starts to leak, this is known as mitral valve disease. The more common type of heart disease affecting larger dog breeds in middle age is Dilated Cardiomyopathy (DCM). The best way to investigate the cause of the heart murmur is with an ultrasound examination of the heart (an echocardiogram).

By the way, after our Max was diagnosed with a Grade 2 murmur, we took the vet's advice and ignored it. However, we are always on alert for a dry, racking cough, which is a sign of fluid in the lungs - so far, it hasn't happened. The good news is that he is now 10 and, as the saying goes: "fit as a butcher's dog."

Obesity in Pugs

Our dogs rely on us to keep them healthy. Virtually every Pug ever born is greedy, so it is up to us as responsible owners to monitor our dog's intake of food. One of the worst things we can do is to allow our Pugs to become overweight - obesity is a life-threatening condition for Pugs.

As with humans, excess weight places extra demands on virtually all the organs of a Pug's body. Couple this with the fact that the breed's conformation (body shape) with its extremely flat face and short neck means that many Pugs' bodies are already under stress - and you have a potential recipe for disaster. When these organs become overloaded due to obesity, disease and even death can occur.

One of the most common complications is the development of diabetes mellitus (sugar diabetes), see the section later in this chapter. And studies have shown that around 25% of overweight dogs develop serious joint complications. The bones, joints, muscles and associated tendons and ligaments all work together to give the dog smooth and efficient movement, and if they have to carry excess weight, they can become damaged. Arthritis can develop and the pain and joint changes associated with hip dysplasia can become markedly more severe – and Pugs are particularly susceptible to hip dysplasia.

Extra tension on joints can also lead to ligament damage. Ligaments are tough, fibrous strands of tissue that hold one bone in proximity to another bone in joints. The knee's anterior cruciate ligament is very prone to strains or tears, and if this happens, surgery is often the consequence.

Certain breeds of dogs, including Pugs, are prone to develop intervertebral disc disease (slipped disc), and carrying extra weight increases the probability of this. As with people, overweight dogs tend to have increased blood pressure (hypertension). The heart has an increased work load since it must pump additional blood to excess tissues, and this can lead to heart failure.

A particular worry for Pug owners is breathing problems caused by obesity; extra fat in the chest restricts the expansion of the lungs and prevents them from functioning properly. To make matters worse, the increased fat tissue puts an increased demand on the lungs to supply oxygen, which is especially serious in Pugs who may already have respiratory problems. Many owners may be unaware of the huge range of other issues obesity brings with it. These include:

- ❖ A general discomfort and reduced quality of life for your dog
- ❖ Lack of stamina
- ❖ Heat intolerance
- ❖ Decreased liver function as fats build up in the liver
- ❖ Increased risk of complications due to anaesthetic
- ❖ Harder for vets to operate on overweight dogs due to all the fat around organs
- ❖ Harder for overweight females to give birth and increased health problems
- ❖ Decreased resistance to viral and bacterial infections
- ❖ Increased risk of skin and coat diseases
- ❖ Increased risk of constipation and flatulence - already a big issue with Pugs
- ❖ Increased risk of cancer
- ❖ Reduced lifespan

Ignore those pleading big brown eyes at mealtimes, your Pug will be much happier and healthier at his or her ideal weight - which should be between 14lbs and 18lbs.

See **Chapter 6 Feeding a Pug** for more information on diets and guidelines on daily amounts.

Overheating Pugs

It's a fact, all brachycephalic dogs overheat more easily than other breeds. Pugs do not cope well with hot, sometimes just warm, temperatures and are prone to heatstroke or hyperthermia.

It's also a fact that dogs can't sweat. Well, only a tiny bit through the pads of their paws. Instead of being able to cool down by sweating all over their body like humans, they have the far less efficient mechanism of panting, which circulates cooling air around their body. Couple this inefficient cooling system with the shortened head of the Pug and you have a potential recipe for disaster. Make no mistake, heat can be a killer for Pugs.

Several airlines refuse to carry Pugs and other brachycephalic breeds because of overheating and breathing issues (the two are related). And in 2014, a family crossing the English Channel on a ferry were devastated to return to their car after 4.5 hours to find their Pug suffering from overheating. He later died. Their other Pug and their Beagle, also in the car for the crossing, were fine. After more than 9,000 people signed a petition, the ferry company is reviewing its policy of not allowing dogs out of the car during transit.

Pugs have been bred to have shortened facial bone structures to give a pushed-in look. However, the soft tissue inside has stayed the same size, which means that there isn't much room for air to circulate inside the dog's mouth and throat.

Some Pugs have elongated palates and extremely narrow nostrils (stenotic nares), which makes breathing difficult, and especially so when they are hot and need to pant. When they try to pant quickly, foam can be produced, which in turn blocks the throat and causes laboured breathing. Eventually they will begin to roar as they try to breathe through the blockage. A dog's normal body temperature is around 100-102.5ºF, (a puppy's normal rectal temperature is 96-100ºF), if this rises to over 106ºF, the dog is suffering from severe heatstroke and can die.

NOTE: As well as dying from overheating, Pugs can also die or get into difficulties when they are highly stressed – again this is related to breathing problems. Do not let your dog get too hot or over-excited or over-exercised. If he is struggling for breath, STOP the activity immediately.

Symptoms of Overheating

- ❖ Panting rapidly and frantically, this may develop into a roaring sound
- ❖ Bright red and floppy tongue
- ❖ Gums may become discoloured
- ❖ He will look tired and distressed, perhaps becoming dizzy
- ❖ He may produce a thick, sticky saliva or foam as his airways become blocked
- ❖ He may have diarrhoea or begin vomiting - sometimes with blood
- ❖ Shock

Action - STAY CALM! Your dog will pick up on your fear if you panic, causing him more stress. Remove the dog from the hot area immediately. Lower his temperature by wetting him thoroughly with **cool or tepid water** (not cold) then increase air movement around him with a fan. Part his fur with your fingers to let the cooling air get to his body.

CAUTION: Using very cold water can actually be counterproductive. Cooling too quickly and especially allowing the dog's body temperature to become too low can cause other life-threatening medical conditions. Similarly, some Pug owners recommend using ice on the body to cool the dog, but many veterinarians advise against this, as it closes the skin pores and could potentially make the situation worse.

Other suggestions from owners include getting your Pug used to eating ice cubes, ice pops or frozen yoghurts from an early age so that if he does start to overheat, you can feed him these and he will readily take them. Another suggestion is that if your dog has started foaming, squirt lemon juice from a plastic lemon into the back of his throat – he will hate it, but the lemon juice will help to break down the foam and clear the throat.

You may also have to reach inside his throat to try and pull out the sticky saliva to clear his airways. This may sound dramatic, but if you think it would save your dog's life, you probably wouldn't hesitate. Many owners in warm climates have found the use of certain products, such as cooling jackets and blankets, to be most helpful. NOTE: Ice collars are not recommended for Pugs, they may restrict the blood flow to the brain and cause other problems, such as seizures.

The rectal temperature of an overheated dog should be checked every five minutes. Do this very carefully, preferably with somebody holding him steady. Use a special rectal thermometer and hold on to it, some dogs have been known to "suck in" the thermometer.

Once the body temperature is down to 103ºF, the cooling measures should be stopped and the dog should be dried thoroughly and covered so he does not continue to lose heat. Even if the dog appears to be recovering, take him to your vet as soon as possible. He should still be examined as he may be dehydrated or have other complications. Allow him access to water or an electrolyte rehydrating solution if he can drink on his own. Do not try to force-feed cold water as he may inhale it or choke.

When you have the emergency situation under control, take him to the vet immediately. He or she will lower your dog's body temperature to a safe range, if you have not already done so, and continue to monitor his temperature. They may administer fluids, and possibly oxygen and may take blood samples to test for clotting. The dog will be monitored for shock, respiratory distress, kidney failure, heart abnormalities and other complications, and treated accordingly.

Dogs with moderate heatstroke often recover without complicated health problems. However, severe heatstroke can cause organ damage that might need ongoing care, such as a special diet prescribed by the vet. Dogs who suffer from heatstroke once have an increased risk of getting it again and owners must take steps to prevent it recurring.

NOTE: Believe it or not, Pugs can also get sunburnt. If yours is to be out in the sun for any length of time, apply a canine sunscreen. Shop around for the best one, some are better than others.

14 Tips to Prevent a Pug Overheating

The main factor in determining whether your dog gets heatstroke is YOU. Being aware of your dog's susceptibility to heat (and stress) is the first step, taking action to prevent it is the second essential step.

Many Pugs love to sunbathe, you need to keep an eye on this and don't let the dog lie for too long in the sun -either inside the house or outdoors. Sometimes 10 or 15 minutes will be enough, a Pug will not realise that he or she is overheating inside so it's up to you to monitor the situation. Pugs Overheating can happen alarmingly quickly, here are some preventative measures:

1. Make sure your dog has a cool place indoors and shade outdoors at all times

2. Reduce exercise in warm weather. On hot days only take your dog outside for short periods – early in the morning and in the evening when temperatures are lower are the best times. Ten minutes is enough for some, while others may enjoy a longer walk, get to know what your dog likes. For some Pugs, anything in the 70s is hot, while others may be fine outdoors for short periods at temperatures up to 80ºF

3. Make sure your dog has access to water 24/7

4. If your dog does not want to go outside, do not force him

5. Have a shady dog toilet area in your yard or garden

6. Take water with you on your walks in warm weather. Watch your dog carefully for indications that he is over-heating, such as heavy panting, loss of energy, and any weakness or stumbling. If he shows signs, stop in a shady spot and give him some water. If symptoms don't subside, take him home and ring the vet

7. NEVER muzzle your Pug

8. NEVER leave him in a parked car, even if you're in the shade or will only be gone a short time. The temperature inside a parked car can quickly reach up to 140ºF

9. On hot days avoid places like the beach and especially concrete or asphalt areas, where heat is reflected and there is no access to shade

10. Put your dog in a cool area of the house. Air conditioning is one of the best ways to keep a dog cool, but is not always reliable. You can freeze water in soda bottles, or place ice and a small amount of water in several resealable food storage bags, wrap them in a towel or tube sock and put them on the floor for your dog to lie on

11. Do not let your dog become over-excited in warm weather, avoid strenuous games or exercise

12. Don't go jogging with a Pug. Most dogs will try to keep up with their owners and this can put stress on the heart or cause them to overheat

13. By the time your Pug starts to feel hot, he's probably already overheating. Keep an eye on your dog, especially puppies and young dogs who may want to run and play for hours. Monitor exercise and play time

14. Do not allow your Pug to become obese. An obese dog is more likely to suffer from heatstroke – as well as many other problems.

Canine Diabetes

This is not an issue which particularly affects Pugs any more than any other type of dog, but can affect dogs of all breeds, sizes and both genders. It does, however, affect obese dogs more than ones of a normal weight and Pugs are prone to obesity.

There are two types: *diabetes mellitus* and *diabetes insipidus*. Diabetes mellitus (sugar diabetes) is the most common form and affects one in 500 dogs. Pugs are regarded as having a moderate risk of contracting this. Thanks to modern veterinary medicine, the condition is now treatable and need not shorten your Pug's lifespan or interfere with his quality of life. Diabetic dogs undergoing treatment now have the same life expectancy as non-diabetic dogs of the same age and gender.

However, if left untreated, the disease can lead to cataracts, increasing weakness in the legs (neuropathy), other ailments and even death. In dogs, diabetes is typically seen anywhere between the ages of four to 14, with a peak at seven to nine years. Both males and females can develop it; unspayed females have a slightly higher risk. The typical canine diabetes sufferer is middle-aged, female and overweight, but there are also juvenile cases.

What is Diabetes?

Diabetes insipidus is caused by a lack of vasopressin, a hormone which controls the kidneys' absorption of water. *Diabetes mellitus* occurs when the dog's body does not produce enough insulin and cannot successfully process sugars.

Dogs, like us, get their energy by converting the food they eat into sugars, mainly glucose. This glucose travels in the dog's bloodstream and individual cells then remove some of that glucose from the blood to use for energy. The substance that allows the cells to take glucose from the blood is a protein called *insulin.*

Insulin is created by beta cells that are located in the pancreas, next to the stomach. Almost all diabetic dogs have Type 1 diabetes: their pancreas does not produce any insulin. Without it, the cells have no way to use the glucose that is in the bloodstream, so the cells 'starve' while the glucose level in the blood rises. Your vet will use blood samples and urine samples to check glucose concentrations in order to diagnose diabetes. Early treatment helps to prevent further complications developing.

Common Symptoms

❖ Extreme thirst
❖ Excessive urination
❖ Weight loss

- ❖ Increased appetite
- ❖ Coat in poor condition
- ❖ Lethargy
- ❖ Vision problems due to cataracts

Cataracts and Diabetes - Some diabetic dogs do go blind. Cataracts may develop due to high blood glucose levels causing water to build up in the eyes' lenses. This leads to swelling, rupture of the lens fibres and the development of cataracts. In many cases, the cataracts can be surgically removed to bring sight back to the dog. Vision is restored in 75% to 80% of diabetic dogs that undergo cataract removal.

However, some dogs may stay blind even after the cataracts are gone, and some cataracts simply cannot be removed. Blind dogs are often able to get around surprisingly well, particularly in a familiar home.

Treatment - Treatment starts with the right diet. Your vet will prescribe meals low in fat and sugars. He will also recommend medication. Many cases of canine diabetes can be successfully treated with diet and medication. More severe cases may require insulin injections. In the newly-diagnosed dog, insulin therapy begins at home.

Normally, after a week of treatment, you return to the vet who will do a series of blood sugar tests over a 12-14 hour period to see when the blood glucose peaks and when it hits its lows. Adjustments are then made to the dosage and timing of the injections. Your vet will explain how to prepare and inject the insulin. You may be asked to collect urine samples using a test strip (a small piece of paper that indicates the glucose levels in urine).

If your dog is already having insulin injections, beware of a 'miracle cure' offered on some internet sites. It does not exist. There is no diet or vitamin supplement which can reduce your dog's dependence on insulin injections because vitamins and minerals cannot do what insulin does in the dog's body. If you think that your dog needs a supplement, discuss it with your vet first to make sure that it does not interfere with any other medication.

Exercise - Managing your dog's diabetes also means managing his activity level. Exercise burns up blood glucose the same way that insulin does. If your dog is on insulin, any active exercise on top of the insulin might cause him to have a severe low blood glucose episode, called **'hypoglycaemia'.**

Keep your dog on a reasonably consistent exercise routine. Your usual insulin dose will take that amount of exercise into account. If you plan to take your dog out for some extra demanding exercise, such as running round with other dogs, give him only half of his usual insulin dose.

FINE FOODS

Menu

"I DON'T SEE TABLE SCRAPS."

Tips

- ❖ You can usually buy specially formulated diabetes dog food from your veterinarian

- ❖ You should feed the same type and amount of food at the same time every day

- ❖ Most vets recommend twice-a-day feeding for diabetic pets. It is OK if your dog prefers to eat more often

- If you have other pets in the home, they should also be placed on a twice-a-day feeding schedule, so that the diabetic dog cannot eat from their bowls. Help your dog to achieve the best possible blood glucose control by not feeding him table scraps or treats between meals

- Watch for signs that your dog is starting to drink more water than usual. Call the vet if you see this happening, as it may mean that the insulin dose needs adjusting.

Remember these simple points:

Food raises blood glucose

Insulin and exercise lower blood glucose

Keep them in balance

For more information on canine diabetes visit **www.caninediabetes.org**

The F Word

We couldn't devote nearly 50 pages to health without mentioning the Puggy F word: farting – or, if you prefer the polite term, flatulence!

There's no avoiding the issue, Pugs are windy beasts. Due to their shape and the way their bodies process food, they produce a lot of gas during and after digestion. It can be unpleasant, smelly and downright embarrassing for owners cooped in a room or car with what seems like enough gas to power the whole country for a month.

Flatulence occurs when gas accumulates in your dog's intestinal tract and colon. This is a normal process that occurs when bacteria break down certain types of food. While it can be disconcerting, the good news is that it is rarely indication of a serious health problem. You might think that it is part and parcel of the joys of owning a Pug, but there are measures you can take to reduce flatulence in your dog.

1. Flatulence is often caused by air that is gulped down when Pugs eat too quickly. Putting a large object in his food dish will force your dog to slow down when eating. The object should be something that is too large for him to pick up in his mouth, like a softball. If you have more than one dog, feed them separately to reduce food competition and gulping. Another option is to raise the feeding bowl to head height

2. Exercise your dog after his meals. Light exercise helps digestion and works out the gas

while you are outside. If your dog is windy during the walk, even better!

3. Some dogs have an intolerance to lactose (dairy products) or grain which causes gas, try and avoid these foods

4. Try switching food. Your brand of dog food may be the culprit, particularly if it is high in soy. Cheap processed dog foods also increase gas. More owners are also looking at switching to a home-cooked or even a raw diet. There is plenty of anecdotal evidence from owners of brachycephalic breeds like the Pug that a raw diet can reduce flatulence. Switch over gradually if you do this, so your dog's digestive system can adapt to the new food, see **Chapter 6 Feeding a Pug** for more details

5. Monitor your dog's food, feed two smaller meals rather than one large meal a day. If you feed table scraps, include them as part of one of these meals, not as well as or in between meals. Neither feeding one huge meal nor constant snacking are good for your Pug

6. A spoonful of yoghurt in the daily feeds helps to keep the balance of good and bad bacteria in balance in the gut

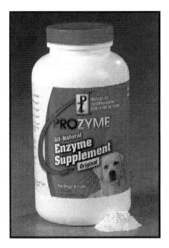

7. You might consider adding **Prozyme** to a feed. Prozyme is a plant-derived enzyme supplement which replaces the natural enzymes that are lost in food processing. It helps digest protein, fat, sugar, starch, and fibre, and enhances the absorption of zinc, selenium, vitamin B6, and linoleic acid.

According to the manufacturer, Prozyme increases absorption of the nutrients in the food. It works once the food is ingested (after mixing the Prozyme with the food; it is not necessary to let the mixture stand before feeding) and is reported to help with immune and digestive disorders, poor coat and excessive shedding, skin problems, joint disorders, weight problems, allergies, lethargy, bloating, flatulence, and coprophagia (stool eating).

Prozyme should be stored in a cool, dry location away from excessive heat and should NOT be used with hot gravy or hot food.

Pugs and Anaesthetic

It is always a concern for owners if their beloved Pug needs to be anaesthetised for a surgical procedure – and it's also a factor to be considered when deciding whether to have them spayed or neutered.

The problem with all brachycephalic dogs is that there is simply too much soft, pink tissue crammed into their short heads. While successive breeding has led to the skulls (and necks) becoming much shorter to create a particularly appealing look, the size of everything inside – such as the tongue, windpipe and palate - has remained the same.

This is why some Pugs' tongues, for example, look enormous - they are out of proportion for the size of the muzzle. In practical terms what this means is that breeds such as Pugs may have difficulty breathing, or at least have smaller airways than other types of dog. Dogs that cope perfectly well on a daily basis may have difficulty with anaesthetic when all their muscles are at rest and the narrow airways effectively become blocked.

Always make sure that the vet or the anaesthetist is familiar with brachycephalic breeds of dogs (as well as Toy breeds), as they react differently to other breeds under anaesthetic. And keep your dog's weight in check, obesity increases the risk of breathing problems. Here are some points to be familiar with before agreeing to surgery. Be sure to ask your vet to outline the extra care he or she will be taking with your Pug.

❖ The vet should have a special anaesthetic procedure or protocol for Pugs and other brachycephalic dogs.

❖ The vet should provide oxygen before anaesthesia to help saturate the dog's lungs with extra oxygen

❖ The Pug protocol should take into account anti-vomiting, anti-inflammatory, anti-anxiety measures and pain management to reduce common complications

❖ Pugs should not be masked, they can become anxious and experience breathing difficulties

❖ The dog should have an endotracheal tube (ET) in his or her windpipe (trachea) to keep the airway open at all times.

❖ The tube should be kept in place as long as possible and until the dog is fully awake

French Bulldogs have similar problems and an Anesthesia Protocol has been developed by Dr Lori Hunt, DVM and Dr Dawn Ruben, DVM for The French Bulldog Rescue Network. www.frenchbulldogrescue.org/adoption-info/faq/anesthesia-policy They recommend AGAINST the use of the following drugs:

➢ Acepromazine

➢ Phenobarbital (injectable anaesthetic)

➢ Xylazine (sedative)

➢ Halothane (gas anaesthetic)

A critical time is the recovery phase after the surgical procedure - and this is where YOU come in. Here are some tips to help your Pug towards a full and speedy recovery:

❖ Keep your dog within sight for 12 to 24 hours after surgery

❖ Monitor the colour of your dog's tongue – pink is good, blue is bad

❖ Keep your Pug well ventilated. If your dog is panting excessively, check his temperature (with a canine thermometer). If it is above 100F turn a fan on and face it towards him

❖ Keep your dog in a quiet, stress-free place, and try and keep him relaxed.

Canine Cancer

This is the biggest single killer of dogs of whatever breed and will claim the lives of one in four dogs. It is the cause of nearly half the deaths of all dogs aged 10 years and older, according to the American Veterinary Medical Association.

Symptoms - Early detection is critical, some things to look out for are:

- ❖ **Swellings anywhere on the body**
- ❖ **Lumps in a dog's armpit or under his jaw**
- ❖ **Sores that don't heal**
- ❖ **Bad breath**
- ❖ **Weight loss**
- ❖ **Poor appetite, difficulty swallowing or excessive drooling**
- ❖ **Changes in exercise or stamina level**
- ❖ **Laboured breathing**
- ❖ **Change in bowel or bladder habits**

If your dog has been spayed or neutered, the risk of certain cancers decreases. These cancers include uterine and breast/mammary cancer in females, and testicular cancer in males (if the dog was neutered before he was six months old). Along with controlling the pet population, spaying is especially important because mammary cancer in female dogs is fatal in about 50% of all cases.

Diagnosis - Just because your dog has a skin growth doesn't mean that it's cancerous. As with humans, tumours may be benign (harmless) or malignant (harmful). Your vet will probably confirm the tumour using X-rays, blood tests and possibly ultrasounds. He or she will then decide whether it is benign or malignant via a biopsy in which a tissue sample is taken from your dog and examined under a microscope. If your dog is diagnosed with cancer, there is hope. Advances in veterinary medicine and technology offer various treatment options, including chemotherapy, radiation and surgery. Unlike with humans, a dog's hair will not fall out with chemotherapy.

Treatment - Canine cancer is growing at an ever-increasing rate. One of the difficulties is that your pet cannot tell you when a cancer is developing, but if cancers can be detected early enough through a physical or behavioural change, they often respond well to treatment.

Over recent years, we have all become more aware of the risk factors for human cancer. Responding to these by changing our habits is having a significant impact on human health. For example, stopping smoking, protecting ourselves from over-exposure to strong sunlight and eating a healthy, balanced diet all help to reduce cancer rates. We know to keep a close eye on ourselves, go for regular health checks and report any lumps and bumps to our doctors as soon as they appear. Increased cancer awareness is definitely improving human health. The same is true with your dog.

While it is impossible to completely prevent cancer from occurring, a healthy lifestyle with a balanced diet and regular exercise can help to reduce the risk. Also, be aware of any new lumps and bumps on your dog's body and any changes in his behaviour.

The success of treatment will depend on the type of cancer, the treatment used and on how early the tumour is found. The sooner treatment begins, the greater the chances of success. One of the best things you can do for your dog is to keep a close eye on him for any tell-tale signs.

This shouldn't be too difficult and can be done as part of your regular handling and grooming. If you notice any new bumps, for example, monitor them over a period of days to see if there is a change in their appearance or size. If there is, then make an appointment to see your vet as soon as possible. It might only be a cyst, but better to be safe than sorry.

Research into earlier diagnosis and improved treatments is being conducted at veterinary schools and companies all over the world. Advances in biology are producing a steady flow of new tests and treatments which are now becoming available to improve survival rates and canine cancer care. If your dog is diagnosed with cancer, do not despair, there are many options and new, improved treatments are constantly being introduced.

Our Happy Ending

We know from personal experience that canine cancer can be successfully treated if it is diagnosed early enough. Our dog was diagnosed with T-cell lymphoma when he was four years old.

We had noticed a black lump on his anus which grew to the size of a small grape. We took him to the vet within the first few days of seeing the lump and, after a test, he was diagnosed with the dreaded T-cell lymphoma. This is a particularly nasty and aggressive form of cancer which can spread to the lymph system and is often fatal for dogs. As soon as the diagnosis was confirmed, our vet Graham operated and removed the lump. He also had to remove one of his anal glands, but as dogs have two this was not a serious worry. Afterwards, we were on tenterhooks, not knowing if another lump would grow or if the cancer had already spread to his lymph system.

After a few months, Max had another blood test and was finally given the all-clear. Max is now happy, healthy and ten years old. We were very lucky. I would strongly advise anyone who suspects that their dog has cancer to get him or her to your local vet as soon as possible.

Disclaimer: The author of this book is not a qualified veterinarian. This chapter is intended to give owners an indication of some of the illnesses which may affect their dogs and the symptoms to look out for. If you have any concerns regarding the health of your dog, our advice is always the same: consult a veterinarian.

11. Skin and Allergies

Allergies are one of the ailments reported by owners of many breeds. This is a complicated topic and a whole book could be written on this subject alone. As with the human population, skin conditions, allergies and intolerances appear to be on the increase.

As far as Pugs are concerned, there is a great deal of variation; the breed as a whole is not one of the ones regarded as being particularly prone to skin issues. While many dogs have no problems at all, some suffer from sensitive skin, allergies, yeast infections and/or skin disorders, causing them to scratch, bite or lick themselves excessively on the paws and other areas. Symptoms may vary from mild itchiness to a chronic reaction.

The many breeders we asked about this topic were split - some have no problems at all with their dogs, while others have had issues. If you haven't already bought your puppy, it would be a question to ask the breeder. One factor is the way the breed has been developed over the years for a distinctive look with rolls of loose skin, or wrinkles. If not properly cared for, Pugs can develop yeast infections and other issues in the folds of the skin.

As with humans, the skin is the dog's largest organ. It acts as the protective barrier between your dog's internal organs and the outside world; it also regulates temperature and provides the sense of touch. Surprisingly, a dog's skin is actually thinner than ours, and it is made up of three layers:

1. **Epidermis** or outer layer, the one that bears the brunt of your dog's contact with the outside world

2. **Dermis** is the extremely tough layer mostly made up of collagen, a strong and fibrous protein. This where blood vessels deliver nutrients and oxygen to the skin, and it also acts as your dog's thermostat by allowing his body to release or keep in heat, depending on the outside temperature and your dog's activity level

3. **Subcutis** is a dense layer of fatty tissue that allows your dog's skin to move independently from the muscle layers below it, as well as providing insulation and support for the skin

Human allergies often trigger a reaction within the respiratory system, causing us to wheeze or sneeze, whereas allergies or hypersensitivities in a dog often cause a reaction in his or her skin.

Skin can be affected from the **inside** by things that your dog eats or drinks.

Skin can be affected from the **outside** by fleas, parasites, inhaled or contact allergies triggered by grass, pollen, man-made chemicals, dust, mould etc. These environmental allergies are especially common in some Terriers as well as the Miniature Schnauzer, Bulldog and certain other breeds.

Like all breeds, a Pug can suffer from food allergies or intolerances as well as environmental allergies. There are also ailments that can be passed on genetically, such as a predisposition to interdigital cysts (interdigital furuncles) - between the toes.

Canine skin disorders are a complex subject. Some dogs can run through fields, digging holes and rolling around in the grass with no after-effects at all. Others may spend most of their time indoors and have an excellent diet, but still experience severe itching.

Skin problems may be the result of one or more of a wide range of causes - and the list of potential remedies and treatments is even longer. It's by no means possible to cover all of them in this chapter. The aim here is to give a broad outline of some of the ailments most likely to affect Pugs and how to deal with them. We have also included remedies tried with some success by ourselves (our dog has skin issues) and other owners of dogs with skin problems as well as advice from a holistic specialist.

This information is not intended to take the place of professional help. We are not animal health experts and you should always contact your veterinarian when your dog appears physically unwell or uncomfortable. This is particularly true with skin conditions:

If a vet can find the source of the problem early on, there is more chance of successfully treating it before it has chance to develop into a more serious condition with secondary issues.

There is anecdotal evidence from some Pug owners that switching to a raw diet or raw meaty bones diet can significantly help some dogs with skin issues. Other owners and breeders have found that their dogs thrive on a diet of kibble. See **Chapter 6. Feeding a Pug** for more information.

One of the difficulties with this type of ailment is that the exact cause is often difficult to diagnose, as the symptoms may be common to other ailments as well. If environmental allergies are involved, some specific tests are available costing hundreds of pounds or dollars.

You will have to take your vet's advice on this, as the tests are not always conclusive and if the answer is dust or pollen, it can be difficult to keep your dog away from the triggers while still having a normal life - unless you and your Pug spend all your time in a spotlessly clean city apartment! It is often a question of managing a skin condition, rather than curing it.

Skin issues and allergies often develop in adolescence or early adulthood, which in a Pug may be anything from a few months to two or three years old. Our dog Max was perfectly normal until he reached two when he began scratching, caused by environmental allergies - most likely pollen. He's now 10 and over the years he's been on various different remedies which have all worked for a time. As his allergies are seasonal, he normally does not have any medication between October and March. But come spring and as sure as daffodils are daffodils, he starts scratching again. Luckily, they are manageable and Max lives a happy, normal life.

Another issue reported by some Pug owners is food allergy or intolerance (there is a difference) – often to grain.

However, allergies and trying to treat them can cause a lot of stress for dogs and owners alike. The number one piece of advice is that if you suspect your Pug has an allergy or skin problem, try to deal with it right away - either via your vet or natural remedies – before the all-too-familiar scenario kicks in and it develops into a chronic (long term) condition.

Whatever the cause, before a vet can diagnose the problem you have to be prepared to tell him or her all about your dog's diet, exercise regime, habits, medical history and local environment. The vet will then carry out a thorough physical examination, possibly followed by further (expensive) tests, before a course of treatment can be prescribed.

Demodectic Mange

Also known as red mange, follicular mange, or puppy mange, this skin disease is known to affect certain breeds, including Pugs, Shar-Peis, Bull-Terrier breeds, Old English Sheepdogs and Dogue de Bordeaux, and normally starts in puppyhood.

It is caused by the tiny mite Demodex canis (pictured). The mites actually live inside the hair follicles on the bodies of virtually every adult dog and most humans without causing any harm or irritation. In humans, the mites are found in the skin, eyelids and the creases of the nose ...try not to think about that!

The demodectic mite spends its entire life on the host dog. Eggs hatch and mature from larvae to nymphs to adults in 20 to 35 days and the mites are transferred directly from the mother to the puppies within the first week of life by direct physical contact. Demodectic mange is not a disease of poorly kept or dirty kennels. It is generally a disease of young dogs with inadequate or poorly developed immune systems (or older dogs suffering from a suppressed immune system).

Virtually every mother carries and transfers mites to her puppies, and most are immune to the mite's effects, but a few puppies are not and they develop full-blown mange. They may have a few (less than five) isolated lesions and this is known as localised mange – often around the head. Or they may have generalised mange which covers the entire body or region of the body. Most lesions in either form develop after four months of age.

Breeder Saran Evans, of Sephina Pugs, Carmarthenshire, UK says: "Pugs are susceptible to demodectic mange. This typically rears its head at around eight to nine months of age - usually when a bitch has her first season, as this appears to cause a dip in the immune system. It begins as a small area of hair loss. If untreated, the Pug will scratch continually and eventually lose the majority of their fur, with the skin becoming inflamed and scaled.

"Demodectic mange is not contagious and is easily treated with Advocate, a spot-on treatment from the vet, but early intervention is necessary."

Symptoms – Bald patches are usually the first sign, usually accompanied by crusty, red skin which sometimes appears greasy or wet. Usually hair loss begins around the muzzle, eyes and other areas on the head. The lesions may or may not itch.

In localised mange a few circular crusty areas appear, most frequently on the head and front legs of three to six-month-old puppies. Most will self-heal as the puppies become older and develop their own immunity, but a persistent problem needs treatment.

With generalised mange there are bald patches over the entire coat, including the head, neck, body, legs, and feet. The skin on the head, side and back is crusty, often inflamed and oozes a clear fluid. The skin itself will often be oily to touch and there is usually a secondary bacterial infection. Some puppies can become quite ill and can develop a fever, lose their appetites and become lethargic. If you suspect your puppy has generalised demodectic mange, get him to a vet straight away.

There is also a condition called pododermatitis, when the mange affects a puppy's paws. It can cause bacterial infections and be very uncomfortable, even painful. The symptoms of this mange include hair loss on the paws, swelling of the paws (especially around the nail beds) and red/hot/inflamed areas which are often infected. Treatment is always recommended, and it can take several rounds to clear it up.

Diagnosis and Treatment – The vet will normally diagnose demodectic mange after he or she has taken a skin scraping or biopsy, in which case the mites can be seen with a microscope. As these mites are present on every dog, they do not necessarily constitute a diagnosis of mange. Only when the mite is coupled with lesions will a diagnosis of mange be made.

Treatment usually involves topical (on the skin) medication and sometimes tablets. Localised demodectic mange often resolves itself as the puppy grows.

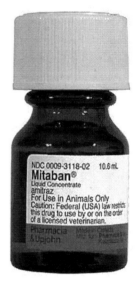

With generalised demodectic mange, treatment can be lengthy and expensive. The vet might prescribe Amitraz anti-parasitic dips every two weeks. It is an organophosphate available only on prescription under the name **Mitaban.** Owners should always wear rubber gloves when treating their dog, and it should be applied in an area with adequate ventilation.

Most dogs with this condition need from six to 14 dips every two weeks. After the first three or four dips, your vet will probably take another skin scraping to check that the mites have gone. Dips continue for one month after the mites have disappeared, but dogs shouldn't be considered cured until a year after their last treatment.

Some dogs, especially Toy breeds like Pugs, don't respond well to Mitaban, as it makes them nauseous. Discuss treatment fully with your vet first. Other options include the heartworm treatment Ivermectin. This isn't approved by the FDA for treating mange, but is often used to do so. It is usually given orally on a daily basis, and is very effective. Another drug is Interceptor (Milbemycin oxime), which can be expensive as it has to be given daily. However, it is effective on up to 80% of the dogs who did not respond to Mitaban dips –but should be given with caution to pups under 21 weeks of age.

Dogs that have the generalised condition may have underlying skin infections, so antibiotics are often given for the first several weeks of treatment. Because the mite flourishes on dogs with suppressed immune systems, it is a good idea to try and get to the root cause of immune system disease, especially if your Pug is older when he or she develops demodectic mange.

Types of Allergies

'*Canine dermatitis*' means inflammation of a dog's skin and it can be triggered by numerous things, but the most common by far is allergies. Vets estimate that one in four dogs at their clinics is there because of some kind of allergy.

Symptoms

- ➢ Chewing on paws
- ➢ Rubbing the face on the carpet
- ➢ Scratching the body
- ➢ Itchy ears, head shaking
- ➢ Hair loss
- ➢ Mutilated skin with sore or discoloured patches or hot spots

A Pug who is allergic to something will show it through skin problems and itching; your vet may call this '*pruritus'*.

It may seem logical that if a dog is allergic to something he inhales, like certain pollen grains, his nose will run; if he's allergic to something he eats, he may vomit, or if allergic to an insect bite, he may develop a swelling. But in practice this is seldom the case. The skin is an organ and with dogs it is this organ which is often affected by allergies. So instead, he will have a mild to severe itching sensation over his body and maybe a chronic ear infection.

Dogs with allergies often chew their feet until they are sore and red. You may see your Pug rubbing his face on the carpet or couch or scratching his belly and flanks. Because the ear glands produce too much wax in response to the allergy, ear infections can occur, with bacteria and yeast - which is a fungus - often thriving in the excessive wax and debris. By the way, if your Pug does develop a yeast infection and you decide to switch to a grain-free diet, try and avoid those which are potato-based, as these contain high levels of starch.

Holistic vet Dr Jodie Gruenstern says: "Grains and other starches have a negative impact on gut health, creating insulin resistance and inflammation. It's estimated that up to 80% of the immune system resides within the gastrointestinal system; building a healthy gut supports a more appropriate immune response. The importance of choosing fresh proteins and healthy fats over processed, starchy diets (such as kibble) can't be overemphasized."

An allergic dog may cause skin lesions or 'hot spots' by constant chewing and scratching. Sometimes he will lose hair, which can be patchy or inconsistent over the body, leaving a mottled appearance. The skin itself may be dry and crusty, reddened, swollen or oily, depending on the dog. It is very common to get secondary bacterial skin infections due to these self-inflicted wounds. An allergic dog's body is reacting to certain molecules called 'allergens.' These may come from:

- ❖ Trees
- ❖ Grass
- ❖ Pollens
- ❖ Foods and food additives, such as specific meats, grains or colourings
- ❖ Milk products

- ❖ Fabrics, such as wool or nylon
- ❖ Rubber and plastics
- ❖ House dust and dust mites
- ❖ Mould
- ❖ Flea bites
- ❖ Chemical products used around the house

These allergens may be **inhaled** as the dog breathes, **ingested** as the dog eats or caused by **contact** with the dog's body when he walks or rolls. However they arrive, they all cause the immune system to produce a protein (IgE), which causes various irritating chemicals, such as histamine, to be released. In dogs these chemical reactions and cell types occur in sizeable amounts only within the skin, hence the scratching.

Inhalant Allergies (Atopy)

The most common allergies in dogs are inhalant and seasonal (at least at first, some allergies may develop and worsen). Substances which can cause an allergic reaction in dogs are similar to those causing problems for humans.

A clue to diagnosing these allergies is to look at the timing of the reaction. Does it happen all year round? If so, this may be mould, dust or some other trigger which is permanently in the environment. If the reaction is seasonal, then pollens may well be the culprit.

A diagnosis can be made by allergy testing - either a blood or skin test where a small amount of antigen is injected into the dog's skin to test for a reaction. The blood test can give false positives, so the skin test is many veterinarians' preferred method.

Whether or not you take this route will be your decision; allergy testing is not cheap, it takes time and may require your dog to be sedated, which is always a risk with Pugs. There's also no point doing it if you are not going to go along with the recommended method of treatment afterwards, which is immunotherapy, or **'hyposensitisation',** and this can also be an expensive and lengthy process.

It consists of a series of injections made specifically for your dog and administered over weeks or months to make him more tolerant of allergens. It may have to be done by a veterinary dermatologist if your vet is not familiar with the treatment. Vets in the US claim that success rates can be as high as 75% of cases. These tests work best when carried out during the season when the allergies are at their worst.

But before you get to this stage, your vet will have had to rule out other potential causes, such as fleas or mites, fungal, yeast or bacterial infections and hypothyroidism. Due to the time and cost involved in skin testing, most mild cases of allergies are treated with a combination of avoidance, fatty acids and antihistamines.

Environmental or Contact Irritations

These are a direct reaction to something the dog physically comes into contact with. It could be as simple as grass, specific plants, dust or other animals. If the trigger is grass or other outdoor materials, the allergies are often seasonal. The dog may require treatment (often tablets, shampoo or localised cortisone spray) for spring and summer, but be perfectly fine with no medication for the other half of the year. This is the case with our dog.

If you suspect your Pug may have outdoor contact allergies, here is one very good tip guaranteed to reduce his scratching: get him to stand in a tray or large bowl of water on your return from a walk. Washing his feet and under his belly will get rid of some of the pollen and other allergens, which in turn will reduce his scratching and biting. Other possible triggers include dry carpet shampoos, caustic irritants, new carpets, cement dust, washing powders or fabric conditioners. If you wash your dog's bedding or if he sleeps on your bed, use a fragrance-free - and if possible hypoallergenic - laundry detergent and avoid fabric conditioner.

The irritation may be restricted to the part of the dog - such as the underneath of the paws or belly - which has touched the offending object. Symptoms are skin irritation - either a general problem or specific hotspots - itching (*pruritis*) and sometimes hair loss. Readers sometimes report to us that their dog will incessantly lick one part of the body, often the paws, bottom, belly or back.

Flea Bite Allergies

These are a very common canine allergy and affect dogs of all breeds. To compound the problem, many dogs with flea allergies also have inhalant allergies. Flea bite allergy is typically seasonal, worse during summer and autumn – peak time for fleas - and is worse in warmer climates where fleas are prevalent.

This type of allergy is not to the flea itself, but to proteins in flea saliva, which are deposited under the dog's skin when the insect feeds. Just one bite to an allergic Pug will cause intense and long-lasting itching. If affected, the dog will try to bite at the base of his tail (impossible for a Pug) and scratch a lot. Most of the damage is done by the dog's scratching, rather than the flea bite, and can result in his fur falling out or skin abrasions.

Some Pugs will develop hot spots. These can occur anywhere, but are often along the back and base of the tail. Flea bite allergies can only be totally prevented by keeping all fleas away from the dog. Various flea prevention treatments are available – see the next section on Parasites. If you suspect your dog may be allergic to fleas, consult your vet for the proper diagnosis and medication.

Diet and Food Allergies

Food is the third most common cause of allergies in dogs. Cheap dog foods bulked up with grains and other ingredients can cause problems. Some Pug owners have reported their dogs having problems with wheat and other grains. If you feed your dog a dry commercial dog food, make sure that it's a high quality, preferably hypoallergenic, one and that the first ingredient listed on the sack is meat or poultry, not grain.

Without the correct food a dog's whole body - not just his skin and coat - will continuously be under stress and this manifests itself in a number of ways. The symptoms of food allergies are similar to those of most allergies:

❖ itchy skin affecting primarily the face, feet, ears, forelegs, armpits and anus
❖ excessive scratching

- ❖ chronic or recurring ear infections
- ❖ hair loss
- ❖ hot spots
- ❖ skin infections that clear up with antibiotics, but return after the antibiotics have finished
- ❖ possible increased bowel movements, maybe twice as many as normal

The bodily process which occurs when an animal has a reaction to a particular food agent is not very well understood, but the veterinary profession does know how to diagnose and treat food allergies. As many other problems can cause similar symptoms to food allergies (and also the fact that many sufferers also have other allergies), it is important that any other problems are identified and treated before food allergies are diagnosed.

Atopy, flea bite allergies, intestinal parasite hypersensitivities, sarcoptic mange and yeast or bacterial infections can all cause similar symptoms. This can be an anxious time for owners as vets try one thing after another to get to the bottom of the allergy.

The normal method for diagnosing a food allergy is elimination. Once all other causes have been ruled out or treated, then a food trial is the next step – and that's no picnic for owners either. See **Chapter 6. Feeding a Pug** for more information. As with other allergies, dogs may have short-term relief by taking fatty acids, antihistamines, and steroids, but removing the offending items from the diet is the only permanent solution.

Interdigital Cysts

Have you ever noticed a fleshy red bump between your dog's toes that looks a bit like an ulcerated sore or a hairless bump? If so, then your Pug could have an interdigital cyst - or 'interdigital furuncle' to give the condition its correct medical term.

These can be very difficult to get rid of, since they are not the primary issue, but often a sign of some other condition. Actually they are not cysts, but the result of **furunculosis**, a condition of the skin which clogs hair follicles and creates chronic infection. They can be caused by a number of factors, including allergies, obesity, poor foot conformation, mites, yeast infections, ingrown hairs or other foreign bodies, and obesity.

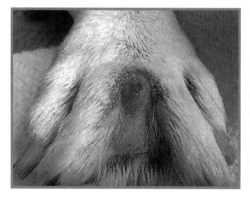

These nasty-looking bumps are painful for your dog and will probably cause him to limp. Vets might recommend a whole range of treatments to get to the root cause of the problem. It can be extremely expensive if your dog is having a barrage of tests or biopsies and even then you are not guaranteed to find the underlying cause. The first thing he or she will probably do is put your dog in an E-collar to stop him licking the affected area, which will never recover properly as long as he's constantly licking it. This again is stressful for your dog. Here are some remedies your vet may suggest:

- ❖ Antibiotics and/or steroids and/or mite killers
- ❖ Soaking his feet in Epsom salts twice daily to unclog the hair follicles
- ❖ Testing him for allergies or thyroid problems
- ❖ Starting a food trial if food allergies are suspected
- ❖ Shampooing his feet
- ❖ Cleaning between his toes with medicated (benzoyl peroxide) wipes
- ❖ A referral to a veterinary dermatologist

❖ Surgery

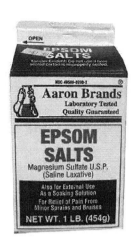

If you suspect your Pug has an interdigital cyst, take him to the vet for a correct diagnosis and then discuss the various options. A course of antibiotics may be suggested initially, along with switching to a hypoallergenic diet if a food allergy is suspected. If the condition persists, many owners get discouraged, especially when treatment may go on for many weeks.

Before you resort to any drastic action, first try soaking your Pug's affected paw in Epsom salts for five or 10 minutes twice a day. After the soaking, clean the area with medicated wipes, which are antiseptic and control inflammation. In the US these are sold under the brand name Stridex pads in the skin care section of any grocery, or from the pharmacy.

If you think the cause may be an environmental allergy, wash your dog's paws and under his belly when you return from a walk, this will help to remove pollen and other allergens from his body.

Surgery can be effective, but it is a drastic option and although it might solve the immediate problem, it will not deal with whatever is triggering the interdigital cysts in the first place. Not only is healing after this surgery a lengthy and difficult process, it also means your dog will never have the same foot as before - future orthopaedic issues and a predisposition to more interdigital cysts are a couple of problems which can occur afterwards.

All that said, your vet *does* understand that interdigital cysts aren't so simple to deal with, but they are always treatable. Get the right diagnosis as soon as possible, limit all offending factors and give medical treatment a good solid try before embarking on more drastic cures.

Acute Moist Dermatitis (Hot Spots)

Acute moist dermatitis or 'hot spots' are not uncommon in Pugs. A hot spot can appear suddenly and is a raw, inflamed and often bleeding area of skin. The area becomes moist and painful and begins spreading due to continual licking and chewing. They can become large, red, irritated lesions in a short pace of time.

The cause is often a local reaction to an insect bite; fleas, ticks, biting flies and even mosquitoes have been known to cause acute moist dermatitis. Other causes of hot spots include:

❖ Allergies - inhalant allergies and food allergies
❖ Mites
❖ Ear infections
❖ Poor grooming
❖ Burs or plant awns
❖ Anal gland disease
❖ Hip dysplasia or other types of arthritis and degenerative joint disease

Diagnosis and Treatment - The good news is that, once diagnosed and with the right treatment, hot spots disappear as soon as they appeared. The underlying cause should be identified and treated, if possible. Check with your vet before treating your Pug for fleas and ticks at the same time as other medical treatment (such as anti-inflammatory medications and/or antibiotics), as he or she will probably advise you to wait. Treatments may come in the form of injections, tablets or creams – or your Pug might need a combination of them. Your vet will probably clip and clean the affected area to help the effectiveness of any spray or ointment and your poor Pug might also have to wear an E-collar until the condition subsides, but usually this does not take long.

Parasites

Fleas

When you see your dog scratching and biting, your first thought is probably: "He's got fleas!" and you may well be right. Fleas don't fly, but they do have very strong back legs and they will take any opportunity to jump from the ground or another animal into your Pug's lovely warm coat. You can sometimes see the fleas if you part your dog's fur.

And for every flea that you see on your dog, there is the awful prospect of hundreds of eggs and larvae in your house or apartment. So if your Pug is unlucky enough to catch fleas, you'll have to treat your environment as well as your dog in order to completely get rid of them.

The best form of cure is prevention. Vets recommend giving dogs a preventative flea treatment every four to eight weeks. This may vary depending on your climate, the season - fleas do not breed as quickly in the cold - and how much time your dog spends outdoors. Once-a-month topical (applied to the skin) insecticides - like Frontline and Advantix - are the most commonly used flea prevention products on the market. You part the skin and apply drops of the liquid on to a small area on your dog's back, usually near the neck. Some kill fleas and ticks, and others just kill fleas - check the details.

It is worth spending the money on a quality treatment, as cheaper brands may not rid your Pug completely of fleas, ticks and other parasites. Sprays, dips, shampoos and collars are other options, as are tablets and injections in certain cases, such as before your dog goes into boarding kennels or has surgery. Incidentally, a flea bite is different from a flea bite allergy.

NOTE: There is considerable anecdotal evidence from dog owners of various breeds that the flea and worm tablet *Trifexis,* available in the US, may cause severe side effects in some dogs. You may wish to read some owners' experiences at: www.max-the-schnauzer.com/trifexis-side-effects-in-schnauzers.html

Ticks – A tick is not an insect, but a member of the arachnid family, like the spider. There are over 850 types of them, divided into two types: hard shelled and soft shelled. Ticks (pictured) don't have wings - they can't fly, they crawl. They have a sensor called Haller's organ which detects smell, heat and humidity to help them locate food, which in some cases is a Pug. A tick's diet consists of one thing and one thing only – blood! They climb up onto tall grass and when they sense an animal is close, crawl on him.

Ticks can pass on a number of diseases to animals and humans, the most well-known of which is Lyme Disease, a serious condition which causes lameness and other problems. Dogs which spend a lot of time outdoors in high risk areas such as woods can have a vaccination against Lime Disease. If you do find a tick on your Pug's coat but are not sure how to get it out, have it removed by a vet or other expert. Inexpertly pulling it out yourself and leaving a bit of the tick behind can be detrimental to your dog's health. Prevention treatment is similar to that for fleas. If your Pug has particularly sensitive skin, he might do better with a natural flea or tick remedy.

Heartworm

Heartworm is a serious and potentially fatal disease in pets in North America and many other parts of the world. It is caused by foot-long worms (heartworms) that live in the heart, lungs and associated blood vessels of affected pets, causing severe lung disease, heart failure and damage to other organs in the body.

The dog is a natural host for heartworms, which means that heartworms living inside the dog mature into adults, mate and produce offspring. If untreated, their numbers can increase, and dogs have been known to harbour several hundred worms in their bodies. Heartworm disease causes lasting damage to the heart, lungs and arteries, and can affect the dog's health and quality of life long after the parasites are gone. For this reason, prevention is by far the best option and treatment—when needed—should be administered as early as possible.

The mosquito plays an essential role in the heartworm life cycle. When a mosquito bites and takes a blood meal from an infected animal, it picks up baby worms which develop and mature into "infective stage" larvae over a period of 10 to 14 days. Then, when the infected mosquito bites another dog, cat or susceptible wild animal, the infective larvae are deposited onto the surface of the animal's skin and enter the new host through the mosquito's bite wound. Once inside a new host, it takes approximately six months for the larvae to mature into adult heartworms. Once mature, heartworms can live for five to seven years in a dog.

In the early stages of the disease, many dogs show few or no symptoms. The longer the infection persists, the more likely symptoms will develop. Symptoms may include:

- ❖ A mild persistent cough
- ❖ Reluctance to exercise
- ❖ Tiredness after moderate activity
- ❖ Decreased appetite
- ❖ Weight loss

As the disease progresses, dogs may develop heart failure and a swollen belly due to excess fluid in the abdomen. Dogs with large numbers of heartworms can develop sudden blockages of blood flow within the heart leading to the life-threatening caval syndrome. This is marked by a sudden onset of laboured breathing, pale gums and dark, bloody or coffee-coloured urine. Without prompt surgical removal of the heartworm blockage, few dogs survive.

Although more common in the south eastern US, heartworm disease has been diagnosed in all 50 states. And because infected mosquitoes can fly indoors, even Pugs which spend most of their time inside the home are at risk. For that reason, the American Heartworm Society recommends that you get your dog tested every year and give your dog heartworm preventive treatment for 12 months of the year.

(Thanks to the American Heartworm Society for assistance with the section)

Ringworm

This is not actually a worm, but a fungus and is most commonly seen in puppies and young dogs. It is highly infectious and often found on the face, ears, paws or tail. The ringworm fungus is most prevalent in hot, humid climates, but surprisingly, most cases occur in autumn and winter. Ringworm infections in dogs are not that common, in one study of dogs with active skin problems, less than 3% had ringworm.

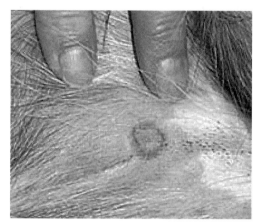

Ringworm is transmitted by spores in the soil and by contact with the infected hair of dogs and cats, which can be typically found on carpets, brushes, combs, toys and furniture. Spores from infected animals can be shed into the environment and live for over 18 months, but fortunately most healthy adult dogs have some resistance and never develop symptoms.

The fungi live in dead skin, hairs and nails - and the head and legs are the most common areas affected. Tell-tale signs are bald patches with a roughly circular shape (see photo). Ringworm is relatively easy to treat with fungicidal shampoos or antibiotics from a vet.

Humans can catch ringworm from pets, and vice versa. Children are especially susceptible, as are adults with suppressed immune systems and those undergoing chemotherapy. Hygiene is extremely important. If your dog has ringworm, wear gloves when handling him and wash your hands well afterwards. And if a member of your family catches ringworm, make sure they use separate towels from everyone else or the fungus may spread. (As an adolescent I caught ringworm from horses at stables where I worked at weekends - much to my mother's horror - and was treated like a leper by the rest of the family until it had cleared up!)

Sarcoptic Mange

Also known as canine scabies, this is caused by the parasite *Sarcoptes scabiei*. This microscopic mite can cause a range of skin problems, the most common of which is hair loss and severe itching. The mites can infect other animals such as foxes, cats and even humans, but prefer to live their short lives on dogs. Fortunately, there are several good treatments for this mange and the disease can be easily controlled.

In cool, moist environments, they live for up to 22 days. At normal room temperature they live from two to six days, preferring to live on parts of the dog with less hair. These are the areas you may see him scratching, although it can spread throughout the body in severe cases.

Diagnosing canine scabies can be somewhat difficult, and it is often mistaken for inhalant allergies. Once diagnosed, there are a number of effective treatments, including selamectin (Revolution), a topical solution applied once a month which also provides heartworm prevention, flea control and some tick protection. Various Frontline products are also effective – check with your vet for the correct ones.

Because your dog does not have to come into direct contact with an infected dog to catch scabies, it is difficult to completely protect him. Foxes and their environment can also transmit the mite, so keep your dog away from areas where you know foxes are present.

Bacterial infection (Pyoderma)

Pyoderma literally means 'pus in the skin' (yuk!) and fortunately this condition is not contagious. Early signs of this bacterial infection are itchy red spots filled with yellow pus, similar to pimples or spots in humans. They can sometimes develop into red, ulcerated skin with dry and crusty patches.

Pyoderma is caused by several things: a broken skin surface, a skin wound due to chronic exposure to moisture, altered skin bacteria, or impaired blood flow to the skin. Dogs have a higher risk of developing an infection when they have a fungal infection or an endocrine (hormone gland) disease such as hyperthyroidism, or have allergies to fleas, food or parasites.

Pyoderma is often secondary to allergic dermatitis and develops in the sores on the skin which happen as a result of scratching. Puppies often develop 'puppy pyoderma' in thinly-haired areas such as the groin and underarms. Fleas, ticks, yeast or fungal skin infections, thyroid disease, hormonal imbalances, heredity and some medications can increase the risk. If you notice symptoms, get your dog to the vet quickly before the condition develops from **superficial pyoderma** into **severe pyoderma**, which is much more unpleasant and takes a lot longer to treat.

Bacterial infection, no matter how bad it may look, usually responds well to medical treatment, which is generally done on an outpatient basis. Superficial pyoderma will usually be treated with a two to six-week course of antibiotic tablets or ointment. Severe or recurring pyoderma looks awful, causes your dog some distress and can take months of treatment to completely cure. Medicated shampoos and regular bathing, as instructed by your vet, are also part of the treatment. It's also important to ensure your dog has clean, dry, padded bedding.

Ear Infections

Infection of the external ear canal (outer ear infection) is called otitis externa and is one of the most common types of infections seen in dogs, including Pugs. The fact that your dog has recurring ear infections does not necessarily mean that his ears are the source of the problem.

One reason may be moisture in the ear canal, allowing bacteria to flourish there. However, many Pugs with chronic or recurring ear infections have inhalant or food allergies or low thyroid function

(hypothyroidism). Sometimes the ears are the first sign of allergy. The underlying problem must be treated or the dog will continue to have chronic ear problems. Tell-tale signs include your dog shaking his head, scratching or rubbing his ears a lot, or an unpleasant odour coming from the ears

If you look inside the ears, you may notice a reddy brown or yellow discharge, it may also be red and inflamed with a lot of wax. Sometimes a dog may appear depressed or irritable; ear infections are painful. In chronic cases the inside of his ears may become crusty or thickened.

Dogs can have ear problems for many different reasons, including:

- ❖ Allergies, such as environmental or food allergies
- ❖ Ear mites or other parasites
- ❖ Bacteria or yeast infections
- ❖ Injury, often due to excessive scratching
- ❖ Hormonal abnormalities, e.g. hypothyroidism
- ❖ The ear anatomy and environment, e.g. excess moisture
- ❖ Hereditary or immune conditions and tumours

Treatment depends on the cause of the ear problem and what other conditions your dog may have. Antibiotics are used for bacterial infections and antifungals for yeast infections. Glucocorticoids, such as dexamethasone, are often included in these medications to reduce the inflammation in the ear. Your vet may also flush out and clean the ear with special drops, something you may have to do daily at home until the infection clears.

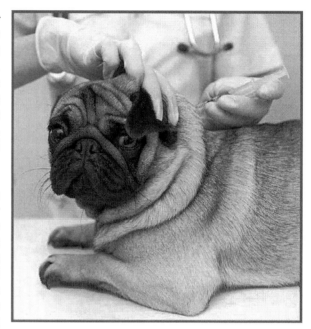

A dog's ear canal is L-shaped, which means it can be difficult to get medication into the lower (horizontal) part of the ear. The best method is to hold the dog's ear flap with one hand and put the ointment or drops in with the other, if possible tilting the dog's head away from you so the liquid flows downwards **with gravity**. Make sure you then hold the ear flap down and massage the medication into the horizontal canal before letting go of your dog, as the first thing he will do is shake his head – and if the ointment or drops aren't massaged in, they will fly out.

Nearly all ear infections can be successfully managed if properly diagnosed and treated. But if an underlying problem remains undiscovered, the outcome will be less favourable. Deep ear infections can damage or rupture the eardrum, causing an internal ear infection and even permanent hearing loss. Closing of the ear canal (*hyperplasia* or *stenosis)* is another sign of severe infection. Most extreme cases of hyperplasia will eventually require surgery as a last resort; the most common procedure is called a *lateral ear resection*.

To avoid or alleviate recurring ear infections, check your dog's ears and clean them regularly, especially if your Pug is one of the very few who enjoys swimming, or after a bath. Be careful not to put anything too far down into your dog's ears. Visit YouTube to see videos of how to correctly clean inside your dog's ears without damaging them. In a nutshell, DO NOT use cotton buds, these are too small and can damage the ear. Some owners recommend regularly cleaning the inside of a Pug's ears with cotton wool and a mixture of water and white vinegar once a week or so.

If your dog appears to be in pain, has smelly ears, or if his ear canals look inflamed, contact your vet straight away. If he has a ruptured or weakened eardrum, ear cleansers and medications could do more harm than good. Early treatment is the best way of preventing a recurrence.

Other Yeast Infections

Brachycephalic (flat faced) breeds of dogs, like Pugs, Bulldogs and French Bulldogs, are at increased risk of getting yeast infections - and not only in their ears. The deep facial wrinkles and skin folds are what help to make the Pug unique. The wrinkles are an attractive feature, but they can also pose a health problem if they aren't kept clean.

If you notice an unpleasant smell from your Pug's face, ears, armpits, paws, groin or body, he may well have a yeast infection – and it's up to you to get rid of it. You should clean underneath the facial folds each week with water or a medicated pad to keep the areas free of debris, bacterial and fungal growth -and, if necessary, the other wrinkles and areas of his body too. If you bathe your Pug, make sure you clean between the skin folds and flush the medicated shampoo out with running water then dry thoroughly.

When a Pug's skin folds aren't checked regularly, the warm, moist pockets can become ideal breeding grounds for infection. Yeast infections are usually easy to diagnose, due to the terrible smell! Wrinkles that have been continuously neglected will become swollen and red, sometimes you might find yellow pus between the folds. You may also notice your Pug rubbing his face on the floor or furniture in an effort to alleviate the irritation.

Your vet may recommend bathing your dog in a medicated shampoo and applying cream to the affected areas. It is important that once your Pug returns to health, you regularly clean his wrinkles.

Canine Acne

This is not uncommon in Pugs and - just as with humans - generally affects teenagers, often between five and eight months of age with canines. Acne occurs when oil glands become blocked causing bacterial infection and these glands are most active in teenagers. Acne is not a major health problem as most of it will clear up once the dog becomes an adult, but it can reoccur. Typical signs are pimples, blackheads or whiteheads around the muzzle, chest or groin. If the area is irritated, then there may some bleeding or pus that can be expressed from these blemishes.

Hormonal Imbalances

These occur in dogs of all breeds. They are often difficult to diagnose and occur when a dog is producing either too much (hyper) or too little (hypo) of a particular hormone. One visual sign is often hair loss on both sides of the dog's body. The condition is not usually itchy. Hormone imbalances can be serious as they are often indicators that glands which affect the dog internally are not working properly. However, some types can be diagnosed by special blood tests and treated effectively.

Some Allergy Treatments

Treatments and success rates vary tremendously from dog to dog and from one allergy to another, which is why it is so important to consult a vet at the outset. Earlier diagnosis is more likely to lead to a successful treatment. Some owners whose Pugs have recurring skin issues find that a course of antibiotics or steroids works wonders for their dog's sore skin and itching. However, the scratching starts all over again when the treatment stops.

Food allergies require patience, a change of diet and maybe even a food trial, and the specific trigger is notoriously difficult to isolate – unless you are lucky and hit on the culprit straight away.

With inhalant and contact allergies, blood and skin tests are available, followed by hypersensitisation treatment.

However, these are expensive and often the specific trigger for many dogs remains unknown. So the reality for many owners of Pugs with allergies is that they manage the ailment with various medications and practices, rather than curing it completely.

Our Personal Experience

After corresponding with numerous other dog owners and consulting our vet, Graham, it seems that our experiences with allergies are not uncommon. Our dog was perfectly fine until he was about two years old when he began to scratch a lot. He seemed to scratch more in spring and summer, which meant that his allergies were almost certainly inhalant or contact-based and related to pollens, grasses or other outdoor triggers.

One option was for Max to have a barrage of tests to discover exactly what he was allergic to. We decided not to do this, not because of the cost, but because our vet said it was highly likely that he was allergic to pollens. If we had confirmed an allergy to pollens, we were not going to stop taking him outside for walks, so the vet treated him on the basis of seasonal inhalant or contact allergies, probably related to pollen.

One recommendation he makes to reduce the itching is to rinse the dog's paws and underneath his belly after a walk in the countryside. This is something he does with his own dogs and has found that the scratching reduces as a result. Regarding medications, Max was at first put on to a tiny dose of Piriton, an antihistamine for hay fever sufferers (human and canine) and for the first few springs and summers, this worked well.

One of the problems with allergies is that they often change and the dog can also build up a tolerance to a treatment – this has been the case over the years with our dog. The symptoms change from season to season, although the main symptoms remain and they are: general scratching, paw biting and ear infections. One year he bit the skin under his tail a lot and this was treated fairly effectively with a cortisone spray. This type of spray is useful if the area of itching is localised, but no good for spraying all over a dog's body.

A couple of years ago he started nibbling his paws for the first time - a habit he persists with - although not to the extent that they become red and raw. Over the years we have tried a number of treatments, all of which have worked for a while, before he comes off the medication in autumn for six months when plants and grasses stop growing outdoors. He manages perfectly fine the rest of the year without any medication.

If we were starting again from scratch, knowing what we know now, I would investigate a raw diet, if necessary in combination with holistic remedies. Our dog is now 10, we feed him a high quality hypoallergenic dry food. His allergies are manageable, he loves his food, is full of energy and otherwise healthy, and so we are reluctant to make such a big change at this point in his life.

According to Graham, more and more dogs appearing in his waiting room every spring with various types of allergies. Whether this is connected to how we breed our dogs remains to be seen. One season he put Max on a short course of steroids. These worked very well for five months, but steroids are not a long-term solution, as prolonged use can cause organ damage.

Another spring Max was prescribed a non-steroid daily tablet called Atopica, sold in the UK only through vets. (The active ingredient is **cyclosporine**, which suppresses the immune system. Some dogs can get side effects, although Max didn't, and holistic practitioners believe that it is harmful to the dog.) This treatment was expensive, but initially extremely effective – so much so that we thought we had cured the problem completely. However, after a couple of seasons on cyclosporine he developed a tolerance to the drug and started scratching again.

A few years ago he went back on the antihistamine Piriton, a higher dose than when he was two years old, and this worked very well again. One advantage of this drug is that is it manufactured by the million for dogs and is therefore very inexpensive.

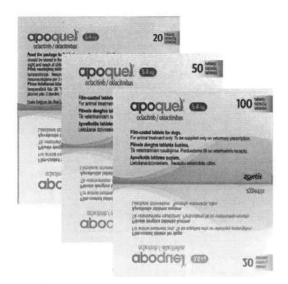

In 2013 the FDA approved Apoquel (oclacitinib) to control itching and inflammation in allergic dogs, and the following we tried it with good results. Max still scratched, but not so much and he is still on Apoquel today for six months of the year. Normally dogs start with a double dose for 10 days to suppress the reaction and then go on to a single tablet a day mixed into one of their feeds. The tablets cost around £1 or $1.50 each, and the treatment has been so successful that the manufacturers can't make it quickly enough, resulting in supply problems, particularly in the US.

Many vets recommend adding fish oils (which contain Omega-3 fatty acids) to a daily feed to keep your dog's skin and coat healthy all year round – whether or not he has problems. We also add a liquid supplement called Yumega Plus, which contains Omegas 3 and 6, to one of his two daily feeds all year round and this definitely seems to help his skin. When the scratching gets particularly bad, we bathe Max in an antiseborrhoeic shampoo called Malaseb twice a week, which also helps.

The main point is that most allergies are manageable. They may change throughout the life of the dog and you may have to alter the treatment. Our Max still scratches, but not as much as when he was younger. He may have allergies, but he wouldn't miss his walks for anything and, all in all, he is one contented canine. We've compiled some anecdotal evidence from our website from owners of dogs with various allergies, here are some of their suggestions for alleviating the problems:

Bathing - Regularly bathing your dog – anything from twice a week to once every two weeks - using shampoos that break down the oils which plug the hair follicles. These shampoos contain antiseborrhoeic ingredients such as benzoyl peroxide, salicylic acid, sulphur or tar. One example is Sulfoxydex shampoo, which can be followed by a cream rinse such as Episoothe Rinse afterwards to prevent the skin from drying out.

Dabbing – Using an astringent such as witch hazel or alcohop on affected areas. We have heard of zinc oxide cream being used to some effect. In the human world, this is rubbed on to mild skin abrasions and acts as a protective coating. It can help the healing of chapped skin and nappy rash in babies. Zinc oxide works as a mild astringent and has some antiseptic properties and is safe to use on dogs, *as long as you do not allow the dog to lick it off*.

Daily supplements - Vitamin E, vitamin A, zinc and omega oils all help to make a dog's skin healthy. Feed a daily supplement which contains some of these, such as fish oil, which provides omega.

Here are some specific remedies from owners. We are not endorsing them, we're just passing on the information. *Check with your vet before trying any new remedies:*

A medicated shampoo with natural tea tree oil has been suggested by one owner. Some have reported that switching to a fish-based diet has helped lessen scratching. Ann G. said: "Try Natural Balance Sweet Potato and Fish formula. My dog Charlie has skin issues and this food has helped him tremendously! Plus he LOVES it!" Others have suggested home-cooked food is best, if you have the time to prepare the food.

This is what another reader had to say: "My 8-month-old dog also had a contact dermatitis around his neck and chest. I was surprised how extensive it was. The vet recommended twice-a-week baths with an oatmeal shampoo. I also applied organic coconut oil daily for a few weeks. This completely cured the dermatitis. I also put a capsule of fish oil with his food once a day and continue to give him twice-weekly baths. His skin is great now."

Several owners have tried coconut oil with some success. Here are a couple of links for articles on the benefits of coconut oils and fish oils, and why it might be worth considering alternating them. Check with your vet first: www.cocotherapy.com/fishoilsvsvirginoil_coconutoil.htm and http://redwhiteandPugs.com/coconut-oil-for-Pugs/

And from another reader: "I have been putting a teaspoon of canola (rapeseed) oil in my dog's food every other day and it has helped with the itching. I have shampooed the new carpet in hopes of removing any of the chemicals that could be irritating her. And I have changed laundry detergent. After several loads of laundry everything has been washed."

Another reader wrote that her dog is being treated for seasonal allergies with half a pill of Claritin a day. Local health food stores may be able to offer advice on suitable ingredients for a diet - for dogs as well as humans.

The Holistic Approach to Allergies

As canine allergies become increasingly common, more and more owners of dogs with allergies and sensitivities are looking towards natural foods and remedies to help deal with the issues. Some others are finding that their dog does well for a time with injections or medication, but then the symptoms slowly start to reappear. A holistic practitioner will look at finding the root cause of the problem and treating that, rather than just treating the symptoms.

Dr Sara Skiwski is a holistic vet working in California. She has written an interesting article on the topic of canine environmental allergies and excerpts from that article are reproduced here.

She says: "Here in California, with our mild weather and no hard freeze in Winter, environmental allergens can build up and cause nearly year-round issues for our beloved pets. Also seasonal allergies, when left unaddressed, can lead to year-round allergies. Unlike humans whose allergy symptoms seem to affect mostly the respiratory tract, seasonal allergies in dogs often take the form of skin irritation/inflammation.

"Allergic reactions are produced by the immune system. The way the immune system functions is a result of both genetics and the environment: Nature versus Nurture. Let's look at a typical case. A puppy starts showing mild seasonal allergy symptoms, for instance a red tummy and mild itching in Spring. Off to the vet!

"The treatment prescribed is symptomatic to provide relief, such as a topical spray. The next year when the weather warms up, the patient is back again - same symptoms but more severe this time. This time the dog has very itchy skin. Again, the treatment is symptomatic - antibiotics, topical spray (hopefully no steroids), until the symptoms resolve with the season change. Fast forward to another Spring... on the third year, the patient is back again but this time the symptoms last longer, (not just Spring but also through most of Summer and into Fall). By year five, all the symptoms are significantly worse and are occurring year-round.

"This is what happens with seasonal environmental allergies. The more your pet is exposed to the allergens they are sensitive to, the more the immune system over-reacts and the more intense and long-lasting the allergic response becomes. What to do?

"In my practice, I like to address the potential root cause at the very first sign of an allergic response, which is normally seen between the ages of 6-9 months old. I do this to circumvent the escalating response year after year. Since the allergen load your environmentally-sensitive dog is most susceptible to is much heavier outdoors, I recommend two essential steps in managing the condition. They are vigilance in foot care as well as fur care.

"What does this mean? A wipe down of feet and fur, especially the tummy, to remove any pollens or allergens is key. This can be done with a damp cloth, but my favorite method is to get a spray bottle filled with Witch Hazel and spray these areas. First, spray the feet then wipe them off with a cloth, and then spray and wipe down the tummy and sides. This is best done right after the pup has been outside playing or walking. This will help keep your pet from tracking the environmental allergens into the home and into their beds. If the feet end up still being itchy, I suggest adding foot soaks in Epsom salts."

Dr Sara also stresses the importance of keeping the immune system healthy by avoiding unnecessary vaccinations or drugs: "The vaccine stimulates the immune system which is the last thing your pet with seasonal environmental allergies needs. I also will move the pet to an anti-inflammatory diet. Foods that create or worsen inflammation are high in carbohydrates. An allergic pet's diet should be very low in carbohydrates, especially grains. Research has shown that 'leaky gut,' or dysbiosis, is a root cause of immune system overreactions in both dog and cats (and some humans).

"Feed a diet that is not processed or minimally processed; one that doesn't have grain and takes a little longer to get absorbed and assimilated through the gut. Slowing the assimilation assures that there are not large spikes of nutrients and proteins that come into the body all at once and overtax the pancreas and liver, creating inflammation.

"A lot of commercial diets are too high in grains and carbohydrates. These foods create inflammation which overtaxes the body and leads not just to skin inflammation, but also to other inflammatory conditions, such as colitis, pancreatitis, arthritis, inflammatory bowel disease, and ear infections. Also, these diets are too low in protein, which is needed to make blood. This causes a decreased blood reserve in the body and in some of these animals this can leads to the skin not being properly nourished, starting a cycle of chronic skin infections which produce more itching."

After looking at diet, check that your dog is free from fleas and then these are some of her suggested supplements:

- ❖ **Raw (Unpasteurised) Local Honey** - an alkaline-forming food containing natural vitamins, enzymes, powerful antioxidants and other important natural nutrients, which are destroyed during the heating and pasteurisation processes.

Raw honey has anti-viral, anti-bacterial and anti-fungal properties. It promotes body and digestive health, is a powerful antioxidant, strengthens the immune system, eliminates allergies, and is an excellent remedy for skin wounds and all types of infections. Bees collect pollen from local plants and their honey often acts as an immune booster for dogs living in the locality.

Dr Sara says: "It may seem odd that straight exposure to pollen often triggers allergies, but that exposure to pollen in the honey usually has the opposite effect. But this is typically what we see. In honey, the allergens are delivered in small, manageable doses and the effect over time is very much like that from undergoing a whole series of allergy immunology injections."

- ❖ **Mushrooms -** make sure you choose the non-poisonous ones! Dogs don't like the taste, you so may have to mask it with another food. Medicinal mushrooms are used to treat and prevent a wide array of illnesses through their use as immune stimulants and modulators, and antioxidants. The most well-known and researched are reishi, maitake, cordyceps, blazei, split-gill, turkey tail and shiitake. The mushrooms stabilise mast cells in the body, which have the histamines attached to them. Histamine is what causes much of the inflammation, redness and irritation in allergies. By helping to control histamine production, the mushrooms can moderate the effects of inflammation and even help prevent allergies in the first place.

Warning! Mushrooms can interact with some over-the-counter and prescription drugs, so do your research or check with your vet first.

- ❖ **Stinging Nettles** - contain biologically active compounds that reduce inflammation. Nettles have the ability to reduce the amount of histamine the body produces in response to an allergen. Nettle tea or extract can help with itching. Nettles not only help directly to decrease the itch but also work overtime to desensitise the body to allergens, helping to reprogramme the immune system.

- ❖ **Quercetin** – is an over-the-counter supplement with anti-inflammatory properties. It is a strong antioxidant and reduces the body's production of histamines.

- ❖ **Omega-3 Fatty Acids** - these help decrease inflammation throughout the body. Adding them into the diet of all pets - particularly those struggling with seasonal environmental allergies – is very beneficial. If your dog has more itching along the top of their back and on their sides, add in a fish oil supplement. Fish oil helps to decrease the itch and heal skin lesions. The best sources of Omega 3s are krill oil, salmon oil, tuna oil, anchovy oil and other fish body oils, as well as raw organic egg yolks. If using an oil alone, it is important to give a vitamin B complex supplement.

- ❖ **Coconut Oil** - contains lauric acid, which helps decrease the production of yeast, a common opportunistic infection. Using a fish body oil combined with coconut oil before inflammation flares up can help moderate or even suppress your dog's inflammatory response.

Dr Sara adds: "Above are but a few of the over-the-counter remedies I like. In non-responsive cases, Chinese herbs can be used to work with the body to help to decrease the allergy threshold even more than with diet and supplements alone. Most of the animals I work with are on a program of Chinese herbs, diet change and acupuncture.

"So, the next time Fido is showing symptoms of seasonal allergies, consider rethinking your strategy to treat the root cause instead of the symptom."

With thanks to Dr Sara Skiwski, of the Western Dragon Integrated Veterinary Services, San Jose, California, for her kind permission to use her writings as the basis for this section.

———————

This chapter has only just touched on the complex subject of skin disorders. As you can see, the causes and treatments are many and varied. One thing is true, whatever the condition, if your Pug has a skin issue, seek a professional diagnosis from a vet as soon as possible before attempting to treat it yourself.

Early diagnosis and treatment can often nip the problem in the bud before it develops into anything more serious. Some skin conditions cannot be completely cured, but they can be successfully managed, allowing your Pug to live a happy, pain-free life.

If you haven't got your Pug yet, ask the breeder if there is a history of skin issues in her bloodlines. Once you have your Pug, remember that good quality diet and attention to cleanliness and grooming go a long way in preventing and managing canine skin problems.

And if you suspect your dog has a problem, it's important to consult a vet straight away before the condition becomes entrenched.

———————

12. Grooming

Although Pugs have a short coat, many new owners do not realise that many shed profusely 365 days of the year.

All fawns and some blacks have a double coat, while well-bred blacks tend to have a single coat which sheds much less. With a double coat the undercoat is softer, while the fine, smooth and short topcoat (which is the guard hair) protects the dog against the elements. The topcoat sheds throughout the year and the soft undercoat sheds twice a year. However, Pugs continue to shed to some degree all year round, so grooming is an ongoing task.

Fawns shed considerably more than blacks with single coats, and there is some anecdotal evidence that unspayed females lose more hair than males, which could be hormonal. Other factors affecting shedding are age, allergies, sudden changes in temperature and nutrition. A healthy skin and coat mean less shedding and you can control it with regular (i.e. more than once a week) grooming and occasional baths with a canine shampoo. A high quality diet also helps, and some owners have found that feeding hypoallergenic kibble or a raw diet improves skin and reduces shedding. Adding a once-daily squirt or spoonful of Omega 3 oil to a feed is also beneficial.

Other benefits of regular brushing are that it removes dead hair and skin, stimulates blood circulation and spreads natural oils throughout the coat, helping to keep it in good condition. If brushed regularly, your dog shouldn't need a bath more than once every three or four months – unless he has a skin condition or is particularly dirty. Time spent grooming is also time spent bonding with your dog. It is this physical and emotional inter-reliance which brings us closer to our pets.

Routine grooming sessions allow you to examine your Pug's wrinkles, ears, tail, teeth, eyes, paws and nails for signs of problems. Often Pugs need more regular personal attention from their owners than many other breeds in order to stay healthy. It's important to get your puppy used to being handled and groomed from an early age; a stubborn adult may not take kindly to being groomed if he is not used to it. And some Pugs are notorious 'screamers' when it comes to nail trimming, so starting early is a good idea.

If you do notice an unpleasant smell (in addition to your Pug's normal gassy emissions) and he hasn't been rolling in something unmentionable, then your dog may have a yeast infection which may entail a visit to the vet, or his anal glands may need squeezing.

One piece of grooming kit favoured by many Pug owners is the Furminator (pictured), a relatively inexpensive and widely available de-shedding and grooming tool. Designed by a professional groomer, it removes the undercoat and loose hair without cutting or damaging the topcoat on double-coated dogs, and is also suitable for single-coated Pugs. Avoid using it on the face, ears and tail as these are sensitive areas. Other options are a bristle brush, a slicker brush (with metal pins, some with rubber ends), a rubber brush or a steel comb. A Puggy favourite is the rubber grooming mitten, which means he gets petted while you groom him.

Brush your dog in the opposite direction a few times to loosen dead hair, then brush from neck to tail, and do the sides from front to back. Don't press too hard with the brush. Gently brush the chest, belly and underneath the neck and unfurl the tail. If you rub your dog down with a damp chamois leather afterwards it will grab any loose hairs.

Bathing

If a Pug's coat and skin get too dirty it can cause irritation, leading to scratching and excessive shedding. It's all a question of getting the balance right, and this will to some extent depend on how much outdoor exercise your Pug gets, what sort of areas he's exercised in and what his natural skin condition is like. A Pug regularly exercising outside may need bathing more often than one living in an apartment and getting little outdoor exercise.

Don't bathe your dog too often as it will cause his coat to dry out; certainly not more than once a month unless you are showing your Pug. (Most show owners also use a conditioner after the shampoo.) The exceptions would be if he has been splashing in puddles, rolling in or eating something disgusting, in which case he might need an extra wash as a dirty coat can lead to bacterial infections.

A dog's coat has a different pH to human hair and only a shampoo recommended for dogs should be used, as human shampoos can lead to skin problems and coat damage. If your Pug has skin problems or allergies, select a **medicated** shampoo with antibacterial, antifungal or anti-itching (which contains antihistamines) properties as it will help to get rid of bacteria and fungi without damaging the coat. If your dog does have issues, your vet will be able to recommend a suitable medicated shampoo. They are also widely available in pet stores and online.

Pugs' ear canals are sensitive to water and so it's a good idea to put a cotton wool ball in each ear before bathing - make sure you do this gently and do not force the cotton wool into the ear canal – and don't forget to remove them afterwards or your Pug will appear even deafer than usual to your commands!

You also have to be extremely careful with the eyes. Some owners recommend administering a drop or two of artificial tears in each eye to offer some limited protection against soap or chemicals in the shampoo.

As with all things Pug, there is a wide variation on how your dog will react to having a bath – some Pugs love the attention, while others hate the water. Make sure you get everything ready before you start and keep your dog's collar on so you have something to hold on to. You can wash your Pug in a bowl, the kitchen sink or the family bath, it doesn't matter. If it's the sink, make sure he can't jump out and injure himself, and it it's the bath, put a non-slip mat in the bottom.

Use lukewarm water and spray it from the neck down to the tail until the coat is completely soaked, avoid wetting the face if you can, but gently wash the ear flaps without getting water in the ear canals. Work the shampoo into your dog's body and legs, not forgetting the underneath, and if it's a medicated shampoo, you may have to leave it on for a few minutes. This is not easy with a lively, aquaphobic Pug, so keep a firm hold - it DOES get better as they get more used to it – especially if they get a treat at the end of the ordeal. Our dog hates being bathed and races round the house like a lunatic afterwards, as though he has just miraculously escaped the most horrific death by drowning in two inches of water!

Rinse your dog thoroughly on top, underneath, on the legs, etc., making sure that all of the soap is out of the coat. Use your hand to squeegee excess water off the coat before putting him on an old towel on the floor and towelling him dry - again, be careful with the eyes. Then stand back as he shakes and gets his revenge by soaking you too! Dry the coat as much as possible, a double coated dog takes a long time to dry naturally. You may want to put the fire on to help him dry out or find him a sunny spot (don't let him overheat). Don't forget to remove the cotton wool balls.

Ear Cleaning

Pugs, like many breeds, are prone to ear infections – predominantly yeast infections. These can usually be detected by a nasty smell coming from the ears or when you see your dog shaking his head a lot. In more severe cases, you may notice redness or a build-up of wax or discharge.

Ear cleaning his should be part of your normal at-home grooming schedule, perhaps once every week to keep infection at bay. Ear canals are generally warm and moist, making them a haven for bacteria. Recurring ear infections can also be a sign of other underlying issues, such as food or environmental allergies.

Checking that the inside of the ears are clean should be a regular part of grooming, see **Chapter 11. Skin and Allergies** on how to clean your dog's ears safely. If your Pug's ears have an unpleasant smell, if he shakes his head or scratches his ears a lot or they look red, consult your vet as simple routine cleaning won't clear up an infection - and ear infections are notoriously difficult to get rid of once the dog has got one. Keeping your Pug's ears clean is the best way to avoid problems starting in the first place. NEVER put anything sharp, or narrow like a cotton bud (which is completely different to a cotton wool ball), inside your dog's ear.

Wrinkle Cleaning

Facial wrinkles and loose skin around the front of the body are part of what makes the breed so unique and appealing. However, the Pug's beauty is more than just skin deep and there are health issues that can occur if the wrinkles are not properly and routinely cleansed. Prevention is better than cure and it's definitely better to keep the skin folds clean than have your dog develop painful problems which later require expensive and time-consuming veterinary attention.

Air cannot circulate in the hidden pockets under the wrinkles and they can become a breeding ground for yeast or bacteria. The skin can become red and infected, and sometimes yellow pus can be seen if not kept clean and - most important – dry. Wipe between the folds of your Pug's skin using a medicated pad or baby wipe with lanolin or aloe to keep the crevices free of debris and bacteria – or you can use a drop of medicated dog shampoo from your vet in a cup of warm water.

Whatever you choose for the task, it is essential that you thoroughly dry the area after cleaning – damp areas are breeding grounds for the aforementioned nasty bugs. Dry with a towel or cloth, don't use talc or corn-starch, which can clump. If the skin is irritated, a dab of petroleum jelly (Vaseline) in the fold after cleaning will soothe the skin and prevent moisture getting in.

NOTE: Overweight Pugs are at greater risk of developing a skin infection because the excess fat makes the wrinkles more pronounced.

It's impossible to say exactly how often to clean the wrinkles on any individual dog, but the short answer is: probably more often than you think. And if a smell is coming off your Pug is enough to make *your* nose wrinkle, you're not doing it often enough.

Moving to the less appealing end of your Pug, let's dive straight in and talk about anal sacs. Sometimes called scent glands, these are a pair of glands located inside your dog's anus that give off a scent when he has a bowel movement. You won't want to hear this, but problems with impacted anal glands are not uncommon in Pugs.

If your dog drags himself along on his rear end ('scooting') or tries to lick or scratch his anus, he could well have impacted anal glands that need squeezing (also called expressing) – either by you if you know how to do it, your vet or a groomer. When a dog passes firm stools the glands normally empty themselves, but soft poo(p) or diarrhoea can mean that not enough pressure is exerted on to the glands to empty them, causing discomfort to the dog. If they become infected, this results in swelling and pain. In extreme cases the anal glands can be removed, but this must be weighed up against the risk of anaesthetising a Pug.

Little red pimples on a dog's face and chin it means he has got acne. A dog can get acne at any age, not just as an adolescent. Plastic bowls can also trigger the condition, which is why stainless steel ones are better. Often a daily washing followed by an application of an antibiotic cream is enough to get rid of the problem. If it persists, consult your vet.

A Pug's skin can dry out, especially with artificial heat in the winter months. If you spot any dry patches, for example on the inner thighs, armpits or a cracked nose, massage a little petroleum jelly or baby oil on to the dry patch.

Eye Care

Like all dogs, a Pug's eyes should be clean and clear. With their protruding eyes, Pugs are particularly prone to eye infections, and if you suspect your dog has one, it needs **immediate** treatment by a vet before the condition escalates and your dog risks losing an eye. Sadly there are far too many one-eyed Pugs around. Cloudy eyes, particularly in an older dog, could be early signs of cataracts. If your Pug gets dust or dirt in his eyes, gently clean them with warm water and cotton wool – NEVER put anything sharp anywhere near your dog's eyes.

Many Pugs suffer from tear staining - often reddish-brown- which is most obvious on fawns and those with more pronounced wrinkles. There are many reasons for tear stains, sometimes it can be perfectly natural, other times it may be a sign of an underlying problem such as an over-active tear duct, diet, or a genetic predisposition caused by the physical structure of the eye.

Excessive tearing results in damp facial hair, which becomes a breeding ground for bacteria and yeast, the most common of which is 'red yeast.' This often makes the tear stains a stronger red-brown colour and may emit a moderate to strong odour. Vets can prescribe medication to treat bacterial and yeast infections. If the tear staining is related to diet, it may take some time to get to the root cause of the problem, see **Chapter 6. Feeding a Pug.**

There are various manufactured products freely available to reduce tear staining, such as EyePack, Angel Tears, NaturVet, Eye Envy and Diamond Eyes, as well as a number of home remedies. One is to add a teaspoon of white cider vinegar to your dog's drinking water to alter his internal pH and control new tear stains. It may take him a while to get used to the new flavour of his water, so start with a tiny bit at a time.

Nail Trimming

Pugs seldom get enough exercise outdoors on hard surfaces to wear their nails down, so they have to be clipped or filed regularly. Nails must be kept short for the paws to remain healthy. Long nails interfere with the dog's gait, making walking awkward or painful and they can also break easily, usually at the base of the nail where blood vessels and nerves are located.

Get your dog used to having his paws inspected from puppyhood. It is also a good opportunity to check for other problems such as cracked pads, thorns, splinters and interdigital cysts. These are swellings between the toes, often due to a bacterial infection. Be prepared: many Pugs dislike having their nails trimmed, so it requires patience and persistence on your part -or a trip to a groomer's (if so, ask her to squeeze your dog's anal sacs while he's there!)

To trim your dog's nails, use a specially designed clipper. Most have safety guards to prevent you cutting the nails too short. Do it before they get too long, if you can hear the nails clicking on the floor, they're too long. You want to trim only the ends, before 'the quick,' which is a blood vessel inside the nail. You can see where the quick ends on a white nail, but not on a dark nail. Clip only the hook-like part of the nail that turns down. Start trimming gently, a nail or two at a time, and your dog will learn that you're not going to hurt him. If you accidentally cut the quick, stop the bleeding with some styptic powder.

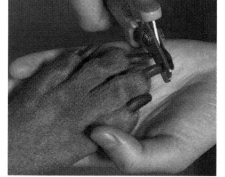

Another option is to file your dog's nails with a nail grinder tool. Some dogs may have tough nails which are hard to trim and this may be less stressful for your dog, with less chance of pain or bleeding. The grinder is like an electric nail file and only removes a small amount of nail at a time. Some owners would rather use one as it is harder to cut the quick, and many dogs prefer them to a clipper – others can't stand the noise. You have to introduce your Pug gradually to the grinder, first let him get used to the noise and then gradually the vibration before you actually begin to grind his nails. If you find it impossible to clip your dog's nails, or you are at all worried about doing it, take him to a vet or a groomer.

Teeth Cleaning

Veterinary studies show that by the age of three, 80% of dogs show signs of gum disease. Symptoms include yellow and brown build-up of tartar along the gum line, red inflamed gums and persistent bad breath. Pugs and other brachycephalic (flat-faced) breeds tend to have more teeth issues than other dogs due to the fact that their 42 teeth are crammed into a smaller space. The crowded teeth often grow at odd angles, trapping food debris and leading to periodontal disease at a far younger age than with other breeds. Establishing good dental hygiene at an early age can save your Pug from years of discomfort and mouth problems and the earlier you begin using home dental products, the longer you can avoid full dentistry under general anaesthetic. A Pug has a natural undershot bite, which means the lower jaw protrudes slightly, which can lead to issues with eating and the position of the tongue.

There are dog chews which specifically promote good chewing habits and dental hygiene. You can give your dog a daily dental treat, such as Dentastix, Whimzees or Greenies, to help keep his mouth and teeth clean. However, you should also regularly brush your Pug's teeth. Take things slowly in the beginning, give him lots of praise and many Pugs will start looking forward to teeth brushing sessions, especially if they like the flavour of the toothpaste. Use a pet toothpaste as the human variety can upset a canine's stomach.

Various brushes, sponges and pads are available - the choice depends on factors such as the health of your dog's gums, the size of his mouth and how good you are at teeth cleaning – and if your dog won't accept any of these there is also a finger toothbrush which you place over your finger and rub his teeth.

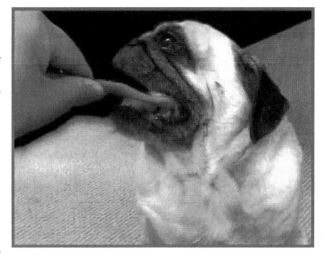

Get your dog used to the toothpaste by letting him lick some off your finger when he is young. If he doesn't like the flavour, try a different one. Continue this until he looks forward to licking the paste – it might be instant or take days. Put a small amount on your finger and gently rub it on one of the big canine teeth at the front of his mouth. Then get him used to the toothbrush or dental sponge - praise him when he licks it –for several days. The next step is to actually start brushing.

Lift his upper lip gently and place the brush at a 45º angle to the gum line. Gently move the brush backwards and forwards. Start just with his front teeth and then gradually do a few more. You don't need to brush the inside of his teeth as his tongue keeps them relatively free of plaque. With a bit of encouragement and patience, it can become a pleasant task for both of you.

Your Pug will be very lucky if he has no dental problems throughout his life. Keeping teeth as clean as possible is one way of helping your dog. A dog can have dental surgery under general anaesthetic, but putting a Pug under is not without risks. Any time your dog needs anaesthesia, ask the vet to check his teeth and perform any necessary cleaning and dentistry at the same time.

As you can see, grooming isn't just about giving your Pug the odd tickle with a brush. Hopefully your dog will thrive without too much extra maintenance, but some Pugs do require that little extra bit of care - and it's up to you to administer it. It's all part of the bargain when you decide the Pug is the dog for you. Sadly too many end up in rescue shelters after their owners couldn't cope with the extra time and expense some of these wonderful little dogs need.

13. The Birds and the Bees

Judging by the number of questions our website receives from owners who ask about the canine reproductive cycle and breeding from their dogs, there is a lot of confusion about the doggie facts of life out there.

Some owners want to know whether they should breed from their dog, while others ask at what age they should have their dog spayed (females) or neutered (males).

Owners of females often ask when she will come on heat, how long this will last and how often it will occur. Sometimes they want to know how you can tell if a female is pregnant or how long a pregnancy lasts. So here, in a nutshell, is a short chapter on the facts of life as far as Pugs are concerned.

Should I Breed From My Pug?

The short and simple answer is: Unless you know exactly what you are doing or have a mentor, **NO, leave it to the experts.** You need specialist knowledge to successfully breed healthy Pugs and many approved breeders will insist that you have your pup spayed or neutered to prevent you from breeding and to protect the integrity of the breed.

The rising popularity and cost of Pugs is tempting more people to consider breeding from their dog. Prices may be as high as £1,500 in the UK for a pet (non-show) Pug and $2,500 in the US. But anyone who thinks it is easy money should bear in mind is that breeding from a Pug is an expensive business when all the fees, tests, care, nutrition and medical expenses have been taken into account, and it's a process fraught with difficulties.

While many Pugs whelp (give birth to puppies) naturally, there are others who have to have a Caesarean, or C-section – especially smaller females. This not only a costly procedure, but you have to know exactly the right time to call a vet in if there's an emergency and you need to know beforehand that your vet will be available if you call in the middle of the night. Breeding Pugs is a high risk occupation if you don't know what you are doing.

If the C-section is performed too late, the puppies can die inside the mother or suffocate. Too early and their lungs may not be fully developed or the mother's milk may not drop, which involved feeding the pups around-the-clock. The C-section itself is also a risky time for the mother. A major survey carried out jointly by the BSAVA (British Small Animal Veterinary Association) and the UK's Kennel Club found that 27.4% of Pugs were born by C-section. The figure is thought to be higher in the USA, where some breeders elect to have the procedure.

C-sections are carried out when the mother is unable to birth all the pups naturally. Sometimes this may be performed for just one puppy at the end of a litter. One main reason is that Pugs are front-loaded; for small dogs they have a large head and wide shoulders. However, their bodies taper off towards the rear and the hips and pelvis are relatively narrow. It is through here that the pups have to pass when being born. Sometimes the pup's head and/or shoulders are too large, or there is a fear that natural whelping (birth) may cause injury to the mother, or the mother simply runs out of steam when pushing. In these cases a Caesarean is performed.

Pups from dams and sires with smaller heads are more likely to be born naturally, and some veterinarians and breeders whose dogs naturally whelp believe that it would not be too difficult to reverse the trend for C-sections. One suggestion is that when puppies are registered with the Kennel Clubs, a note should be added to their pedigree recording whether their birth was natural or by C-section. Breeders would then be able to factor this information into their choice of future breeding stock and, over a few generations, selective breeding of easy-birth dogs would increase the percentage of natural whelping within the breed.

Having puppies takes a lot out of female Pugs and some first-time mothers are not very good with their little ones. In the beginning, most breeders do not let their Pug mothers and puppies out of their sight, day or night. According to the breeders we contacted, raising a litter of puppies literally takes over a breeder's life for the first few weeks. Here's what some said:

Linda and Kim Wright, of Wright's Pugs, Springport, Michigan, gives an idea of some of the initial care needed: "I provide around the clock watch for my litters for the first two weeks. When whelping naturally, you have to remove the sacks, as the breed's flat face makes it near impossible for the mothers to do this. Solid food is not fed until at least four weeks of age because the puppies are more likely to inhale it with their flat faces than other breeds with longer muzzles. And with their round bodies, the mothers may lay on a puppy without noticing." Our photo shows Linda and Kim's Anna with her pups just after birth.

Breeder Erin Ford, of Fur N Feathers, Florida, gets up every two hours in the night to check on the female and her litter. She also uses a heating pad to keep the pups in a constant ambient temperature.

Carly Firth, of Mumandau Pugs, Greater Manchester, UK, said: "In my experience I have to say, Pugs aren't the easiest to whelp and require us humans to intervene, as opposed to some breeds – such as gundogs - which are quite content getting on with it alone. I do often think this is the case with the mating process too! They do need some assistance at times. Typically when the pups are born, I will sleep on my sofa next to the whelping box for up to two weeks. It's important that the pups feed regularly from the dam. As with most litters, you'll get some stronger and greedier than others, so it's important the others get their share and don't just give up.

"My bitch isn't the most maternal to start with, and will often cop out of being with her babies at first, but after 24 hours her maternal instinct seems to kick in and results in her obsessively cleaning them. Although this is a good thing, she can become quite keen when it comes to their umbilical cords. Some dams will attempt to chew them off the pups, which can result in the pups having a slight hernia. The other downside for us is my girl likes to gather the pups up in a bundle and sit on them. In her little head she thinks she's keeping them warm, but in fact she could suffocate them. But generally they can get out from under her, she just needs a reminder. Maybe it's me being an over-protective mum, but my maternal instincts kick in too, and my body won't leave her until I know the pups and her are capable on their own."

Donna Shank and Brenda Schuettenberg, of RoKuCiera Pugs, California, said: "C-section is becoming more prevalent as we breed faster-maturing dogs. We want the large head and stout bone and end up with pelvic openings that can't accommodate the bulk if we want the breed to stay in the 14-18 pound range, as stated in the standard. I have girls that can free whelp, their pups do not mature as quickly.... They do well enough in puppy classes, but not in Bred-By or open classes as they don't look 'adult' until 24 to 30 months."

Sue Wragg, of Glammarags Pugs, UK, added: "The puppies themselves aren't difficult to rear, but although most Pugs are good mothers, they can be clumsy and lie on their puppies if they aren't watched, so most breeders don't leave the bitch alone with the puppies."

There are many other details to be taken into consideration, such as sexually transmitted diseases

like herpes, hormone tests, monitoring the pregnant female and veterinary expenses. In short, breeding Pugs is a complex issue – if you want a healthy mother and pups, that is. It is expensive, time-consuming and requires knowledge. That's why the breed societies discourage regular dog owners from breeding from their pets.

If you are determined to breed from your Pug, you must first learn a lot about the breed. Visit shows and talk to breeders, a good breeder is one whose main aim is to improve the breed by producing healthy puppies with good temperaments and conformation. Our photo shows three generation of Pugs bred by Laura Libner, of Loralar Pugs, Michigan, USA.

Before deciding to breed from your dog, ask yourself these questions:

1. **Did you get your Pug from a breeder?** Dogs sold in pet stores and on general sales websites are seldom good specimens of the breed and are often unhealthy.

2. **Did you get a three to five-generation pedigree with your Pug?** A reputable breeder will always provide a pedigree so that you can see your dog's lineage.

3. **Does your Pug have a good temperament? Does he or she socialise well with people and other animals?** If you can't tell, take the dog out to training classes. The instructor can help you evaluate the dog's temperament. Dogs with poor temperaments should not be bred from, regardless of how good they look.

4. **Is your Pug a good, quiet breather, particularly during moderate exercise and in warm weather?** Pugs with poor airways can have problems in hot weather or with stress or exercise. If you can't tell, have your vet check your dog's respiratory system.

5. **Can your Pug move with ease and sustain a vigorous and active trot?** A variety of orthopaedic problems, such as hip dysplasia and luxating patella, can contribute to poor movement and may have an inheritable basis. Compare your dog's gait with that of other Pugs, or have a reputable breeder help you evaluate it.

6. **Has a vet checked your Pug's hips and patellae (knee caps) and found them to be sound? Have X-rays been done?** You should know your dog's hip score before deciding to breed.

7. **Are your dog and his or her close relatives free from a history of back trouble?** Hemivertebrae are a common issue within the breed. They do not always cause problems unless they protrude into the spinal canal or impinge on the spinal nerves. However, Pugs with many malformed vertebrae or prematurely degenerated discs should not be used for breeding.

8. **Has your Pug been tested for, and found to be free of, infectious diseases?** There are infections of the reproductive tract that can be transmitted during a natural mating - or from dog to bitch during artificial insemination - and can also prevent or terminate pregnancy or cause problems for the puppies.

9. **Is your Pug in general good health, and free of major health problems?** An unhealthy female is more likely to have trouble with pregnancy and whelping, and certain health problems could be inherited by the puppies from either parent.

10. **Does your Pug conform to the breed standard?** Do not breed a Pug who is not a good specimen of the breed, hoping that somehow the puppies will conform better to the standard. Read and study the standard, talk with experienced breeders and ask them for an honest assessment of your dog.

11. **Is your Pug a colour other than fawn or black?** If so, he or she is actually a crossbreed, with blood from another breed, as all true Pugs are either fawn or black. Under no circumstances should you breed from this dog - no matter how cute he looks - as his ancestry is unknown.

12. **Have you had your Pug's eyes examined by an ophthalmologist within the last year and found to be normal?** There are several eye conditions in Pugs that are thought to be inheritable. Only a specialised vet can detect some of these.

13. **Is your female two years old or older and at least in her second heat cycle?** Females should not be bred until they are fully physically mature, they are able to carry a litter to term, and are robust enough to recover quickly from a C-section, should it be necessary, and then nurse a litter for several weeks.

14. **Are you financially able to provide good veterinary care for the mother and puppies, particularly if complications occur?** The tests for infections, eye and orthopaedic examinations can be expensive, and that's in addition to routine veterinary care and the added costs of pre-natal care and immunisations for puppies. If you are not prepared to make a financial commitment to a breeding that could end up costing you a significant amount of money, then do not breed from your Pug.

15. **Do you have the time to provide full-time care for the mother and puppies if necessary?** As you have read from breeders, caring for the mother and new-borns is a 24/7 job in the beginning.

16. **Will you be able to find good homes for however many puppies there should be and will you be prepared to take them back if necessary?** This is an important consideration for good breeders, who will not let their precious puppies go to any old home. They want to be sure that the new owners will take good care of their Pugs for their lifetime.

In the UK, Pugs are on a "watch list" of dogs which have had physical traits bred into them which have inadvertently led to health problems. Today's reputable breeders are continually looking at ways of improving the health of the breed through selective breeding.

Responsible breeding is backed up by genetic information and screening as well as a thorough knowledge of the desired traits of the Pug. It is definitely not an occupation for the amateur hobbyist. Breeding is not just about the look of the dogs; health and temperament are important factors too. Many dog lovers do not realise that the single most important factor governing health and certain temperament traits is genetics.

Having said that, experts are not born, they learn their trade over many years. Our photo shows five generations of Sandra Mayoh's Drumlinfold Pugs, North Yorkshire, England (yes, a fawn Pug can produce a black puppy and vice versa!) Anyone who is seriously considering getting into the specialised art of Pug breeding should first spend time researching the breed and its genetics. Make sure you are going into breeding for the right reasons.

Don't breed Pugs to make money or to get puppies just like your perfect Pug, and certainly not to show the kids "the miracle of birth." If you are determined to go into breeding, then do so for the right reason - to improve the breed. Learn all you can beforehand, read books, visit dog shows and make contact with established breeders. Find yourself a mentor - ideally a successful breeder with a proven track record who is registered with the breed club and/or Kennel Club in your country - and make sure you have a vet who is familiar with brachycephalic breeds.

Committed Pug breeders use their skills and knowledge to produce healthy pups with good temperaments which conform to breed standards and ultimately improve the breed.

Females and Heat

Just like all other animal and human females, a female Pug has a menstrual cycle - or to be more accurate, an oestrus cycle. This is the period when she is ready (and willing!) for mating and is more commonly called **heat** or being **on heat**, **in heat** or **in season**.

A female Pug has her first cycle from about six to nine months old. However, there are some bloodlines with longer spans between heat cycles and the female may not have her first heat until she is anywhere from 10 months to one year old.

She will generally come on heat every six to eight months, though it may be even longer between cycles, and the timescale becomes more erratic with old age. It can also be irregular with young dogs when cycles first begin.

Heat will last on average from 12 to 21 days, although it can be anything from just a few days up to four weeks. Within this period there will be several days which will be the optimum time for her to get pregnant. This middle phase of the cycle is called the *oestrus*. The third phase, called *diestrus*, then begins. During this time, her body will produce hormones whether or not she is pregnant. Her body thinks and acts like she is pregnant. All the hormones are present; only the puppies are missing. This can sometimes lead to what is known as a 'false pregnancy'.

Pug breeders normally wait until a female has been in heat at least twice before breeding from her. Some believe that two years old is the right age for a first litter, while others think it is prudent to wait until she is a little older - especially as a pregnancy will draw on her calcium reserves which she needs for her own growing bones. Responsible Pug breeders limit the number of litters from each female, as breeding can take a lot out of them.

While a female is on heat, she produces hormones which attract male dogs. Because dogs have a sense of smell hundreds of times stronger than ours, your girl on heat is a magnet for all the males in the neighbourhood. They may congregate around your house or follow you around the park, waiting for their chance to prove their manhood – or mutthood in their case.

Don't expect your precious Pug princess to be fussy. Her hormones are raging when she is on heat and during her most fertile days, she is ready, able and … very willing! As she approaches the optimum time for mating, you may notice her short tail bending slightly to one side. She will also start to urinate more frequently. This is her signal to all those virile male dogs out there that she is ready for mating.

The first visual sign you may notice is when she tries to lick her swollen rear end – or vulva to be more precise. She will then bleed, this is sometimes called spotting. It will be a light red or brown at the beginning of the heat cycle, then some bitches bleed a lot after the first week. Some females Pugs can bleed quite heavily, this is normal. But if you have any concerns about her bleeding, contact your vet to be on the safe side. She may also start to "mate" with your leg or other dogs. These are all normal signs of heat.

Pug breeding requires specialised knowledge on the part of the owner, but this does not stop a female on heat from being extremely interested in attention from any old mutt. To avoid an unwanted pregnancy, you must keep a close eye on your female and not allow her to freely wander where she may come into contact with other dogs when she is on heat.

Unlike women, female dogs do not go through the menopause and can have puppies even when they are quite old. However, a litter for an elderly Pug can also result in complications.

If you don't want your female Pug to get pregnant, you should have her spayed. In North America and Europe, humane societies, animal shelters and rescue groups urge dog owners to have their pets spayed or neutered to prevent unwanted litters which contribute to too many animals in the rescue system or, even worse, euthanasia. Normally all dogs from rescue centres and shelters are spayed or neutered. Many responsible breeders also encourage early spaying and neutering – and some may even specify it in the puppy's sale contract.

Spaying

Spaying is the term used to describe the removal of the ovaries and uterus (womb) of a female dog so that she cannot become pregnant. Although this is a routine operation, it is major abdominal surgery and she has to be anaesthetised. A popular myth is that a female dog should have her first heat cycle before she is spayed, but this is not the case. Even puppies can be

spayed. You should consult your vet for the optimum time, should you decide to have your dog done.

If spayed before her first heat cycle, one of the advantages is that your dog will have an almost zero risk of mammary cancer (the equivalent of breast cancer in women). Even after the first heat, spaying reduces the risk of this cancer by 92%.

Some vets claim that the risk of mammary cancer in unspayed female dogs can be as high as one in four. Some females may put weight on easier after spaying and will require slightly less food afterwards. As with any major procedure, there are pros and cons.

Spaying is a much more serious operation for a female than neutering is for a male. This is because it involves an internal abdominal operation, whereas the neutering procedure is carried out on the male's testicles, which are outside his abdomen.

For:

➢ Spaying prevents infections, cancer and other diseases of the uterus and ovaries.
➢ Your dog will have a greatly reduced risk of mammary cancer. It reduces hormonal changes which can interfere with the treatment of diseases like diabetes or epilepsy.
➢ Spaying can reduce behaviour problems, such as roaming, aggression to other dogs, anxiety or fear.
➢ It eliminates the risk of the potentially fatal disease pyometra (a secondary infection that occurs as a result of hormonal changes in the female's reproductive tract), which affects unspayed middle-aged females.
➢ A spayed dog does not contribute to the pet overpopulation problem.

Against:

➢ Complications can occur, including an abnormal reaction to the anaesthetic, bleeding, stitches breaking and infections. This is not common.
➢ Occasionally there can be long-term effects connected to hormonal changes. These may include weight gain, urinary incontinence or less stamina and these problems can occur years after a female has been spayed.
➢ Older females may suffer some urinary incontinence, but it only affects a few spayed females. Discuss it with your vet.
➢ Cost. This can range from $160 - $480 in the USA and £100 to £300 in the UK.
➢ Pugs are sensitive to anaesthesia – select a vet who is familiar with Pugs, or at least brachycephalic (flat faced) breeds.

If you talk to your vet or a volunteer at a rescue shelter, they will say that the advantages of spaying far outweigh any disadvantages. If you have a female puppy, you can discuss with your vet whether, and at what age, spaying would be a good idea for your Pug when you take her in for her vaccinations.

Neutering

Neutering male dogs involves castration; the removal of the testicles. This can be a difficult decision for some owners, as it causes a drop in the pet's testosterone levels, which some humans – males in particular! - feel affects the quality of their dog's life.

Fortunately, dogs do not think like people and male dogs do not miss their testicles or the loss of sex. Our own experience is that our dog Max is much happier having been neutered. We decided to have him neutered after he went missing three times on walks – he ran off on the scent of a female on heat. Fortunately, he is micro-chipped and has our phone number on a tag on his collar and we were lucky that he was returned to us on all three occasions.

Unless you specifically want to breed from or show your dog, or he has a special job, neutering is recommended by animal rescue organisations and vets. Guide Dogs for the Blind, Hearing Dogs for Deaf People and Dogs for the Disabled are routinely neutered and this does not impair their ability to perform their duties.

There are countless unwanted puppies, especially in the US, many of which are destroyed. There is also the problem of a lack of knowledge from the owners of some breeding dogs, resulting in the production of puppies with congenital health or temperament problems.

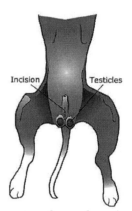
Incision   Testicles

Neutering is usually performed around puberty, i.e. about six months old. It can, however, be done at any age over eight weeks, provided both testicles have descended. The operation is a relatively straightforward procedure. Dogs neutered before puberty tend to grow a little larger than dogs done later. This is because testosterone is involved in the process which stops growth, so the bones grow for longer without testosterone.

The neutering operation for a male is much less of a major operation than spaying for a female. Complications are less common and less severe than with spaying a female. Although he will feel tender afterwards, your dog should return to his normal self within a couple of days.

When he comes out of surgery, his scrotum (the sacs which held the testicles) will be swollen and it may look like nothing has been done. But it is normal for these to slowly shrink in the days following surgery. Here are the main pros and cons:

For:

- ➢ Behaviour problems such as aggression and wandering off are reduced.
- ➢ Unwanted sexual behaviour, such as mounting people or objects, is usually reduced or eliminated.
- ➢ Testicular problems such as infections, cancer and torsion (painful rotation of the testicle) are eradicated.
- ➢ Prostate disease, common in older male dogs, is less likely to occur.
- ➢ A submissive entire (uncastrated) male dog may be targeted by other dogs. After he has been neutered, he will no longer produce testosterone and so will not be regarded as much of a threat by the other males, so he is less likely to be bullied.
- ➢ A neutered dog is not fathering unwanted puppies.

Against:

- ➢ As with any surgery, there can be bleeding afterwards, you should keep an eye on him for any blood loss after the operation. Infections can also occur, generally caused by the dog licking the wound, so try and prevent him doing this. If he persists, use an E collar. In the **vast majority** of cases, these problems do not occur.
- ➢ Some dogs' coats may be affected, but supplementing their diet with fish oil can compensate for this.
- ➢ Cost. This starts at around $130 in the US, £80 in the UK.
- ➢ Pugs are sensitive to anaesthesia – select a vet who is familiar with the breed.

Myths - Here are some common myths about neutering and spaying:

Neutering or spaying will spoil the dog's character - There is no evidence that any of the positive characteristics of your dog will be altered. He or she will be just as loving, playful and loyal. Neutering may reduce aggression or roaming, especially in male dogs, because they are no longer competing to mate with a female.

A female needs to have at least one litter - There is no proven physical or mental benefit to a female having a litter. Pregnancy and whelping (giving birth to puppies) can be stressful and can have complications. In a false pregnancy, a female is simply responding to the hormones in her body.

Mating is natural and necessary - Dogs are not humans, they do not think emotionally about sex or having and raising a family. Because Pugs like the company of humans so much, we tend to ascribe human emotions to them. Unlike humans, their desire to mate or breed is entirely physical, triggered by the chemicals called hormones within their body. Without these hormones – i.e. after neutering or spaying – the desire disappears or is greatly reduced.

Male dogs will behave better if they can mate - This is simply not true; sex does not make a dog behave better. In fact it can have the opposite effect. Having mated once, a male may show an increased interest in females. He may also consider his status elevated, which may make him harder to control or call back.

Pregnancy

A canine pregnancy will normally last for 61 to 65 days - typically 63 days – regardless of the size or breed of the dog. Sometimes pregnancy is referred to as the *"gestation period."*

There is now a blood test available which measures levels *relaxin*. This is a hormone produced by the ovary and the developing placenta, and pregnancy can be detected by monitoring relaxin levels as early as 22 to 27 days after mating. The levels are high throughout pregnancy and then decline rapidly after the female has given birth.

After 45 days, X-rays can confirm the pregnancy. X-rays also give the breeder an idea of the number of puppies, they can help if the bitch has had previous whelping problems, and also give the vet more information if a C-section is to be performed. Here are some of the signs of pregnancy:

- ➢ After mating, many females become more affectionate. (However, some will become uncharacteristically irritable and maybe even a little aggressive)

- The female may produce a slight clear discharge from her vagina about one month after mating

- Her appetite will increase in the second month of pregnancy

- She may seem slightly depressed and/or show a drop in appetite. These signs can also mean there are other problems, so you should consult your vet

- Her teats (nipples) will become more prominent, pink and erect 25 to 30 days into the pregnancy. Later on, you may notice a fluid coming from them

- After about 35 days, or seven weeks, her body weight will noticeably increase

- Her abdomen will become noticeably larger from around day 40, although first-time mums and females carrying few puppies may not show as much

- Many pregnant females' appetite will increase in the second half of pregnancy

- Her nesting instincts will kick in as the delivery date approaches. She may seem restless or scratch her bed or the floor

- During the last week of pregnancy, females often start to look for a safe place for whelping. Some seem to become confused, wanting to be with their owners and at the same time wanting to prepare their nest.

(Our photo shows Linda and Kim Wright's Ch. Aramis Wright As Rain with a female puppy who was born naturally, i.e. without a C-section)

Even if the female is having a C-section, she should still be allowed to nest in a whelping box with layers of newspaper, which she will scratch and dig as the time approaches.

However, natural birthing – or free whelping - can present problems for some Pugs and should only be attempted by experienced breeders with a Pug-savvy vet on call. And even then they will not leave the pregnant female unattended when she is near her time.

If your female becomes pregnant – either by design or accident - your first step should be to consult a veterinarian familiar with Pugs straight away. Pregnant Pugs simply cannot be left to get on with it like many other breeds.

False Pregnancies

As many as 50% or more of intact (unspayed) females may display signs of a false pregnancy. In the wild it was common for female dogs to have false pregnancies and to lactate (produce milk). This female would then nourish puppies if their own mother died.

False pregnancies occur 60 to 80 days after the female was in heat - about the time she would have given birth – and are generally nothing to worry about for an owner. The exact cause is unknown. However, hormonal imbalances are thought to play an important role. Some dogs have shown symptoms within three to four days of spaying. Typical symptoms include:

- ➢ Mothering or adopting toys and other objects
- ➢ Making a nest
- ➢ Producing milk (lactating)
- ➢ Appetite fluctuations
- ➢ Barking or whining a lot
- ➢ Restlessness, depression or anxiety
- ➢ Swollen abdomen
- ➢ She might even appear to go into labour

Try not to touch your dog's nipples, as touch will stimulate further milk production. If she is licking herself repeatedly, she may need an Elizabethan collar (a large plastic collar from the vet) to minimise stimulation.

Under no circumstances should you restrict your Pug's water supply to try and prevent her from producing milk. This is dangerous as she can become dehydrated.

Some unspayed bitches may have a false pregnancy with each heat cycle. Spaying during a false pregnancy may actually prolong the condition, so better to wait until the false pregnancy is over and then have her spayed to prevent it happening again. False pregnancy is not a disease, but an exaggerated response to normal hormonal changes. Owners should be reassured that even if left untreated, the condition almost always resolves itself.

However, if your Pug appears physically ill or the behavioural changes are severe enough to worry you, visit your vet. He or she may prescribe tranquilisers to relieve anxiety, or diuretics to reduce milk production and relieve fluid retention. In rare cases, hormone treatment may be necessary. Generally, dogs experiencing false pregnancies do not have serious long-term problems, as the behaviour disappears when the hormones return to their normal levels in two to three weeks.

One exception is pyometra, a disease mainly affecting unspayed middle-aged females, caused by a hormonal abnormality. Pyometra follows a heat cycle in which fertilisation did not occur and the dog typically starts showing symptoms within two to four months. These are excessive drinking and urination, with the female trying to lick a white discharge from her vagina. She may also have a slight temperature. If the condition becomes severe, her back legs will become weak, possibly to the point where she can no longer get up without help.

Pyometra is serious if bacteria take a hold and in extreme cases it can be fatal. It is also relatively common and needs to be dealt with promptly by a vet, who will give the dog intravenous fluids and antibiotics for several days. In most cases this is followed by spaying.

NOTE: If you are offered a Pug puppy which seems very large, or has an unusual or "rare" coat colour, or has a tattoo, it has probably been bred from an imported Pug and does not conform to breed standards. There are often issues regarding the welfare of these mothers and puppies, as well as the long-term health of the puppies. Many imports are not properly screened for heritable diseases or breathing problems.

Sometimes pups are kept in concrete buildings during the critical early period for socialisation. Our advice is to AVOID imported puppies at all costs – no matter what colour they are and how cute they look. You could be storing up a lot of trouble for yourself in the future when you find you have an unhealthy or unsocialised dog with behaviour issues.

14. Rescuing a Pug

Are you thinking of adopting a Pug from a rescue organisation? What could be kinder and more rewarding than giving a poor, abandoned dog a happy and loving home for the rest of his or her life?

Not much really; adoption saves lives. The problem of homeless dogs is truly depressing, it's bad enough in the UK, but even worse in America. The sheer numbers in kill shelters is hard to comprehend; Randy Grim states in "Don't Dump The Dog" that 1,000 dogs are being put to sleep every hour in the US.

There are many reasons why a dog may end up in rescue. The owners may have died, divorced, moved home or got a new job. The dog may have been used for breeding in a 'puppy mill' and has outlived her usefulness to the breeder – in this case the poor animal will probably need a lot of socialising as she will be unused to much human contact. She also might not be housetrained.

Through a lack of knowledge or effort on the part of the previous owner, a rescue dog may have behaviour issues. And another common reason for Pugs to end up homeless is health. Sadly the Pug is among the most expensive breeds when it comes to vets' bills – which some owners simply don't consider before getting a dog. A rescue Pug may have breathing, skin, eye, allergies, infections or other health issues - or the dog may simply be suffering from neglect in the form of malnutrition, worms and parasites. It's hard to believe that these are all-too-frequent scenarios in the 21st century.

If you decide to offer a home to one of these poor souls, you need to do it with your eyes wide open. Offering a home to a rescue Pug is often not recommended if you are a first-time dog owner. The Pug – even a healthy, well behaved one - is a breed which requires some specialist care, and many rescues are very needy. It can be like living with a permanent toddler, so ask yourself if you are prepared for that level of commitment.

Some Pugs may have issues with humans, dogs, other animals or children and will require a great deal of time and patience from their new owners if they are to be rehabilitated. Some may never learn to live with small children or other animals. Many Pugs available for adoption are older and, although you can teach an old dog new tricks and good manners, it is not as easy as with a puppy.

There is, however, a ray of sunshine for some of these dogs. Every year many thousands of people in North America, the UK and countries all around the world adopt a rescue dog and the story often has a happy ending.

The Dog's Point of View

But if you are serious about adopting a Pug, then you should do so with the right motives and prepared for a ride which may not always be smooth – especially in the beginning when you are both getting to know each other and fit in with each others' lives. If you're expecting a perfect dog, you could be in for a shock. Rescue Pugs can and do become wonderful additions to the household, but often the outcome is down to you and how much time and patience you can devote to your new arrival.

Pugs make outstanding companion dogs, however, many of them in rescue centres are traumatised. Some dogs from puppy mills may have been kept on concrete or in cages without stimulation, toys, daily walks and little or no contact with the outside world. And those rescues from families don't understand why they have been abandoned by their beloved owners and in the beginning often arrive with problems of their own until they adjust to being part of a loving family home again.

Do not consider adopting a Pug - or any other dog - unless you are 100% committed to making it work and you are prepared to be there for the long haul. Ask yourself a few questions before you take the plunge:

❖ Am I prepared to accept and deal with any problems - such as bad behaviour, shyness, aggression, chewing or making a mess in the house - which the dog may display when he or she initially arrives in my home?
❖ How much time am I willing to spend with my new pet to help him or her integrate into normal family life?
❖ Can I take time off work in the beginning to be at home and help the new arrival settle in?
❖ Am I prepared to take on a new addition to my family that may live for many years?
❖ Can I afford the vets' bills if my rescue Pug has or develops health problems?

Think about the implications before taking on a rescue dog - try and look at it from the dog's point of view. What could be worse for an unlucky Pug than to be abandoned again if things don't work out between you?

Other Considerations

Adopting a rescue dog is a big commitment for all involved. It is not a cheap way of getting a Pug and shouldn't be viewed as such. It will probably cost you several hundred pounds or dollars. You'll have adoption fees to pay and often vaccination and veterinary bills as well as worm and flea medication and spaying or neutering. Make sure you're aware of the full cost before committing. Many rescue Pugs have had difficult lives. You need plenty of time to help them rehabilitate. Some may have initial problems with housebreaking. Others may need socialisation with people as well as other dogs.

It may take the dog up to two months just to get used to being in your home with you and your family and during this initial period, the dog will require intensive supervision, patience and care - can you give it? Even if you are serious about adopting, you may have to wait a while until a suitable dog comes up. One way of finding out if you, your family and home are suitable is to volunteer to become a foster home for one of the rescue centres. Fosters offer temporary homes until a forever home becomes available It's a shorter term arrangement, but still requires commitment and patience. Or you could help by becoming a fundraiser to generate cash to keep these very worthy rescue groups providing such a wonderful service.

And it's not just the dogs that are screened - you'll have to undergo a screening by the rescue organisation to ensure you are suitable. You might even have to provide references. To give you some idea of the hoops you have to jump through before being considered suitable, The UK's Pug Dog Welfare & Rescue Organisation (PDWRA) has kindly allowed us to publish questions from their adoption form for prospective owners:

❖ If your property is rented, have you established that you are permitted to keep a dog?
❖ Do you have your own garden?
❖ Is your garden secure?
❖ If not secure, where will the dog be exercised?
❖ Please explain your reasons for wanting to adopt a Pug
❖ Please tell us about your knowledge and experience of Pugs
❖ In your own words please tell us why we should pick you to adopt a rescue Pug.
❖ Do you own a Pug now?
❖ Have you owned a Pug in the past?
❖ If yes to the above, what happened to it?
❖ Do you have any other dogs or pets?
❖ If yes to the above, are all your existing dogs and bitches neutered?
❖ If you have other dogs or pets, what are they?
❖ Have you ever had to give up or re-home one of your pets?
❖ If yes to the above, please give details.
❖ Where will the Pug be kept during the day?
❖ Where will the Pug be kept at night?
❖ Where will the Pug be kept during holidays?
❖ Where will the Pug be kept during absences from home or illness? NOTE: It must be fully understood that the Pug must NOT be kept outside.
❖ Number in the household: Adults, Children.
❖ If children in the household please state ages.
❖ Do you work? Full-time? Part-time?
❖ If yes to the above, how long will the dog be left during the day? Hours?
❖ Will you permit a Trustee/appointed agent to visit your home?

You then have to sign a declaration agreeing to the following: In the event of my obtaining a Pug through The Pug Dog Welfare & Rescue Association, I understand that:

1. I shall be required to sign their adoption form
2. The Pug is intended solely as a pet and is not to be used for breeding
3. No papers are given with the Pug, I am responsible for the Pug in every way
4. I am willing for one of the Welfare Trustees to keep in touch with me and to visit me occasionally
5. In the event of my being unable to keep the Pug, it must be returned to The Pug Dog Welfare & Rescue Association
6. I agree to have my adopted Pug spayed or neutered as required
7. I agree to have my adopted Pug micro chipped to PDWRA

RESCUING & REHOMING PUGS THROUGHOUT THE UK

According to Jo-Anne Cousins, a leading figure in canine rescue and former President of IDOG Rescue, often the situations leading to a dog ending up in rescue can be summed up in one phrase: **unrealistic expectations.**

She said: "In many situations, dog ownership was something that the family went into without fully understanding the time, money and commitment that it takes to raise a dog. While they may have spent hours on the internet pouring over cute puppy photos, they probably didn't read any puppy training books or look into actual costs of regular vet care, training and boarding."

Some of the most common reasons for Pugs ending up in rescue are:

❖ Finances –the owners can no longer afford to keep the dog
❖ Health issues – the owner has not got the money and/or time needed to deal with them
❖ Lifestyle changes, such as new partner, new job, or moving home
❖ Poor behaviour, such as chewing, biting or not being housetrained
❖ Lack of time, what may have seemed like a great gift becomes too much of a burden when owners realise how much time and care a dog requires.

The following article 'So You Want a Pug?' gives a great insight into some of the challenges facing new owners and is reproduced with kind permission of The Pug Dog Welfare & Rescue Association.

So You Want A Pug?

"You want a Pug. You've wanted one for years. You hopefully have done some research and think this is the breed for you. Well, read on. There are some things about Pugs that aren't in all the books and that may make a Pug a bad fit for you.

Let me start by saying that no two Pugs are alike. Don't assume that because your neighbour's Pug is a slug, yours will be. It's a HUGE mistake to judge all Pugs by your experience with one or two. They can vary quite a bit in energy, intelligence and temperament, ranging from go-with-the-flow to I'm-in-charge-of-everything. Gross generalizations that tend to be true:

❖ Blacks tend to be busier and have more attitude than fawns

❖ Females tend to be pushier and more in your face than males

❖ Males tend to be more laid back and easy going than females

There are exceptions to all of the above.

Pug Puppies

No doubt you've read about how Pugs are sweet, affectionate, cuddly and low energy. So you will be rightfully horrified when you find that your puppy is a whirling dervish of energy who snuggles for 30 seconds and then is off again to race around the house, leaving destruction in his or her path. Pug puppies are no different from any other puppy. Expect nipping, chewing, gnawing, jumping, pulling on your trouser legs, shoe destroying, and general mayhem.

Here's the reality. NO puppy is a couch potato. They are all lunatics. Some more than others. You likely won't have a couch potato Pug until at least the age of two and your Pug may NEVER be a couch potato. Pugs from reputable breeders are more likely to have the Pug temperament eventually, but even they will be devils as a puppy. If your puppy is from the internet, a pet store, a newspaper ad, then it's up for grabs what kind of temperament you may end up with. You might get a Pug that has the solid and stable temperament that is the signature of the breed, but you might also end up with a high drive, high energy Pug that won't settle down for several years, if ever.

One of the best ways to wear a puppy out (or any busy dog) is to engage them in activities that make them work and think. This is why obedience classes are so great – it may only be an hour, but that's a hard hour of learning and really takes the 'edge' off of a busy dog.

Pugs are and were bred to be companion animals. They need people. If you are going to be gone for long periods of time and/or be too tired to engage with your Pug when you get home from work, then a Pug probably isn't the dog for you. And Pug puppies will need you to engage with them. They will demand it (as will most adults). Just like children, puppy brains need stimulation and activity to develop. A puppy left crated for eight to ten hours will be absolutely manic by the time you get home and will need you to devote the remainder of the evening to them. They are often referred to as a Velcro dog, so if you don't want a dog that is going to be wherever you are all the time (including in the bathroom!), then rethink getting a Pug.

Housetraining

Pugs will not be housetrained in a month or two months or even six months. Some pick it up quickly, but most take a year or longer and may still not be 100% reliable. And most Pugs won't ask to go out. You might be able to train them to ask, but in my experience, most Pugs don't learn this or if they do learn it, they figure it equals a treat (assuming you give a treat to your dog after going outside). You may end up with a Pug that asks for food as opposed to letting you know they want to go out.

Pugs generally will not just go outside and do their business while you sit nice and warm in the kitchen and have a coffee. If they are outside, you'd better be outside, too. Most will not excrete outside without your company and encouragement. Many will also try to fake you out by pretending to pee. Maddening? You bet, but these quirks are part of the charm of the breed.

While some Pugs can last all day while you're at work, most can't and none should be expected to. When was the last time you had to hold your bowels or bladder for eight to ten hours at a stretch? So if you are contemplating a Pug (or small breed dog) then be sure that you can afford to have someone come in and let the dog out or make arrangements for the dog to excrete in an 'approved' spot.

Punishing a Pug for an accident is not an effective method of housetraining. Praise for appropriate toileting will win the day – eventually – but scolding, yelling, hitting, or rubbing the dog's nose in the mess will not housetrain the dog and will likely create a dog that will become a sneaky excreter. There are many good books and articles on housetraining.

Be prepared that if you have a Pug puppy, you may well have to get up at night – two, three or four times a night – until they are six months or older.

Pug Quirks

Pugs have a variety of quirks that drive some people nuts. They are nosey, inquisitive, and often right underfoot. Many are tremendously food-driven and will consume things that you don't consider edible. I'm not kidding. They will eat sticks, rocks, coins, screws, plastic caps off of bottles. You name it, they will eat it. They figure out quickly that the command "drop it" means you're going to take it away so many will swallow the forbidden object rather than give it up.

It is your job to Pug proof your home to avoid tragedy. Many have tissue and toilet paper addictions that they have all their lives. I have known several to think eating used tissue is a true delight and will go out of their way to access it. I never trust any Pug around any food source, rubbish bin or even cabinets that they can open.

Quite a few will 'table surf'. If they can get on to your dining room or kitchen table, they will. And they will consume whatever is up there.

Pugs are often quite tactile. Many are obsessive lickers – of themselves, you, the other dogs or cats, the kids, the carpet, your pillow. It's a Pug thing. Many use their paws more like hands than paws. Quite a few are "swatters" and will use their paws to whack you or other animals – generally to play or get attention.

Pugs can be quite vocal and can be barkers, howlers, moaners and grumblers. I have known of many that were vocal in the extreme and would carry on protracted conversations with their owners. As a breed, they have the widest assortment of noises I've ever heard. And some snore very, very loudly.

Pugs are tough little dogs that have no clue how small they are. Most will not initiate a fight, but many will vigorously defend themselves or others if a fight starts. Most are hopelessly outclassed in the fighting department and will get seriously hurt.

As a deeply food-driven breed, you may have issues with food aggression and resource guarding. Make sure that you do research on working with these issues.

Many Pugs are not fans of inclement weather and will resist excreting outside in the cold, rain or wind. Some are fine, but in my experience, many will refuse (or try to refuse) to excrete outdoors. Some will simply use your floors, some will hold their bowels and bladder for frighteningly long periods of time too.

Few Pugs will show any remorse or other indication that they know they did wrong by excreting in the house. Some will, but most will happily pee on my floors and look at you like "What? I went to the door and you weren't there so I used the floor. Get over it".

No dog can be trained to be "traffic smart". And don't fool yourself that you can do this or that your neighbourhood is safe. Pugs (any dog, in my opinion) should not be off lead in any environment where they can get away from you and end up on the road or lost. They can be remarkably fast and it only takes a second for a dog to be hit by a car.

They have a remarkable capacity for bodily excretions. Expect to get snot blown in your face regularly, eye boogers to be wiped on your new white blouse/pillow/trousers and to find the foul smell of anal gland excretions on your furniture or lap sometime.

Pugs are Smart

Pugs are often tagged as dumb dogs. Most aren't. In fact, most are smart enough and stubborn enough to figure out how to get their way or how to outlast you. Positive training, setting rules and boundaries are crucial with this breed if you don't want to end up with a thug. Since they are often very food driven, treats are very effective in training Pugs.

And they are dogs. Let's remember that. They aren't little people, much as we like to think of them that way. They need to do dog things – go to parks, meet other dogs, play and have fun. Just as you wouldn't raise a human child in isolation with no rules, it isn't good for a Pug to be raised in isolation where there are no rules or boundaries. Pugs are very adept at figuring out what you will and will not tolerate and will test the limits. You don't need to be a dictator, but all dogs like to know what the routine is and like a predictable world.

Pug Energy

While they aren't sporting dogs, all Pugs need exercise. Yes, quite a few would prefer to laze on the sofa all day, but that isn't good for them. There are Pugs that excel at agility, and at obedience. They don't have to be slugs and most importantly, they shouldn't get FAT. This can be a real struggle as they always act like they haven't eaten in a week, have pitiful, soulful eyes and for some reason some of them just seem to think of food and put on weight. It really is important to remember that they need the right amount of food for the activity level of the dog. You don't do your dog any kindness by letting them get obese; you will shorten their life significantly.

As mentioned earlier, they can be wildly busy puppies and many first-time Pug owners get very discouraged. They may slow down with time and age, but you need to be sure that your Pug, regardless of energy level, gets exercise and mental stimulation.

Pug Health

This, more than any other issue, is often the undoing of a Pug owner. Like all purebred dogs, Pugs have some health issues that may crop up and they are often expensive health issues. DO YOUR RESEARCH on the breed and especially on where you are getting your Pug. Rescues generally have a good idea of the health issues facing a given dog – don't assume that a rescued Pug is going to be a health nightmare.

You do put yourself at risk for expensive health issues with Pugs from pet shops, internet ads and the newspaper. Most reputable breeders will have genetic testing going back generations. It's no guarantee that your Pug won't have an issue, but it does decrease the odds.

Pugs are prone to issues specific to brachycephalic (flat faced) breeds (breathing, eyes, folds of skin) and are prone to issues of the toy breeds generally (luxating patella, dental problems, trachea). And then there is Pug Dog Encephalitis (PDE) that is Pug-specific.

Pugs have a very high rate of allergies – food being a big one – grains in particular. Pugs need a high quality diet. Shop brought kibble may not cut it and you can avoid a host of future problems if you start off feeding your Pug a good diet, whether raw or a premium kibble.

Pugs have a high rate of vaccine reactions. Be watchful and conservative in your vaccination protocol.

Think seriously about insurance for your Pug. It can be a life saver, literally. If you don't or won't get insurance, then have a plan for what you will do when the first £2,500 vet bill crops up. It can happen. An eye injury in a Pug can go from simple scratch to serious ulcer in 24 hours and need a corneal graft that will run you into some serious cash. Be prepared for this so that you aren't sitting at the vet's trying to figure out what to do because you can't afford the vet care needed.

They Are A High Maintenance Breed

Don't get me wrong. I love Pugs, but they are, to my mind, a high maintenance breed. They need and want a lot of attention. They moult like maniacs. I'm not kidding about the moult. It's downright astonishing. They can be bossy, stubborn, and full of naughtiness. They require a fair bit of watching and managing in terms of safety, health and general training. They can and will get themselves into trouble – by dashing into the road (if off the lead) to get a piece of squashed sandwich, chewing on your power cords, opening up your cupboards (which you thought were safe) and 7.5 kg bag of kibble, and jumping off of a height and snapping a leg bone.

They tend to need some pretty regular cleaning of nose folds, eye areas and are notoriously fussy about having their nails trimmed. You can see some real dramatic behaviour around nail clipping in particular. I've known several Pugs to start screaming as if they were being killed before the nail trimming even started...

They do a thing called Reverse Sneezing. Read up about it and save yourself a trip to the emergency vet. All Pugs do it.

This is one of the most affectionate and overtly loving breeds I've ever owned. To me, they are worth the effort, expense and time that they require. They are clowns and comics and will provide hours of laughter and entertainment. But as a Pug owner, you MUST be aware of the care involved in this breed."

If you haven't been put you off with all of the above ... Congratulations, you may be just the family or person that poor homeless Pug is looking for. So how to find one?

There are many dedicated people out there who give up their time free of charge to help find loving and permanent homes for Pugs which would often otherwise be put down (euthanized). There are networks of these worthy people who have set up excellent rescue services for Pugs.

You might also find yourself in a position where you have to rehome your Pug. Here are some of the main rescue charities:

Pug Rescue Organisations

This is by no means an exhaustive list, but it does cover some of the main organisations involved. Other online resources are the Pet Finder website at www.petfinder.com and Adopt a Pet site at www.adoptapet.com Some dogs listed with the Pug-specific rescue organisations are also advertised on these websites If you do visit these websites, you cannot presume that the descriptions are 100% accurate, even when they have been given in good faith, and we advise you to check out the health credentials of the dog and its parents.

NEVER buy a puppy or an adult dog from eBay, Craig's List, Preloved, Gumtree or any of the other advertising websites which sell old cars, washing machines, golf clubs etc. You might think you are getting a cheap Pug, but in the long run you will pay the price.

If the dog had been well bred and properly cared for, he or she would not be advertised on a website such as this. If you buy or get a free one, you may be storing up a whole load of trouble for yourselves in terms of behavioural, temperament and/or health issues due to poor breeding and/or training.

NEVER buy a Pug from a pet shop. Good Pug breeders never sell their puppies to pet shops.

UK Rescue

The Pug Dog Welfare & Rescue Association (PDWRA) is a registered charity run entirely by volunteers, set up in 1973 under the original name of The Pug Dog Welfare Association.

The group says: "PDWRA operates throughout the whole of the UK and has a maximum of twelve Trustees, who are able to assist a Pug in need in any part of the country. Should any further assistance be required, such as vetting a possible new home and help with transport, the Trustees can call upon members of Friends of Welfare, whose contribution since this group was first formed has been invaluable.

"Each year we rehome and rescue many Pugs. In 2014, around 170 Pugs were surrendered to PDWRA for rehoming, an increase yet again on previous years. Earlier in the year the Trustees decided that the time had come to operate our rehoming system on a regional basis; there are now six regional areas.

"We seldom have Pugs waiting for homes, and therefore we do not have a kennel or rescue centre anywhere in the UK. On occasions, however, we do have Pugs in need of nursing care and temporary fostering, and again the assistance of members of Friends of Welfare is invaluable.

"Please note that, with the exception of any Pugs requiring nursing care or temporary fostering as mentioned above, no surrendered Pugs awaiting rehoming are kept at the homes of our Trustees or Friends of Welfare. We therefore request that you do not contact us to ask if you can come and view the available Pugs."

PDWRA encourages potential adopters to become Friends of Welfare to help raise or donate money to the charity and in certain cases to help with the work of the charity.

The PDWRA website is at http://pugwelfare-rescue.org.uk and the email address for anyone interested in adoption is adoption@pugwelfare-rescue.org.uk. If you are interesting in helping out or becoming a Friend of Welfare, then email secretary@pugwelfare-rescue.org.uk.

The **Wales & West of England Pug Dog Club** also runs a rescue service. For a list of the club's volunteers involved in rescue on a county-wide basis, visit the Kennel Club's directory page at: www.thekennelclub.org.uk/services/public/findarescue/Default.aspx?breed=6164

USA Rescue Groups

The Pug Dog Club of America (PDCA) has an online list of chapter groups which help to rescue Pugs at: http://pugs.org/pug-rescue-directory

There are also a number of regional rescue groups in the USA, many of which rescue and rehome Pugs outside of state boundaries.

Alabama Pug Rescue and Adoption Inc. (APRA) http://www.alabamapugrescue.org email pugsrescued@aol.com

Arkansas Pug Rescue of Northwest Arkansas

Arizona Pug Adoption and Rescue Network (APARN) www.aparn.org email info@aparn.org

California – Pugs 'N Pals www.pugdogrescue.com Tel 949-262-PUGD(7843) Newport Beach

Pug Rescue of Sacramento www.pugpros.org email rescue@pugpros.org Tel 925-974-PUGS (7847) or 916-484-4158

Pug Rescue San Diego County www.pugbutts.com email info@pugsandiego.com Tel (619) 685-3580

Pugsavers North California & North Nevada www.pugsavers.com email rescue@pugsavers.com

Colorado Pug Rescue http://copugrescue.org

Connecticut, Maine, Massachusetts, New Hampshire, Rhode Island, Vermont PRONE (Pug Rescue of New England) www.pugrescueofnewengland.org

Yankee Pug Dog Club email mfdux@att.net

Delaware Valley Pug Club Rescue www.delawarevalleypugclub.org/html/rescue.html also NJ, PA

Florida Pug Rescue of Florida http://pugrescueofflorida.org email pugrescueofflorida@gmail.com

Compassionate Pug Rescue (South Florida) www.compassionatepugrescue.com email cpr@compassionatepugrescue.com

Idaho Pugs Rescue email RedsPugs@aol.com

Illinois MOPS Pug Rescue & Adoption, Rescue for Great Lakes Pug Club, email gotpug21@yahoo.com

Indiana Central Indiana Pug Club email djaymdee@aol.com

Northern Illinois Pug Rescue and Adoption www.northernillinoispugrescue.org

Iowa, Kansas, Oklahoma Midwest Pug Rescue www.mnmidwestpugrescue.com email mnmprinfo@gmail.com

Kentucky Kentuckiana Pug Rescue www.kentuckianapugs.com email adoptionskentucky@kentuckianapugs.com (Indiana - pugcrazy3@att.net)

Maryland Pug Dog Club of Maryland www.pugdogclubofmd.org email Mail4Pugs@aol.com

Michigan Pug Rescue www.michiganpugrescue.com email pugluv@michiganpugrescue.com Tel (248) 473-8389

Mid Michigan Pug Club and Rescue www.midmichiganpugclub.com email adoptpugs@hotmail.com

Pug Rescue Network http://pugrescuenetwork.com

Minnesota Midwest Pug Rescue www.mnmidwestpugrescue.com email mnpugrescue@yahoo.com or MNMPRinfo@gmail.com

Nebraska Pug Partners of Nebraska www.pugpartners.com Tel 1-888-509-1940

Nevada KC's Pug Rescue www.rescuepugs.com email info@rescuepugs.com

New York Pug Dog Club of Greater New York, Inc. email Joe@therhythmdogs.com

North Carolina Pug Rescue of North Carolina www.pugrescuenc.org Tel 336-312-2983 email pugrescueofnc@gmail.com or chris@pugrescuenc.org

Mid Atlantic Pug Rescue www.midatlanticpugrescue.org Serving NC, SC, VA, MD, WV and Eastern TN email maprapplications@yahoo.com

Ohio Pug Rescue www.ohiopugrescue.com also **Kentucky** email Pugcrazy247@aol.com

Oklahoma Homeward Bound Pugs www.homewardboundpugs.com Tel 405-706-1492 email homewardboundpugs@cox.net

Texas Pug Hearts of Houston www.pugheartshouston.org email info@pughearts.com

Dallas Fort Worth Pug Rescue http://dfwpugs.com email molly_klimek@yahoo.com

Pug Club of Greater San Antonio email brindun@austin.rr.com

Virginia Old Dominion Pug Club email JDPugtales@aol.com

Washington Seattle Pugs www.seattlepugs.com email rescue@seattlepugs.com

Puget Sound Pug Rescue email JenCarton@aol.com

Grays Harbor Pug and Boston Terrier Rescue email puglady@hotmail.com

Wisconsin MOPS Pug Rescue & Adoption email gotpug21@yahoo.com

Canada Rescue

Pug Club of Canada Rescue www.pugcanada.com/Pug%20Rescue/rescue.html

Pug and Boxer Rescue (Moncton, New Brunswick area) email meredith26@hotmail.com

---

**Saving one Pug will not change the world
But it will change the world for one Pug**

With special thanks to The Pug Dog Welfare & Rescue Association for their considerable input into this chapter and kind permission to reproduce PDWRA material http://pugwelfare-rescue.org.uk

15. Caring for Older Dogs

As your Pug gets older, his or her body and mind will start to slow down. Physically, joints may become stiffer and organs, such as heart or liver, may not function as effectively.

On the mental side - just like with humans - your dog's memory, ability to learn and awareness will all start to dim. You may also notice that your faithful companion doesn't see or hear as well as he or she used to – or (s)he might become a bit more grumpy or stubborn. On the other hand, they might not be hard of hearing at all, they might just be conveniently choosing to ignore some of your commands!

You can help ease your mature dog into old age gracefully by keeping an eye on him, noticing the changes and taking action to help him as much as possible.

This might involve a visit to the vet for supplements and/or medications, modifying your dog's environment, a change of diet and slowly reducing the amount of daily exercise. Our breeders have some excellent advice for all owners of elderly Pugs later in this chapter.

Much depends on the individual dog. Just as with humans, a dog of ideal weight who has been active and stimulated all of his or her life is likely to age slower than an overweight couch potato.

Keeping Pugs at that ideal weight is even more challenging - and important – as they age. Their metabolisms slow down, making it easier for them to put on weight unless their daily calories are reduced. At the same time extra weight is placing additional, unwanted stress on their joints and organs, making them all work harder than they should. In fact, obesity is one of the main issues with older Pugs.

We normally talk about dogs being old when they reach the last third of their lives. So how long do Pugs live and when do they become old?

The Kennel Club is rather vague when it comes to the lifespan of the Pug, it says: "over 10 years," other organisations put it at 12 to 15 years. Much of it depends of the genetic health of your Pug, his or her bloodlines and how well you take care of your dog. Most overweight dogs will not live as long as slimmer ones.

There was a wide variation in opinions from our breeders, with the consensus being that the lifespan could be anywhere from 12 to 18 years old. Generally, anything over 11 or 12 years old was considered to be a good age. When you get your puppy, ask the breeder how long the Pugs in her bloodline live. Well looked after with no major health issues, you can expect your puppy to live as long.

Physical and Mental Signs of Aging

If your Pug is in or approaching the last third of his life, here are some signs that his body is feeling its age:

❖ Your dog is putting on weight - more than normal

❖ He gets up from lying down more slowly, he goes up and down stairs more slowly, he can no longer jump on to the couch or bed. These are all signs that his joints are stiffening, often due to arthritis

❖ He has generally slowed down and no longer seems as keen to go out on his walks. He tires more easily on a walk

❖ He doesn't want to go outside in bad weather - although with Pugs, this is a general trait throughout their lives!

❖ He has the occasional 'accident' (incontinence) inside the house

❖ He is getting grey hairs, particularly around the muzzle

❖ He urinates more frequently

❖ He drinks more water

❖ He gets constipated

❖ The foot pads thicken and nails may become more brittle

❖ He has one or more lumps or fatty deposits on his body. (Our 10-year-old dog developed two on his head recently and we took him straight to the vet, who performed an operation to remove them. They were benign (harmless), but you should always get them checked out ASAP in case they are an early form of cancer.)

❖ Pugs are not very good at regulating their temperature when they are young, and this ability can deteriorate with age

❖ He doesn't hear as well as he used to

❖ His eyesight may deteriorate – if his eyes appear cloudy he is probably developing cataracts and you should see your vet as soon as you notice the signs

❖ He has bad breath (halitosis), which could be a sign of dental or gum disease. Brush his teeth regularly and give him a daily dental stick, such as Dentastix or similar. If the bad breath persists, get him checked out by a vet

❖ Inactive dogs may develop callouses on the elbows, especially if they lie down on hard surfaces – although this is more common with larger breeds

It's not just your dog's body which deteriorates, his mind does too. It's all part of the normal aging process. Here are some symptoms - your dog may display some, all or none of these signs of mental deterioration:

❖ His sleep patterns change, an older dog may be more restless at night and sleepy during the day

❖ He barks more

❖ He stares at objects or wanders aimlessly around the house

❖ He forgets or ignores commands or habits he once knew well, such as housetraining and coming when called

❖ He displays increased anxiety or aggressiveness

❖ Some dogs may become more clingy and dependent, often resulting in separation anxiety, while others become less interested in human contact

Understanding the changes happening to your dog and acting on them compassionately and effectively will help your dog's passage through his senior years. Your dog has given you so much pleasure over the last few years, now he or she needs you to give that bit of extra care for a happy, healthy old age.

You can also help your Pug to stay mentally active by playing games (not too rough) and getting new toys to stimulate interest.

Helping Seniors

The first thing you can do is to monitor your dog and be on the lookout for any changes in actions or behaviour. Then there are lots of things you can do for him.

Food and Supplements - As dogs age they need less calories and less protein, so many owners switch to a food specially formulated for older dogs. These are labelled "Senior," "Aging" or "Mature." Check the labelling, some are specifically for dogs aged over eight, others may be for 12-year-old dogs.

If you are not sure if a senior diet is necessary for your Pug, talk to your vet the next time you are there for vaccinations or a check-up. Remember, if you do change the brand, switch the food gradually over a week to 10 days. Unlike with humans, a dog's digestive system cannot cope with sudden changes of diet.

Consider feeding your Pug a supplement, such as Omega-3 fatty acids for the brain and coat, or one to help joints. There are also medications and homeopathic remedies to help relieve anxiety. Check with your vet before introducing anything new.

Exercise – Take the lead from your dog, if he doesn't want to walk as far, then don't. But if your dog doesn't want to go out at all, you will have to coax him out. ALL senior dogs need exercise, not only to keep their joints moving, but also to keep their heart, lungs and joints exercised.

Weight – no matter how old your Pug is, he still needs a waist. Maintaining a healthy weight with a balanced diet and regular, often gentler, exercise are the two of the most important things you can do for your dog.

Environment – Make sure your Pug has a nice soft place to rest his old bones, which may mean adding an extra blanket to his bed. This should be in a place which is not too hot or cold, as he may not be able to regulate his body temperature as well as when he was younger. If his eyesight is failing, move obstacles out of his way, reducing the chance of injuries.

He will need a helping hand or even a little ramp to get in and out of the car, on to the couch – or your bed! Make sure he has plenty of time to sleep and is not pestered and/or bullied by young children, younger dogs or other animals.

Consult a Professional - If your dog is showing any of the following signs, get him checked out by your vet:

> ➢ Increased urination or drinking - this can be a sign of something amiss, such as reduced liver or kidney function, Cushing's disease or diabetes

> ➢ Constipation or not urinating regularly could be a sign of something not functioning properly with the digestive system or organs

> ➢ Incontinence, which could be a sign of a mental or physical problem

> ➢ Cloudy eyes, which could be cataracts

> ➢ Lumps or bumps on the body -which are most often benign but can occasionally be malignant

> ➢ Decreased appetite – Pugs love their food and loss of appetite is often a sign of an underlying problem

> ➢ Excessive sleeping or a lack of interest in you and your dog's surroundings

> ➢ Diarrhoea or vomiting

> ➢ A darkening and dryness of skin that never seems to get any better - this can be a sign of hypothyroidism

> ➢ Any other out-of-the-ordinary behaviour for your dog. A change in patterns or behaviour is often your dog's way of telling you that all is not well.

The Last Lap

Huge advances in veterinary science have meant that there are countless procedures and medications which can prolong the life of your dog, and this is a good thing.

But there comes a time when you have to let go. If your dog is showing all the signs of aging, has an ongoing medical condition from which he or she cannot recover, or is showing signs of pain, mental anxiety or distress and there is no hope of improvement, then the dreaded time has come to say goodbye.

You owe it to him or her.

There is no point keeping an old dog alive if all they have to look forward to is pain and death.

I'm even getting upset as I write this, as I think of parting from my 10-year-old dog not too many years into the future, as well as the wonderful dogs we have had in the past. But we have their lives in our hands and we can give them the gift of passing away peacefully and humanely at the end when the time is right.

Losing our beloved companion, our best friend, a member of the family, is truly heart-breaking for many owners. But one of the things we realise at the back of our minds when we get that lively little puppy is the pain that comes with it, knowing that we will live longer than him or her and that we will probably have to make this most painful of decisions at some point. It's the worst thing about being a dog owner.

If your Pug has had a long and happy life, then you could not have done any more. You were a great owner and your dog was lucky to have you. Remember all the good times you had together. And try not to rush out and buy another dog; wait a few weeks or months to grieve for your Pug. Assess your current life and lifestyle and, if your situation is right, only then consider getting another dog and all that that entails in terms of time, commitment and expense. Dogs are sensitive, often intuitive, creatures. One coming into a happy, stable household will get off to a much better start in life than a dog entering a home full of grief.

Whatever you decide to do, put the dog first.

What the Pug Experts Say

Let's not dwell on the end stages of our dog's life, but focus on what we can do to keep him or her fit and healthy as the years roll by.

J. Candy Schlieper, of Candyland Pugs, Ohio, has been breeding Pugs for 30 years, so she knows a thing or two about elderly dogs. Here's our interview:

At what age would you say a Pug becomes a senior – i.e. time to look at changing to a senior diet? "Any dog over the age of seven."

What do you feed your older Pugs? "I feed most of my older Pugs a raw diet."

Do you feed any supplements to your older dogs - or anything else which helps them as they age? "I feed Brewer's Yeast with garlic and Prozyme to all of my adult dogs."

Are there any health issues particular to older Pugs? "Eye issues as they age can get worse without the proper treatment."

How about behavioural changes? "I haven't seen any behavioral changes in this breed as they age. They are still very sweet and loving dogs."

Do you have any advice for owners of older Pugs or tips you can pass on? "Be sure to check eyes on a regular basis and get appropriate meds if needed. Don't allow them to run a lot with younger dogs, that could cause an older dog to become injured.

"They don't need as much exercise as they age, but a short walk each day, if they have been built up to it, is always a good thing for this breed. Try to keep them on the slimmer size so they don't get too heavy, which causes them more health problems."

We have lots of wonderful photographs in this book, but Candy's photo, here, of her 17-year-old Pug Norma pictured enjoying her 16th birthday is an absolute favourite!

Breeder Catherine Jones-Kyle, of Dixie Darlings, Tennessee, says: "At about six we change their food to a venison and sweet potato sensitive systems food and add a joint formula to their daily vitamin. At about nine we start looking at their overall health and digestive function and decide if we need to make a change to a senior formula."

Catherine feeds her dogs vitamins from being puppies: "At four weeks the puppies start getting a multi vitamin. We use NuVet and they get it as their morning treat. We encourage our families to continue giving the puppies the vitamins, most of our families do since we've seen such great results in our own dogs. They also get a little coconut oil with their food once a day starting with a ¼ teaspoon as puppies, gradually going up to about a tablespoon once they are fully grown."

She believes that weight is a major factor with older Pugs: "If they are overweight they can have exacerbated breathing issues and joint issues. Keep your Pugs with in a weight range of 16 to 20 pounds. Give them a tablespoonful of coconut oil daily in their food and keep them on a good multi vitamin with added joint benefits.

"A Pug's behaviour rarely changes with age, the biggest change is their activity level. They tend to sleep a little more and prefer a quiet day on the couch to a lot of activity. Get a set of pet stairs so they can get into bed or onto the couch without having to jump, this really pays off if you get the stairs as puppies and they use them from the beginning. Their joints won't have as much stress on them and they will have less of a chance of suffering from arthritis later in life."

Pug Dog Club of America member Brenda Shuettenberg and her mother Donna Shank, of RoKuCiera Pugs, California, have been breeding Pugs since 1962 when they got their first fawn girl. They had their first litter of fawn Pugs in 1964 and the first litter of blacks two years later. Brenda said: "I'd consider a senior diet any time after the dog is aged six or seven. I start looking for changes in the overall dog: teeth, gums, energy level, coat. Do they have a problem chewing their food? Do they gain weight too easily with the same exercise? If yes, then it may be time for a change. Boogie is 13 and we just changed his diet due to chewing issues.

"The short answer to what we feed our older dogs is 'whatever they will eat,' but in reality we feed a dry kibble as much as possible. Our really old guys get a stew of mackerel, peas, cooked carrots, stewed tomato and boiled rice and/or oatmeal twice per day.

"Because we live in a desert area we add salmon/pollock oil (just because they all love fish, it could be olive, coconut, safflower oil) to all the dogs' feeds once per day. As they age and we notice signs of arthritis, we start adding a glucosamine and chondroitin tablet crushed into their food or as a treat once or twice per day as necessary....then with vet approval they will get aspirin or stronger meds when they becomes needed."

Asked about health issues for elderly Pugs she said: "Rear quarter ataxia, or a wasting of the muscling in the rear, causing them to lose the use of the rear legs. Some become incontinent of bowel and bladder. Also loss of teeth and eyesight due to cataracts, both can be dealt with, with the help of a good veterinarian. A vet well used to dealing with the geriatric pet population is a real blessing for both owner and animal."

Here are her tips for owners: "Just love them, keep them as healthy as possible and a bit on the lean side, and treat them as you would want your family to treat you in your old age. Recognise when it is the right time to let them go, don't prolong the suffering, and hold them while you say good-bye and they pass over the rainbow bridge to await your arrival on the other side when it is your time."

Brenda's tips are obviously working. Pictured is her Ch. Ceil's Black Bottom Boogie. He's now 13 and, according to Brenda: "He still chases the girls hoping for a date!"

Laura Libner, of Loralar Pugs, Grand Rapids, Michigan, has been breeding Pugs since 1999. She says: "A Pug becomes a senior around seven or eight years of age, but it truly depends on the individual dog. I feed my mature Pugs an all-stages diet. I usually just feed a little less if they are less active. I don't as yet feed any supplements, but I'm thinking about starting something for senility as I have one that is becoming a bit that way lately."

Asked about health or behaviour issues she said: "It depends on the dog - a couple I have had have suffered elongated palate symptoms as they have gotten on in years. I'm not sure if it was exacerbated by intubations over the years for dental procedures or C-sections, but it seems to worsen when a few I've had have become older. Behaviourally, Pugs can become less tolerant of the younger dogs and in general - especially if their vision becomes impaired, etc.

She added: "Keep older dogs groomed and pampered as you would your younger ones. Just because they are older doesn't mean they still don't enjoy being clean and kept groomed. Try to keep them as exercised as you can, also as they merge into their golden years."

Breeder Sue Wragg, of Glammarags Pugs, Cheshire, UK, said: "It's difficult to say when a Pug becomes a senior really, as I think they differ as individuals. They usually seem to slow down a bit at about eight or nine and certainly are much more dignified by the time they get to 10. Pugs' teeth are something of a challenge - they hate having them cleaned and many have dreadful teeth which can be troublesome as they get older.

"I don't actually change to a senior diet, as I feed raw. But as they get older I probably chop it up a bit more finely, or mince chicken wings, necks etc. as they struggle to chew. I do add Yumega to oldies' food if they're a bit stiff and arthritic, or Petcetera Coat & Skin supplement to anyone looking a bit grizzled. These both contain Omega 3 and 6 and fish oils of various types. Coconut oil is supposed to be the new in thing, but I haven't yet tried it.

"We try to maintain their weight at a steady level as they get older, and as they take less exercise this means cutting back a bit on the amount of food they are given. Fat old dogs can sometimes struggle with breathing issues if the weather is hot and, of course, excess weight isn't good for hearts or joints.

"Many older Pugs benefit from a trip to the vet's for a dental clean and polish (and sometimes removal of particularly bad teeth). This definitely improves the dog breath! Old fashioned Pugs with very bulbous eyes can suffer with dry eye in later life, again this can be treated with special drops from the vet, but it is something we are trying to breed away from as we try to produce Pugs with less bulbous and vulnerable eyes. As with most breeds, some older Pugs suffer from joint pains and stiffness, but I don't think this is particularly a Pug thing, more just an old dog thing.

"I can't say I have noticed any behavioural changes - my oldies still like to go for walks, love their food and cuddles, but perhaps at a calmer pace then when they were young. They still want to be in the thick of everything, but just not at 100mph as they did in their youth!

"My only advice to anyone with an older Pug would be to keep their teeth clean, monitor their weight so they don't get too fat (particularly if they have been neutered) and perhaps cut the distances of walks down a bit. Pugs are indoor dogs so nice soft beds are usually provided, but I think they are especially appreciated by oldies who enjoy snuggling into a soft bed after their exercise." (Pictured is Sue's Frank, who is looking forward to a long and happy life!)

Sandra Mayoh, of Drumlinfold Pugs, North Yorkshire added: "I think it's time to look at a senior diet when the dog reaches seven years or so. I feed my Pugs more of the same complete adult diet with extra tripe and titbits, and sometimes carrots, which they love. I haven't had to feed supplements, but the eldest is now 10 and may need a little help due to becoming a little stiffer.

"As Pugs get older they may suffer from loss of hearing – or selective hearing! They also become sun worshippers. As for tips, I think it's important for older dogs to have their own space to retreat to."

16. Showing and Judging Pugs in the UK

In this chapter, Robert Hitchcock, of Bobitch Pugs, Derbyshire, shares his knowledge of the UK show and judging system. Robert has exhibited and bred Pugs for 18 years, producing several champions, and is an approved Championship Show judge for the breed:

There are three main types of dog shows in the UK:
> Limit Shows,
> Open Shows
> Championship Shows

For these shows, all exhibitors have to enter in advance of the show date, usually around four weeks prior.

Limit shows are 'limited' to members of the club, be that general canine society, breed club and also to dogs who have not won the Challenge Certificate (CC) winners.

The idea of limit shows is to give newcomers chance to be part of a dog club and compete in a friendly atmosphere, or for more established exhibitors to bring out young hopefuls without the competition from the 'big winners'.

These types of shows are also a good learning ground for new, up-and-coming judges to get the chance to judge and get their hands on a good number of dogs. And, in the absence of the top winners, it's not unusual for youngsters to take top awards at these shows.

The next level of shows is Open Shows. Like the Limit Show, these can be either breed-specific or all-breed shows.

Again, a friendly atmosphere usually prevails and it is here where up-and-coming judges finely tune their skills as breed-specific judges or for those slightly more adventurous, to learn about other breed which are of interest to them. Championship Show judges also officiate at Open Shows, as it is a requirement of the Kennel Club for group and Best in Show judges to award challenge certificates in at least one breed.

All breed Open Shows these days are usually held on the 'group system.' This is where the Best of Breeds in each scheduled breed, compete head-to-head in their respective groups with the other Best of Breed winners.

There are seven groups in the UK, Working, Pastoral, Hound, Terrier, Gundog, Toy and Utility, Pugs being in the Toy group. The group winner then represents his group in the challenge for Best in Show and goes head-to-head with the other six group winners.

The best dog from these seven, in the judge's opinion, is awarded Best in Show. The same happens with each best puppy from each breed; it competes with best puppies from the other breeds within its group and each puppy group winner goes on to compete for the Best Puppy in Show title.

Championship Shows are the more serious end of the dog show scale, more classes are scheduled for each breed, and judges must have completed their required training and passed several exams as required by the Kennel Club in order to judge at this level. These types of shows are also generally considerably more expensive to enter.

The classes usually scheduled might be: Minor Puppy, Puppy, Junior, Graduate, Yearling, Post Graduate, Limit and Open. Often there might be a Veteran class for dogs over seven years of age. The classes are separate for males and females. The exhibitor enters the class for which each dog they are showing is eligible. Some classes are restricted by age and some by previous wins, the more the dog has won, the higher class it must enter.

Males are judged first and the judge carefully works his way through each class, assessing each dog with a hands-on examination. He or she also watches each exhibit move - usually in a triangle - to assess rear end movement, side gait and front movement as the exhibit comes back toward the judge, not against the others in the class, but against the breed standard (see **Chapter 3**).

The judge then places the exhibits in each class based on their merits and de-merits, first to fifth, however fourth place is termed reserve and fifth place is 'very highly commended' or VHC. Each class progresses until the judge ends up with winners from each class. These are then called back into the ring as 'unbeaten dogs' and they compete for the honour of Best Male.

The judge carefully considers the merits and demerits of each exhibit. As we all know, the perfect specimen is yet to be born, but the dog which, in the judge's opinion is closest to perfection, closest to the breed standard, will be awarded the CC (Challenge Certificate). The exhibit who is awarded the challenge certificate is of such outstanding merit as to be called a champion.

The second best male is awarded a Reserve CC and should also be of such quality that if the CC winner is disqualified, he would be moved up one place and be awarded the Challenge Certificate. The same process takes place with the females until we have our best male and best female. These two are then called back into the ring and challenge each other for the honour of Best of Breed.

In the UK, dogs must win three Challenge Certificates from three different judges at three different shows in order for the dog to claim the Champion title. One of those certificates must be awarded after the age of twelve months. If the dog wins three (or more) CCs before the age of twelve months, he must wait until he is one year old and hopefully wins another CC before he can be called a Champion.

So, we have looked at how a dog becomes a Champion, there are two more titles on offer in the UK which dogs can gain.

Firstly, the Junior Warrant, or JW. This award can be gained by young dogs between the ages of six and 18 months. Six months being the youngest a dog can be exhibited.

The dog must gain 25 points, from both Open and Championship Shows. A class win at a Championship Show gains three points and a class win at an Open Show gains one point. However, three exhibits must be present in each class where points are being claimed from. Junior Warrant claim forms are available to download from the Kennel Club website.

The third title on offer is the Show Certificate of Merit or ShCM. This was introduced by the Kennel Club in 2003 in an effort to encourage exhibitors back to Open Shows. Much like the Junior

Warrant, the exhibit collects 25 points for various wins, only from Open Shows. Points can be accrued from Best of Breed wins, group placings and Best in Show awards.

When one has been lucky enough to have campaigned a dog to all three titles, his full kennel name will look something like this: Ch. Nutbush City Limits JW ShCM.

Becoming a Judge

The five UK breed clubs, The Pug Dog Club, The Northern Pug Dog Club, The Scottish Pug Dog Club, The Wales and West of England Pug Dog Club and The West Pennine Pug Dog Club each have two representatives, who make up the Pug Breed Council. The council meets a couple of times a year and is responsible for judges' education, health and positive promotion of the breed.

Becoming a Championship judge takes many years. Judges start off being able to judge three classes only and, ideally, this only happens after several years of successfully exhibiting of the breed, after which a dog show society offers an invitation to judge in an honorary capacity.

New judges are encouraged to attend the basic Pug judging assessment, normally held annually by one or more of the five breed clubs. This includes a very informative talk on the breed given by a Championship Show judge. He or she describes detailed points of the breed standard using live models and often a PowerPoint presentation. Candidates then sit a multi-choice exam based on the talk and the breed standard.

Successful candidates can then apply to be included on the judges list C.

In order to move up to the next level - judging list B - a candidate must have judged a certain number of dogs from a certain amount of classes over a five year period.

This is a deliberately slow process, as it's very important that up-and-coming judges learn the finer points of the breed and to hone their skills. So, after five years on the C list, assuming one has fulfilled the necessary criteria, a judge is moved up to the B list, entitling him or her to judge more than three classes.

He or she might be offered a breed club Open or Limit Show, but the same process applies, more dogs and classes must be judged and the next level of seminar must be attended and passed in order to move up the lists. This takes a further two years.

The advanced assessment is very detailed; candidates have to assess five exhibits. They all watch the dogs move at the same time, so they all see the same thing. Each candidate then makes a manual examination of each dog - as though judging at a show - and then writes a detailed critique about each dog and places them (theoretically) in order of merit, 1st to VHC.

This is done on paper which is then handed in for marking to the assessors, who are all Championship Show judges. The assessors have all previously judged the same dogs and watched the dogs move at the same time as the candidates. Between them they have agreed the merits and demerits of each dog and in what order they should be placed.

Successful candidates then move up to the A3 list. Here they can accept a Championship Show judging appointment. (Show societies often work three years in advance). From starting out as a novice judge and learning one's craft to awarding that first set of Challenge Certificates often takes a minimum of 10 years.

New judges are encouraged by the clubs and the Breed Council, who play a vital role in getting the best out of new judges through their education seminars. Without new, young up-and-coming judges, the dog showing sport would die out. At the same time, candidates are encouraged to take their time to learn the art of becoming a good judge.

Some people are natural judges, they just have the eye for a good dog and can easily find the best dogs in any breed; others less so.

Personal Preference

The breed standard **(Chapter 3)** is a blueprint of how the perfect Pug - should he ever be born - should look like. This is quite loose and open to some degree of individual interpretation. Judges have, to some degree, their own views and opinions on parts of the standard, which is why different dogs win each week.

For example, the breed standard quotes:

EYES - Dark, relatively large, round in shape, soft and solicitous in expression, very lustrous, and when excited, full of fire. Never protruding, exaggerated or showing white when looking straight ahead. Free from obvious eye problems.

Some judges will have differing opinions of how dark is dark? How large is relatively large? Applying this to the whole breed standard, this is why we see different Pugs winning. Judges also have particular likes and dislikes, must haves or must have nots.

My personal pet hate is white or unpigmented nails. However if the runaway winner of a class was superb and fitted the standard in every way but had white nails, I would still place the dog first. Judging is a matter of compromise to some degree and the whole dog must be taken into account. It is up to the judge to weigh up the merits and demerits of each exhibit and place it where it should be.

Colour can be another contentious issue. As we know the Pug comes in four colours and four colours only: **fawn, black, apricot and silver**. Apricot and silver are variations of fawn.

Black Pugs should be blue-black rather than brown-black, and most breeders of black Pugs understand that top quality blacks should have a single coat and blue skin. Although this is not mentioned in the breed standard, it is a feature which good black breeders aim for. Some judges simply don't understand blacks and often a superb black is put down the line in favour of a mediocre fawn.

Similarly with apricots, the standard doesn't mention how dark an apricot coat should be. We see very pale apricots with just a slight warm hue, through to really dark, almost red, apricots. A famous old breeder said: "Apricot is like sunlight, silver like moonlight."

This is something I think should be spoken about in more in depth about at seminars, but when judging, personal preference plays a part, particularly in a class where the quality is so good and the judge finds himself splitting hairs.

Becoming a judge can be very rewarding if you are prepared to put in the time to learn your craft. The Kennel Club has a list of approved judges for Pugs, and if you are considering becoming a judge, then one of the breed clubs or the Breed Council will be happy to help you start out on the right track. Visit: www.thekennelclub.org.uk/services/public/judge/list.aspx?id=Pug

---

Written for the New Pug Handbook by Robert Hitchcock. Copyright Robert Hitchcock 2015.

No part of this article may be reproduced without express permission of Robert Hitchcock and the Canine Handbooks.

Photographs show Robert judging at Leeds Championship Dog Show and Robert together with his wife, Holly, joint owner of Bobitch Pugs.

Useful Contacts

http://pugs.org Pug Dog Club of America (PDCA)

http://pugs.org/breeder-directory List of approved PDCA breeders state by state

http://pugdogclub.org.uk Pug Dog Club (UK)

http://www.pugcanada.com Pug Club of Canada

http://pugwelfare-rescue.org.uk The Pug Dog Welfare & Rescue Association (UK)

http://pugs.org/pug-rescue-directory Pug Dog Club of America Rescue Directory

www.thekennelclub.org.uk The Kennel Club UK

http://www.thekennelclub.org.uk/services/public/acbr/Default.aspx?breed=Pug List of Kennel Club assured breeders of Pugs in the UK

http://www.champdogs.co.uk/breeds/pug/breeders List of UK Pug breeders (not all are Kennel Club registered - check)

www.akc.org American Kennel Club

https://www.apps.akc.org/apps/classified/search/landing_puppy.cfm?breed_code=512 AKC classified ads for Pug breeders

www.ckc.ca Canadian Kennel Club

www.ukcdogs.com United Kennel Club (North America)

http://ankc.org.au Australian National Kennel Council

www.apdt.co.uk Association of Pet Dog Trainers UK

www.apdt.com Association of Pet Dog Trainers USA

www.cappdt.ca Canadian Association of Professional Pet Dog Trainers

www.dogfoodadvisor.com Useful information on grain-free and hypoallergenic dogs foods

www.akcreunite.org Helps find lost or stolen dogs in USA, register your Pug's microchip

Pug internet forums and Facebook groups are also a good source of information from other owners, including:

http://www.pugvillage.com/forum
http://pugworld.co.uk

Contributing Breeders

UK: (listed alphabetically)

Holly Attwood, Taftazini, Sheffield, South Yorkshire, England

Deborah Beecham, Fizzlewick Pugs, Gwent, South Wales

Melanie Clark and Tony Glover, Pugginpugs, Gainsborough, Lincolnshire, England

Saran Evans, Sephina Pugs, Carmarthenshire, Wales

Carly Firth, Mumandau Pugs, Bolton, Greater Manchester, England

Linda Guy, Londonderry Pugs, Londonderry, Northern Ireland

Robert and Holly Hitchcock, Bobitch Pugs, Belper, Derbyshire, England

Sandra Mayoh, Drumlinfold Pugs, York, North Yorkshire, England

Sue Wragg, Glammarags Pugs, Cheshire, England, England

MALTA:

Deborah Hayman, Fawnydawn Pugs, Malta

USA:

Erin Ford, Fur-N-Feathers, Deland, Florida

Roberta Kelley-Martin, HRH Pugs, Chico, California

Catherine Jones-Kyle, Dixie Darlings, Leipers Fork, Tennessee

Laura Libner, Loralar Pugs, Grand Rapids, Michigan

J. Candy Schlieper, CandyLand Pugs, Tipp City, Ohio

Donna Shank and Brenda Shuettenberg, RoKuCiera Pugs, North Highlands, California

Kim and Linda Wright, Wright's Pugs, Springport, Michigan

Disclaimer

This book has been written to provide helpful information on Pugs. It is not meant to be used, nor should it be used, to diagnose or treat any medical condition. For diagnosis or treatment of any animal medical problem, consult a qualified veterinarian. The author is not responsible for any specific health or allergy conditions that may require medical supervision and is not liable for any damages or negative consequences from any treatment, action, application or preparation, to any person reading or following the information in this book. References are provided for informational purposes only and do not constitute endorsement of any websites or other sources.

Author's Note: For ease of reading the masculine pronoun 'he' is intended to represent both male and female dogs.

If you care for dogs and would like to learn more, follow us on Twitter **@CanineHandbooks**

Made in the USA
Columbia, SC
27 September 2020